ANNUAL EDITIONS DEVELOPING WORLD 11/12

2011 Custom Edition

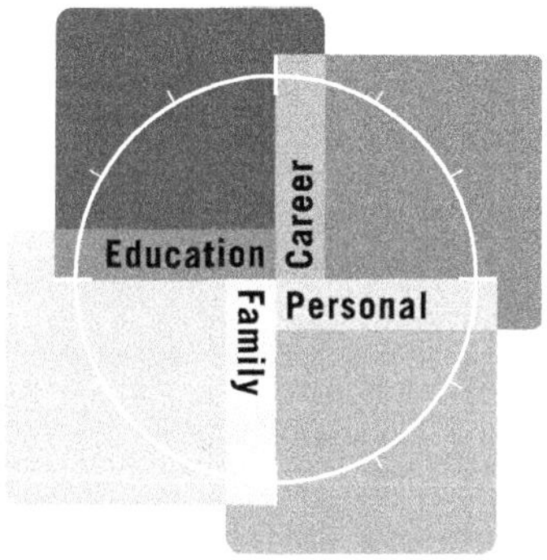

Taken from:
Annual Editions: Developing World, Twenty-first Edition
Robert J. Griffiths

STRAYER UNIVERSITY

McGRAW-HILL LEARNING SOLUTIONS

BOSTON BURR RIDGE, IL DUBUQUE, IA NEW YORK SAN FRANCISCO ST. LOUIS
BANGKOK BOGOTÁ CARACAS LISBON LONDON MADRID
MEXICO CITY MILAN NEW DELHI SEOUL SINGAPORE SYDNEY TAIPEI TORONTO

The McGraw-Hill Companies

ANNUAL EDITIONS: DEVELOPING WORLD 11/12
TWENTY-FIRST EDITION

This book is a McGraw-Hill Learning Solutions textbook and contains select material from *Annual Editions: Developing World 11/12*, Twenty-first Edition by Robert J. Griffiths. Copyright © 2011, 2010 by The McGraw-Hill Companies, Inc. Previous edition(s) 1989-2009. Reprinted with permission of the publisher. Many custom published texts are modified versions or adaptations of our best-selling textbooks. Some adaptations are printed in black and white to keep prices at a minimum, while others are in color.

4 5 6 7 8 9 0 QDB QDB 14 13 12

ISBN-13: 978-0-07-747279-5
ISBN-10: 0-07-747279-9

Learning Solutions Manager: Aimee Tait
Learning Solutions Representative: Nada Mraovic
Production Editor: Lynn Nagel
Printer/Binder: Quad/Graphics
Cover Photo Credit: Man carrying straw © Connie Coleman/Getty Images

Editors/Academic Advisory Board

Members of the Academic Advisory Board are instrumental in the final selection of articles for each edition of ANNUAL EDITIONS. Their review of articles for content, level, and appropriateness provides critical direction to the editors and staff. We think that you will find their careful consideration well reflected in this volume.

ANNUAL EDITIONS: Developing World 11/12
21st Edition

EDITOR

Robert J. Griffiths
University of North Carolina

ACADEMIC ADVISORY BOARD MEMBERS

Preface

In publishing ANNUAL EDITIONS we recognize the enormous role played by the magazines, newspapers, and journals of the public press in providing current, first-rate educational information in a broad spectrum of interest areas. Many of these articles are appropriate for students, researchers, and professionals seeking accurate, current material to help bridge the gap between principles and theories and the real world. These articles, however, become more useful for study when those of lasting value are carefully collected, organized, indexed, and reproduced in a low-cost format, which provides easy and permanent access when the material is needed. That is the role played by ANNUAL EDITIONS.

The developing world continues to play an increasingly important role in world affairs. It is home to the vast majority of the world's population and it has an increasingly significant impact on the international economy. From the standpoint of international security, developing countries are not only sites of frequent conflicts and humanitarian crises, but also a source of continuing concern related to international terrorism. Developing countries also play a critical role in the efforts involved to protect the global environment.

The developing world demonstrates considerable ethnic, cultural, political, and economic diversity, thus making generalizations about such a diverse group of countries difficult. Increasing differentiation among developing countries further complicates our comprehension of the challenges of modernization, development, and globalization that they face. A combination of internal and external factors shape the current circumstances throughout the developing world, and issues of peace and security, international trade and finance, debt, poverty, the environment, human rights, and gender illustrate the complexity of these challenges as well as the effects of globalization and the growing interdependence between nations. The ways in which these issues interrelate suggest the need for greater understanding of the connections between developing and industrialized countries. There continues to be significant debate about the best way to address the challenges faced by the developing world.

The developing world competes for attention on an international agenda that is often dominated by relations between the industrialized nations. Moreover, the domestic concerns of the industrial countries frequently overshadow the plight of the developing world. The twenty first edition of *Annual Editions: Developing World* seeks to provide students with an understanding of the diversity and complexity of the developing world and to acquaint them with the challenges that these nations confront. I remain convinced of the need for greater awareness of the problems that confront the developing world and that the international community must make a commitment to effectively address these issues, especially because of the increasingly important role developing countries are playing in international affairs. I hope that this volume contributes to students' knowledge and understanding of current trends in the developing world and the implications of these developments and serves as a catalyst for further discussion.

Over fifty percent of the articles in this edition are new. I chose articles that I hope are both interesting and informative and that can serve as a basis for further student research and discussion. The units deal with what I regard as the major issues facing the developing world. In addition, I have attempted to suggest the similarities and differences between developing countries, the nature of their relationships with the industrialized nations, and the different perspectives that exist regarding the causes of and approaches to meet the issues.

I would again like to thank McGraw-Hill for the opportunity to put together a reader on a subject that is the focus of my teaching and research. I would also like to thank those who have sent in the response forms with their comments and suggestions. I have tried to take these into account in preparing the current volume. No book on a topic as broad as the developing world can be completely comprehensive. There certainly are additional and alternative readings that might be included. Any suggestions for improvement are welcome. Please complete and return the postage-paid article rating form at the end of the book with your comments.

Robert J. Griffiths
Editor

Contents

UNIT 1
Understanding the Developing World

The concepts in bold italics are developed in the article. For further expansion, please refer to the Topic Guide.

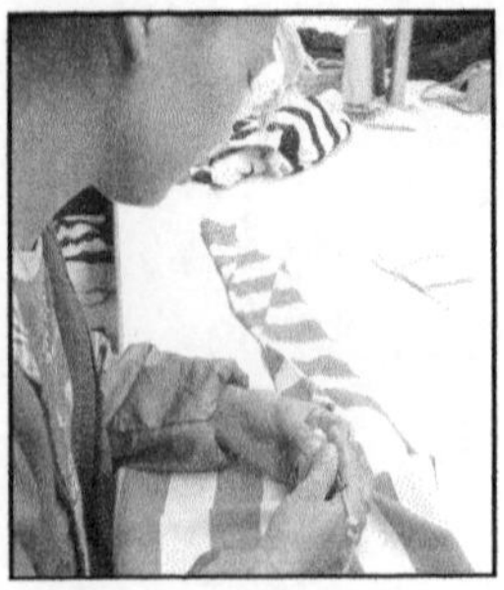

UNIT 2
Political Economy and the Developing World

The concepts in bold italics are developed in the article. For further expansion, please refer to the Topic Guide.

UNIT 3
Conflict and Instability

The concepts in bold italics are developed in the article. For further expansion, please refer to the Topic Guide.

UNIT 4
Political Change in the Developing World

The concepts in bold italics are developed in the article. For further expansion, please refer to the Topic Guide.

The concepts in bold italics are developed in the article. For further expansion, please refer to the Topic Guide.

UNIT 5
Population, Resources, Environment, and Health

The concepts in bold italics are developed in the article. For further expansion, please refer to the Topic Guide.

UNIT 6
Women and Development

The concepts in bold italics are developed in the article. For further expansion, please refer to the Topic Guide.

The concepts in bold italics are developed in the article. For further expansion, please refer to the Topic Guide.

Correlation Guide

The *Annual Editions* series provides students with convenient, inexpensive access to current, carefully selected articles from the public press. **Annual Editions: Developing World 11/12** is an easy-to-use reader that presents articles on important topics such as *democracy, foreign aid, human rights,* and many more. For more information on *Annual Editions* and other *McGraw-Hill Contemporary Learning Series* titles, visit www.mhhe.com/cls.

This convenient guide matches the units in **Annual Editions: Developing World 11/12** with the corresponding chapters in one of our best-selling McGraw-Hill Political Science textbooks by Rourke/Boyer.

Annual Editions: Developing World 11/12	International Politics on the World Stage, Brief, 8/e by Rourke/Boyer
Unit 1: Understanding the Developing World	**Chapter 1:** Thinking and Caring about World Politics **Chapter 2:** The Evolution of World Politics **Chapter 4:** Nationalism: The Traditional Orientation **Chapter 5:** Globalism: The Alternative Orientation
Unit 2: Political Economy and the Developing World	**Chapter 3:** Levels of Analysis and Foreign Policy **Chapter 5:** Globalism: The Alternative Orientation **Chapter 11:** International Economics: The Alternative Road
Unit 3: Conflict and Instability	**Chapter 9:** Pursuing Security
Unit 4: Political Change in the Developing World	**Chapter 6:** Power, Statecraft, and the National State: The Traditional Structure **Chapter 7:** Intergovernmental Organizations: Alternative Governance
Unit 5: Population, Resources, Environment, and Health	**Chapter 8:** International Law and Human Rights **Chapter 10:** National Economic Competition: The Traditional Road **Chapter 11:** International Economics: The Alternative Road **Chapter 12:** Preserving and Enhancing the Biosphere
Unit 6: Women and Development	**Chapter 8:** International Law and Human Rights

Topic Guide

This topic guide suggests how the selections in this book relate to the subjects covered in your course. You may want to use the topics listed on these pages to search the Web more easily.

On the following pages a number of websites have been gathered specifically for this book. They are arranged to reflect the units of this Annual Editions reader. You can link to these sites by going to www.mhhe.com/cls.

All the articles that relate to each topic are listed below the bold-faced term.

Internet References

The following Internet sites have been selected to support the articles found in this reader. These sites were available at the time of publication. However, because websites often change their structure and content, the information listed may no longer be available. We invite you to visit www.mhhe.com/cls for easy access to these sites.

Annual Editions: Developing World 11/12

General Sources

Council on Foreign Relations
www.cfr.org
Independent, non-partisan membership and research organization providing information on world affairs and United States Foreign policy.

Foreign Policy in Focus (FPIF): Progressive Response Index
http://fpif.org/progresp/index_body.html
This index is produced weekly by FPIF, a "think tank without walls," which is an international network of analysts and activists dedicated to "making the U.S. a more responsible global leader and partner by advancing citizen movements and agendas." This index lists volume and issue numbers, dates, and topics covered by the articles.

Nordic Africa Institute
www.nai.uu.se
Center for research, documentation, and information on Africa.

People & Planet
www.peopleandplanet.org
People & Planet is an organization of student groups at universities and colleges across the United Kingdom. Organized in 1969 by students at Oxford University, it is now an independent pressure group campaigning on world poverty, human rights, and the environment.

United Nations System Web Locator
www.unsystem.org
This is the website for all the organizations in the United Nations family. According to its brief overview, the United Nations, an organization of sovereign nations, provides the machinery to help find solutions to international problems or disputes and to deal with pressing concerns that face people everywhere, including the problems of the developing world, through the UN Development Program at www.undp.org and UNAIDS at www.unaids.org.

United States Census Bureau: International Summary Demographic Data
www.census.gov/ipc/www/idb
The International Data Base (IDB) is a computerized data bank containing statistical tables of demographic and socioeconomic data for all countries of the world.

UNIT 1: Understanding the Developing World

Africa Index on Africa
www.afrika.no/index
A complete reference source on Africa is available on this website.

African Studies WWW (U. Penn)
www.sas.upenn.edu/African_Studies/AS.html
The African Studies Center at the University of Pennsylvania supports this ongoing project that lists online resources related to African Studies.

United Nations Development Program
http://undp.org
The UN's global development network advocating change and connecting countries to knowledge, experience, and resources.

UNIT 2: Political Economy and the Developing World

Center for Third World Organizing
www.ctwo.org
The Center for Third World Organizing (CTWO, pronounced "C-2") is a racial justice organization dedicated to building a social justice movement led by people of color. CTWO is a 20-year-old training and resource center that promotes and sustains direct action organizing in communities of color in the United States.

ENTERWeb
www.enterweb.org
ENTERWeb is an annotated meta-index and information clearinghouse on enterprise development, business, finance, international trade, and the economy in this age of cyberspace and globalization. The main focus is on micro-, small-, and mediumscale enterprises, cooperatives, and community economic development both in developed and developing countries.

International Monetary Fund (IMF)
www.imf.org
The IMF was created to promote international monetary cooperation, to facilitate the expansion and balanced growth of international trade, to promote exchange stability, to assist in the establishment of a multilateral system of payments, to make its general resources temporarily available under adequate safeguards to its members experiencing balance of payments difficulties, and to shorten the duration and lessen the degree of disequilibrium in the international balances of payments of members.

TWN (Third World Network)
www.twnside.org.sg
The Third World Network is an independent, nonprofit international network of organizations and individuals involved in issues relating to development, the Third World, and North-South issues.

U.S. Agency for International Development (USAID)
www.usaid.gov
USAID is an independent government agency that provides economic development and humanitarian assistance to advance U.S. economic and political interests overseas.

The World Bank
www.worldbank.org
The International Bank for Reconstruction and Development, frequently called the World Bank, was established in July 1944 at the UN Monetary and Financial Conference in Bretton Woods, New Hampshire. The World Bank's goal is to reduce poverty and improve living standards by promoting sustainable growth and investment in people. The bank provides loans, technical assistance, and policy guidance to developing country members to achieve this objective.

Internet References

World Trade Organization (WTO)
www.wto.org

The WTO is promoted as the only international body dealing with the rules of trade between nations. At its heart are the WTO agreements, the legal ground rules for international commerce and for trade policy.

UNIT 3: Conflict and Instability

The Carter Center
www.cartercenter.org

The Carter Center is dedicated to fighting disease, hunger, poverty, conflict, and oppression through collaborative initiatives in the areas of democratization and development, global health, and urban revitalization.

Center for Strategic and International Studies (CSIS)
www.csis.org

For four decades, the Center for Strategic and International Studies (CSIS) has been dedicated to providing world leaders with strategic insights on, and policy solutions to, current and emerging global issues.

Conflict Research Consortium
http://conflict.colorado.edu

The site offers links to conflict- and peace-related Internet sites.

Institute for Security Studies
www.iss.co.za

This site is South Africa's premier source for information related to African security studies.

International Crisis Group
www.crisisgroup.org

A leading independent, non-partisan research organization focused on the prevention and resolution of conflict.

PeaceNet
www.igc.org/peacenet

PeaceNet promotes dialogue and sharing of information to encourage appropriate dispute resolution, highlights the work of practitioners and organizations, and is a proving ground for ideas and proposals across the range of disciplines within the conflict resolution field.

Refugees International
www.refintl.org

Refugees International provides early warning in crises of mass exodus. It seeks to serve as the advocate of the unrepresented—the refugee. In recent years, Refugees International has moved from its initial focus on Indochinese refugees to global coverage, conducting almost 30 emergency missions in the last 4 years.

UNIT 4: Political Change in the Developing World

Center for Research on Inequality, Human Security, and Ethnicity
www.crise.ox.ac.uk

Information on multiethnic societies and the conditions that promote human security.

Latin American Network Information Center—LANIC
www.lanic.utexas.edu

According to Latin Trade, LANIC is "a good clearinghouse for Internet-accessible information on Latin America."

ReliefWeb
www.reliefweb.int/w/rwb.nsf

ReliefWeb is the UN's Department of Humanitarian Affairs clearinghouse for international humanitarian emergencies.

UNIT 5: Population, Resources, Environment, and Health

Earth Pledge Foundation
www.earthpledge.org

The Earth Pledge Foundation promotes the principles and practices of sustainable development—the need to balance the desire for economic growth with the necessity of environmental protection.

EnviroLink
http://envirolink.org

EnviroLink is committed to promoting a sustainable society by connecting individuals and organizations through the use of the World Wide Web.

Greenpeace
www.greenpeace.org

Greenpeace is an international NGO (nongovernmental organization) that is devoted to environmental protection.

Linkages on Environmental Issues and Development
www.iisd.ca/linkages

Linkages is a site provided by the International Institute for Sustainable Development. It is designed to be an electronic clearinghouse for information on past and upcoming international meetings related to both environmental issues and economic development in the developing world.

Population Action International
www.populationaction.org

According to its mission statement, Population Action International is dedicated to advancing policies and programs that slow population growth in order to enhance the quality of life for all people.

World Health Organization (WHO)
www.who.ch

The WHO's objective, according to its website, is the attainment by all peoples of the highest possible level of health. Health, as defined in the WHO constitution, is a state of complete physical, mental, and social well-being and not merely the absence of disease or infirmity.

The Worldwatch Institute
www.worldwatch.org

The Worldwatch Institute advocates environmental protection and sustainable development.

UNIT 6: Women and Development

WIDNET: Women in Development NETwork
www.focusintl.com/widnet.htm

This site provides a wealth of information about women in development, including the Beijing '95 Conference, WIDNET statistics, and women's studies.

Women Watch/Regional and Country Information
www.un.org/womenwatch

The UN Internet Gateway on the Advancement and Empowerment of Women provides a rich mine of information.

UNIT 1

Understanding the Developing World

Unit Selections

1. **The New Face of Development,** Carol Lancaster
2. **How Development Leads to Democracy: What We Know about Modernization,** Ronald Inglehart and Christian Welzel
3. **The New Population Bomb,** Jack A. Goldstone
4. **The Ideology of Development,** William Easterly
5. **The Case against the West: America and Europe in the Asian Century,** Kishore Mahbubani

Learning Outcomes

After reading this unit you should be able to:

- Discuss the complexity and diversity of developing countries.
- Describe the changes in the emphasis of development over time.
- Outline the connection between democracy and development.
- Explain the ways that demographic and economic changes are likely to have an impact on the power and influence of both developing and industrialized countries.
- Contrast the differences between the traditional model of development and one that emphasizes the input of those who are the focus of development efforts.
- Analyze the argument that the West's global influence is declining.

Student Website

www.mhhe.com/cls

Internet References

Africa Index on Africa
www.afrika.no/index

African Studies WWW (U. Penn)
www.sas.upenn.edu/African_Studies/AS.html

United Nations Development Program
http://undp.org

The diversity of the countries that make up the developing world has always made it difficult to characterize and understand these countries and their role in international affairs. The task has become even more difficult as further differentiation among developing countries has occurred. "Developing world" is a catch-all term that lacks precision and explanatory power. It is used to describe societies that are desperately poor as well as those rich in resources. The term also refers to societies ranging from traditional to modern and from authoritarian to democratic. To complicate things even further, there is also debate over what actually constitutes development. For some, it is economic growth or progress towards democracy, while for others it involves greater empowerment and dignity. There are also differing views on why progress toward development has been uneven. The West tends to see the problem as stemming from poor governance, institutional weakness, and failure to embrace free-market principles. Critics from the developing world cite the legacy of colonialism and the nature of the international political and economic structures as the reasons for the lack of development. Not only are there differing views on the causes of lagging development, but there is also considerable debate on how best to tackle these issues. The Millennium Development Goals (MDGs) seek to eradicate extreme poverty and hunger and address issues of education, health, gender, and the environment. Progress in this effort so far has been uneven. This has contributed to the debate on the best way to achieve development. Critics maintain that the top-down ideology of development epitomized in the MDGs focuses attention at the macro level of development and impedes the emergence of local, grassroots solutions. The emphasis of development has shifted as well; it now extends beyond the traditional focus on poverty reduction to include issues like civil and political rights, human security, and environmental sustainability. Reflecting this broader emphasis is a growing list of actors that includes non-governmental organizations and philanthropic organizations involved in development efforts. In any case, lumping together the 120-plus nations that make up the developing world obscures the disparities in size, population, resources, forms of government, level of industrialization, distribution of wealth, ethnicity, and a host of other indicators that makes it difficult to categorize and generalize about this large, diverse group of countries.

© Paul Springett/Alamy Images RF

Despite their diversity, most nations of the developing world share some characteristics. Many developing countries have large populations, with annual growth rates that often exceed 2 percent. Although there has been some improvement, poverty continues to be widespread in both rural and urban areas, with rural areas often containing the poorest of the poor. While the majority of the developing world's inhabitants continue to live in the countryside, there is a massive rural-to-urban migration under way, cities are growing rapidly, and some developing countries are approaching urbanization rates similar to those of industrialized countries. Wealth is unevenly distributed, making education, employment opportunities, and access to health care luxuries that only a few enjoy. Corruption and mismanagement are too common. With very few exceptions, these nations share a colonial past that has affected them both politically and economically. A critical perspective from the developing world charges that the neocolonial structure of the international economy and the West's political, military, and cultural links with the developing world amount to continued domination.

The roots of the diverging views between the rich and the poor nations on development emerged shortly after the beginning of the independence era. The neocolonial viewpoint encouraged efforts to alter the international economic order during the 1970s. While the New International Economic Order (NIEO) succumbed to neoliberalism in the 1980s, developing countries still frequently seek solidarity in their interactions with the West. The efforts to extract concessions from the industrialized countries in the negotiations on the Doha Trade Round illustrated this effort. Moreover, developing countries still view Western prescriptions for development skeptically and chafe under the Washington Consensus, which dictates the terms for the access to funds from international financial institutions and foreign aid. Furthermore, some critics suggest that Western development models result in inequitable development and give rise to cultural imperialism. In contrast to the developing world's criticism of the West, industrial countries continue to maintain the importance of institution-building and following the Western model that emphasizes a market-oriented approach to development. As the developing world comes to play a more prominent role in economic, security, and environmental issues, the West's ability to dictate the terms on which development occurs will diminish.

There is a clear difference of opinion between the industrialized countries and the developed world on issues ranging from economic development to governance. While the West has always had an advantage in determining the agenda for development, the influence of the industrialized countries may wane as demographic and economic changes bring about a shift in power. Ultimately the development process will be shaped primarily by the countries experiencing it. The industrialized countries can, however, continue to contribute to this process although it may require re-evaluation of policies on trade and technology transfer, along with more emphasis on innovative and effective aid.

The New Face of Development

As the traditional development challenge of reducing poverty is increasingly met, a new challenge for the twenty-first century emerges: that of ensuring a livable, peaceful, and prosperous world.

CAROL LANCASTER

A number of trends in international development that were already emerging at the end of the last millennium—including the introduction of new actors and technologies, the increasing role of private investment, and the remarkable reduction in poverty in countries such as China and India—have become even more apparent as we approach the end of the current decade. These trends go to the core of what development is, how it is achieved, and who is involved in promoting it. In combination, they suggest that international development in the future will likely be very different from what it has been in the past.

The world first turned its attention to the challenge of international development in the decades immediately after World War II, as the cold war began and decolonization got under way. How, the international community asked itself, could growth be accelerated and poverty reduced in newly independent, less developed nations? Wealthy countries increasingly engaged in promoting economic progress in developing countries (primarily through foreign aid), and also established professional agencies, both bilateral and multilateral, to allocate and manage development assistance. The motives for the developed countries' actions, of course, were not purely altruistic. They sought to promote their national interests (such as the containment of Soviet influence); to ensure that decolonization proceeded smoothly; to preserve spheres of influence in former colonies; to expand their own exports; and to secure sources of raw materials abroad.

During the 40 years between 1960 and 2000, the international aid and development regime depended on rich countries' providing concessional economic assistance. They provided such assistance either directly to recipient governments, or indirectly, through international institutions. The aid was targeted toward agreed-upon projects like roads, government-provided agricultural services, primary education, and health care. Rich countries' trade and investment policies were understood to be an important part of the development equation, but they tended to be much less prominent than development aid itself, since trade and investment usually involved powerful domestic interests within rich countries, a circumstance that constrained their use for development purposes.

Over the same period, the ways in which aid was used to promote development underwent an evolution. In the 1960s, the primary emphasis was on encouraging economic growth by providing funds for infrastructure and other projects meant to expand national production. In the 1970s, the main focus was direct action to alleviate poverty, with aid devoted to projects that would meet the basic needs of the poor in developing countries (including basic education, primary health care, and development of small farms). In the 1980s, the emphasis was on fostering growth through budgetary support for economic reforms and "structural adjustment."

The 1990s turned out to be a transition decade for development. With the end of the cold war and the breakup of the Soviet Union, many of the former communist bloc countries began a transition to free markets and democratic governance. Aid-giving governments turned their attention, and their aid, to furthering this transition. A wave of democratization washed over other parts of the world as well, including sub-Saharan Africa, and democracy became increasingly linked with development in the minds of many development practitioners. Democracy, it was now argued, was a key facilitator of development, and thus foreign aid was increasingly used to promote political development.

At the same time, rising concerns over transnational problems, such as environmental deterioration and infectious diseases (especially HIV/AIDS), expanded the development discourse. Conflict prevention and mitigation became part of the broadening framework of international development as civil conflicts erupted in a number of countries, especially in Africa, and it became obvious that economic progress required peaceful conditions. Finally, the development dialogue renewed its emphasis on poverty reduction, partly because of the "associational revolution"—an explosion of civil society organizations, in both rich and poor countries. Many of these organizations were interested in bettering the human condition.

The continued evolution of information technologies will empower the poor, probably in ways we cannot foresee.

And so, between the postwar period and the year 2000, much changed. In particular, the notion of development expanded to include a much wider range of issues. Yet the core focus remained poverty reduction, and the primary instrument for achieving it remained government-based economic assistance.

An Elastic Idea

Today, international development has become an even more elastic concept, as ideas about what constitutes development, how it is best achieved, and who should be part of the process continue to evolve. Starting from the early years of the international development era a half-century ago, development was thought of as a means to improve the material conditions of life. That is, public and private investment would promote growth, which in turn would eventually reduce or even eliminate poverty. This basic concept remains at the heart of development, but there have been some important additions.

"Human development" is now part of the equation, meaning that education, health, life expectancy, and other indicators of well-being are given greater attention. Political rights are also considered a key aspect of development, in part to ensure that the poor and excluded have a political voice. Some have incorporated "human security," as well, including security against economic deprivation and against physical violence, actual or threatened. "Sustainable development," or economic progress that does not affect the environment too harshly, is another element in the welter of ideas that currently define development. Some in recent years have defined development as the freedom to choose a fulfilling life.

This trend is likely to continue. Development will have at its core the reduction of severe poverty as long as that problem endures; but it will also continue to evolve to reflect changing global beliefs about the basic requirements of a decent human life and about how to meet those requirements.

Western economists have always believed that the driver of development is private investment—on the theory that because it increases productivity, production, growth, incomes, and jobs, it will ultimately eliminate poverty. Others, however, have taken the view that the market is unable to create equitable development and that state intervention is necessary to direct and hasten economic progress. This state-versus-market tension was evident during the cold war, with the socialist and capitalist models doing battle. The same philosophical difference is part of the debate between those who emphasize macroeconomic growth (for example, through structural adjustment) and those who emphasize direct interventions to reduce poverty. From an institutional perspective, this tension has been reflected in the often differing approaches of the World Bank and nongovernmental organizations (NGOs) toward promoting development.

In recent years, something of a consensus has emerged. It is now broadly accepted that private investment and well functioning markets are essential to sustaining long-term growth, and that the state cannot do it alone. But it is also generally recognized that without a well-functioning state, markets cannot produce sustained growth and reduce poverty.

When the era of international development began, the major actors were states, along with international institutions like the World Bank. Rich states shaped world trade policies and the special trade arrangements (for example, the Generalized System of Preferences) that affected the trade of poor countries. Not much foreign investment in poor countries was carried out, and even then it was sometimes unwelcome. Essentially, the governments of rich countries provided aid to the governments of poor countries. It was, in the language of telecommunications, a "one-to-one" world.

This has changed. Governments still play a major role but they are joined by civil society organizations, both in developed and developing countries. These groups deliver services, funded both by governments and through private giving, and advocate for more action to improve the lives of the poor. Growing numbers of corporations are investing large amounts in poor countries. They are also funding development activities on their own, often in public-private partnerships that also involve governments of rich countries and NGOs. These activities are part of corporate social responsibility programs, or even part of businesses' marketing strategies.

The scale of global philanthropy has grown over time, and the number of philanthropic organizations funding development activities has also grown. The Gates Foundation is the most prominent of the new foundations but there are many others. Countless so-called social entrepreneurs have come on the scene as well. These are individuals in developed and developing countries who create NGOs to tackle development problems—as well as "venture philanthropists" who create enterprises with double and triple bottom lines, enterprises that aim to do good while doing well. (An example would be an equity fund that combines investing with providing technical assistance to small enterprises that have few alternatives for capital or training.)

These actors have created a "many-to-many" development space that promises to grow in the coming decades. Also contributing to many-to-many development is the growing flow of remittances from immigrants working in rich countries to their families in poor countries. Indeed, the flow of remittances exceeds the global total of foreign aid by a considerable amount.

The Technology Revolution

All these trends have been facilitated by new information technologies. We are living, in fact, in the midst of several technology revolutions—information technology, biotechnology, nano-technology, and materials technology. All of these hold the promise of radically changing not only our lives but also the lives of the poor in developing countries.

Information technology is already connecting many inhabitants of developing nations to the internet, as computers become increasingly affordable in poor countries. Cell phones are being used for banking, medical investigations, market updates, and obtaining all manner of otherwise out-of-reach information (as well as for political networking). The continued evolution of information technologies will empower the poor, probably in ways we cannot foresee. It has already provided new means for financial support to reach the poor through NGOs operating in developing countries, as wealthy people contribute through internet portals. This innovation cuts out middlemen and encourages direct giving. The internet has also facilitated the transfer of remittances from rich to poor countries. And it permits the poor to network as never before, an opportunity that will surely be seized even more in the future as cell phones come to resemble computers and become more affordable for all.

The biological revolution promises gains in medicine and agriculture, though these are not without controversy. The benefits have not yet reached a large enough scale to have a major impact on the lives of the poor, but this seems only a matter of time. Nanotechnology fosters miniaturization that, among other things, will make more powerful and cheaper cell phones possible. And advances in materials technology could lead to the production of commodities especially designed for difficult environments, an encouraging prospect for the poor living in those environments.

The Third World's End

During much of the past 40 years, people spoke and wrote about the "Third World"—the many developing countries that were an arena of competition between the United States and the Soviet Union. The Soviet Union, of course, is gone. But so is any semblance of shared poverty among the 150 or so countries comprising Asia, Africa, and Latin America. China has provided the most dramatic example of a poor country achieving rapid growth through manufacturing and exporting. In the past 25 years, China's development has lifted a quarter of a billion people out of poverty. This is a degree of economic progress, even with all of its accompanying problems, that is historically unprecedented. China is in fact now a major source of trade, aid, and investment for countries in Africa, Latin America, and elsewhere in Asia.

Economic progress in India—the other country with large-scale poverty and a population in excess of a billion—is increasingly evident as well. There, development is based to a large extent on the export of services. Poverty has fallen somewhat in Latin America, too, as many economies there diversify and grow. This means that the world's hard-core poverty and development problem is now concentrated in sub-Saharan Africa.

In many countries in sub-Saharan Africa, little economic progress has been achieved since independence. The difficulties standing in the way of the region's advancement include a difficult climate and the heavy disease load that comes with being located in the tropics. Also, many sub-Saharan nations are small and landlocked. Others are resource-rich but have found these resources to be a curse (Nigeria with its oil; Sierra Leone with its diamonds; the Democratic Republic of Congo [DRC] with its copper, cobalt, and other minerals).

One discerns a real opportunity—for the first time in history—to eradicate severe poverty worldwide.

Governments in these countries have long exhibited incompetence and corruption, and their resources have made it possible for them to provide little accountability to their citizens. Discontent has often led to violent conflict, which has been further stoked by competition for the control of resources. Civil conflicts in the DRC, Sierra Leone, and elsewhere have killed large numbers of people, created even more refugees and displaced persons, and destroyed national assets. Nigeria continues to teeter on the brink of a political abyss, the DRC continues to be plagued by internal war, and Somalia is still a collapsed state—with predictable effects on development.

But not all the news out of Africa is gloomy. Economic growth in India and China has increased demand, and thus prices, for the raw materials that many African countries export. Economic management in Africa, at least in most places, is better than it has been in several decades. Democratic development—or political openness, anyway—is greater than it has been during much of the period since independence.

Corruption, on the other hand, remains a major problem in many African countries. Additionally, China's extraordinary success in producing cheap manufactured goods appears to have left African countries—which lack the cheap, productive labor that China has—with few opportunities to attract the investment that might lead them into world manufacturing markets. In short, Africa is experiencing some new economic opportunities but also some new challenges.

Global Challenges

Beginning in the 1990s, major powers began to take greater note of global and transnational problems when they calculated their foreign policy and foreign aid policies. For much of that decade, the focus of this set of concerns, known as global public goods, was the environment—pollution, loss of plant and animal species, and loss of the ozone layer. While these transnational concerns (other than the ozone layer) have not abated, two more have joined them: infectious disease (above all HIV/AIDS) and climate change (which was not yet such a prominent concern in the 1990s).

The Bush administration has promised an extraordinary amount of aid to fight HIV/AIDS worldwide—$30 billion over the coming five years. Concern over this disease has risen in the United States as its global impact has become ever more evident, above all in Africa. The American religious right—long skeptical of the appropriateness and efficacy of foreign aid—has embraced fighting HIV/AIDS as the duty of Christians to aid those, especially women and children, who are suffering through no fault of their own. Although allocations of assistance so far have not kept pace with pledges, it is possible that fighting this disease will become the largest element in US foreign aid in the future.

But the next US president will also need to confront the issue of climate change, the reality and probable impact of which can no longer be ignored. That impact, incidentally, is expected to be particularly damaging to many of the world's poor countries. It seems likely, given that the governments of rich countries only have so much money to spend on development, that some development money will be shifted over the coming decades to fund activities intended to combat global warming—perhaps some of it as incentive payments to encourage governments to reduce greenhouse gas emissions.

Beyond climate change, two other trends may produce major development challenges in decades to come: the continuing growth of the world's population and the economic growth in China, India, and elsewhere. Global population is expected to continue expanding over the coming years—with nearly all of the growth taking place in the world's poor countries. Increased population will mean additional greenhouse gas emissions, as well as additional pressure on supplies of food, water, and energy. Economic growth, though it is hoped for and expected, will exacerbate those pressures, especially as demand for superior foods—meats instead of grains—increases. (A widely observed growth pattern is that as people's incomes rise they demand more protein in their diets in the form of meat and fish. But producing one pound of beef requires eight pounds of grain, and this increases pressures on food production systems.)

As for water, pressures on supply are already evident in Africa, the Middle East, northern China, and the Indian subcontinent. Where adequate water supplies cannot be procured, threats to human health and well-being emerge, along with threats to peace, stability, and income growth. Severe tensions over water already exist in the Middle East, and such situations are likely to become more common as population continues to increase. Meanwhile, a growing world population will use more fossil fuels, which will not only lead to progressively higher petroleum prices but will also exacerbate global warming.

These trends suggest that the combination of worldwide population growth and income growth needs to be managed carefully if the planet is to remain livable for our children and grandchildren. This challenge may prove the greatest of the twenty-first century.

An additional problem affecting development worldwide will be movements of people. The populations of many rich countries, and China as well, are growing at or below the replacement rate (with the United States, for reasons that are not entirely clear, a notable exception). The average age of people in these countries is rising, and this means that the dependency ratio is rising as well—each worker is in effect supporting more people. Unsurprisingly, the demand for additional workers is growing in these economies, and immigration from poorer countries to richer ones—from China to Japan, from North Africa and sub-Saharan Africa to Europe, and from Latin America to the United States—has exploded. Much of this immigration is illegal.

This movement of people has delivered benefits both to host countries and to countries of origin. It allows necessary work to be carried out in host countries while immigrants are able to send home remittances that finance consumption and investment there. This seems like a win-win arrangement—except that some citizens of the host countries experience the arrangement as a threat to their identities and ways of life. Even in the United States, where national identity is based on the idea of republican democracy rather than ethnicity, religion, or language, tensions surrounding immigration are increasingly evident.

Such tensions, in the United States and also in Japan and Europe, threaten sometimes to erupt into social strife (as indeed has occurred in recent years in France). It is not clear what will happen as the irresistible force of immigration continues to collide with the immovable object of host-country resistance, but certainly if the remittance economy and access to labor are constrained, international development will suffer a setback.

After Poverty

Since the end of the cold war, because we no longer live in a bipolar world, we have lacked a certain clarity that allowed us to order our international relations and forge domestic consensus on urgent problems. Today's world has a single major power—and many complex problems that are beyond that power's ability to resolve. International development is one of them.

Nevertheless, within this complex and fluid world, one discerns a real opportunity—for the first time in history—to eradicate severe poverty worldwide. The resources and know-how are available and much progress has already been made, especially in China and, increasingly, in India. It will not be easy to "make poverty history" over the coming decades. A great deal needs to be achieved in education, investment, and governance, and in addition we must address the issue of migrations of people away from areas of the world with too few resources to sustain a minimally acceptable standard of living. The obstacles may be insuperable in some cases. But the opportunities are there.

Meanwhile, as the traditional development challenge of reducing poverty is increasingly met, a new development challenge for the twenty-first century emerges: that of ensuring a livable, peaceful, and prosperous world. This will require addressing the global problems that arise when growing populations and rising incomes collide with limited resources.

Assess Your Progress

1. What trends account for the current perspective on international development?
2. How has the view of international development changed over the past five decades?
3. How would you define the terms human development, human security, and sustainable development?
4. What actors have increasingly come to play a role in development?
5. What global challenges are likely to affect development in the future?

Carol Lancaster is an associate professor at Georgetown University's Walsh School of Foreign Service and director of the university's Mortara Center for International Studies. A former deputy administrator of the US Agency for International Development, she is author of the forthcoming *George Bush's Foreign Aid: Revolution or Chaos?* (Center for Global Development, 2008).

How Development Leads to Democracy

What We Know about Modernization

RONALD INGLEHART AND CHRISTIAN WELZEL

In the last several years, a democratic boom has given way to a democratic recession. Between 1985 and 1995, scores of countries made the transition to democracy, bringing widespread euphoria about democracy's future. But more recently, democracy has retreated in Bangladesh, Nigeria, the Philippines, Russia, Thailand, and Venezuela, and the Bush administration's attempts to establish democracy in Afghanistan and Iraq seem to have left both countries in chaos. These developments, along with the growing power of China and Russia, have led many observers to argue that democracy has reached its high-water mark and is no longer on the rise.

That conclusion is mistaken. The underlying conditions of societies around the world point to a more complicated reality. The bad news is that it is unrealistic to assume that democratic institutions can be set up easily, almost anywhere, at any time. Although the outlook is never hopeless, democracy is most likely to emerge and survive when certain social and cultural conditions are in place. The Bush administration ignored this reality when it attempted to implant democracy in Iraq without first establishing internal security and overlooked cultural conditions that endangered the effort.

The good news, however, is that the conditions conducive to democracy can and do emerge—and the process of "modernization," according to abundant empirical evidence, advances them. Modernization is a syndrome of social changes linked to industrialization. Once set in motion, it tends to penetrate all aspects of life, bringing occupational specialization, urbanization, rising educational levels, rising life expectancy, and rapid economic growth. These create a self-reinforcing process that transforms social life and political institutions, bringing rising mass participation in politics and—in the long run—making the establishment of democratic political institutions increasingly likely. Today, we have a clearer idea than ever before of why and how this process of democratization happens.

The long-term trend toward democracy has always come in surges and declines. At the start of the twentieth century, only a handful of democracies existed, and even they fell short of being full democracies by today's standards. There was a major increase in the number of democracies following World War I, another surge following World War II, and a third surge at the end of the Cold War. Each of these surges was followed by a decline, although the number of democracies never fell back to the original base line. By the start of the twenty-first century, about 90 states could be considered democratic.

Although many of these democracies are flawed, the overall trend is striking: in the long run, modernization brings democracy. This means that the economic resurgence of China and Russia has a positive aspect: underlying changes are occurring that make the emergence of increasingly liberal and democratic political systems likely in the coming years. It also means that there is no reason to panic about the fact that democracy currently appears to be on the defensive. The dynamics of modernization and democratization are becoming increasingly clear, and it is likely that they will continue to function.

The Great Debate

The concept of modernization has a long history. During the nineteenth and twentieth centuries, a Marxist theory of modernization proclaimed that the abolition of private property would put an end to exploitation, inequality, and conflict. A competing capitalist version held that economic development would lead to rising living standards and democracy. These two visions of modernization competed fiercely throughout much of the Cold War. By the 1970s, however, communism began to stagnate, and neither economic development nor democratization was apparent in many poor countries. Neither version of utopia seemed to be unfolding, and critics pronounced modernization theory dead.

Since the end of the Cold War, however, the concept of modernization has taken on new life, and a new version of modernization theory has emerged, with clear implications for our understanding of where global economic development is likely to lead. Stripped of the oversimplifications of its early versions, the new concept of modernization sheds light on ongoing cultural changes, such as the rise of gender equality the recent wave of democratization, and the democratic peace theory.

For most of human history, technological progress was extremely slow and new developments in food production were offset by population increases—trapping agrarian economies in a steady-state equilibrium with no growth in living standards. History was seen as either cyclic or in long-term decline from a past golden age. The situation began to change with the Industrial Revolution and the advent of sustained economic growth—which led to both the capitalist and the communist visions of modernization. Although the ideologies competed fiercely, they were both committed to economic growth and social progress and brought mass participation in politics. And each side believed that the developing nations of the Third World would follow its path to modernization.

At the height of the Cold War, a version of modernization theory emerged in the United States that portrayed underdevelopment as a direct consequence of a country's psychological and cultural traits. Underdevelopment was said to reflect irrational traditional religious and communal values that discouraged achievement. The rich Western democracies, the theory went, could instill modern values and bring progress to "backward" nations through economic, cultural, and military assistance. By the 1970s, however, it had become clear that assistance had not brought much progress toward prosperity or democracy—eroding confidence in this version of modernization theory, which was increasingly criticized as ethnocentric and patronizing. It came under heavy criticism from "dependency theorists," who argued that trade with rich countries exploits poor ones, locking them into positions of structural dependence. The elites in developing countries welcomed such thinking, since it implied that poverty had nothing to do with internal problems or the corruption of local leaders; it was the fault of global capitalism. By the 1980s, dependency theory was in vogue. Third World nations, the thinking went, could escape from global exploitation only by withdrawing from global markets and adopting import-substitution policies.

More recently, it has become apparent that import-substitution strategies have failed: the countries least involved in global trade, such as Cuba, Myanmar (also called Burma), and North Korea, have not been the most successful—they have actually grown the least. Export-oriented strategies have been far more effective in promoting sustained economic growth and, eventually, democratization. The pendulum, accordingly, has swung back, and a new version of modernization theory has gained credibility. The rapid economic development of East Asia, and the subsequent democratization of South Korea and Taiwan, seem to confirm its basic claims: producing for the world market enables economic growth; investing the returns in human capital and upgrading the work force to produce high-tech goods brings higher returns and enlarges the educated middle class; once the middle class becomes large and articulate enough, it presses for liberal democracy—the most effective political system for advanced industrial societies. Nevertheless, even today, if one mentions modernization at a conference on economic development, one is likely to hear a reiteration of dependency theory's critique of the "backward nations" version of modernization theory, as if that were all there is to modernization theory—and as if no new evidence had emerged since the 1970s.

The New Modernization

In retrospect, it is obvious that the early versions of modernization theory were wrong on several points. Today, virtually nobody expects a revolution of the proletariat that will abolish private property, ushering in a new era free from exploitation and conflict. Nor does anyone expect that industrialization will automatically lead to democratic institutions; communism and fascism also emerged from industrialization. Nonetheless, a massive body of evidence suggests that modernization theory's central premise was correct: economic development does tend to bring about important, roughly predictable changes in society, culture, and politics. But the earlier versions of modernization theory need to be corrected in several respects.

First, modernization is not linear. It does not move indefinitely in the same direction; instead, the process reaches inflection points. Empirical evidence indicates that each phase of modernization is associated with distinctive changes in people's worldviews. Industrialization leads to one major process of change, resulting in bureaucratization, hierarchy, centralization of authority, secularization, and a shift from traditional to secular-rational values. The rise of postindustrial society brings another set of cultural changes that move in a different direction: instead of bureaucratization and centralization, the new trend is toward an increasing emphasis on individual autonomy and self-expression values, which lead to a growing emancipation from authority.

Thus, other things being equal, high levels of economic development tend to make people more tolerant and trusting, bringing more emphasis on self-expression and more participation in decision-making. This process is not deterministic, and any forecasts can only be probabilistic, since economic factors are not the only influence; a given country's leaders and nation-specific events also shape what happens. Moreover, modernization is not irreversible. Severe economic collapse can reverse it, as happened during the Great Depression in Germany, Italy, Japan, and Spain and during the 1990s in most of the Soviet successor states. Similarly, if the current economic crisis becomes a twenty-first-century Great Depression, the world could face a new struggle against renewed xenophobia and authoritarianism.

Second, social and cultural change is path dependent: history matters. Although economic development tends to bring predictable changes in people's worldviews, a society's heritage—whether shaped by Protestantism, Catholicism, Islam, Confucianism, or communism—leaves a lasting imprint on its worldview. A society's value system reflects an interaction between the driving forces of modernization and the persisting influence of tradition. Although the classic modernization theorists in both the East and the West thought that religion and ethnic traditions would die out, they have proved to be highly resilient. Although the publics of industrializing societies are becoming richer and more educated, that is hardly creating a uniform global culture. Cultural heritages are remarkably enduring.

Third, modernization is not westernization, contrary to the earlier, ethnocentric version of the theory. The process of industrialization began in the West, but during the past few decades, East Asia has had the world's highest economic growth rates, and Japan leads the world in life expectancy and some other aspects of modernization. The United States is not the model for global cultural change, and industrializing societies in general are not becoming like the United States, as a popular version of modernization theory assumes. In fact, American society retains more traditional values than do most other high-income societies.

Fourth, modernization does not automatically lead to democracy. Rather, it, in the long run, brings social and cultural changes that make democratization increasingly probable. Simply attaining a high level of per capita GDP does not produce democracy: if it did, Kuwait and the United Arab Emirates would have become model democracies. (These countries have not gone through the modernization process described above.) But the emergence of postindustrial society brings certain social and cultural changes that are specifically conducive to democratization. Knowledge societies cannot function effectively without highly educated publics that have become increasingly accustomed to thinking for themselves. Furthermore, rising levels of economic security bring a growing emphasis on a syndrome of self-expression values—one that gives high priority to free choice and motivates political action. Beyond a certain point, accordingly, it becomes difficult to avoid democratization, because repressing mass demands for more open societies becomes increasingly costly and detrimental to economic effectiveness. Thus, in its advanced stages, modernization brings social and cultural changes that make the emergence and flourishing of democratic institutions increasingly likely.

The core idea of modernization theory is that economic and technological development bring a coherent set of social, cultural, and political changes. A large body of empirical evidence supports this idea. Economic development is, indeed, strongly linked to pervasive shifts in people's beliefs and motivations, and these shifts in turn change the role of religion, job motivations, human fertility rates, gender roles, and sexual norms. And they also bring growing mass demands for democratic institutions and for more responsive behavior on the part of elites. These changes together make democracy increasingly likely to emerge, while also making war less acceptable to publics.

Evaluating Values

New sources of empirical evidence provide valuable insights into how modernization changes worldviews and motivations. One important source is global surveys of mass values and attitudes. Between 1981 and 2007, the World Values Survey and the European Values Study carried out five waves of representative national surveys in scores of countries, covering almost 90 percent of the world's population. (For the data from the surveys, visit www.worldvaluessurvey.org.) The results show large cross-national differences in what people believe and value. In some countries, 95 percent of the people surveyed said that God was very important in their lives; in others, only 3 percent did. In some societies, 90 percent of the people surveyed said they believed that men have more of a right to a job than women do; in others, only 8 percent said they thought so. These cross-national differences are robust and enduring, and they are closely correlated with a society's level of economic development: people in low-income societies are much likelier to emphasize religion and traditional gender roles than are people in rich countries.

These values surveys demonstrate that the worldviews of people living in rich societies differ systematically from those of people living in low-income societies across a wide range of political, social, and religious norms. The differences run along two basic dimensions: traditional versus secular-rational values and survival versus self-expression values. (Each dimension reflects responses to scores of questions asked as part of the values surveys.)

The shift from traditional to secular-rational values is linked to the shift from agrarian to industrial societies. Traditional societies emphasize religion, respect for and obedience to authority, and national pride. These characteristics change as societies become more secular and rational. The shift from survival to self-expression values is linked to the rise of postindustrial societies. It reflects a cultural shift that occurs when younger generations emerge that have grown up taking survival for granted. Survival values give top priority to economic and physical security and conformist social norms. Self-expression values give high priority to freedom of expression, participation in decision-making, political activism, environmental protection, gender equality, and tolerance of ethnic minorities, foreigners, and gays and lesbians. A growing emphasis on these latter values engenders a culture of trust and tolerance in which people cherish individual freedom and self-expression and have activist political orientations. These attributes are crucial to democracy—and thus explain how economic growth, which takes societies from agrarian to industrial and then from industrial to postindustrial, leads to democratization. The unprecedented economic growth of the past 50 years has meant that an increasing share of the world's population has grown up taking survival for granted. Time-series data from the values surveys indicate that mass priorities have shifted from an overwhelming emphasis on economic and physical security to an emphasis on subjective well-being, self-expression, participation in decision-making, and a relatively trusting and tolerant outlook.

Both dimensions are closely linked to economic development: the value systems of high-income countries differ dramatically from those of low-income countries. Every nation that the World Bank defines as having a high income ranks relatively high on both dimensions—with a strong emphasis on both secular-rational and self-expression values. All the low-income and lower-middle-income countries rank relatively low on both dimensions. The upper-middle-income countries fall somewhere in between. To a remarkable degree, the values and beliefs of a given society reflect its level of economic developments—just as modernization theory predicts.

This strong connection between a society's value system and its per capita GDP suggests that economic development tends to produce roughly predictable changes in a society's beliefs and values, and time-series evidence supports this hypothesis. When one compares the positions of given countries in successive waves of the values surveys, one finds that almost all the countries that experienced rising per capita GDPs also experienced predictable shifts in their values.

The values survey evidence also shows, however, that cultural change is path dependent; a society's cultural heritage also shapes where it falls on the global cultural map. This map shows distinctive clusters of countries: Protestant Europe, Catholic Europe, ex-communist Europe, the English-speaking countries, Latin America, South Asia, the Islamic world, and Africa. The values emphasized by different societies fall into a remarkably coherent pattern that reflects both those societies' economic development and their religious and colonial heritage. Still, even if a society's cultural heritage continues to shape its prevailing values, economic development brings changes that have important consequences. Over time, it reshapes beliefs and values of all kinds—and it brings a growing mass demand for democratic institutions and for more responsive elite behavior. And over the quarter century covered by the values surveys, the people of most countries placed increasing emphasis on self-expression values. This cultural shift makes democracy increasingly likely to emerge where it does not yet exist and increasingly likely to become more effective and more direct where it does.

Development and Democracy

Fifty years ago, the sociologist Seymour Martin Lipset pointed out that rich countries are much more likely than poor countries to be democracies. Although this claim was contested for many years, it has held up against repeated tests. The causal direction of the relationship has also been questioned: Are rich countries more likely to be democratic because democracy makes countries rich, or is development conducive to democracy? Today, it seems clear that the causality runs mainly from economic development to democratization. During early industrialization, authoritarian states are just as likely to attain high rates of growth as are democracies. But beyond a certain level of economic development, democracy becomes increasingly likely to emerge and survive. Thus, among the scores of countries that democratized around 1990, most were middle-income countries: almost all the high-income countries already were democracies, and few low-income countries made the transition. Moreover, among the countries that democratized between 1970 and 1990, democracy has survived in every country that made the transition when it was at the economic level of Argentina today or higher; among the countries that made the transition when they were below this level, democracy had an average life expectancy of only eight years.

The strong correlation between development and democracy reflects the fact that economic development is conducive to democracy. The question of why, exactly, development leads to democracy has been debated intensely, but the answer is beginning to emerge. It does not result from some disembodied force that causes democratic institutions to emerge automatically when a country attains a certain level of GDP. Rather, economic development brings social and political changes only when it changes people's behavior. Consequently, economic development is conducive to democracy to the extent that it, first, creates a large, educated, and articulate middle class of people who are accustomed to thinking for themselves and, second, transforms people's values and motivations.

Today, it is more possible than ever before to measure what the key changes are and how far they have progressed in given countries. Multivariate analysis of the data from the values surveys makes it possible to sort out the relative impact of economic, social, and cultural changes, and the results point to the conclusion that economic development is conducive to democracy insofar as it brings specific structural changes (particularly the rise of a knowledge sector) and certain cultural changes (particularly the rise of self-expression values). Wars, depressions, institutional changes, elite decisions, and specific leaders also influence what happens, but structural and cultural change are major factors in the emergence and survival of democracy.

Modernization brings rising educational levels, moving the work force into occupations that require independent thinking and making people more articulate and better equipped to intervene in politics. As knowledge societies emerge, people become accustomed to using their own initiative and judgment on the job and are also increasingly likely to question rigid and hierarchical authority.

Modernization also makes people economically more secure, and self-expression values become increasingly widespread when a large share of the population grows up taking survival for granted. The desire for freedom and autonomy are universal aspirations. They may bc subordinated to the need for subsistence and order when survival is precarious, but they take increasingly high priority as survival becomes more secure. The basic motivation for democracy—the human desire for free choice—starts to play an increasingly important role. People begin to place a growing emphasis on free choice in politics and begin to demand civil and political liberties and democratic institutions.

Effective Democracy

During the explosion of democracy that took place between 1985 and 1995, electoral democracy spread rapidly throughout the world. Strategic elite agreements played an important role in this process, facilitated by an international environment in which the end of the Cold War opened the way for democratization. Initially, there was a tendency to view any regime that held free and fair elections as a democracy. But many of the new democracies suffered from massive corruption and failed to apply the rule of law, which is what makes democracy effective. A growing number of observers today thus emphasize the inadequacy of "electoral demomcy," "hybrid democracy," "authoritarian democracy," and other forms of sham democracy in which mass preferences are something that political elites can largely ignore and in which they do not decisively influence government decisions. It is important, accordingly, to distinguish between effective and ineffective democracies.

The essence of democracy is that it empowers ordinary citizens. Whether a democracy is effective or not is based on not only the extent to which civil and political rights exist on paper but also the degree to which officials actually respect these rights. The first of these two components—the existence of rights on paper—is measured by Freedom House's annual rankings: if a country holds free elections, Freedom House tends to rate it as "free," giving it a score at or near the top of its scale. Thus, the new democracies of eastern Europe receive scores as high as those of the established democracies of western Europe, although in-depth analyses show that widespread corruption makes these new democracies far less effective in responding to their citizens' choices. Fortunately, the World Bank's governance scores measure the extent to which a country's democratic institutions are actually effective. Consequently, a rough index of effective democracy can be obtained by multiplying these two scores: formal democracy, as measured by Freedom House, and elite and institutional integrity, as measured by the World Bank.

Effective democracy is a considerably more demanding standard than electoral democracy. One can establish electoral democracy almost anywhere, but it will probably not last long if it does not transfer power from the elites to the people. Effective democracy is most likely to exist alongside a relatively developed infrastructure that includes not only economic resources but also widespread participatory habits and an emphasis on autonomy. Accordingly, it is closely linked to the degree to which a given public emphasizes self-expression values. Indeed, the correlation between a society's values and the nature of the country's political institutions is remarkably strong.

Virtually all the stable democracies show strong self-expression values. Most Latin American countries are underachievers, showing lower levels of effective democracy than their publics' values would predict. This suggests that these societies could support higher levels of democracy if the rule of law were strengthened there. Iran is also an underachiever—a theocratic regime that allows a much lower level of democracy than that to which its people aspire. Surprising as it may seem to those who focus only on elite-level politics, the Iranian public shows relatively strong support for democracy. Conversely, Cyprus, Estonia, Hungary, Poland, Latvia, and Lithuania are overachievers, showing higher levels of democracy than their publics' values would predicts—perhaps reflecting the incentives to democratize provided by membership in the European Union.

But do self-expression values lead to democracy, or does democracy cause self-expression values to emerge? The evidence indicates that these values lead to democracy. (For the full evidence for this claim, see our book *Modernization, Cultural Change, and Democracy.*) Democratic institutions do not need to be in place for self-expression values to emerge. Time-series evidence from the values surveys indicates that in the years preceding the wave of democratization in the late 1980s and early 1990s, self-expression values had already emerged through a process of an intergenerational change in values—not only in the Western democracies but also within many authoritarian societies. By 1990, the publics of East Germany and Czechoslovakia—which had been living under two of the most authoritarian regimes in the world—had developed high levels of self-expression values. The crucial factor was not the political system but the fact that these countries were among the most economically advanced countries in the communist world, with high levels of education and advanced social welfare systems. Thus, when the Soviet leader Mikhail Gorbachev renounced the Brezhnev Doctrine, removing the threat of Soviet military intervention, they moved swiftly toward democracy.

In recent decades, self-expression values have been spreading and getting stronger, making people more likely to directly intervene in politics. (Indeed, unprecedented numbers of people took part in the demonstrations that helped bring about the most recent wave of democratization.) Does this mean that authoritarian systems will inevitably crumble? No. A rising emphasis on self-expression values tends to erode the legitimacy of authoritarian systems, but as long as determined authoritarian elites control the army and the secret police, they can repress pro-democratic forces. Still, even repressive regimes find it costly to check these tendencies, for doing so tends to block the emergence of effective knowledge sectors.

Modern Strategy

This new understanding of modernization has broad implications for international relations. For one thing, it helps explain why advanced democracies do not fight one another. Recent research provides strong empirical support for the claim that they do not, which goes back to Adam Smith and Immanuel Kant. Since they emerged in the early nineteenth century, liberal democracies have fought a number of wars, but almost never against one another. This new version of modernization theory indicates that the democratic peace phenomenon is due more to cultural changes linked to modernization than to democracy per se.

In earlier periods of history, democracies fought one another frequently. But the prevailing norms among them have evolved over time, as is illustrated by the abolition of slavery, the gradual expansion of the franchise, and the movement toward gender equality in virtually all modern societies. Another cultural change that has occurred in modern societies—which tend to be democracies—is that war has become progressively less acceptable and people have become more likely to express this preference and try to affect policy accordingly. Evidence from the World Values Survey indicates that the publics of high-income countries have much lower levels of xenophobia than do the publics of low-income countries, and they are much less willing to fight for their country than are the publics of low-income countries. Moreover, economically developed democracies behave far more peacefully toward one another than do poor democracies, and economically developed democracies are far less prone to civil war than are poor democracies.

Modernization theory has both cautionary and encouraging implications for U.S. foreign policy. Iraq, of course, provides a cautionary lesson. Contrary to the appealing view that democracy can be readily established almost anywhere, modernization theory holds that democracy is much more likely to flourish under certain conditions than others. A number of factors made it unrealistic to expect that democracy would be easy to establish in Iraq, including deep ethnic cleavages that had been exacerbated by Saddam Hussein's regime. And after Saddam's defeat, allowing physical security to deteriorate was a particularly serious mistake. Interpersonal trust and tolerance flourish when people feel secure. Democracy is unlikely to survive in a society torn by distrust and intolerance, and Iraq currently manifests the highest level of xenophobia of any society for which data are available. A good indicator of xenophobia is the extent to which people say they would not want to have foreigners as neighbors. Across 80 countries, the median percentage of those surveyed who said this was 15 percent. Among Iraqi Kurds, 51 percent of those polled said they would prefer not to have foreigners as neighbors. Among Iraqi Arabs, 90 percent of those polled said they would not want foreigners as neighbors. In keeping with these conditions, Iraq (along with Pakistan and Zimbabwe) shows very low levels of both self-expression values and effective democracy.

Modernization theory also has positive implications for U.S. foreign policy. Supported by a large body of evidence, it points to the conclusion that economic development is a basic driver of democratic change—meaning that Washington should do what it can to encourage development. If it wants to bring democratic change to Cuba, for example, isolating it is counterproductive. The United States should lift the embargo, promote economic development, and foster social engagement with, and other connections to, the world. Nothing is certain, but empirical evidence suggests that a growing sense of security and a growing emphasis on self-expression values there would undermine the authoritarian regime.

Similarly, although many observers have been alarmed by the economic resurgence of China, this growth has positive implications for the long term. Beneath China's seemingly monolithic political structure, the social infrastructure of democratization is emerging, and it has progressed further than most observers realize. China is now approaching the level of mass emphasis on self-expression values at which Chile, Poland, South Korea, and Taiwan made their transitions to democracy. And, surprising as it may seem to observers who focus only on elite-level politics, Iran is also near this threshold. As long as the Chinese Communist Party and Iran's theocratic leaders control their countries' military and security forces, democratic institutions will not emerge at the national level. But growing mass pressures for liberalization are beginning to appear, and repressing them will bring growing costs in terms of economic inefficiency and low public morale. On the whole, increasing prosperity for China and Iran is in the United States' national interest.

More broadly, modernization theory implies that the United States should welcome and encourage economic development around the world. Although economic development requires difficult adjustments, its long-term effects encourage the emergence of more tolerant, less xenophobic, and ultimately more democratic societies.

Assess Your Progress

1. What is modernization? How does this process make democratization more likely?
2. How has modernization theory evolved over time?
3. What changes in emphasis need to be made to ensure modernization's continued relevance?
4. What values are important to democracy?
5. What is the connection between economic development and democracy?

Ronald Inglehart is Professor of Political Science at the University of Michigan and Director of the World Values Survey. **Christian Welzel** is Professor of Political Science at Jacobs University Bremen, in Germany. They are the co-authors of *Modernization, Cultural Change, and Democracy.*

The New Population Bomb

The Four Megatrends that Will Change the World

JACK A. GOLDSTONE

Forty-two years ago, the biologist Paul Ehrlich warned in *The Population Bomb* that mass starvation would strike in the 1970s and 1980s, with the world's population growth outpacing the production of food and other critical resources. Thanks to innovations and efforts such as the "green revolution" in farming and the widespread adoption of family planning, Ehrlich's worst fears did not come to pass. In fact, since the 1970s, global economic output has increased and fertility has fallen dramatically, especially in developing countries.

The United Nations Population Division now projects that global population growth will nearly halt by 2050. By that date, the world's population will have stabilized at 9.15 billion people, according to the "medium growth" variant of the UN's authoritative population database World Population Prospects: The 2008 Revision. (Today's global population is 6.83 billion.) Barring a cataclysmic climate crisis or a complete failure to recover from the current economic malaise, global economic output is expected to increase by two to three percent per year, meaning that global income will increase far more than population over the next four decades.

But twenty-first-century international security will depend less on how many people inhabit the world than on how the global population is composed and distributed: where populations are declining and where they are growing, which countries are relatively older and which are more youthful, and how demographics will influence population movements across regions.

These elements are not well recognized or widely understood. A recent article in *The Economist,* for example, cheered the decline in global fertility without noting other vital demographic developments. Indeed, the same UN data cited by *The Economist* reveal four historic shifts that will fundamentally alter the world's population over the next four decades: the relative demographic weight of the world's developed countries will drop by nearly 25 percent, shifting economic power to the developing nations; the developed countries' labor forces will substantially age and decline, constraining economic growth in the developed world and raising the demand for immigrant workers; most of the world's expected population growth will increasingly be concentrated in today's poorest, youngest, and most heavily Muslim countries, which have a dangerous lack of quality education, capital, and employment opportunities; and, for the first time in history, most of the world's population will become urbanized, with the largest urban centers being in the world's poorest countries, where policing, sanitation, and health care are often scarce.

Taken together, these trends will pose challenges every bit as alarming as those noted by Ehrlich. Coping with them will require nothing less than a major reconsideration of the world's basic global governance structures.

Europe's Reversal of Fortunes

At the beginning of the eighteenth century, approximately 20 percent of the world's inhabitants lived in Europe (including Russia). Then, with the Industrial Revolution, Europe's population boomed, and streams of European emigrants set off for the Americas. By the eve of World War I, Europe's population had more than quadrupled. In 1913, Europe had more people than China, and the proportion of the world's population living in Europe and the former European colonies of North America had risen to over 33 percent.

But this trend reversed after World War I, as basic health care and sanitation began to spread to poorer countries. In Asia, Africa, and Latin America, people began to live longer, and birthrates remained high or fell only slowly. By 2003, the combined populations of Europe, the United States, and Canada accounted for just 17 percent of the global population. In 2050, this figure is expected to be just 12 percent—far less than it was in 1700. (These projections, moreover, might even understate the reality because they reflect the "medium growth" projection of the UN forecasts, which assumes that the fertility rates of developing countries will decline while those of developed countries will increase. In fact, many developed countries show no evidence of increasing fertility rates.)

The West's relative decline is even more dramatic if one also considers changes in income. The Industrial Revolution made Europeans not only more numerous than they had been but also considerably richer per capita than others worldwide. According to the economic historian Angus Maddison, Europe, the United States, and Canada together produced about 32 percent of the world's GDP at the beginning of the nineteenth century. By 1950, that proportion had increased to a remarkable 68 percent of the world's total output (adjusted to reflect purchasing power parity).

This trend, too, is headed for a sharp reversal. The proportion of global GDP produced by Europe, the United States, and Canada fell from 68 percent in 1950 to 47 percent in 2003 and will decline even more steeply in the future. If the growth rate of per capita income (again, adjusted for purchasing power parity) between 2003 and 2050 remains as it was between 1973 and 2003—averaging 1.68 percent annually in Europe, the United States, and Canada and 2.47 percent annually in the rest of the world—then the combined GDP of Europe, the United States, and Canada will roughly double by 2050, whereas the GDP of the rest of the world will grow by a factor of five. The portion of global GDP produced by Europe, the United States, and Canada in 2050 will then be less than 30 percent—smaller than it was in 1820.

These figures also imply that an overwhelming proportion of the world's GDP growth between 2003 and 2050—nearly 80 percent—will occur outside of Europe, the United States, and Canada. By the middle of this century, the global middle class—those capable of purchasing durable consumer products, such as cars, appliances, and electronics—will increasingly be found in what is now considered the developing world. The World Bank has predicted that by 2030 the number of middle-class people in the developing world will be 1.2 billion—a rise of 200 percent since 2005. This means that the developing world's middle class alone will be larger than the total populations of Europe, Japan, and the United States combined. From now on, therefore, the main driver of global economic expansion will be the economic growth of newly industrialized countries, such as Brazil, China, India, Indonesia, Mexico, and Turkey.

Aging Pains

Part of the reason developed countries will be less economically dynamic in the coming decades is that their populations will become substantially older. The European countries, Canada, the United States, Japan, South Korea, and even China are aging at unprecedented rates. Today, the proportion of people aged 60 or older in China and South Korea is 12–15 percent. It is 15–22 percent in the European Union, Canada, and the United States and 30 percent in Japan. With baby boomers aging and life expectancy increasing, these numbers will increase dramatically. In 2050, approximately 30 percent of Americans, Canadians, Chinese, and Europeans will be over 60, as will more than 40 percent of Japanese and South Koreans.

Over the next decades, therefore, these countries will have increasingly large proportions of retirees and increasingly small proportions of workers. As workers born during the baby boom of 1945–65 are retiring, they are not being replaced by a new cohort of citizens of prime working age (15–59 years old). Industrialized countries are experiencing a drop in their working-age populations that is even more severe than the overall slowdown in their population growth. South Korea represents the most extreme example. Even as its total population is projected to decline by almost 9 percent by 2050 (from 48.3 million to 44.1 million), the population of working-age South Koreans is expected to drop by 36 percent (from 32.9 million to 21.1 million), and the number of South Koreans aged 60 and older will increase by almost 150 percent (from 7.3 million to 18 million). By 2050, in other words, the entire working-age population will barely exceed the 60-and-older population. Although South Korea's case is extreme, it represents an increasingly common fate for developed countries. Europe is expected to lose 24 percent of its prime working-age population (about 120 million workers) by 2050, and its 60-and-older population is expected to increase by 47 percent. In the United States, where higher fertility and more immigration are expected than in Europe, the working-age population will grow by 15 percent over the next four decades—a steep decline from its growth of 62 percent between 1950 and 2010. And by 2050, the United States' 60-and-older population is expected to double.

All this will have a dramatic impact on economic growth, health care, and military strength in the developed world. The forces that fueled economic growth in industrialized countries during the second half of the twentieth century—increased productivity due to better education, the movement of women into the labor force, and innovations in technology—will all likely weaken in the coming decades. College enrollment boomed after World War II, a trend that is not likely to recur in the twenty-first century; the extensive movement of women into the labor force also was a one-time social change; and the technological change of the time resulted from innovators who created new products and leading-edge consumers who were willing to try them out—two groups that are thinning out as the industrialized world's population ages.

Overall economic growth will also be hampered by a decline in the number of new consumers and new households. When developed countries' labor forces were growing by 0.5–1.0 percent per year, as they did until 2005, even annual increases in real output per worker of just 1.7 percent meant that annual economic growth totaled 2.2–2.7 percent per year. But with the labor forces of many developed countries (such as Germany, Hungary, Japan, Russia, and the Baltic states) now shrinking by 0.2 percent per year and those of other countries (including Austria, the Czech Republic, Denmark, Greece, and Italy) growing by less than 0.2 percent per year, the same 1.7 percent increase in real output per worker yields only 1.5–1.9 percent annual overall growth. Moreover, developed countries will be lucky to keep productivity growth at even that level; in many developed countries, productivity is more likely to decline as the population ages.

A further strain on industrialized economies will be rising medical costs: as populations age, they will demand more health care for longer periods of time. Public pension schemes for aging populations are already being reformed in various industrialized countries—often prompting heated debate. In theory, at least, pensions might be kept solvent by increasing the retirement age, raising taxes modestly, and phasing out benefits for the wealthy. Regardless, the number of 80- and 90-year-olds—who are unlikely to work and highly likely to require nursing-home and other expensive care—will rise dramatically. And even if 60- and 70-year-olds remain active and employed, they will require procedures and medications—hip replacements, kidney transplants, blood-pressure treatments—to sustain their health in old age.

All this means that just as aging developed countries will have proportionally fewer workers, innovators, and consumerist young households, a large portion of those countries' remaining economic growth will have to be diverted to pay for the medical bills and pensions of their growing elderly populations. Basic services, meanwhile, will be increasingly costly because fewer young workers will be available for strenuous and labor-intensive jobs. Unfortunately, policymakers seldom reckon with these potentially disruptive effects of otherwise welcome developments, such as higher life expectancy.

Youth and Islam in the Developing World

Even as the industrialized countries of Europe, North America, and Northeast Asia will experience unprecedented aging this century, fast-growing countries in Africa, Latin America, the Middle East, and Southeast Asia will have exceptionally youthful populations. Today, roughly nine out of ten children under the age of 15 live in developing countries. And these are the countries that will continue to have the world's highest birthrates. Indeed, over 70 percent of the world's population growth between now and 2050 will occur in 24 countries, all of which are classified by the World Bank as low income or lower-middle income, with an average per capita income of under $3,855 in 2008.

Many developing countries have few ways of providing employment to their young, fast-growing populations. Would-be laborers, therefore, will be increasingly attracted to the labor markets of the aging developed countries of Europe, North America, and Northeast Asia. Youthful immigrants from nearby regions with high unemployment—Central America, North Africa, and Southeast Asia, for example—will be drawn to those vital entry-level and manual-labor jobs that sustain advanced economies: janitors, nursing-home aides, bus drivers, plumbers, security guards, farm workers, and the like. Current levels of immigration from developing to developed countries are paltry compared to those that the forces of supply and demand might soon create across the world.

These forces will act strongly on the Muslim world, where many economically weak countries will continue to experience dramatic population growth in the decades ahead. In 1950, Bangladesh, Egypt, Indonesia, Nigeria, Pakistan, and Turkey had a combined population of 242 million. By 2009, those six countries were the world's most populous Muslim-majority countries and had a combined population of 886 million. Their populations are continuing to grow and indeed are expected to increase by 475 million between now and 2050—during which time, by comparison, the six most populous developed countries are projected to gain only 44 million inhabitants. Worldwide, of the 48 fastest-growing countries today—those with annual population growth of two percent or more—28 are majority Muslim or have Muslim minorities of 33 percent or more.

It is therefore imperative to improve relations between Muslim and Western societies. This will be difficult given that many Muslims live in poor communities vulnerable to radical appeals and many see the West as antagonistic and militaristic. In the 2009 Pew Global Attitudes Project survey, for example, whereas 69 percent of those Indonesians and Nigerians surveyed reported viewing the United States favorably, just 18 percent of those polled in Egypt, Jordan, Pakistan, and Turkey (all U.S. allies) did. And in 2006, when the Pew survey last asked detailed questions about Muslim-Western relations, more than half of the respondents in Muslim countries characterized those relations as bad and blamed the West for this state of affairs.

But improving relations is all the more important because of the growing demographic weight of poor Muslim countries and the attendant increase in Muslim immigration, especially to Europe from North Africa and the Middle East. (To be sure, forecasts that Muslims will soon dominate Europe are outlandish: Muslims compose just three to ten percent of the population in the major European countries today, and this proportion will at most double by midcentury.) Strategists worldwide must consider that the world's young are becoming concentrated in those countries least prepared to educate and employ them, including some Muslim states. Any resulting poverty, social tension, or ideological radicalization could have disruptive effects in many corners of the world. But this need not be the case; the healthy immigration of workers to the developed world and the movement of capital to the developing world, among other things, could lead to better results.

Urban Sprawl

Exacerbating twenty-first-century risks will be the fact that the world is urbanizing to an unprecedented degree. The year 2010 will likely be the first time in history that a majority of the world's people live in cities rather than in the countryside. Whereas less than 30 percent of the world's population was urban in 1950, according to UN projections, more than 70 percent will be by 2050.

Lower-income countries in Asia and Africa are urbanizing especially rapidly, as agriculture becomes less labor intensive and as employment opportunities shift to the industrial and service sectors. Already, most of the world's urban agglomerations—Mumbai (population 20.1 million), Mexico City (19.5 million), New Delhi (17 million), Shanghai (15.8 million), Calcutta (15.6 million), Karachi (13.1 million), Cairo (12.5 million), Manila (11.7 million), Lagos (10.6 million), Jakarta (9.7 million)—are found in low-income countries. Many of these countries have multiple cities with over one million residents each: Pakistan has eight, Mexico 12, and China more than 100. The UN projects that the urbanized proportion of sub-Saharan Africa will nearly double between 2005 and 2050, from 35 percent (300 million people) to over 67 percent (1 billion). China, which is roughly 40 percent urbanized today, is expected to be 73 percent urbanized by 2050; India, which is less than 30 percent urbanized today, is expected to be 55 percent urbanized by 2050. Overall, the world's urban population is expected to grow by 3 billion people by 2050.

This urbanization may prove destabilizing. Developing countries that urbanize in the twenty-first century will have far lower per capita incomes than did many industrial countries when they first urbanized. The United States, for example, did not reach 65 percent urbanization until 1950, when per capita income was nearly $13,000 (in 2005 dollars). By contrast, Nigeria, Pakistan, and the Philippines, which are approaching similar levels of urbanization, currently have per capita incomes of just $1,800–$4,000 (in 2005 dollars).

According to the research of Richard Cincotta and other political demographers, countries with younger populations are especially prone to civil unrest and are less able to create or sustain democratic institutions. And the more heavily urbanized, the more such countries are likely to experience Dickensian poverty and anarchic violence. In good times, a thriving economy might keep urban residents employed and governments flush with sufficient resources to meet their needs. More often, however, sprawling and impoverished cities are vulnerable to crime lords, gangs, and petty rebellions. Thus, the rapid urbanization of the developing world in the decades ahead might bring, in exaggerated form, problems similar to those that urbanization brought to nineteenth-century Europe. Back then, cyclical employment, inadequate policing, and limited sanitation and education often spawned widespread labor strife, periodic violence, and sometimes—as in the 1820s, the 1830s, and 1848—even revolutions.

International terrorism might also originate in fast-urbanizing developing countries (even more than it already does). With their neighborhood networks, access to the Internet and digital communications technology, and concentration of valuable targets, sprawling cities offer excellent opportunities for recruiting, maintaining, and hiding terrorist networks.

Defusing the Bomb

Averting this century's potential dangers will require sweeping measures. Three major global efforts defused the population bomb of Ehrlich's day: a commitment by governments and nongovernmental organizations to control reproduction rates; agricultural advances, such as the green revolution and the spread of new technology; and a vast increase in international trade, which globalized markets and thus allowed developing countries to export foodstuffs in exchange for seeds, fertilizers, and machinery, which in turn helped them boost production. But today's population bomb is the product less of absolute growth in the world's population than of changes in its age and distribution. Policymakers must therefore adapt today's global governance institutions to the new realities of the aging of the industrialized world, the concentration of the world's economic and population growth in developing countries, and the increase in international immigration.

During the Cold War, Western strategists divided the world into a "First World," of democratic industrialized countries; a "Second World," of communist industrialized countries; and a "Third World," of developing countries. These strategists focused chiefly on deterring or managing conflict between the First and the Second Worlds and on launching proxy wars and diplomatic initiatives to attract Third World countries into the First World's camp. Since the end of the Cold War, strategists have largely abandoned this three-group division and have tended to believe either that the United States, as the sole superpower, would maintain a Pax Americana or that the world would become multipolar, with the United States, Europe, and China playing major roles.

Unfortunately, because they ignore current global demographic trends, these views will be obsolete within a few decades. A better approach would be to consider a different three-world order, with a new First World of the aging industrialized nations of North America, Europe, and Asia's Pacific Rim (including Japan, Singapore, South Korea, and Taiwan, as well as China after 2030, by which point the one-child policy will have produced significant aging); a Second World comprising fast-growing and economically dynamic countries with a healthy mix of young and old inhabitants (such as Brazil, Iran, Mexico, Thailand, Turkey, and Vietnam, as well as China until 2030); and a Third World of fast-growing, very young, and increasingly urbanized countries with poorer economies and often weak governments.

To cope with the instability that will likely arise from the new Third World's urbanization, economic strife, lawlessness, and potential terrorist activity, the aging industrialized nations of the new First World must build effective alliances with the growing powers of the new Second World and together reach out to Third World nations. Second World powers will be pivotal in the twenty-first century not just because they will drive economic growth and consume technologies and other products engineered in the First World; they will also be central to international security and cooperation. The realities of religion, culture, and geographic proximity mean that any peaceful and productive engagement by the First World of Third World countries will have to include the open cooperation of Second World countries.

Strategists, therefore, must fundamentally reconsider the structure of various current global institutions. The G-8, for example, will likely become obsolete as a body for making global economic policy. The G-20 is already becoming increasingly important, and this is less a short-term consequence of the ongoing global financial crisis than the beginning of the necessary recognition that Brazil, China, India, Indonesia, Mexico, Turkey, and others are becoming global economic powers. International institutions will not retain their legitimacy if they exclude the world's fastest-growing and most economically dynamic countries. It is essential, therefore, despite European concerns about the potential effects on immigration, to take steps such as admitting Turkey into the European Union. This would add youth and economic dynamism to the EU—and would prove that Muslims are welcome to join Europeans as equals in shaping a free and prosperous future. On the other hand, excluding Turkey from the EU could lead to hostility not only on the part of Turkish citizens, who are expected to number 100 million by 2050, but also on the part of Muslim populations worldwide.

NATO must also adapt. The alliance today is composed almost entirely of countries with aging, shrinking populations and relatively slow-growing economies. It is oriented toward the Northern Hemisphere and holds on to a Cold War structure that cannot adequately respond to contemporary threats. The young and increasingly populous countries of Africa, the Middle East, Central Asia, and South Asia could mobilize insurgents much more easily than NATO could mobilize the troops it would need if it were called on to stabilize those countries. Long-standing NATO members should, therefore—although it would require atypical creativity and flexibility—consider the logistical and demographic advantages of inviting into the alliance countries such as Brazil and Morocco, rather than countries such as Albania. That this seems far-fetched does not minimize the imperative that First World countries begin including large and strategic Second and Third World powers in formal international alliances.

The case of Afghanistan—a country whose population is growing fast and where NATO is currently engaged—illustrates the importance of building effective global institutions. Today, there are 28 million Afghans; by 2025, there will be 45 million; and by 2050, there will be close to 75 million. As nearly 20 million additional Afghans are born over the next 15 years, NATO will have an opportunity to help Afghanistan become reasonably stable, self-governing, and prosperous. If NATO's efforts fail and the Afghans judge that NATO intervention harmed their interests, tens of millions of young Afghans will become more hostile to the West. But if they come to think that NATO's involvement benefited their society, the West will have tens of millions of new friends. The example might then motivate the approximately one billion other young Muslims growing up in low-income countries over the next four decades to look more kindly on relations between their countries and the countries of the industrialized West.

Creative Reforms at Home

The aging industrialized countries can also take various steps at home to promote stability in light of the coming demographic trends. First, they should encourage families to have more children. France and Sweden have had success providing child care, generous leave time, and financial allowances to families with young children. Yet there is no consensus among policymakers—and certainly not among demographers—about what policies best encourage fertility.

More important than unproven tactics for increasing family size is immigration. Correctly managed, population movement can benefit developed and developing countries alike. Given the dangers of young, underemployed, and unstable populations in developing countries, immigration to developed countries can provide economic opportunities for the ambitious and serve as a safety valve for all. Countries that embrace immigrants, such as the United States, gain economically by having willing laborers and greater entrepreneurial spirit. And countries with high levels of emigration (but not so much that they experience so-called brain drains) also benefit because emigrants often send remittances home or return to their native countries with valuable education and work experience.

One somewhat daring approach to immigration would be to encourage a reverse flow of older immigrants from developed to developing countries. If older residents of developed countries took their retirements along the southern coast of the Mediterranean or in Latin America or Africa, it would greatly reduce the strain on their home countries' public entitlement systems. The developing countries involved, meanwhile, would benefit because caring for the elderly and providing retirement and leisure services is highly labor intensive. Relocating a portion of these activities to developing countries would provide employment and valuable training to the young, growing populations of the Second and Third Worlds.

This would require developing residential and medical facilities of First World quality in Second and Third World countries. Yet even this difficult task would be preferable to the status quo, by which low wages and poor facilities lead to a steady drain of medical and nursing talent from developing to developed countries. Many residents of developed countries who desire cheaper medical procedures already practice medical tourism today, with India, Singapore, and Thailand being the most common destinations. (For example, the international consulting firm Deloitte estimated that 750,000 Americans traveled abroad for care in 2008.)

Never since 1800 has a majority of the world's economic growth occurred outside of Europe, the United States, and Canada. Never have so many people in those regions been over 60 years old. And never have low-income countries' populations been so young and so urbanized. But such will be the world's demography in the twenty-first century. The strategic and economic policies of the twentieth century are obsolete, and it is time to find new ones.

Assess Your Progress

1. What demographic and economic shifts are currently under way worldwide?
2. What helps to explain economic shifts in the industrialized countries?
3. Where is population growing most rapidly? What are the implications of this growth?
4. What will be the impact of increasing urbanization?
5. What effect will demographic changes have on international institutions?

Jack A. Goldstone is **Virginia E.** and **John T. Hazel, Jr.**, Professor at the George Mason School of Public Policy.

The Ideology of Development

The failed ideologies of the last century have come to an end. But a new one has risen to take their place. It is the ideology of Development—and it promises a solution to all the world's ills. But like Communism, Fascism, and the others before it, Developmentalism is a dangerous and deadly failure.

WILLIAM EASTERLY

A dark ideological specter is haunting the world. It is almost as deadly as the tired ideologies of the last century—communism, fascism, and socialism—that failed so miserably. It feeds some of the most dangerous trends of our time, including religious fundamentalism. It is the half-century-old ideology of Developmentalism. And it is thriving.

Like all ideologies, Development promises a comprehensive final answer to all of society's problems, from poverty and illiteracy to violence and despotic rulers. It shares the common ideological characteristic of suggesting there is only one correct answer, and it tolerates little dissent. It deduces this unique answer for everyone from a general theory that purports to apply to everyone, everywhere. There's no need to involve local actors who reap its costs and benefits. Development even has its own intelligentsia, made up of experts at the International Monetary Fund (IMF), World Bank, and United Nations.

The power of Developmentalism is disheartening, because the failure of all the previous ideologies might have laid the groundwork for the opposite of ideology—the freedom of individuals and societies to choose their destinies. Yet, since the fall of communism, the West has managed to snatch defeat from the jaws of victory, and with disastrous results. Development ideology is sparking a dangerous counterreaction. The "one correct answer" came to mean "free markets," and, for the poor world, it was defined as doing whatever the IMF and the World Bank tell you to do. But the reaction in Africa, Central Asia, Latin America, the Middle East, and Russia has been to fight against free markets. So, one of the best economic ideas of our time, the genius of free markets, was presented in one of the worst possible ways, with unelected outsiders imposing rigid doctrines on the xenophobic unwilling.

The backlash has been so severe that other failed ideologies are gaining new adherents throughout these regions. In Nicaragua, for instance, IMF and World Bank structural adjustments failed so conspicuously that the pitiful Sandinista regime of the 1980s now looks good by comparison. Its leader, Daniel Ortega, is back in power. The IMF's actions during the Argentine financial crisis of 2001 now reverberate a half decade later with Hugo Chávez, Venezuela's illiberal leader, being welcomed with open arms in Buenos Aires. The heavy-handed directives of the World Bank and IMF in Bolivia provided the soil from which that country's neosocialist president, Evo Morales, sprung. The disappointing payoff following eight structural adjustment loans to Zimbabwe and $8 billion in foreign aid during the 1980s and 1990s helped Robert Mugabe launch a vicious counterattack on democracy. The IMF-World Bank-Jeffrey Sachs application of "shock therapy" to the former Soviet Union has created a lasting nostalgia for communism. In the Middle East, $154 billion in foreign aid between 1980 and 2001, 45 structural adjustment loans, and "expert" advice produced zero per capita GDP growth that helped create a breeding ground for Islamic fundamentalism.

This blowback against "globalization from above" has spread to every corner of the Earth. It now threatens to kill sensible, moderate steps toward the freer movement of goods, ideas, capital, and people.

Development's Politburo

The ideology of Development is not only about having experts design your free market for you; it is about having the experts design a comprehensive, technical plan to solve all the problems of the poor. These experts see poverty as a purely technological problem, to be solved by engineering and the natural sciences, ignoring messy social sciences such as economics, politics, and sociology.

Sachs, Columbia University's celebrity economist, is one of its main proprietors. He is now recycling his theories of overnight shock therapy, which failed so miserably in Russia, into promises of overnight global poverty reduction. "Africa's problems," he has said, "are . . . solvable with practical and proven technologies." His own plan features hundreds of expert interventions to solve every last problem of the poor—from green manure, breast-feeding education, and bicycles to solar-energy systems, school uniforms for aids orphans, and windmills. Not to mention such critical interventions as "counseling and information services for men to address their reproductive health needs." All this will be done, Sachs says, by "a united and effective United Nations country team, which coordinates in one place the work of the U.N. specialized agencies, the IMF, and the World Bank."

Under Developmentalism, an end to starvation, tyranny, and war are thrown in like a free toaster.

So the admirable concern of rich countries for the tragedies of world poverty is thus channeled into fattening the international aid bureaucracy, the self-appointed priesthood of Development. Like other ideologies, this thinking favors collective goals such as national poverty reduction, national economic growth, and the global Millennium Development Goals, over the aspirations of individuals. Bureaucrats who write poverty-reduction frameworks outrank individuals who actually reduce poverty by, say, starting a business. Just as Marxists favored world revolution and socialist internationalism, Development stresses world goals over the autonomy of societies to choose their own path. It favors doctrinaire abstractions such as "market-friendly policies," "good investment climate," and "pro-poor globalization" over the freedom of individuals.

Development also shares another Marxist trait: It aspires to be scientific. Finding the one correct solution to poverty is seen as a scientific problem to be solved by the experts. They are always sure they know the answer, vehemently reject disagreement, and then later change their answers. In psychiatry, this is known as Borderline Personality Disorder. For the Development Experts, it's a way of life. The answer at first was aid-financed investment and industrialization in poor countries, then it was market-oriented government policy reform, then it was fixing institutional problems such as corruption, then it was globalization, then it was the Poverty Reduction Strategy to achieve the Millennium Development Goals.

One reason the answers keep changing is because, in reality, high-growth countries follow a bewildering variety of paths to development, and the countries with high growth rates are constantly changing from decade to decade. Who could be more different than successful developers such as China and Chile, Botswana and Singapore, Taiwan and Turkey, or Hong Kong and Vietnam? What about the many countries who tried to emulate these rising stars and failed? What about the former stars who have fallen on hard times, like the Ivory Coast, which was one of the fastest developers of the 1960s and 1970s, only to become mired in a civil war? What about Mexico, which saw rapid growth until 1980 and has had slow growth ever since, despite embracing the experts' reforms?

The experts in Developmentalism's Politburo don't bother themselves with such questions. All the previous answers were right; they were just missing one more "necessary condition" that the experts have only just now added to the list. Like all ideologies, Development is at the same time too rigid to predict what will work in the messy real world and yet flexible enough to forever escape falsification by real-world events. The high church of Development, the World Bank, has guaranteed it can never be wrong by making statements such as, "different policies can yield the same result, and the same policy can yield different results, depending on country institutional contexts and underlying growth strategies." Of course, you still need experts to figure out the contexts and strategies.

Resistance Is Futile

Perhaps more hypocritical yet is Development's simple theory of historical inevitability. Poor societies are not just poor, the experts tell us, they are "developing" until they reach the final stage of history, or "development," in which poverty will soon end. Under this historiography, an end to starvation, tyranny, and war are thrown in like a free toaster on an infomercial. The experts judge all societies on a straight line, per capita income, with the superior countries showing the inferior countries the image of their own future. And the experts heap scorn on those who resist the inevitabilities on the path to development.

One of today's leading Developmentalists, *New York Times* columnist Thomas Friedman, can hardly conceal his mockery of those who resist the march of history, or "the flattening of the world." "When you are Mexico," Friedman has written, "and your claim to fame is that you are a low-wage manufacturing country, and some of your people are importing statuettes of your own patron saint from China, because China can make them and ship them all the way across the Pacific more cheaply than you can produce them . . . you have got a problem. [T]he only way for Mexico to thrive is with a strategy of reform . . . the more Mexico just sits there, the more it is going to get run over." Friedman seems blissfully unaware that poor Mexico, so far from God yet so close to American pundits, has already tried much harder than China to implement the experts' "strategy of reform."

The self-confidence of Developmentalists like Friedman is so strong that they impose themselves even on those who accept their strategies. This year, for instance, Ghana celebrated its 50th anniversary as the first black African nation to gain independence. Official international aid donors to Ghana told its allegedly independent government, in the words of the World Bank: "We Partners are here giving you our pledge to give our best to make lives easier for you in running your country." Among the things they will do to make your life easier is to run your country for you.

Unfortunately, Development ideology has a dismal record of helping any country actually develop. The regions where the ideology has been most influential, Latin America and Africa, have done the worst. Luckless Latins and Africans are left chasing yesterday's formulas for success while those who ignored the Developmentalists found homegrown paths to success. The nations that have been the most successful in the past 40 years did so in such a variety of different ways that it would be hard to argue that they discovered the "correct answer" from development ideology. In fact, they often conspicuously violated whatever it was the experts said at the time. The East Asian tigers, for instance, chose outward orientation on their own in the 1960s, when the experts' conventional wisdom was industrialization for the home market. The rapid growth of China over the past quarter century came when it was hardly a poster child for either the 1980s Washington Consensus or the 1990s institutionalism of democracy and cracking down on corruption.

What explains the appeal of development ideology despite its dismal track record? Ideologies usually arise in response to tragic situations in which people are hungry for clear and comprehensive solutions. The inequality of the Industrial Revolution bred Marxism, and the backwardness of Russia its Leninist offshoot. Germany's defeat and demoralization in World War I birthed Nazism. Economic hardship accompanied by threats to identity led to both Christian and Islamic fundamentalism. Similarly, development ideology appeals to those who want a definitive, complete answer to the tragedy of world poverty and inequality. It answers the question, "What is to be done?" to borrow the title of Lenin's 1902 tract. It stresses collective social outcomes that must be remedied by collective, top-down action by the intelligentsia, the revolutionary vanguard, the development expert. As Sachs explains, "I have . . . gradually come to understand through my scientific research and on the ground advisory work the awesome power in our generation's hands to end the massive suffering of the extreme poor . . . although introductory economics textbooks preach individualism and decentralized markets, our safety and prosperity depend at least as much on collective decisions."

Freeing the Poor

Few realize that Americans in 1776 had the same income level as the average African today. Yet, like all the present-day developed nations, the United States was lucky enough to escape poverty before there were Developmentalists. In the words of former IMF First Deputy Managing Director Anne Krueger, development in the rich nations "just happened." George Washington did not have to deal with aid partners, getting structurally adjusted by them, or preparing poverty-reduction strategy papers for them. Abraham Lincoln did not celebrate a government of the donors, by the donors, and for the donors. Today's developed nations were free to experiment with their own pragmatic paths toward more government accountability and freer markets. Individualism and decentralized markets were good enough to give rise to penicillin, air conditioning, high-yield corn, and the automobile—not to mention better living standards, lower mortality, and the iPod.

The opposite of ideology is freedom, the ability of societies to be unchained from foreign control. The only "answer" to poverty reduction is freedom from being told the answer. Free societies and individuals are not guaranteed to succeed. They will make bad choices. But at least they bear the cost of those mistakes, and learn from them. That stands in stark contrast to accountability-free Developmentalism. This process of learning from mistakes is what produced the repositories of common sense that make up mainstream economics. The opposite of Development ideology is not anything goes, but the pragmatic use of time-tested economic ideas—the benefits of specialization, comparative advantage, gains from trade, market-clearing prices, trade-offs, budget constraints—by individuals, firms, governments, and societies as they find their own success.

History proves just how much good can come from individuals who both bear the costs and reap the benefits of their own choices when they are free to make them. That includes local politicians, activists, and businesspeople who are groping their way toward greater freedom, contrary to the Developmentalists who oxymoronically impose freedom of choice on other people. Those who best understood the lessons of the 20th century were not the ideologues asking, "What is to be done?" They were those asking, "How can people be more free to find their own solutions?"

The ideology of Development should be packed up in crates and sent off to the Museum of Dead Ideologies, just down the hall from Communism, Socialism, and Fascism. It's time to recognize that the attempt to impose a rigid development ideology on the world's poor has failed miserably. Fortunately, many poor societies are forging their own path toward greater freedom and prosperity anyway. That is how true revolutions happen.

Assess Your Progress

1. What are the features of developmentalism?
2. What actors are responsible for pushing the ideology of development?
3. What is the alternative to the developmentalist model?

William Easterly is professor of economics at New York University.

The Case against the West

America and Europe in the Asian Century

KISHORE MAHBUBANI

There is a fundamental flaw in the West's strategic thinking. In all its analyses of global challenges, the West assumes that it is the source of the solutions to the world's key problems. In fact, however, the West is also a major source of these problems. Unless key Western policymakers learn to understand and deal with this reality, the world is headed for an even more troubled phase.

The West is understandably reluctant to accept that the era of its domination is ending and that the Asian century has come. No civilization cedes power easily, and the West's resistance to giving up control of key global institutions and processes is natural. Yet the West is engaging in an extraordinary act of self-deception by believing that it is open to change. In fact, the West has become the most powerful force preventing the emergence of a new wave of history, clinging to its privileged position in key global forums, such as the UN Security Council, the International Monetary Fund, the World Bank, and the G-8 (the group of highly industrialized states), and refusing to contemplate how the West will have to adjust to the Asian century.

Partly as a result of its growing insecurity, the West has also become increasingly incompetent in its handling of key global problems. Many Western commentators can readily identify specific failures, such as the Bush administration's botched invasion and occupation of Iraq. But few can see that this reflects a deeper structural problem: the West's inability to see that the world has entered a new era.

Apart from representing a specific failure of policy execution, the war in Iraq has also highlighted the gap between the reality and what the West had expected would happen after the invasion. Arguably, the United States and the United Kingdom intended only to free the Iraqi people from a despotic ruler and to rid the world of a dangerous man, Saddam Hussein. Even if George W. Bush and Tony Blair had no malevolent intentions, however, their approaches were trapped in the Western mindset of believing that their interventions could lead only to good, not harm or disaster. This led them to believe that the invading U.S. troops would be welcomed with roses thrown at their feet by happy Iraqis. But the twentieth century showed that no country welcomes foreign invaders. The notion that any Islamic nation would approve of Western military boots on its soil was ridiculous. Even in the early twentieth century, the British invasion and occupation of Iraq was met with armed resistance. In 1920, Winston Churchill, then British secretary for war and air, quelled the rebellion of Kurds and Arabs in British-occupied Iraq by authorizing his troops to use chemical weapons. "I am strongly in favor of using poisoned gas against uncivilized tribes," Churchill said. The world has moved on from this era, but many Western officials have not abandoned the old assumption that an army of Christian soldiers can successfully invade, occupy, and transform an Islamic society.

Many Western leaders often begin their speeches by remarking on how perilous the world is becoming. Speaking after the August 2006 discovery of a plot to blow up transatlantic flights originating from London, President Bush said, "The American people need to know we live in a dangerous world." But even as Western leaders speak of such threats, they seem incapable of conceding that the West itself could be the fundamental source of these dangers. After all, the West includes the best-managed states in the world, the most economically developed, those with the strongest democratic institutions. But one cannot assume that a government that rules competently at home will be equally good at addressing challenges abroad. In fact, the converse is more likely to be true. Although the Western mind is obsessed with the Islamist terrorist threat, the West is mishandling the two immediate and pressing challenges of Afghanistan and Iraq. And despite the grave threat of nuclear terrorism, the Western custodians of the nonproliferation regime have allowed that regime to weaken significantly. The challenge posed by Iran's efforts to enrich uranium has been aggravated by the incompetence of the United States and the European Union. On the economic front, for the first time since World War II, the demise of a round of global trade negotiations, the Doha Round, seems imminent. Finally, the danger of global warming, too, is being mismanaged.

Yet Westerners seldom look inward to understand the deeper reasons these global problems are being mismanaged. Are there domestic structural reasons that explain this? Have Western democracies been hijacked by competitive populism and structural short-termism, preventing them from addressing long-term challenges from a broader global perspective?

Fortunately, some Asian states may now be capable of taking on more responsibilities, as they have been strengthened by implementing Western principles. In September 2005, Robert Zoellick, then U.S. deputy secretary of state, called on China to become a "responsible stakeholder" in the international system. China has responded positively, as have other Asian states. In recent decades, Asians have been among the greatest beneficiaries of the open multilateral order created by the United States and the other victors of World War II, and few today want to destabilize it. The number of Asians seeking a comfortable middle-class existence has never been higher. For centuries, the Chinese and the Indians could only dream of such an accomplishment; now it is within the reach of around half a billion people in China and India. Their ideal is to achieve what the United States and Europe did. They want to replicate, not dominate, the West. The universalization of the Western dream represents a moment of triumph for the West. And so the West should welcome the fact that the Asian states are becoming competent at handling regional and global challenges.

The Middle East Mess

Western Policies have been most harmful in the Middle East. The Middle East is also the most dangerous region in the world. Trouble there affects not just seven million Israelis, around four million Palestinians, and 200 million Arabs; it also affects more than a billion Muslims worldwide. Every time there is a major flare-up in the Middle East, such as the U.S. invasion of Iraq or the Israeli bombing of Lebanon, Islamic communities around the world become concerned, distressed, and angered. And few of them doubt the problems origin: the West.

The invasion and occupation of Iraq, for example, was a multidimensional error. The theory and practice of international law legitimizes the use of force only when it is an act of self-defense or is authorized by the UN Security Council. The U.S.-led invasion of Iraq could not be justified on either count. The United States and the United Kingdom sought the Security Council's authorization to invade Iraq, but the council denied it. It was therefore clear to the international community that the subsequent war was illegal and that it would do huge damage to international law.

This has created an enormous problem, partly because until this point both the United States and the United Kingdom had been among the primary custodians of international law. American and British minds, such as James Brierly, Philip Jessup, Hersch Lauterpacht, and Hans Morgenthau, developed the conceptual infrastructure underlying international law, and American and British leaders provided the political will to have it accepted in practice. But neither the United States nor the United Kingdom will admit that the invasion and the occupation of Iraq were illegal or give up their historical roles as the chief caretakers of international law. Since 2003, both nations have frequently called for Iran and North Korea to implement UN Security Council resolutions. But how can the violators of UN principles also be their enforcers?

One rare benefit of the Iraq war may be that it has awakened a new fear of Iran among the Sunni Arab states. Egypt, Jordan, and Saudi Arabia, among others, do not want to deal with two adversaries and so are inclined to make peace with Israel. Saudi Arabia's King Abdullah used the opportunity of the special Arab League summit meeting in March 2007 to relaunch his long-standing proposal for a two-state solution to the Israeli-Palestinian conflict. Unfortunately, the Bush administration did not seize the opportunity—or revive the Taba accords that President Bill Clinton had worked out in January 2001, even though they could provide a basis for a lasting settlement and the Saudis were prepared to back them. In its early days, the Bush administration appeared ready to support a two-state solution. It was the first U.S. administration to vote in favor of a UN Security Council resolution calling for the creation of a Palestinian state, and it announced in March 2002 that it would try to achieve such a result by 2005. But here it is 2008, and little progress has been made.

The United States has made the already complicated Israeli-Palestinian conflict even more of a mess. Many extremist voices in Tel Aviv and Washington believe that time will always be on Israel's side. The pro-Israel lobby's stranglehold on the U.S. Congress, the political cowardice of U.S. politicians when it comes to creating a Palestinian state, and the sustained track record of U.S. aid to Israel support this view. But no great power forever sacrifices its larger national interests in favor of the interests of a small state. If Israel fails to accept the Taba accords, it will inevitably come to grief. If and when it does, Western incompetence will be seen as a major cause.

Never Say Never

Nuclear nonproliferation is another area in which the West, especially the United States, has made matters worse. The West has long been obsessed with the danger of the proliferation of weapons of mass destruction, particularly nuclear weapons. It pushed successfully for the near-universal ratification of the Biological and Toxin Weapons Convention, the Chemical Weapons Convention, and the Nuclear Nonproliferation Treaty (NPT).

But the West has squandered many of those gains. Today, the NPT is legally alive but spiritually dead. The NPT was inherently problematic since it divided the world into nuclear haves (the states that had tested a nuclear device by 1967) and nuclear have-nots (those that had not). But for two decades it was reasonably effective in preventing horizontal proliferation (the spread of nuclear weapons to other states). Unfortunately, the NPT has done nothing to prevent vertical proliferation, namely, the increase in the numbers and sophistication of nuclear weapons among the existing nuclear weapons states. During the Cold War, the United States and the Soviet Union agreed to work together to limit proliferation. The governments of several countries that could have developed nuclear weapons, such as Argentina, Brazil, Germany, Japan, and South Korea, restrained themselves because they believed the NPT reflected a fair bargain between China, France, the Soviet Union, the United Kingdom, and the United States (the five official nuclear weapons states and five permanent members of the UN Security Council) and the rest of the world. Both sides agreed that the world would be safer if the five nuclear states took steps to reduce their arsenals and worked toward the eventual goal of universal disarmament and the other states refrained from acquiring nuclear weapons at all.

So what went wrong? The first problem was that the NPT's principal progenitor, the United States, decided to walk away from the postwar rule-based order it had created, thus eroding the infrastructure on which the NPT's enforcement depends. During the time I was Singapore's ambassador to the UN, between 1984 and 1989, Jeane Kirkpatrick, the U.S. ambassador to the UN, treated the organization with contempt. She infamously said, "What takes place in the Security Council more closely resembles a mugging than either a political debate or an effort at problem-solving." She saw the postwar order as a set of constraints, not as a set of rules that the world should follow and the United States should help preserve. This undermined the NPT, because with no teeth of its own, no self-regulating or sanctioning mechanisms, and a clause allowing signatories to ignore obligations in the name of "supreme national interest," the treaty could only really be enforced by the UN Security Council. And once the United States began tearing holes in the fabric of the overall system, it created openings for violations of the

NPT and its principles. Finally, by going to war with Iraq without UN authorization, the United States lost its moral authority to ask, for example, Iran to abide by Security Council resolutions.

Another problem has been the United States'—and other nuclear weapons states'—direct assault on the treaty. The NPT is fundamentally a social contract between the five nuclear weapons states and the rest of the world, based partly on the understanding that the nuclear powers will eventually give up their weapons. Instead, during the Cold War, the United States and the Soviet Union increased both the quantity and the sophistication of their nuclear weapons: the United States' nuclear stockpile peaked in 1966 at 31,700 warheads, and the Soviet Union's peaked in 1986 at 40,723. In fact, the United States and the Soviet Union developed their nuclear stockpiles so much that they actually ran out of militarily or economically significant targets. The numbers have declined dramatically since then, but even the current number of nuclear weapons held by the United States and Russia can wreak enormous damage on human civilization.

The nuclear states' decision to ignore Israel's nuclear weapons program was especially damaging to their authority. No nuclear weapons state has ever publicly acknowledged Israel's possession of nuclear weapons. Their silence has created a loophole in the NPT and delegitimized it in the eyes of Muslim nations. The consequences have been profound. When the West sermonizes that the world will become a more dangerous place when Iran acquires nuclear weapons, the Muslim world now shrugs.

India and Pakistan were already shrugging by 1998, when they tested their first nuclear weapons. When the international community responded by condemning the tests and applying sanctions on India, virtually all Indians saw through the hypocrisy and double standards of their critics. By not respecting their own obligations under the NPT, the five nuclear states had robbed their condemnations of any moral legitimacy; criticisms from Australia and Canada, which have also remained silent about Israel's bomb, similarly had no moral authority. The near-unanimous rejection of the NPT by the Indian establishment, which is otherwise very conscious of international opinion, showed how dead the treaty already was.

The world has lost its trust in the five nuclear weapons states and now sees them as the NPT's primary violators.

From time to time, common sense has entered discussions on nuclear weapons. President Ronald Reagan said more categorically than any U.S. president that the world would be better off without nuclear weapons. Last year, with the NPT in its death throes and the growing threat of loose nuclear weapons falling into the hands of terrorists forefront in everyone's mind, former Secretary of State George Shultz, former Defense Secretary William Perry, former Secretary of State Henry Kissinger, and former Senator Sam Nunn warned in *The Wall Street Journal* that the world was "now on the precipice of a new and dangerous nuclear era." They argued, "Unless urgent new actions are taken, the U.S. soon will be compelled to enter a new nuclear era that will be more precarious, psychologically disorienting, and economically even more costly than was Cold War deterrence." But these calls may have come too late. The world has lost its trust in the five nuclear weapons states and now sees them as the NPT's primary violators rather than its custodians. Those states' private cynicism about their obligations to the NPT has become public knowledge.

Contrary to what the West wants the rest of the world to believe, the nuclear weapons states, especially the United States and Russia, which continue to maintain thousands of nuclear weapons, are the biggest source of nuclear proliferation. Mohamed ElBaradei, the director general of the International Atomic Energy Agency, warned in *The Economist* in 2003, "The very existence of nuclear weapons gives rise to the pursuit of them. They are seen as a source of global influence, and are valued for their perceived deterrent effect. And as long as some countries possess them (or are protected by them in alliances) and others do not, this asymmetry breeds chronic global insecurity." Despite the Cold War, the second half of the twentieth century seemed to be moving the world toward a more civilized order. As the twenty-first century unfurls, the world seems to be sliding backward.

Irresponsible Stakeholders

After leading the world toward a period of spectacular economic growth in the second half of the twentieth century by promoting global free trade, the West has recently been faltering in its global economic leadership. Believing that low trade barriers and increasing trade interdependence would result in higher standards of living for all, European and U.S. economists and policymakers pushed for global economic liberalization. As a result, global trade grew from seven percent of the world's GDP in 1940 to 30 percent in 2005.

But a seismic shift has taken place in Western attitudes since the end of the Cold War. Suddenly, the United States and Europe no longer have a vested interest in the success of the East Asian economies, which they see less as allies and more as competitors. That change in Western interests was reflected in the fact that the West provided little real help to East Asia during the Asian financial crisis of 1997–98. The entry of China into the global marketplace, especially after its admission to the World Trade Organization, has made a huge difference in both economic and psychological terms. Many Europeans have lost confidence in their ability to compete with the Asians. And many Americans have lost confidence in the virtues of competition.

There are some knotty issues that need to be resolved in the current global trade talks, but fundamentally the negotiations are stalled because the conviction of the Western "champions" of free trade that free trade is good has begun to waver. When Americans and Europeans start to perceive themselves as losers in international trade, they also lose their drive to push for further trade liberalization. Unfortunately, on this front at least, neither China nor India (nor Brazil nor South Africa nor any other major developing country) is ready to take over the West's mantle. China, for example, is afraid that any effort to seek leadership in this area will stoke U.S. fears that it is striving for global hegemony. Hence, China is lying low. So, too, are the United States and Europe. Hence, the trade talks are stalled. The end of the West's promotion of global trade liberalization could well mean the end of the most spectacular economic growth the world has ever seen. Few in the West seem to be reflecting on the consequences of walking away from one of the West's most successful policies, which is what it will be doing if it allows the Doha Round to fail.

At the same time that the Western governments are relinquishing their stewardship of the global economy, they are also failing to take the lead on battling global warming. The awarding of the Nobel Peace Prize to former U.S. Vice President Al Gore, a longtime environmentalist, and the UN's Intergovernmental Panel on Climate Change confirms there is international consensus that global warning is a real threat. The most assertive advocates for tackling this problem come from the U.S. and European scientific communities, but the greatest resistance to any effective action is coming from the U.S. government. This has left the rest of the world confused and puzzled. Most people believe that the greenhouse effect is caused mostly by the flow of current emissions. Current emissions do aggravate the problem, but the fundamental cause is the stock of emissions that has accumulated since the Industrial Revolution. Finding a just and equitable solution to the problem of greenhouse gas emissions must begin with assigning responsibility both for the current flow and for the stock of greenhouse gases already accumulated. And on both counts the Western nations should bear a greater burden.

The West has to learn to share power and responsibility for the management of global issues with the rest of the world.

When it comes to addressing any problem pertaining to the global commons, such as the environment, it seems only fair that the wealthier members of the international community should shoulder more responsibility. This is a natural principle of justice. It is also fair in this particular case given the developed countries' primary role in releasing harmful gases into the atmosphere. R. K. Pachauri, chair of the Intergovernmental Panel on Climate Change, argued last year, "China and India are certainly increasing their share, but they are not increasing their per capita emissions anywhere close to the levels that you have in the developed world." Since 1850, China has contributed less than 8 percent of the world's total emissions of carbon dioxide, whereas the United States is responsible for 29 percent and western Europe is responsible for 27 percent. Today, India's per capita greenhouse gas emissions are equivalent to only 4 percent of those of the United States and 12 percent of those of the European Union. Still, the Western governments are not clearly acknowledging their responsibilities and are allowing many of their citizens to believe that China and India are the fundamental obstacles to any solution to global warming.

Washington might become more responsible on this front if a Democratic president replaces Bush in 2009. But people in the West will have to make some real concessions if they are to reduce significantly their per capita share of global emissions. A cap-and-trade program may do the trick. Western countries will probably have to make economic sacrifices. One option might be, as the journalist Thomas Friedman has suggested, to impose a dollar-per-gallon tax on Americans' gasoline consumption. Gore has proposed a carbon tax. So far, however, few U.S. politicians have dared to make such suggestions publicly.

Temptations of the East

The Middle East, nuclear proliferation, stalled trade liberalization, and global warming are all challenges that the West is essentially failing to address. And this failure suggests that a systemic problem is emerging in the West's stewardship of the international order—one that Western minds are reluctant to analyze or confront openly. After having enjoyed centuries of global domination, the West has to learn to share power and responsibility for the management of global issues with the rest of the world. It has to forgo outdated organizations, such as the Organization for Economic Cooperation and Development, and outdated processes, such as the G-8, and deal with organizations and processes with a broader scope and broader representation. It was always unnatural for the 12 percent of the world population that lived in the West to enjoy so much global power. Understandably, the other 88 percent of the world population increasingly wants also to drive the bus of world history.

First and foremost, the West needs to acknowledge that sharing the power it has accumulated in global forums would serve its interests. Restructuring international institutions to reflect the current world order will be complicated by the absence of natural leaders to do the job. The West has become part of the problem, and the Asian countries are not yet ready to step in. On the other hand, the world does not need to invent any new principles to improve global governance; the concepts of domestic good governance can and should be applied to the international community. The Western principles of democracy, the rule of law, and social justice are among the world's best bets. The ancient virtues of partnership and pragmatism can complement them.

Democracy, the foundation of government in the West, is based on the premise that each human being in a society is an equal stakeholder in the domestic order. Thus, governments are selected on the basis of "one person, one vote." This has produced long-term stability and order in Western societies. In order to produce long-term stability and order worldwide, democracy should be the cornerstone of global society, and the planet's 6.6 billion inhabitants should become equal stakeholders. To inject the spirit of democracy into global governance and global decision-making, one must turn to institutions with universal representation, especially the UN. UN institutions such as the World Health Organization and the World Meteorological Organization enjoy widespread legitimacy because of their universal membership, which means their decisions are generally accepted by all the countries of the world.

The problem today is that although many Western actors are willing to work with specialized UN agencies, they are reluctant to strengthen the UN's core institution, the UN General Assembly, from which all these specialized agencies come. The UN General Assembly is the most representative body on the planet, and yet many Western countries are deeply skeptical of it. They are right to point out its imperfections. But they overlook the fact that this imperfect assembly enjoys legitimacy in the eyes of the people of this imperfect world. Moreover, the General Assembly has at times shown more common sense and prudence than some of the most sophisticated Western democracies. Of course, it takes time to persuade all of the UN's members to march in the same direction, but consensus building is precisely what gives legitimacy to the result. Most countries in the world respect and abide by most UN decisions because they believe in the authority of the UN. Used well, the body can be a powerful vehicle for making critical decisions on global governance.

The world today is run not through the General Assembly but through the Security Council, which is effectively run by the five permanent member states. If this model were adopted in the United States, the U.S. Congress would be replaced by a selective council comprised of only the representatives from the country's five most powerful states. Would the populations of the other 45 states not deem any such proposal absurd? The West must cease its efforts to prolong its undemocratic management of the global order and find ways to effectively engage the majority of the world's population in global decision-making.

Another fundamental principle that should underpin the global order is the rule of law. This hallowed Western principle insists that no person, regardless of his or her status, is above the law. Ironically, while being exemplary in implementing the rule of law at home, the United States is a leading international outlaw in its refusal to recognize the constraints of international law. Many Americans live comfortably with this contradiction while expecting other countries to abide by widely accepted treaties. Americans react with horror when Iran tries to walk away from the NPT. Yet they are surprised that the world is equally shocked when Washington abandons a universally accepted treaty such as the Comprehensive Test Ban Treaty.

The Bush administration's decision to exempt the United States from the provisions of international law on human rights is even more damaging. For over half a century, since Eleanor Roosevelt led the fight for the adoption of the Universal Declaration of Human Rights, the United States was the global champion of human rights. This was the result of a strong ideological conviction that it was the United States' God-given duty to create a more civilized world. It also made for a good ideological weapon during the Cold War: the free United States was fighting the unfree Soviet Union. But the Bush administration has stunned the world by walking away from universally accepted human rights conventions, especially those on torture. And much as the U.S. electorate could not be expected to tolerate an attorney general who broke his own laws from time to time, how can the global body politic be expected to respect a custodian of international law that violates these very rules?

Finally, on social justice, Westerns nations have slackened. Social justice is the cornerstone of order and stability in modern Western societies and the rest of the world. People accept inequality as long as some kind of social safety net exists to help the dispossessed. Most western European governments took this principle to heart after World War II and introduced welfare provisions as a way to ward off Marxist revolutions seeking to create socialist societies. Today, many Westerners believe that they are spreading social justice globally with their massive foreign aid to the developing world. Indeed, each year, the members of the Organization for Economic Cooperation and Development, according to the organization's own estimates, give approximately $104 billion to the developing world. But the story of Western aid to the developing world is essentially a myth. Western countries have put significant amounts of money into their overseas development assistance budgets, but these funds' primary purpose is to serve the immediate and short-term security and national interests of the donors rather than the long-term interests of the recipients.

Some Asian countries are now ready to join the West in becoming responsible custodians of the global order.

The experience of Asia shows that where Western aid has failed to do the job, domestic good governance can succeed. This is likely to be Asia's greatest contribution to world history. The success of Asia will inspire other societies on different continents to emulate it. In addition, Asia's march to modernity can help produce a more stable world order. Some Asian countries are now ready to join the West in becoming responsible custodians of the global order; as the biggest beneficiaries of the current system, they have powerful incentives to do so. The West is not welcoming Asia's progress, and its short-term interests in preserving its privileged position in various global institutions are trumping its long-term interests in creating a more just and stable world order. Unfortunately, the West has gone from being the world's primary problem solver to being its single biggest liability.

Assess Your Progress

1. According to Kishore Mahbubani, how is the West's strategic thinking flawed?
2. How did the U.S. invasion of Iraq affect the Middle East region? What was its impact on international law?
3. How has western policy contributed to the undermining of the Nuclear Nonproliferation Treaty?
4. How do recent western trade and environmental policies affect prospects for progress on these issues?
5. What does Mahbubani argue the West must do to address the challenges that face the international system?

Kishore Mahbubani is Dean of the Lee Kuan Yew School of Public Policy at the National University of Singapore. This essay is adapted from his latest book, *The New Asian Hemisphere: The Irresistible Shift of Global Power to the East* (Public Affairs, 2008).

UNIT 2
Political Economy and the Developing World

Unit Selections

Learning Outcomes

After reading this unit you should be able to:

- Describe the obstacles to economic growth and stability in developing countries.
- Explain the growing influence of developing countries in the international economy.
- Outline the impact of the recent financial crisis on developing countries.
- Discuss the nature of the international trade system and describe the differences between industrialized and developing countries on trade issues.
- Recognize the changes in funding and disbursement of development aid and the issues associated with these activities.
- Describe the nature of worldwide food production and distribution.
- Analyze the advantages and disadvantages of microfinance.
- Assess the arguments for debt reduction in the poorest developing countries and reparations for Haiti in the aftermath of its devastating earthquake.

Student Website

www.mhhe.com/cls

Internet References

Center for Third World Organizing
www.ctwo.org

ENTERWeb
www.enterweb.org

International Monetary Fund (IMF)
www.imf.org

TWN (Third World Network)
www.twnside.org.sg

U.S. Agency for International Development (USAID)
www.usaid.gov

The World Bank
www.worldbank.org

World Trade Organization (WTO)
www.wto.org

Economic issues are one of the most pressing concerns of the developing world. Economic growth and stability are essential to tackle the various problems confronting developing countries. Even though the developing world is beginning to play a larger role in the global economy, many countries still continue to struggle to achieve consistent economic growth. Although there is some indication that the number of people below the poverty line is decreasing worldwide, over a billion people still live on less than a dollar a day. Economic inequality between the industrial countries and much of the developing world persists. This is especially true of the poorest countries that have become further marginalized due to their limited participation in the global economy. Substantial inequality within developing countries is also obvious. The elite's access to education, capital, and technology has significantly widened the gap between the rich and the poor. Since their incorporation into the international economic system during colonialism, the majority of developing countries have been primarily suppliers of raw materials, agricultural products, and inexpensive labor. Dependence on commodity exports means that developing countries have had to deal with fluctuating, and frequently declining, prices for their exports. At the same time, prices for imports have remained constant or have increased. At best, this decline in terms of trade has made development planning difficult; at worst, it has led to economic stagnation and decline. Although industrialization in China and India boosted demand for primary products over the past few years, the recent global economic decline has resulted in falling demand and lower prices for commodities. In the meantime, domestic constraints may prevent India from further boosting its economic growth. Clearly, dependence on export of raw materials and agricultural goods is not an ideal long-term strategy for economic success.

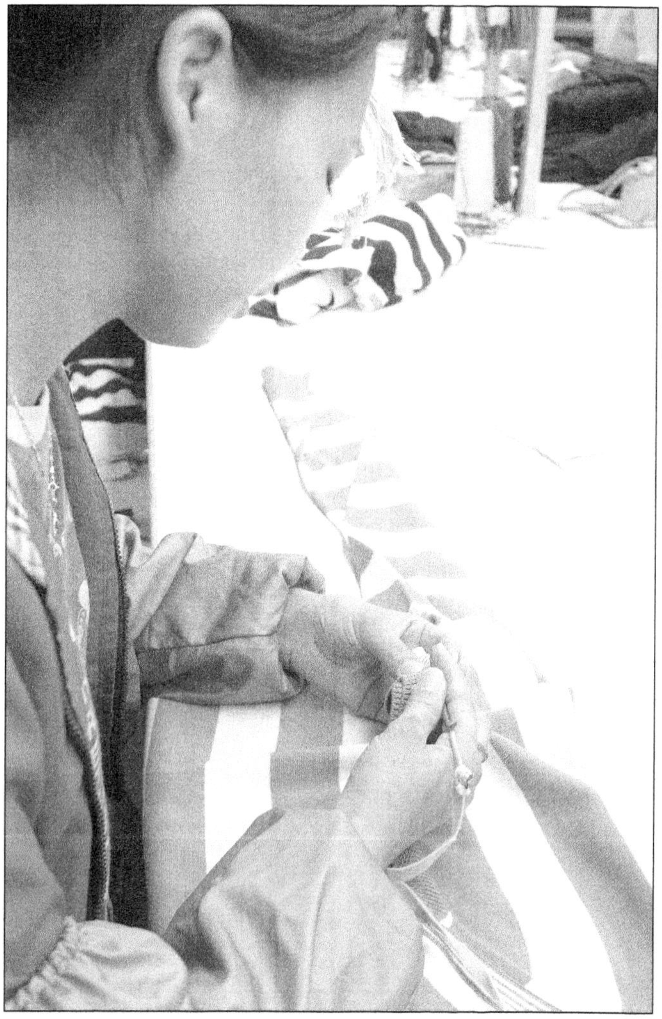

With a few exceptions, most of the developing nations have had limited success in breaking out of this dilemma through the process of diversifying their economies. Efforts at industrialization and export of light manufactured goods have led to competition with the less efficient industries of the industrialized world. The response of industrialized countries has often been protectionism and demands for trade reciprocity, which can overwhelm the markets of the developing countries. The economic situation in the developing world, however, is not entirely attributable to colonial legacy and protectionism on the part of industrialized countries. Developing countries have sometimes constructed their own trade barriers. In addition, industrialization schemes involving heavy government direction were often ill-conceived or have resulted in corruption and mismanagement. Industrialized countries frequently point to these inefficiencies in calling for market-oriented reforms, but the emphasis on privatization does not adequately recognize the role of the state in developing countries' economies; and privatization may result in foreign control of important sectors of the economy, as well as a loss of jobs. The World Trade Organization (WTO) was established to standardize trade regulations and increase international trade, but critics charge that the WTO continues to be dominated by the wealthy industrial countries. Developing world countries also assert that they are often shut out of trade negotiations, that they must accept deals dictated by the wealthy countries, and that they lack sufficient resources to effectively participate in the wide range of forums and negotiations that take place around the world. Moreover, developing countries charge that the industrialized countries are selective in their efforts to dismantle trade barriers and emphasize only those trade issues that reflect their interests. Delegates from poor countries walked out of the 2003 WTO ministerial meeting in Cancún, Mexico protesting the rich countries' reluctance to eliminate agricultural subsidies and their efforts to dominate the agenda. Neither the 2005 Hong Kong WTO ministerial meeting nor the 2006 talks in Geneva made much progress on forming a comprehensive international trade agreement. Further talks in 2007 and 2008 also failed to produce an agreement, largely due to disagreement over agricultural trade. It seems increasingly unlikely that the Doha round will produce a broad agreement further liberalizing trade and the failure of these negotiations may have an adverse impact on the WTO.

During the 1970s, developing countries' prior economic performance and the availability of petrodollars encouraged extensive commercial lending. The worldwide recession in the early 1980s left many developing countries unable to meet their debt obligations and international financial institutions became the lenders of last resort. Access to the World Bank and International Monetary Fund became conditional on the adoption of structural adjustment programs that involved steps such as reduced public expenditures, devaluation of currencies, and export promotion, all geared to debt reduction. The consequences of these programs have been painful for developing countries, resulting in declining public services, higher prices, and greater reliance on primary production. Eliminating the debt of the world's poorest countries was a major focus of the G-8 summit in July 2005 but whether the promised debt relief will have the desired effect remains to be seen. The recent global economic crisis will certainly have an impact on trade, aid, and investment.

Despite a renewed interest in foreign aid after the September 11th attacks, the effectiveness of this assistance remains uneven. Some are calling for a re-evaluation of aid that takes into account broader goals, the greater number of actors involved, and provides better ways to measure effectiveness. Efforts to raise more revenue for development aid have led to innovative financing schemes. The money raised by small taxes on airline tickets and voluntary contributions associated with the sale of certain products can then be channeled to developing countries to help fight disease and boost economic activity. In the meantime, the emergence of non-governmental organizations as major players in the disbursement of aid has become a controversial trend. Critics argue that this lets incompetent governments escape responsibility and scrutiny. While microloans have been credited with helping to reduce poverty, criticism has emerged regarding the cost of these loans and the emergence of large banks and financial institutions as providers of these funds. The amount of development aid available as well as its effectiveness and administration continue to be controversial topics.

Globalization has produced differing views regarding the benefits and costs of this trend for the developing world. Advocates claim that closer economic integration, especially through trade and financial liberalization, increases economic prosperity in developing countries and encourages good governance, transparency, and accountability. Critics respond that globalization favors the powerful nations and through the international financial institutions, imposes difficult and perhaps counterproductive policies on the struggling economies. They also charge that globalization undermines workers' rights and causes environmental degradation. Moreover, most of the benefits of globalization have gone to those countries that are already growing—leaving the poorest even further behind.

Industrial Revolution 2.0

In the corner offices of New York and Tokyo, business leaders cling to the notion that their designs, technologies, and brands are cutting edge. Increasingly, however, that just isn't so. In industries ranging from steel and cement to automobiles and electronics, "Third World companies" are poised to overtake their Western rivals. Get ready for the biggest firms you've never heard of to become household names.

ANTOINE VAN AGTMAEL

For a few minutes, I held the future in my hand. The third-generation cell phone in my palm made a BlackBerry look like a Model T Ford. Looking down at the color video screen, I could see the person on the other end of the line. The gadget, which fit easily into my pocket, could check local traffic, broadcast breaking television news, and play interactive computer games across continents. Internet and e-mail access were a foregone conclusion. So were downloading music and watching video clips.

None of this would be all that surprising were it not for where I was standing. I wasn't visiting Apple Computers in Cupertino, California, or Nokia headquarters outside Helsinki. It was January 2005, and I was in Taiwan, standing in the research lab of High Tech Computer Corporation (HTC). The innovative Taiwanese company employs 1,100 research engineers, invented the iPAQ pocket organizer (which it sold to Hewlett-Packard), and developed a series of advanced handheld phones for companies such as Palm, Verizon, and Vodafone. All around me were young, smart, ambitious engineers. They represented the cream of the crop of Taiwanese universities with, in some cases, years of experience in international firms. They were hard at work testing everything from sound quality in a sophisticated acoustics studio to the scratch resistance of newly developed synthetic materials.

I was being shown not just the prototype of a new smart phone but the prototype of a new kind of company—savvy, global, and, most important, well ahead of its nearest competitors in the United States and Europe. My experience in Taiwan is not that unusual. From Asia to Latin America, companies that many still regard as "Third World" makers of cheap Electronics or producers of raw materials are emerging as competitive firms capable of attaining world-class status. Only a decade ago, the attention of the international business community was focused on a new economy backed by hot tech firms in California and Tokyo. But the reality of the current global dynamic is that, more likely than not, the next Microsoft or General Electric will come from the "new economies" of Asia, Latin America, and Eastern Europe, not the United States, Europe, or Japan.

Today, emerging-market countries account for 85 percent of the world's population but generate just 20 percent of global gross national product. By 2035, however, the combined economies of emerging markets will be larger than (and by the middle of this century, nearly double) the economies of the United States, Western Europe, or Japan. The reality of globalization—which is only slowly and reluctantly sinking in—is that outsourcing means more than having "cheap labor" toil away in mines, factories, and call centers on behalf of Western corporations. Yet in the West, business leaders and government officials cling to the notion that their companies lead the world in technology, design, and marketing prowess.

Just as the Industrial Revolution turned American companies from imitators to innovators, emerging-market multinationals will do the same.

Increasingly, that just isn't so. South Korea's Samsung is now a better recognized brand than is Japan's Sony. Its research and development budget is larger than that of America's Intel. And its 2005 profits exceeded those of Dell, Motorola, Nokia, and Philips, Mexico's CEMEX is now the largest cement company in the United States, the second largest in the United Kingdom, and the third largest in the world. The gas reserves of Russian giant Gazprom are larger than those of all the major oil companies combined, and its market capitalization—or total stock value—is larger than that of Microsoft. South Korean engineers are helping U.S. steel companies modernize their outdated plants. New proprietary drugs are being developed in Indian and Slovenian labs, where researchers are no longer content to turn out high volumes of low-cost generics for sale in the United States and Europe. New inventions in consumer electronics and wireless technology are moving from Asia to the United States and Europe, not just the other way around.

The growth in emerging-market companies has been nothing short of astounding. In 1988, there were just 20 companies in emerging markets' with sales topping $1 billion. Last year, there were 270, including at least 38 with sales exceeding $10 billion. In 1981, the total value of all stocks listed on stock exchanges in emerging markets was $80 billion. That was less than the market capitalization of the largest emerging-market firm, Samsung, in 2005. Over the past quarter century, the total market capitalization of emerging markets as a group has risen to more than $5 trillion. Twenty-five years ago, portfolio investors had invested less than a few hundred-million dollars in emerging-market firms. Today, annual portfolio investment flows of more than $60 billion constitute the leading edge of a trend. Fifty-eight of the Fortune 500 top global corporations are from emerging markets, and many of them are more profitable than their peers in the West. The era of emerging-market companies being nothing more than unsophisticated makers of low-cost, low-tech products has ended.

Lifting the Veil

Most people are blissfully unaware that companies from emerging markets already play a major part in their lives by making much of what they eat, drink, and wear. One reason that these new multinationals have flown below the radar of so many executives, as well as the general public, is that companies such as Taiwan-based Yue Yuen and Hon Hai remain deliberately hidden in the shadows. Even though Yue Yuen produces the actual shoes for Nike and Hon Hai makes much of what can be found inside Dell computers, Apple iPods, and Sony PlayStations, the bigger brands continue to control the distribution and marketing. When will they remove their veil? These firms' prevailing invisibility—a conscious stealth strategy in some cases—does not mean that they are powerless, less profitable, or that they will be content to have a low profile forever. It won't be long before the biggest companies you have never heard of become household names.

Companies like Samsung, LG, and Hyundai, all based in South Korea, began by making products efficiently and cheaply. Now, they have recognized brand names, a high-quality image, world-class technology, and appealing designs. China's Haier, the country's leading producer of household appliances, is following in their footsteps. In fact, it is already better known than GE, Sony, or Toyota by hundreds of millions of consumers in China, India, and other emerging markets. Firms such as Haier have not relied on big brand names to reach consumers in the United States and Europe. Instead, they used niche products such as small refrigerators and wine coolers to get their lines into big-box stores such as Walmart. And as time goes on, more emerging-market firms will overtake the long-established Western companies that they now supply.

That has already happened in a number of industries ranging from semiconductors to beer. Samsung now holds the No. 1 global market position not only in semiconductors used in hard disks and flash memory cards but also in flat-screen monitors used for computers and televisions. In 2004, China's Lenovo purchased IBM's ThinkPad brand. In a wholly different industry, Brazilian investment bankers merged domestic beer companies in 1999 and then swapped shares with Europe's largest beer giant, Interbrew, to form a new entity that is now managed by a Brazilian CEO. Meanwhile, Corona beer, produced by Mexico's Modelo, is now the leading imported beer brand in the United States. Elsewhere, the global supply chain is turning upside-down, with Western companies selling components services and to multinationals from emerging markets. GE, for instance, sells jet engines to Brazilian plane manufacturer Embraer. Other smart firms will soon follow suit. Just as the rise of the United States after the Industrial Revolution turned American companies from imitators into innovators, emerging-market multinationals will increasingly do the same.

For many of these firms, the road to success included weathering global financial crises. These economic shocks squeezed out many emerging-market companies. The ensuing Darwinian struggle for survival left only battle-hardened firms still standing. As newcomers, emerging multinationals had to fight for shelf space against preconceived notions of inferior product quality (a bias that wasn't always without justification). When the financial crises were over, a few world-class companies had carved out leading roles. Today, more than 25 emerging-market multinationals have attained a leading global market share in their respective industries. Fifteen command the No. 1 market share—and they are no longer limited to a narrow slice of low-tech industries. The truth is, emerging multinationals now maintain dominant market positions in some of the world's fastest-growing industries. Consider Samsung, which is the global market leader in flash memory cards used in iPods, cameras, and mobile phones. The memory card market was worth $370 million in 2000. This year, it is valued at $13 billion. In fact, more than half of all emerging-market companies of world-class status operate in capital-intensive or technology-oriented industries, where high rates of spending on research and development are required to remain competitive.

Nothing to Lose

But the road to success has not been easy. Emerging-market multinationals did not succeed simply by following textbook practices and solutions. Contrary to popular belief, it is unconventional thinking, adaptability, a global mind-set, and disciplined ambition—not natural resources or the advantage of lowcost labor—that have been the crucial ingredients for their success. As newcomers, emerging-market firms could only wrestle away market share from deeply entrenched incumbents through audacious solutions. Their success hinged upon novel thinking that was widely ridiculed by competitors from the rich world. In many cases, emerging multinationals became

From Small-Time to Prime-Time

A growing number of companies in emerging markets now enjoy the No. 1 global market share for their products. Here's a look at some of the industries they dominate.

Company	Industry	Country
Samsung Electronics	Flat-screen televisions	South Korea
Aracruz Celulose	Market pulp for paper products	Brazil
Sasol	Synthetic fuels	South Africa
TSMC	Logic semiconductors	Taiwan
Yue Yuen	Athletic and casual shoes	Hong Kong
MISC	Liquified natural gas shipping	Malaysia
Embraer	Regional jet aircraft	Brazil
Gazprom	Natural gas	Russia
Hon Hai	Electronics manufacturing by contract	Taiwan
Tenaris	Oil pipes	Argentina

successful only by following the opposite of tried and true textbook policies. Two of the best examples are Taiwan's HTC and Argentina's Tenaris.

By the 1990s, Taiwanese companies had carved out a leading position in notebook computers and various PC accessories. But they were way behind on smaller, more cutting-edge personal digital assistants (PDAS) and smart phones. Until 1997, that is, when a group of Taiwanese engineers got together and decided that the future was elsewhere. Instead of making knockoff organizers or cheap cell phones, the engineers at HTC designed the stylish iPAQ, the first PDA to challenge Palm's unrivaled position. The iPAQ had elements that Palm and other manufacturers had studiously avoided—a Microsoft operating system, an Intel chip, and a Sony screen, all technologies that mobile companies had hitherto considered inferior. But HTC recognized that wireless technology would soon turn PDAS into pocket PCS, combining cell phones with e-mail and Internet access. That insight helped them land a contract to become the primary manufacturer of the Treo PDA and inspired them to embark on a leapfrogging effort by designing a whole series of versatile handhelds and smart phones that eventually became the chief Windows-based competitors of BlackBerry.

A similarly innovative approach was taken in Argentina by oil-pipe manufacturer Siderca. Realizing that government protection had led to technological mediocrity and a poor global image, Siderca CEO Paolo Rocca decided that global oil giants wanted more than top-quality pipes. They wanted suppliers that could react quickly to their needs anywhere in the world, able to deliver a pipe to a remote oil well in the middle of Nigeria on short notice. Siderca already had loose alliances with companies in Brazil, Italy, Japan, Mexico, and Romania. Rocca transformed this ad hoc group of companies into a well-oiled machine that was able to integrate researchers from far-flung subsidiaries to invent sophisticated pipes that were increasingly in demand for deep-ocean and arctic drilling operations. He also introduced high-tech systems that enabled the company to deliver its pipes "just in time" to the major oil companies, a feat that took leading, rich-world players such as Mannesmann several years to match. When Rocca was finished, the small "club" of traditional Western oil-pipe makers had lost its stranglehold on the market.

Emerging markets now control the bulk of the world's foreign exchange reserves and energy resources.

Other examples abound. Take Aracruz, in Brazil. The company used eucalyptus trees to make market pulp, even though it had generally been looked down upon before as "filler pulp" while the "real" pulp was made from slow-growing pine trees. In Mexico, CEMEX began a global acquisition spree by taking over two Spanish cement producers after it was locked out of the U.S. market by anti-dumping laws. The company's CEO, Lorenzo Zambrano, says, "For Spaniards, the idea of a Mexican company coming to Spain and changing top management was unthinkable."

Superior execution and an obsession with quality are now hallmarks of virtually all of the world-class companies based in emerging markets. That has helped feed a mind-set in which emerging multi-nationals are no longer content with being viewed as leading Chinese, Korean, Mexican, or Taiwanese companies. They aspire to be global, and this aspiration is rapidly becoming a reality.

Back to the Future?

Those who recall the Cold War may be forgiven for entertaining a sense of déjà vu. The launch of Sputnik in 1957 prompted anxieties that the West was falling behind. Two decades later, the overwhelming success of Japanese firms Toyota and Sony resulted in alarmed cries that "the Japanese are winning." Similar calls, proclaiming that the Chinese and the Indians are winning, can be heard today. But those who speak of winners and losers are regarding the global economy as a zero-sum game. There is ample reason to believe that is not the case—not based on naive internationalism, but on the well-justified belief that, in the current global economic order, both sides can come out ahead.

Many emerging multinationals are already owned by shareholders from all over the world. Foreign shareholders own 52 percent of Samsung, 71 percent of CEMEX, 57 percent of Hon Hai, and 54 percent of India-based Infosys. As a group, emerging multinationals can claim about 50 percent of their ownership as being foreign. Emerging multinationals are also becoming significant employers in the United States and Europe, as well as attractive prospective employers for business school graduates and scientists. More than 30,000 people in the United States and Europe work for CEMEX, many more than the company employs in Mexico. Its management meetings are conducted in English, because more than half of the firm's employees do not speak Spanish. Hyundai just opened a plant in Alabama, creating 2,000 American jobs; its regional suppliers employ an additional 5,500 workers. Haier makes most of its refrigerators for the U.S. market at a plant in North Carolina.

Of course, the road ahead for these emerging-market winners will not be without setbacks. Motorola's Razr cell phone has already helped the firm recover much of the ground it lost to Samsung. CEMEX's aggressive acquisition strategy may have worked, but the takeover bids of other emerging multinationals have failed, including Haier's bid to buy Maytag. Others have fallen flat, such as the Taiwanese company BenQ's failure to turn around Germany's Siemens Mobile. The very fact that the Latin and Asian financial crises are receding in memory and that new public offerings by Chinese and Russian companies are often oversubscribed could tempt these emerging competitors to rest on their laurels. An unexpected crisis or decline in China's growth could deliver a blow to the economy that many consider the anchor of the developing world. And a growing list of innovative companies—such as Amazon, Apple, Google, Qualcomm, and Toyota, with its new hybrid car in Japan—reveals that the rich world's creativity is far from dead.

Still, the larger trends are clear. In recent years, it has become apparent that the dominance of the United States as a superpower is resulting in its deepening dependence on foreign money, foreign resources, foreign professionals, and, increasingly, foreign technology. Only 25 years ago, most sophisticated investors scoffed at the notion of investing even a tiny portion of respectable retirement funds or endowments in developing-world companies. Just as the conventional wisdom then wrongly depicted emerging markets as "Third World," today it is all too common to underestimate the leading companies from these markets. Emerging markets now control the bulk of the world's foreign exchange reserves and energy resources. They are growing faster than the United States and many European countries (and have been for decades). Most have budget and trade surpluses, and a few are even recognized as major economic powers.

Standing inside a research lab in China, South Korea, or Taiwan, it is painfully clear just how stymieing Western protectionism has been for Western companies. Such measures led to a false sense of security, a reluctance to streamline, and a lack of innovative thinking in industries ranging from steel and automobiles, to electronics and cement. As Western firms spent the 1980s and 90s protecting themselves from foreign exports, emerging multinationals built campuses of bright, young software engineers in India and incredibly efficient mining operations in Brazil and Chile. Instead of denying the new reality, the West must formulate a creative response to this global shift of power. That task is now the central economic challenge of our time.

Assess Your Progress

1. How is economic and technological power shifting worldwide?
2. What accounts for the success of emerging market multinational corporations?
3. How does ownership of emerging market multinationals reflect globalization's influence?

ANTOINE VAN AGTMAEL, known for coining the term "emerging markets," is founder and chief investment officer of Emerging Markets Management L.L.C. He is the author of *The Emerging Markets Century: How a New Breed of World Class Companies is Taking over the World* (New York: Free Press, 2007).

A Tiger Despite the Chains

The State of Reform in India

Powerful political interests still stand in the way of India's realizing its economic potential.

RAHUL MUKHERJI

India's rapid and sustained economic growth since 1991 has occurred in an environment in which industrialists, trade unions, bureaucrats, farmers, and nongovernmental organizations wield considerable political power. Two decades ago, India was stereotyped as a "soft" state, quite unlike the fast-growing "tiger" economies of East Asia. India was deemed incapable of disciplining powerful social actors in order to promote its competitiveness.

This perception seemed confirmed when the economic growth that the country enjoyed in the 1980s, which was fueled by greater opportunities for private companies in a closed economy, became unsustainable in 1991 amid a balance of payments crisis. That crisis was driven by fiscal profligacy, a rise in the price of oil during the Gulf War in 1990, and India's heavy dependence on foreign commercial borrowings.

And yet, substantial economic reforms did occur after 1991, and they helped transform India's economy. How did this happen? New policy ideas gradually replaced old ones, which had emphasized economic self-sufficiency and trade pessimism. Also, reforming statesmen such as Prime Minister P. V. Narasimha Rao and Finance Minister (now Prime Minister) Manmohan Singh, along with reforming technocrats like Montek Ahluwalia and Chakravarthy Rangarajan, took advantage of the balance of payments crisis to alter fundamentally the rules of economic engagement in India.

Since 1991, the Indian economy has experienced an average growth rate in excess of 6 percent per year. Between 2003 and 2007, the economy grew at an average rate of 9 percent. It weathered the recent global financial crisis with greater ease than most countries' economies, and it continued to grow at a 6.7 percent clip in 2008–2009. India's current finance minister, Pranab Mukherjee, expects the figure to be 7.2 percent in 2009–2010. After the global downturn has ended, a return to a 9 percent growth rate seems likely.

But why does the Indian economy not grow at double-digit rates like China's does? It is because numerous political challenges still get in the way. Powerful constituencies such as trade unions, rich farmers, and politicians and bureaucrats still pose substantial obstacles to investment.

Trade unions, rich farmers, and politicians and bureaucrats still pose obstacles to investment.

In addition, economic reform has not yet benefited enough Indians for the country to harness the potential of its youthful workforce. Substantial resources have been pledged in areas such as literacy promotion and employment generation, yet the government so far has been unable to reach targeted populations efficiently. For India, which has more poverty than any other nation in the world, improvement in the human condition is not just an end in itself—it is a means toward sustaining a high-growth trajectory.

Reform and Rejuvenation

The government's response to the foreign exchange crisis in July and August of 1991 constituted a watershed in India's economic history. A number of significant policy decisions taken at that time subsequently improved the country's competitiveness in the global economy.

First, India devalued the rupee by about 20 percent, thereby making Indian exports cheaper in the world market. (In 1994, the rupee was made fully convertible in the capital account, which meant that exporters could easily access foreign exchange at the market rate.) Second, the government overturned an intrusive regulatory framework that had evolved since 1951, a framework that required industrialists to seek state permission before embarking on commercial enterprises. Third, the government abolished stringent regulations on capacity expansion in any company worth more than 1 billion rupees. Fourth, the foreign investment limit in most sectors was raised from 40 percent to 51 percent.

India's growth story owes a great deal to entrepreneurs who took advantage of the new industrial deregulation and export orientation of the 1990s. The country's ratio of trade to gross domestic product (GDP), which had been constant at about 16 percent between 1980–81 and 1990–91, jumped to 54 percent by 2008. Information technology exports surged from $194 million in 1991–92 to $6.54 billion in 2001–02, and to $50.4 billion in 2008–09.

The information technology service company Infosys, which began with an initial investment of $250 in 1981, was worth $4 billion in 2008. Tata Steel retrenched its workforce and invested $2.5 billion to transform itself from a top-fifty steel company in the world to one of the leading five. The Tata Group, in search of technology and markets, bought the Anglo-Dutch steel maker Corus Group in 2007 for $12.1 billion.

Successful companies have generated substantial personal wealth for a few individuals. Mukesh Ambani, a tycoon in several industries, is the fourth-richest person in the world, with a fortune of $29 billion. According to the latest rankings in *Forbes,* four other Indian entrepreneurs rank among the top fifty billionaires.

Linking domestic competitiveness with global acquisitions has become characteristic of many of India's best companies. These include Bharat Forge (automobile parts), Tata Motors (cars), Wipro (information technology), Dr. Reddy's (pharmaceuticals), and Tata Tea (fast-moving consumer goods).

In 2006–07, Indian companies spent $12.8 billion on acquisitions of overseas companies, compared with China's $16.1 billion. This represented a substantial amount, considering that the Chinese economy is two and a half times the size of the Indian economy. Moreover, a large share of Chinese investment was accounted for by state-owned companies pursuing natural resources, whereas India's investments were made by private companies in search of technology, brand names, and markets.

Financial Returns

The government also successfully reformed India's banks and stock markets to create the financial environment necessary for growth. The Reserve Bank of India improved the supervision of banks and systematically subjected them to international best practices. This led to a substantial reduction in bad debts and an improvement in profitability. Indeed, India's banking system is today better regulated than China's.

The government viewed stock markets as critical for raising resources for Indian companies. So, when the brokers of the Bombay Stock Exchange refused to accept international best practices, the Ministry of Finance in 1993 created a modern and computerized national stock exchange. Competition from the national exchange forced the Bombay exchange to acquiesce to the reforms suggested by the Ministry of Finance. Substantial reforms in trading norms followed, in 2003.

The booming markets quickly became an attractive investment proposition for Indians and foreigners alike. India's stock markets attracted $24.2 billion from foreign institutional investors between 1992–93 and 2002–03. This figure was a little higher than the foreign direct investment ($24.1 billion) registered during the same period.

Foreign investment was impaired because the business environment for multinational companies was more hostile in India than in China. India had enormous entrepreneurial potential waiting to be unleashed in 1991, whereas China had no private sector when it initiated its economic reforms. Partly as a result, India's government and companies were more cautious than China about allowing foreign investment. In 1993, an informal group of industrialists calling themselves the Bombay Club made the case that foreign investment was detrimental to India. Many a productive investment was blocked by regulations governing joint ventures with foreign partners and by the need for state-level intervention in matters related to obtaining land, water, electricity, road infrastructure, and a variety of such amenities.

This business environment for foreign investors is changing gradually. Successful Indian businesses that began as relatively small entrepreneurial endeavors have needed foreign capital and technology to compete with larger companies. For example, the Hero Group, a bicycle manufacturer, partnered with Honda to become a leading producer of motorized two-wheelers. Bharti's partnership with SingTel helped it become India's leading telecom service provider. Whereas India attracted $24.1 billion in foreign direct investment between 1992–93 and 2002–03, in a single recent year (2008–09) it attracted $27.3 billion.

The Telecom Boom

It is well known that India's telecom boom has contributed substantially to the country's growth. Less widely known perhaps has been the impact of government actions on telecommunications. India has more than 500 million telephone lines and is adding between 8 and 10 million lines every month, in what is considered the world's fastest-growing telecom market. Indian companies offer the cheapest rates in the world. But it was the Indian state's response to the balance of payments crisis of 1991 that created conditions favorable for private sector participation and growth in the telecom field. The government proved it was serious about withdrawing from commercially viable sectors in order to reduce substantial fiscal deficits.

In the early 1990s, private sector activity in the absence of appropriate regulation sowed the seeds for companies to experience investment crises later in the decade. This could have driven telecom service providers to bankruptcy. But the government again responded, first in 1997, by creating the Telecom Regulatory Authority of India, then in 2000 by further empowering the regulators.

The success of Indian telecommunications owes much to the spread of wireless telephone. By 2008, 90 percent of the Indian market was using wireless technology. Two principal factors made this possible. First, the sector's transformation from a government monopoly in 1991 to one in which 80 percent of the market is now served by private companies drove telecommunications providers to become more efficient. Technological advances in mobile technology further fueled growth. (Private companies enjoyed the first mover's advantage in cellular services because the government had not predicted the potential of this technology in the early 1990s.)

Second, competent regulation promoted competition among service providers, which exerted downward pressure on tariffs. Today the penetration of mobile telephones in the smaller cities and villages holds great promise of opening up new opportunities for the poorer people of India.

Remaining Fetters

Notwithstanding India's economic performance over the past two decades, powerful interest groups—in particular, trade unions, wealthy farmers, and government bureaucracies—continue to present substantial challenges to the promotion of the nation's competitiveness and overall development. They constitute the principal reasons that India is unable to grow as rapidly as China.

India's labor unions, though they represent less than 10 percent of the workforce, have successfully thwarted a social contract that would benefit the majority of Indian workers and boost the country's productivity. Trade unions in many European countries, with memberships that protect more than 70 percent of the labor force, have promoted a business environment in which labor is productive and contributes to the industrial sector's competitiveness. Labor laws in India, on the other hand, protect a minority of workers and turn a blind eye to the majority in the unorganized sector who work under exploitative conditions.

Legal protection for labor, moreover, increases with the size of the enterprise. The government's regulatory framework thus forces industrial enterprises either to reduce their scale or become more capital-intensive. This is a disincentive for reaping economies of scale in a labor-abundant economy like India's.

The political power of the unions can be judged from the fact that even severe economic crises and fiscal and external pressures have not made an impact on laws that create perverse incentives. India is in dire need of more widely inclusive unions that pledge productivity in return for social protection. This represents a significant challenge for promoting competitiveness in labor-intensive activities, an essential condition for generating more employment.

India's rich farmer lobby is another potent political force and hindrance to growth and development. This lobby benefits from fertilizer and power subsidies that do not help marginal farmers and that crowd out public investments in areas such as irrigation and rural roads. The subsidies also contribute handsomely to India's fiscal deficits.

To be sure, public investment is essential in a sector that constitutes less than 20 percent of GDP yet employs a majority of the population. Average annual growth in the country's agricultural sector dipped from 3.4 percent in the 1980s to 2.9 percent in the 1990s. The sector witnessed zero or negative growth in three of the first four years of the new millennium. Policy makers have tried to give agriculture serious attention since 2004.

But the political power of the wealthy farmers has stalled reforms, particularly in the power sector. Farmers in many Indian states do not pay electricity bills. In states such as Andhra Pradesh and Tamil Nadu, the agricultural lobby can bring down governments that seek to impose even a subsidized tariff. Consequently, the losses of state-owned power companies have increased from $4.8 billion in 2005–06 to $7.1 billion in 2008–09.

The private sector hesitates to play an enthusiastic role in a business environment in which obtaining revenues is a major challenge. And the power sector's losses not only impose a burden on the public treasury; they also increase costs for industry, which has to subsidize the free power delivered to farmers.

India's poorer farmers, meanwhile, are unable to benefit from these subsidies because their farms depend on canal irrigation and diesel pumps. Farmers who consume free electricity to run electric hand pumps pay a price anyway, in the form of poor power quality and frequent transformer burnouts.

Land acquisition can also be a major bottleneck for productive investment in India. Political mobilization at the local level often impedes acquisition of land for industrial enterprises. To give one example, Tata Motors faced a slew of challenges when it wanted to make an iconic investment in the world's cheapest car, the Nano. Such was the level of politically motivated opposition to the setting up of a Nano factory in Singur, in the eastern state of West Bengal, that one of the most highly respected captains of Indian industry, Ratan Tata, had to shift the location of the factory from Singur to Pantnagar, in the northern state of Uttarakhand.

Laws that govern the acquisition of land contain serious flaws. The colonial-era Land Acquisition Act gives the government absolute power to acquire any piece of land. But protests in places like Singur and Nandigram in West Bengal point to the need to win the consent of the local population. The government needs to devise a regulatory framework that allows for adequate compensation and makes the acquirers of land work toward improving the living conditions of those who will be displaced as a result of commercial activity.

Within an appropriate regulatory framework, productive investment can be a win-win situation for the investor and for displaced people. Investment-friendly states such as Gujarat, Tamil Nadu, Haryana, and Andhra Pradesh have found ways to win consent for land acquisitions in the absence of a national regulatory framework; as a result, they have been able to attract more investment and grow rapidly.

Government in the Way

Even more than trade unions and obstructive rural interests, the government itself is often the worst enemy of competitiveness in India. For example, the ports that carry 95 percent of the country's trade by volume could benefit from better regulation of private investment. India's ports charge higher fees and take a longer time to provide services than do ports in Dubai, Colombo, and Singapore. Larger vessels often dock in other countries' more efficient ports and use smaller vessels to ship merchandise to India because of the inadequacy of that nation's port infrastructure. Indian ports thus lose business, and Indian exports and imports face higher transaction costs.

The government's regulation of private sector participation in ports is primitive compared to its regulation of the telecom sector. Bidding procedures regarding ports, for example, encourage private players to make unreasonably high bids to secure contracts that may not be commercially viable. Tariff-making procedures do not aid the realization of scale economies. And the governance of most major ports is controlled by port trusts, which are run by government servants who do not respect commercial considerations. The terminal charges for private operators are competitive, but high port costs result from additional charges levied by the port trusts.

The government has dragged its feet in other areas as well. The civil aviation sector lacks an independent regulator, and Air India continues to lose money. The United Progressive Alliance government, in office since 2004, has been averse to the privatization of a loss-making airline. As a consequence, precious taxpayers' money is diverted from developmental projects. The case of Air India reflects a trend in which disinvestment in loss-making public companies has taken a back seat in recent years.

In contrast, allowing a greater role for commercial considerations in Indian Railways six years ago catapulted the rail system from bankruptcy to substantial profits. Yet the populist inclinations of the government's new railway minister may overturn this legacy. Likewise, the development of national highways and private sector participation in roads have also slowed in recent years. These infrastructure areas are vital for India's economic growth, and the government is constricting their development.

Sharing Growth

India's rapid economic growth needs to involve a larger proportion of the citizenry. The government's inattention to areas such as literacy promotion and employment generation has helped produce unacceptable levels of absolute poverty. Most economists believe that about 26 percent of the Indian people in 1999 lived below the poverty line, under unacceptable conditions, when the same figure for China was about 10 percent.

The economic reforms of the early 1990s clearly reduced poverty levels from what they would have been without the reforms. But it is also apparent that the benefits of rapid economic growth trickle down too slowly in India. Moreover, it may not be politically feasible to sustain a social environment in which a few of the richest individuals in the world coexist with a vast population that lives on less than $2 a day.

India produces more engineers than the United States, but its literacy rate in 2001 was 61 percent, far lower than in China—or, for that matter, in Sri Lanka, where more than 90 percent of the population is literate. India's policy elite during the 1990s ignored the need to abolish child labor and promote literacy. The prevailing view was that poor people could keep their children at work to augment their family incomes, and that literacy for such Indians was not critical.

This view has changed over time. India's Supreme Court linked the right to education and the right to life in 1993. In the new millennium, the government has pledged substantially greater resources for literacy promotion, a commitment that was evident in the Right to Education Act of 2009. More than 96 percent of Indian children aged 6 to 14 years were enrolled in school in 2006–07. This suggests that the literacy picture in India is undergoing a belated transformation.

The major challenge facing literacy promotion is the low quality of government schools. Teacher absenteeism rates in India's public schools are among the highest in the world. And the children of poor parents have no exit options. Cheap private schools serve the lower middle class and the relatively better off among the poor. Policy makers are debating whether school vouchers for the poor may be a better option than spending large sums of money on government schools that are largely dysfunctional. States like Madhya Pradesh have been able to reduce teacher absenteeism by involving village governments in the governance of schools and by keeping teachers on renewable contracts.

High levels of unemployment and underemployment also pose a significant challenge for poverty alleviation. The Mahatma Gandhi National Rural Employment Guarantee Act (NREGA) of 2005 is the most ambitious welfare program in India. It guarantees 100 days of paid work to all who seek employment. Employment is generated by the creation of public goods such as water tanks, roads, and schools, especially in rural areas. Public works are monitored by local village governments.

According to NREGA, 47.2 million families have benefited so far from this scheme, over 50 percent of whom are from socially and economically marginalized castes and tribes, and 48 percent of the beneficiaries are women. Rajasthan has the best implementation record, and India's poorest states—including Bihar, Chhattisgarh, and Madhya Pradesh—are among NREGA's top five beneficiaries. This program seems to be making a dent in poverty, notwithstanding some corruption problems.

Corruption has been the bane of India's poverty reduction efforts. Funds provided for employment generation schemes are often siphoned off to benefit richer families. In 2003–04, over $90 million out of a $158 million food subsidy did not reach a single family whose economic status was considered below the official poverty line. Meanwhile, teacher absenteeism impairs literacy initiatives, and health worker absenteeism weakens health programs.

The current government has taken two significant steps in an effort to improve service delivery for Indian citizens. First, the Right to Information Act of 2005 replaced the Official Secrets Act of 1923, which had made it legally impossible to obtain information vital for punishing corruption within the government. Social activists such as Aruna Roy helped bring about this reform. Roy had resigned from the civil service and started a "social audit," whereby poorer people who were supposed to benefit from public services began to assess government programs. The Right to Information Act is a powerful weapon that has been successfully deployed to catch corruption in high places.

Second, the Unique Identification Authority of India, initiated in 2009, will provide every resident with a card that will carry essential data about the individual. The card is designed to empower citizens such that they should easily be able to access essential public services. The authority is headed by Nandan Nilekani, who gave up his chief executive's job at Infosys to help devise the system. The new card will eliminate the need for multiple identification cards, such as one card for NREGA employment benefits and another that certifies a person's status as living below the official poverty line.

The Road Ahead

India's growth story has largely been driven by the gradual development of new policy ideas—ideas whose value became more apparent during financial crises, which facilitated their consolidation. Gaining political support for new ideas has taken time; indeed, ideas such as autarkic development and public control over the economy could not be quickly or easily replaced by ones that emphasize the role of private companies and international trade. New ideas have also been resisted by political constituencies that benefited from the old ideas.

The transformation of policy ideas and politics has made India's corporate sector more efficient. It has engendered better service provision in appropriately regulated areas such as telecommunications, banks, and stock markets. In these arenas, the government's role has contributed to India's rise as a rapidly emerging economy.

Predatory propensities within the government hinder the development of roads, railways, and airlines.

But powerful political interests still stand in the way of India's realizing its economic potential. The country's trade unions have successfully opposed a legal framework that could benefit more workers and spur labor-intensive industrialization. Rich farmers make unreasonable demands for power and fertilizer subsidies that crowd out essential public investment in rural areas. The predatory propensities of politicians and bureaucrats prevent India's ports from achieving their potential. Similar predatory propensities within the government hinder the development of vital infrastructure such as roads, railways, and airlines.

Growth has made welfare more affordable, and democratic pressures are making it essential.

India's growth has preceded the creation of a welfare state. Growth has made welfare more affordable, and democratic pressures are making it essential. In advanced industrial welfare states, capitalism arrived before democracy. The welfare state was born because of democratic pressures on the propertied classes after substantial surplus accumulation had already occurred. A similar phenomenon is occurring now in India.

Legal and institutional developments such as the Right to Education Act, the Mahatma Gandhi National Rural Employment Guarantee Act, the Right to Information Act, and the Unique Identification Authority of India point to the pressures from below that are today demanding redistribution of wealth and consolidating the idea that the Indian citizen has certain rights to services, which the state is obliged to provide. Going forward, efforts to reduce poverty could have a significant impact, not only in spreading the benefits of growth more widely, but also in sustaining India's rapid economic development.

Assess Your Progress

1. What accounts for India's rapid and sustained recent economic growth?
2. What factors prevent India from matching China's dramatic economic growth?
3. What role does the government play in limiting competitiveness in India?
4. How might India's growth benefits be more widespread?

Rahul Mukherji, an associate professor at the National University of Singapore, is the editor of *India's Economic Transition: The Politics of Reforms* (Oxford University Press, 2007).

The Poor Man's Burden

Eighty years ago, a depression changed the way we think about poverty. It took decades for the world to recover and to remember that if people are given freedom, they will prosper. Now, in the wake of another massive meltdown, the fear that shocked us into depending on government to fix poverty is spreading once again—and threatening to undo many of the gains we've made.

WILLIAM EASTERLY

Will Richard Fuld, the disgraced CEO of the now defunct Lehman Brothers, go down in history as the father of Bolivian socialism? If we learn the wrong lessons from the global financial Crash of 2008, he very well could.

That's because the crash arrived at a crucial moment in the global fight to reduce poverty. For Bolivia—and so many other countries like it—the crash represents much more than a temporary downturn; it could mean the end of one of the greatest openings for prosperity in decades. Amid today's gloom, it is easy to forget we have just witnessed half a century of the greatest mass escape from poverty in human history. The proportion of the world's population living in extreme poverty in 2008 (those earning less than a $1 a day) was a fifth of what it was in 1960. In 2008, the income of the average citizen of the world was nearly three times higher than it was in 1960. But those tremendous gains are now in peril. For this crash hit many poor countries from Asia to Africa to Latin America that are still experimenting with political and economic freedom—but have yet to fully embrace it and experience its benefits. For decades, these countries have struggled tremendously to realize the potential of individual creativity as opposed to the smothering hand of the state. And it even seemed that the power of individual liberty might be winning.

It wasn't happening because experts had handed out some blueprint for achieving economic growth to governments and then down to their people. What happened instead was a Revolution from Below—poor people taking initiative without experts telling them what to do. We saw such surprising success stories as the family grocer in Kenya who became a supermarket giant, the Nigerian women who got rich making tie-dyed garments, the Chinese schoolteacher who became a millionaire exporting socks, and the Congolese entrepreneur who started a wildly successful cellphone business in the midst of his country's civil war. Perhaps not coincidentally, the share of countries enjoying greater levels of economic and political freedom steadily and simultaneously shot upward.

Then came the crash.

Today, global economic calamity risks aborting that hopeful Revolution from Below. As India's Prime Minister Manmohan Singh warned late last fall, "It would be a great pity if this growing support for open policies in the developing world is weakened" because of the crash. Singh understands that the risk of a backlash against individual freedom is far more dangerous than the direct damage to poor countries caused by a global recession, falling commodity prices, or shrinking capital flows. We're already seeing this dangerous trend in Latin America. In Bolivia, President Evo Morales has openly crowed about the failure of Fuld's Lehman Brothers and other Wall Street giants: The capitalist "models in place are not a good solution for humanity . . . because [they are] based on injustice and inequality." Socialism, he said, will be the solution—in Bolivia, the state "regulates the national economy, and not the free market." The leaders of Argentina, Bolivia, Brazil, Ecuador, Nicaragua, Honduras, Paraguay, Venezuela, and even tiny Dominica to varying degrees align with these anticapitalist pretensions, all seemingly vindicated by the Crash of 2008. And it's not confined to Latin America: Vladimir Putin blamed the U.S. financial system for his own populist mismanagement of Russia's even more catastrophic crisis. A spreading fire of statism would find plenty of kindling already stacked in the Middle East, the former Soviet Union, Africa, and Asia. And there are many Western "development" experts who would eagerly fan the flames with their woolly, paternalistic thinking.

To Jeffrey Sachs, perhaps the foremost of these experts, the crash is an opportunity to gain support for the hopelessly utopian Millennium Development Goals of reducing poverty, achieving gender equality, and improving the general state of the planet through a centrally planned, government-led Big Push. "The US could find $700 billion for a bailout of its corrupt and errant banks but couldn't find a small fraction of that for the world's poor and dying," he wrote in September. "The laggards in the struggle for the [goals] are not the poor countries . . . the laggards are the rich world." To Sachs and his acolytes, poor people can't prosper without Western-country plans—and the crash only serves to turn Western governments inward. Therefore, progress on poverty is bound to suffer. To governments of poor countries that have failed to give their people the freedom needed to prosper, the neglect of Western governments is an easy excuse. So the gospel of Sachs and his disciples, though terribly condescending and wrong-headed, could attract many converts in the coming months.

A Depressing History

At least we've been here before—and we have a chance to avoid the philosophical traps we fell into after the last calamity that did so much harm to our economic system. But so far, there have been strikingly similar reactions to the crashes of 1929 and 2008. In both cases, when stocks registered some of their largest percentage declines on record, highly leveraged firms and individuals who had placed large bets using complex financial securities that few understood lost everything. The failure of gigantic financial firms spread panic. Complaints about the greedy and reckless rich escalated; a shift toward protectionism and government interventionism appeared inevitable even where free markets once reigned supreme. Authoritarian populists abroad mocked the U.S. system. The catastrophe seemed to threaten democratic capitalism everywhere.

So far, there have been strikingly similar reactions to the crashes of 1929 and 2008.

The difference is today we know that after a long and scary Great Depression, democratic capitalism did survive. And the U.S. economy returned to exactly the same long-run trend path it was on before the Depression.

We also know that, for another important part of the world, democratic capitalism did not hold up so well. In many ways, that failure stemmed from a misguided overreaction on the part of a new, influential field of economics that was highly skeptical of capitalism, was deeply traumatized by economic calamity, and considered much of the world "underdeveloped." Born in the aftermath of the Depression, "development economics" grew on a foundation of bizarre misconceptions and dangerous assumptions.

This approach to poor-country development, promulgated by the economists who took up its cause in the 1950s, had four unfortunate lasting consequences, the effects of which we're still reckoning with today in the midst of the latest big crash.

First, seeing Depression-style unemployment in every part of the world led these economists to assume that poor countries simply had too many people who were literally producing nothing. A U.N. report in 1951, produced by a group of economists, including future Nobel laureate Arthur Lewis, estimated that fully half of the farming population of Egypt produced nothing. The insulting assumption that poor people had "zero" productivity led these economists to think that individual freedoms for the poor should not be the foundation for wealth creation, as they had been during the Industrial Revolution, when the state had played a secondary, supportive role. And because governments seemed to successfully take on a larger role during the Depression, development economists assumed that granting extensive powers to the state was the surest path to progress. A 1947 U.N. report on development gave equivalent approval to state action in democratic capitalist countries like Chile, enslaved Soviet satellites like Poland, African colonies of the British and French, and apartheid South Africa, ignoring the vast differences in individual liberty between these places.

Second, these thinkers lost faith in bottom-up economic development that was "spontaneous, as in the classical capitalist pattern" (as a later history put it), preferring instead development "consciously achieved through state planning." After all, the Five-Year Plans of the 1930s Soviet Union had avoided the Depression, at an appalling but then ignored cost in lives and human rights. This thinking was so universal that Gunnar Myrdal (who would later win a Nobel Prize in economics) claimed in 1956: "Special advisors to underdeveloped countries who have taken the time and trouble to acquaint themselves with the problem . . . all recommend central planning as the first condition of progress."

Third, these economists grew to believe that the most important factor in reducing poverty was the amount of money invested in the tools to do so. After all, if there were simply too many people, they reasoned, the binding constraint on growth must be the lack of physical equipment. As a result, this line of economic philosophy would forever stress the volume of investment over the efficiency of using those resources; would be stubbornly indifferent as to whether it was the state or individuals who made the investments; would always stress the total amount of aid required to finance investment as the crucial ingredient in escaping poverty; and would ignore the role of a dynamic financial system in allocating investment resources to those private uses where they would get the highest return.

Fourth, the collapse of international trade during the Depression made development economists skeptical about trade as an engine of growth. So in Africa, for example, they pushed for heavy taxes on export crops like cocoa to finance domestic industrialization. In Latin America, Raúl Prebisch pushed import-substituting industrialization instead of export-led growth. This strategy was supposed to help developing countries in Africa and Latin America escape a presumed "poverty trap." But the only "trap" it kept them out of was the greatest global trade boom in history following World War II, which fueled record growth in Asia, Europe, and the United States.

By the 1980s, the state-led plans had clearly failed. The wreckage of unsuccessful state enterprises, bankrupt state banks, and inefficient hothouse industries behind protectionist walls—all of which culminated in African and Latin American debt crises that destroyed growth—became too obvious to ignore. These factors, plus East Asia's rise to power in global markets, finally fueled a counterrevolution in development thinking that favored free markets and individual liberty. By the new millennium, the long record of failure of the top-down development experts triggered a well-deserved collapse of confidence in top-downplanning. It had taken nearly 50 years for the world to recognize the damage that the state-led, expert-directed, antifreedom agenda had done to the world's poor. Today, the only remaining holdouts among the top-down experts are so utopian that they are safely insulated from reality.

A 5(0)-Year Plan

Today, just when we were getting over the long, toxic legacy of the Depression and its misguided emphasis on statist plans to fight poverty, this financial crash threatens to take us back to the bad old days. To avoid such a return, we must keep some principles in mind.

First, we must not fall into the trap of protectionism—neither unilaterally nor multilaterally, neither in rich countries nor poor. Protectionism will just make the recession spread further and deeper, as it did during the Depression.

Second, when changing financial regulations to repair the excesses of the past several years, don't strangle the financial system altogether. You can't have a Revolution from Below without it. This lesson is especially salient as Washington bails out Wall Street banks and failing industries and intervenes in the U.S. financial sector to an unprecedented degree. This bailout might turn out to be the bitter medicine that saves "finance capitalism" from a stronger form of anticapitalism, but in developing countries, open economies are still an open question.

Third, keep slashing away at the enormous red tape that is left over from previous harebrained attempts at state direction of the economy. Learn from the combined dismal track record of state-owned enterprises but also from the unexpected success stories: Private entrepreneurs are far better than the government at picking industries that can be winners in the global economy. Although fierce opposition will be inevitable, to adopt these policies would be to turn the bad hand we've been dealt into an outright losing one.

Fourth, don't look to economists to create "development strategies," and don't back up such experts with external coercion like IMF and World Bank conditions on loans. Such efforts will be either a waste of local politicians' time or positively harmful. Jeffrey Sachs alone can take partial credit for the rise of two xenophobic rulers hostile to individual liberty—Evo Morales and Vladimir Putin—after his expert advice backfired in Bolivia and Russia. If like-minded experts couldn't get it done in the 50 years after the Great Depression, they can't do it in the next 50 years. Nothing in the current crash changes these common-sense principles.

Driving the Right Way

In the coming months and years, the world's economists, politicians, and average consumers could find it incredibly easy to fall again for the wrongheaded policies of the past century. But if we are truly to continue the miraculous exodus from poverty that was under way before this traumatic crash, we ought to keep in mind stories like that of Chung Ju-yung.

The son of North Korean peasant farmers, Chung had to leave school at 14 to support his family. He held jobs as a railway construction laborer, a dockworker, a bookkeeper, and a deliveryman for a rice shop in Seoul. At 22, he took over the rice shop, but it failed. He then started A-Do Service garage, but that failed, too. In 1946, at age 31, Chung tried once again to start an auto repair service in Seoul. At last, his enterprise succeeded, largely through the contracts he won to repair U.S. Army vehicles. As his success continued, Chung diversified into construction, and his company kept growing rapidly. In 1968, he started manufacturing cars.

He named his company Hyundai. It became one of the largest companies contributing to South Korea's rise. His first effort to export cars to the United States in 1986 brought ridicule because of the cars' poor quality. The Asian crisis of 1997-98 led to a partial breakup of the Hyundai Group, but the Hyundai Motor Company continues to thrive. Chung died in 2001, but his dreams for the U.S. market came true. By 2008, Hyundai cars had received awards in the United States for the highest level of quality from *Consumer Reports*.

However terrifying the latest crash may be, let's never forget that it is the Chungs of the world that will end poverty—not the Depression-inspired regression into statism.

Want to Know More?

William Easterly's most recent book, *The White Man's Burden: Why the West's Efforts to Aid the Rest Have Done So Much Ill and So Little Good* (New York: Oxford University Press, 2006), criticizes Western approaches to global poverty. In **"The Ideology of Development"** (*Foreign Policy* July/August 2007), Easterly warns of the dangers of "Developmentalism."

Easterly's chief economic adversaries, Jeffrey Sachs and Paul Collier, take a more aid-oriented approach. Sachs's *Common Wealth: Economics for a Crowded Planet* (New York: Penguin Press, 2008) and Collier's *The Bottom Billion: Why the Poorest Countries Are Failing and What Can Be Done About It* (New York: Oxford University Press, 2008) offer policy solutions for the world's most pressing problems.

For a look at one of the earliest and most prescient (and now forgotten) economists to advocate the potential of free markets as a tool for development, read S. Herbert Frankel's *Some Conceptual Aspects of International Economic Development of Underdeveloped Territories* (Princeton: Princeton University, 1952). For a more well-known early critique of development, see P.T. Bauer's *Dissent on Development* (Cambridge: Harvard University Press, 1976).

Assess Your Progress

1. What impact might the 2008–2009 global financial crisis have on developing countries?
2. According to William Easterly, what accounts for the rapid decline in poverty rates in developing countries?
3. How might the economic slowdown affect open economic policies?
4. What steps must be taken to avoid a return to statist plans geared toward fighting poverty?

William Easterly is professor of economics at New York University.

Cotton: The Huge Moral Issue

World cotton prices have dropped to an historic low: the reason being the immoral continuation of EU and US trade subsidies that allow non-competitive and inefficient farming to continue. While the recent WTO meeting in Hong Kong failed to resolve the issue, the livelihoods of West Africa's 12 million cotton farmers will soon be destroyed if subsidies are not slashed. This is a huge moral issue.

KATE ESHELBY

Seydou, dressed in a ripped T-shirt that hangs off his shoulders, looked at me blankly as I questioned him about the effects of US subsidies on his only source of income, cotton farming. "I don't know about cotton in the US but I know cotton prices have fallen here in Burkina Faso," he lamented.

The farmers working in the cotton fields of Burkina Faso, often in remote locations, have little knowledge of the intricacies of world markets. What they do know is that the price they receive for their cotton harvests—essential for basic necessities such as medicines and school fees—is dropping fast.

The end of cotton farming in Burkina Faso and other cotton producing West African countries is rapidly approaching. World cotton prices have dropped to an historic low: the reason being the immoral continuation of EU and US trade subsidies that allow non-competitive and inefficient farming to continue.

Cotton subsidies in richer countries cause over production, artificially distorting world markets. And who suffers? The poor countries, whose economies are wholly dependent on the cotton trade.

In Burkina Faso, a former French colony in West Africa, cotton is the country's main cash crop. It is the primary source of foreign income, making up one-third of export earnings, and the lifeblood for the majority of farmers. Here cotton is grown on small, family-owned farms, seldom bigger than five hectares. One farmer, called Yacouba, explains: "I also grow maize and groundnuts on the farm, to feed my family, but cotton is my only source of cash."

In contrast, US cotton operations are enormous and yet, unlike Burkina Faso, cotton is a minimal proportion of its GDP. Ironically, the US subsidies are concentrated on the biggest, and richest, farms. One such farm based in Arkansas has 40,000 acres of cotton and receives subsidies equivalent to the average income of 25,000 people in Burkina Faso.

The benefits of subsidies only reach a small number of people in the US and other Western countries, whereas two million people in Burkina Faso, one of the world's poorest countries with few other natural resources, depend on cotton for survival.

The farms in Burkina Faso are very productive, it is cheaper and more economical to grow cotton there than in the US. "I have to take out loans each year to buy enough insecticides and fertilisers for my cotton," says Yacouba. "They are very expensive so we have to work hard to ensure we get a good harvest. Each year I worry whether I will earn enough to pay back the loans." Burkinabe farmers are forced to be efficient, also prevailing against climatic uncertainties and limited infrastructure—all this, with no support from subsidies.

Fields are prepared by plough and both seed planting and picking are done by hand, which explains why cotton is also vital for providing jobs—being very labour intensive. Yacouba explains: "My family works on the farm throughout the year, but during harvesting we bring in extra help." Pickers are dotted around the fields surrounding him, plucking the cotton balls from the shoulder-high plants. Some of the women have children tied to their backs and the sacks of cotton are steadily placed under the shade of a giant baobab tree. This scene is in stark contrast to the US where huge, computerised harvesters pick the cotton and aerial spraying administers the chemicals required.

The meeting (in mid-December 2005) of the World Trade Organisation (WTO) in Hong Kong was to address this farcical situation as part of the Doha "development" talks. But nothing much came out of it. Burkina Faso is still resting its hopes on cotton subsidies being eliminated, or at least reduced, in order to save its fundamental crop from demise. The Doha negotiations, launched in 2001, are intended to show that trade could benefit the world's poor. But subsidies are a global injustice, and create major imbalances in world trade—it is argued they should only be available for products that are not exported, and targeted towards family and small-scale farmers.

The US gives approximately $3.4bn a year in subsidies to its 25,000 cotton farmers; this is more than the entire GDP of Burkina Faso. Subsidies dramatically increased in the US after the 2002 Farm Act and as a result US cotton production has recently reached historic highs. It is now the world's second largest cotton producer, after China, and the biggest exporter—an easy achievement because US cotton prices no longer bear any relation to production costs.

Current world cotton prices are in decline due to global over-production, fuelled by agricultural subsidies. EU and US taxpayers and consumers pay farmers billions of dollars to overproduce for a stagnant market. These surpluses are then dumped overseas, often in developing countries, destroying their markets and driving down world prices.

The livelihoods of West Africa's 12 million cotton farmers will soon be destroyed if subsidies are not slashed. This is a huge moral issue. It is simple—Burkina Faso cannot compete against heavily subsidised exports.

In March 2004, a WTO panel ruled that the majority of US cotton subsidies were illegal. The WTO agreements state that "domestic support should have no, or at most minimal trade-distorting effects on production." The US tried to appeal against this decision but it was overruled.

If Africa took just 1% more in world trade, it would earn $70bn more annually—three times what it now receives in aid. In 2003, Burkina Faso received $10m in US aid, but lost $13.7m in cotton export earnings, as a result of US subsidies. No country ever grew rich on charity, it is trade that holds the key to generating wealth. Fair trade would give the Burkinabe cotton farmers a decent opportunity to make a living by selling their produce, at a decent price, to the richer world; enabling them to work their way out of poverty.

The US was legally required to eliminate all trade-distorting subsidies by 21 September 2005, according to a WTO ruling. President George Bush keeps saying he will cut subsidies, but actions are louder than words. The delay is partly due to a long-standing arm wrestle between the US and the EU, neither of whom will budge. The British prime minister, Tony Blair, does seem to want to abolish EU subsidies, but the French argue that subsidies are not even negotiable. Despite four years of haggling, negotiators are still at loggerheads. Numerous reports have been compiled, many meetings held and yet scant progress has been made—and things are only getting worse for the Burkinabe cotton farmers.

"Both the US and EU brag about their boldness, but the actual reform they propose is minuscule, tiny fractions of their massive farm support. The negotiations have recently moved into the finger-pointing phase in which rich countries criticise the inadequacy of each other's proposals. Meanwhile, poor countries await something real," says Issaka Ouandago, from Oxfam's office in Burkina Faso.

Oxfam has been supporting the struggle of African cotton farmers in their campaign known as the "Big Noise", and are hoping to gather a petition of one million signatures against cotton subsidies. "We can only hope the US reform their subsidy programmes and stop dumping cheap cotton onto the world market," Ouandago continues. "Despite their WTO commitments to reduce trade-distorting subsidies, the EU and US have used loopholes and creative accounting to continue. Such practices are undermining the fragile national economics of countries that depend on cotton."

The rich countries have to come forward with more, otherwise the Doha Round will achieve nothing, as the meeting in Hong Kong proved—although developing countries have less political power, they are still capable of blocking the negotiations if they don't get what they want. In the last WTO meeting, held in Geneva, July 2004, negotiations on US cotton subsidies were supposed to be kept separate from broader agricultural negotiations—this did not happen. It was a blow for Burkina Faso and other West Africa countries who produce mainly cotton and are less interested in other commodities. A subcommittee on cotton was set up to "review" the situation, but the EU and US have not taken this committee seriously.

With the emergence of the G20 alliance, some developing countries, such as India and Brazil, are now powerful enough to resist pressures, but African countries have previously never been centre stage. West African cotton producers are, however, becoming far stronger as a group. "We have become more united to make our voice heard. Our aim is to gather all African cotton producers together," explains Yao, a member of the National Union of Cotton Producers in Burkina Faso.

The only reason Burkinabe cotton farmers are still surviving is that producer prices have been maintained at a minimum level-175 CFA per kg of cotton seed is the minimum price the farmers need to break even, prices never go below this, despite being above current world prices.

In recent years, the Burkinabe cotton companies used their profits from previous harvests to support the farmers; these savings are now depleted. The full effects of world prices have, therefore, not yet been felt by the farmers, the worst is to come—once the prices are forced to drop below this minimum, the farmers can no longer survive.

Leaving the house of Seydou, I wonder about his fate. A pile of bright-white cotton sits drying in the glaring sun, in front of his mud house. Inside the walls are bare, except for a single cross; a bundle of clothes hang from a rope and a pile of maize is stacked in the corner. "I cannot afford to buy things because cotton prices keep fluctuating," he says. "I know cotton grows well here but prices are down so I cannot send my youngest son to school. This makes me sad. I know his only chance of a good future is school."

In Burkina Faso, cotton is the country's biggest interest and essential to its economy, so it prays that cotton is addressed more seriously and given the attention it deserves. As the sun sets, the workers leave the fields, holding sacks of cotton above their heads. A donkey cart trundles by, carrying a mound of cotton—kicking up a trail of red earth. Their livelihoods depend on the decisions made at the WTO.

Assess Your Progress

1. How do subsidies hurt cotton producers in poor countries?
2. In what ways do subsidies push down prices?
3. How might elimination of subsidies boost African trade and prosperity prospects?
4. What has allowed Burkina Faso's cotton producers to survive? Can this be sustained?

R.I.P, WTO

PAUL BLUSTEIN

Someday historians may look back on 2010 as the year the global trade system died—or contracted a terminal illness. A pledge by world leaders to complete the Doha round of global trade negotiations this year looks increasingly likely to end in yet another flop, and that would deal a crushing blow to the trade system as we know it.

Of course, commerce will continue across national borders, and one-off deals between countries will still happen. But the slow-but-steady, across-the-board opening of markets that has fueled growth for decades is grinding to a halt. After eight painful years of standstill and failure, with each meeting just a shoveling of intractable problems forward to the next, the Doha talks might collapse once and for all in 2010, possibly taking the World Trade Organization (WTO) down in the process.

Yes, negotiators could once again defer the day of reckoning by setting a new deadline and resolving to try again later—just as they've already done in Cancún, Geneva (three times), Hong Kong, and Potsdam. But they're running out of chances. No less an authority than Stuart Harbinson, the former WTO General Council chairman who played a key role in the round's launch in 2001, wrote recently: "This time... the crisis is real. Too many deadlines have come and gone and the WTO simply cannot afford a repeat. The fundamental credibility of the institution is now at stake.... 2010 is a real deadline."

That's dangerous, because for all its failings, the WTO is a rare international organization that works as intended. The Geneva-based trade group is the current embodiment of the system established after World War II to prevent a reversion to 1930s-style protectionism and trade wars. Its rules keep a lid on its member countries' import barriers, and members take their trade disputes to WTO tribunals rather than imposing tit-for-tat sanctions on each other's goods. In addition, the WTO is the guardian of the most-favored-nation principle, which requires members to treat each other's products in a nondiscriminatory fashion—a valuable bulwark against the sorts of trade blocs that can lead to friction or even military conflict.

If Doha falls apart, the WTO's ability to continue performing its vital functions would be imperiled. If it can't forge new agreements, how long before it loses its authority to arbitrate disputes? The trade body won't disintegrate overnight, but the danger is that its tribunals will be weakened to the point where member countries start ignoring WTO rulings and flouting their commitments.

Without negotiated settlements of contentious issues, litigation will almost surely spread like wildfire—a potentially explosive situation. On climate change, for example, some in the United States and Europe want to impose "green tariffs" on goods from countries that aren't reducing their carbon emissions fast enough (read: China and India). In the absence of clear rules, China and India would have plenty of leeway to challenge such tariffs, putting WTO tribunals in the terribly awkward position of having to decide: Are such tariffs illegal, meaning that free trade trumps saving the planet? Or, if the tariffs are legal, should the Chinese and Indians have the right to slap duties on goods from Western countries, which they blame for creating the global warming problem in the first place?

Sadly, even in a best-case scenario for 2010, with Doha ending in a deal, the global trading regime might still be doomed. The round's initial goals—making globalization work for the billions left behind by eliminating the farm subsidies and tariffs that adversely affect the world's poor—have become so laughably implausible that completing what's left of an agreement will prompt a painful reckoning. The deal on the table has been so watered down by negotiations that it cannot be credibly said to work wonders for the poor, or even effect much change in how global trade takes place. The gap between the result and the initial aspirations will prompt legitimate questions about why so much time was required and whether the WTO has any future as a negotiating forum.

Even in a best-case scenario, with Doha ending in a deal, the global trading regime might still be doomed.

What an irony that would be for President Barack Obama. Despite making multilateralism a keystone of his foreign policy, he may preside over the marginalization of the most successful multilateral institution of all.

Assess Your Progress

1. What important roles does the WTO play?
2. What threatens to undermine the WTO's ability to facilitate trade?
3. What was the Doha round of trade talks supposed to accomplish?

Paul Blustein a journalist at the Brookings Institution's Global Economy and Development Program, is author of *Misadventures of the Most Favored Nations: Clashings Egos, Inflated Ambitions, and the Great Shambles of the World Trade System.*

Taking the Measure of Global Aid

International development assistance has in effect been assigned a new grand purpose: managing interdependencies in a globalized world.

JEAN-MICHEL SEVERINO AND OLIVIER RAY

"Official development assistance"—the standard measure of aid that governments and multilateral institutions provide to developing countries—is dying. Not that it ever really existed, in the sense of neatly representing a global fight against poverty that comprised common objectives and means. And not that international solidarity itself has diminished: More money, not less, is being poured each year into what can be called global development policies.

Still, an outdated concept of development—one based on illusions about the unity, clarity, and purity of the international community's goals—is giving way to a complex new mix of public policies that attempts to promote global public goods and confront the development challenges of a globalized world. The aid deck has been reshuffled by a triple revolution in objectives, players, and instruments.

This sudden metamorphosis of international development aid presents a problematic question: What is the relevance of global standards such as the widely cited objective of allocating 0.7 percent of donor countries' gross domestic product (GDP) to official development assistance (ODA)? Understanding why this benchmark is senseless may give us a clue as to why it is not reached. In any case, it is high time for new measures to guide development assistance policies.

The New World Order

The first of the revolutions that have recently swept through international development aid is a drastic expansion of the goals assigned to assistance. Development aid has always served a wide range of economic, political, social, and cultural objectives. Yet, for most of its existence, its main driving force was geopolitical. The initiators of aid were nation-states: European nations, by financing expensive economic development projects, retained some say in the political and economic lives of their former colonies. During the cold war, too, development aid served to purchase influence in the global south. Indeed, a race for influence ran parallel to the global arms race. Vast sums were disbursed to keep regions in the right camp.

Then came the fall of the Berlin Wall and the collapse of most communist states. In this new world order, economic liberalism prevailed on all continents and in virtually all countries. The widespread embrace of trade and markets as the engines of development created a major identity crisis for official development assistance, and this period was characterized by large decreases in official development flows. ODA for the United States, France, and the United Kingdom was halved in the space of seven years.

For much of the 1990s, development assistance budgets were used largely to refinance developing countries' public debts, contain humanitarian crises, and address the most troubling social consequences of structural adjustment programs. Aid became much more people-centered and much less growth-oriented. An increasing share of ODA went to social sectors, while budgets for infrastructure and agriculture were sliced. And because north-south relations were no longer perceived as strategic, states happily gave up the monopoly over aid they once enjoyed—such that decreases in public aid flows were partly compensated for by increases in private aid.

Since the turn of the century, however, the international community has come to discover other, less appealing characteristics of the "new world order." For many, the terrorist attacks of September 11, 2001, manifested the interdependency between developed and developing nations in terms of global security. Since then, much ODA has been poured into the Iraqs and Afghanistans of the world. Vast amounts of money have been dedicated to "failed" states. Conflict prevention and conflict management have become high-level items on the international development agenda.

Globalization has introduced other challenges as well. It has increased the risk that transmittable diseases will spread via commercial trade and international travel. It has accelerated global warming and the loss of biodiversity. In recent years it helped provoke an international food crisis and a period of soaring energy prices. The global financial meltdown that began in America illustrated that, in an integrated world economy, misguided policy choices in one country can penalize the system as a whole.

The global has not subsumed or transcended the local. Rather, local challenges have become an integral part of global stakes.

This new set of global problems has compounded the historic challenges of poverty and inequality. Contrary to what many early analysts of globalization expected, transcended the local. Rather, local challenges have become an integral part of global stakes. For all of these reasons, international development assistance has in effect been assigned a new grand purpose: managing interdependencies in a globalized world.

Everyone's an Actor

A second revolution in development assistance is an impressive expansion, in both number and range, of the players involved in the "market" for aid. The end of the state monopoly has sparked a boom in private giving. Nongovernmental organizations (NGOs)—left-wing and conservative, secular and faith-based, small and large—have mushroomed in all industrialized countries, and have come to represent a considerable proportion of north-south financial transfers. Businesses have also emerged as a growing component of international transfers.

Organizations and special funds dedicated to development have flourished and proliferated as never before. Behind each of these lies a respectable international concern, but many of them also represent lobbies that resist aid restructuring and streamlining. And because overall cash transfers have not increased as fast as have the entities involved, the average size of projects and operations has decreased sharply.

Recipient states too have contributed to making the international landscape more complex. Political liberalization in many developing countries has led to the birth of civil society organizations, themselves on the receiving end of an increasing share of development funds. Local governments are also taking on a greater role as political decentralization—enabled by democratization, urbanization, and demographic growth—advances throughout the world. Local businesses and financial institutions have likewise been increasingly involved.

This changing and ever-denser institutional environment is commonly considered a problem for both the efficiency and the coherence of public policy. Indeed, the costs of coordinating the activities of multiple stakeholders with differing agendas have skyrocketed over the past decade. In some cases, the gains realized from having more actors involved are outweighed by policy incoherence and coordination costs.

But the bustling creativity of new development actors has also unleashed forms of innovation that would probably not have come about had conservative public administrations continued to monopolize policy. For instance, philanthropic foundations have brought modern business practices to international development. In any case, this change is not something that can be curbed significantly: Whether we applaud or lament it, the genie is out of the bottle. Tomorrow's major development challenges will need to be resolved in this new, tumultuous environment.

A New Tool Kit

The third revolution that has swept through development assistance involves the tools with which problems are addressed. In the days when aid was about geopolitics and states, the lion's share of ODA was accounted for by sovereign grants and loans. These were largely channeled to infrastructure and agriculture projects. When compassion and private solidarity came to drive the field, smaller-scale projects in the social sector grew in importance, along with large-scale debt relief.

A section of the international aid community, tasked with finding solutions to increasingly globalized ills and representing new and diverse combinations of actors, has already moved far beyond "old school" development aid. Over the space of a decade, international development assistance has witnessed an astonishing proliferation of complex instruments: new taxation or quasi-taxation mechanisms (such as taxes on airline tickets); increased investment in risk capital; countercyclical/contingent lending instruments; and so forth.

Moreover, the way in which projects are evaluated has undergone a dramatic shift. Old school ODA typically consisted of loans and grants that subsidized the start-up costs of projects whose recurrent operational costs were meant to be borne by the beneficiaries. The idea was to avoid donor dependency. This principle, that projects needed to be financially and economically viable, became one of the cornerstones of development assistance. Although projects conceived in this way continue to exist—and justly so, since the needs to which they respond have not disappeared—economic viability and discrete transfers have often been set aside in recent years to allow for longer-term, recurrent transfers.

Today no one asks whether projects funding the education of Mali's children or providing access to clean water for Haiti's urban dwellers are economically viable.

Today no one asks whether projects funding the education of Mali's children or providing access to clean water for Haiti's urban dwellers are economically viable. The efficiency of a program is now evaluated according to the improvements brought to a targeted population's basic living standard. In a way, the logic of economic investment has been replaced by one of long-term social redistribution.

A similar paradigmatic shift in the instruments of aid has occurred because of the need to protect and finance global public goods. International health, for example, responds to the logic of the weakest link: Pandemics tend to break out in countries with the lowest capacity for prevention, early warning, and emergency treatment. If the world is to defend itself from global pandemics, it will need to strengthen the weakest links. The same goes for certain climate change efforts. Thus, nations cooperate to achieve a global public good, sharing the burden of action according to actors' capacity to pay. This requires mobilizing more stable sources of funding and finding appropriate disbursement mechanisms.

Let us be clear: This new creativity in development aid should not—cannot—aspire to replace traditional aid channels and resources. Many traditional development problems require traditional development solutions. But the diversification of tools and resources is both vital and natural.

Sins of Mismeasurement

This triple revolution in goals, actors, and instruments amounts to enormous change. But surprisingly, it has not yet affected the way that the international development community measures financial volumes dedicated to development aid. The new daily practice of aid in the twenty-first century is now well established, yet assessment of national contributions and their impacts has largely stuck to old school methods.

The problem in a nutshell is that the Development Assistance Committee (DAC) of the Organization for Economic Cooperation and Development (OECD) continues to measure development assistance by adding up OECD member states' grants, certain types of loans, and a whole series of "other" expenses whose link to development financing is at times tenuous. Indeed, it is hard to find other examples of public policies whose performance is assessed so little on the basis of results and so much on the basis of expenses, themselves measured so imperfectly. Still, the DAC's figures continue to serve as the basis for official and highly publicized promises of development aid.

The OECD's measure of ODA, which was created to gauge a relatively narrow set of activities aimed at promoting the convergence of former colonies' economies with their former masters', has become the only benchmark to assess official north-south financial flows. Yet it suffers from three deadly sins: It measures expenditures not remotely relevant to what really matters; it fails to capture the resources that are dedicated to specific ends; and it does not align costs with outcomes. In fact, only a minority of expenses included under ODA actually translates into fresh funds for development programs in the world's poorest nations.

To start with, the administrative overhead of donor states counts as aid—which clearly is not the best incentive for achieving resource-efficient aid bureaucracies. ODA figures include items such as grants offered to students from the developing world who study in a donor nation—even when they never return to their home countries to work. Also included are the costs of caring for political refugees from developing nations, and emergency relief and food aid sent to zones of natural disaster or conflict. The importance of such expenses is undeniable, but their link to countries' long-term economic and social development is very indirect.

Debt relief is also included: In 2005 it represented a record-high 25 percent of ODA. While it is true that debt restructuring has been helpful to many developing nations, allowing them to recover essential margins of maneuver in their national budgets, debt forgiveness sometimes does not represent a real budgetary cost to donors, since they do not actually expect to be paid back. There is also something awkward about counting the cancellation of loans that at the time they were granted would not have counted as ODA—as is the case with Iraq's sovereign debt, which was largely amassed to pay for weaponry during the Iran-Iraq War.

Conversely, ODA's second sin is that it misses a whole range of items that contribute meaningfully to financing development assistance. For one thing, development aid from non-OECD countries appears nowhere in statistics on international development—other than in very approximate and unofficial estimates. Yet non-OECD states represent a growing share of development aid.

China's aid to Africa is a case in point. Beijing has become one of the major contributors to the financing of infrastructure in sub-Saharan Africa. The very generous aid policies of oil-rich Arab states are not included either. In the same vein, although private giving to development efforts is now estimated as equal to half of (the inflated) official totals of official development assistance, this contribution does not appear in official measures of development aid.

Moreover, many of the innovative tools that have been designed in recent decades to finance development do not count toward ODA, which only takes into consideration grants and loans with a grant element of at least 25 percent. Failing to include new tools in measures of development assistance reduces the incentive for countries to use them. Likewise, many activities are not captured because they are deemed too remote from the so-called core of the development agenda expressed in the Millennium Development Goals. This is the case, for instance, with some peace-building and post-conflict activities, the training of international police forces, and the construction of prisons.

Costs and Benefits

The third deadly sin of ODA is its failure to address a number of crucial types of questions, thereby preventing a better appraisal of donor efforts and a more efficient alignment of expenditures with outcomes. First, what are the overall funds mobilized to finance global development policy—regardless of their origin and delivery method? The international community is ill-equipped today to assess its own efforts according to this most basic benchmark.

Second, what outputs and impacts are achieved through the projects and programs that are financed? How many children gain access to vaccinations? How many square kilometers of rain forest are saved from destruction? Because ODA measures only financial inputs, and because it does not identify the policy goals that are sought, it is absolutely mute on the question of impacts.

Third, what are the budgetary costs to donor states of development aid? Although this seems the most logical benchmark for comparing states' contributions to international development, such figures are nowhere to be found. Grants of course relate directly to budgetary costs, but official data do not capture the fiscal expenditures represented by tax exemptions that help NGOs and foundations appeal to public generosity (and the desire to avoid inheritance taxes).

Finally, what are the administrative costs of delivering development policies? DAC standards allow for declaring administrative costs, but these figures are then mixed into the broader hodgepodge of ODA. And no one is able to identify clearly how much money is spent in the field and how much is spent outside developing countries.

The Name's the Thing

What are our options for escaping the current impasse and steering global development policy as efficiently as possible? Four goals can be identified: first, giving things appropriate names, since proper naming and counting are crucial to building a sound foundation for global policies; second, devising estimates of the overall funding made available for particular goals, whatever the provenance of the funding; third, aligning policy goals with measures of results, laying aside for good the bureaucratic focus on expenditures; and fourth, assessing the budgetary costs of official aid so that we can benchmark governments' efforts.

To address the first goal, we suggest forgetting about ODA. Why not move toward a new concept: global policy finance (GPF)? This measure would include all funding devoted to the three core components of sustainable development: achieving convergence between northern and southern economies; providing better access to essential services across the world; and providing global public goods (environmental protection, international health, and so on).

Although GPF would encompass activities that go beyond old school economic development objectives and delivery methods, it would in no way exclude them. This broader scope would recognize that the nature of what the international community is undertaking has changed, and thus what needs to be measured has changed.

Regarding the second goal, our statistics should estimate the overall financing provided toward an agreed set of objectives for international development assistance. These figures should disregard financing's provenance and the share of grant money, and give us a measure of the overall sum that can be invested in the policy. Such a measure would provide a first yardstick of the financing gap for each type of policy goal (such as fighting climate change, or eradicating a given disease).

As to the third goal, we should devise a way to measure the development results of specific development activities or other global public policies. This would encourage innovation and allow us to concentrate on what ultimately matters: impact. An agreed methodology would allow us to compare the results of very different actions, be they systemic, programmatic, or project-oriented. Each actor in development aid, whatever its nature (public or private, from a traditional or an emerging donor nation, and so on), would be able to report the results of its development activities according to this methodology. Results would be open to verification.

Regarding the fourth goal, we could establish a metric such as "official global public finance" that would tabulate states' budgetary efforts toward a set of agreed global causes. This would measure public resources earmarked for financing global policies—no matter the instruments through which they are channeled. This approach would encourage countries to leverage their instruments so as to enhance the impact per dollar spent.

Times Change

These are bold changes in policy formulation and measurement, and implementing them would have important consequences on, among other things, communications. The target of spending 0.7 percent of GDP on development assistance has played an important role in public debates, and it has helped in the naming and shaming of countries that perform badly. Defining a policy objective according to its budgetary inputs is, as we have suggested, problematic. However, preserving some sort of easy-to-communicate minimum benchmark is important.

Thus, one could retain the figure of 0.7 percent, but, for example, specify that it should be applied only to a certain category of actions (for instance, promoting access to essential services). Alternately, we could alter the target (for instance, to 1 percent or 1.5 percent of GDP) and include all the development objectives—promoting economic growth, human welfare, and global public goods.

Another question is whether the DAC should continue to exist. It should, but its scope should be extended. Many countries and organizations that currently do not want to or cannot join the OECD would be willing to participate in a forum where global development policies are debated, standards set, and evaluations processed.

Such a group would probably look very different from the current DAC. It would therefore need a new name, such as "Global Policy Funding Forum." The UN would have a crucial role to play in this reorganization: A joint venture between the DAC and the UN Development Program might provide the best platform for such global engagement. The Bretton Woods institutions would also have an active role to play.

Changes such as these will not happen overnight, nor will they happen by themselves. At some stage, a set of actors will need to take the initiative and clarify the emerging global policy of development assistance by making it more inclusive—and better measured, evaluated, and communicated. To declare the death of ODA is neither to claim victory over poverty nor to admit defeat. Rather it is a statement of reality, an admission that times change. Moving from ODA to GPF would be to recognize that policies, actors, and instruments also change over time—and that an administrative measuring instrument created several decades ago needs serious revamping if we are to face effectively the global policy challenges of this century.

Assess Your Progress

1. What three developments are changing the nature of development aid?
2. How has the agenda of development expanded?
3. What important new actors are now involved in international development?
4. What are the new sources of development assistance?
5. How should the effectiveness of international development aid be evaluated?

Jean-Michel Severino is managing director of France's international development agency, and was formerly vice president for Asia at the World Bank. **Olivier Ray** is his adviser in charge of research. This article is adapted from a Center for Global Development working paper.

The New Colonialists

Only a motley group of aid agencies, international charities, and philanthropists stands between some of the world's most dysfunctional states and collapse. But for all the good these organizations do, their largesse often erodes governments' ability to stand up on their own. The result: a vicious cycle of dependence and too many voices calling the shots.

MICHAEL A. COHEN, MARIA FIGUEROA KÜPÇÜ, AND PARAG KHANNA

Even on their best days, the world's failed states are difficult to mistake for anything but tragic examples of countries gone wrong. A few routinely make the headlines—Somalia, Iraq, Congo. But alongside their brand of extreme state dysfunction exists an entirely separate, easily missed class of states teetering on the edge. In dozens of countries, corrupt or feeble governments are proving themselves dangerously incapable of carrying out the most basic responsibilities of statehood. These countries—nations such as Botswana, Cambodia, Georgia, and Kenya—might appear to be recovering, even thriving, developing countries, but like their failed-state cousins, they are increasingly unable, and perhaps unwilling, to fulfill the functions that have long defined what it means to be a state.

What—or who—is keeping these countries from falling into the abyss? Not so long ago, former colonial masters and superpower patrons propped them up. Today, however, the thin line that separates weak states from truly failed ones is manned by a hodgepodge of international charities, aid agencies, philanthropists, and foreign advisors. This armada of nonstate actors has become a powerful global force, replacing traditional donors' and governments' influence in poverty-stricken, war-torn world capitals. And as a measure of that influence, they are increasingly taking over key state functions, providing for the health, welfare, and safety of citizens. These private actors have become the "new colonialists" of the 21st century.

In much the same way European empires once dictated policies across their colonial holdings, the new colonialists—among them international development groups such as Oxfam, humanitarian nongovernmental organizations (NGOs) like Doctors Without Borders, faith-based organizations such as Mercy Corps, and megaphilanthropies like the Bill & Melinda Gates Foundation—direct development strategies and craft government policies for their hosts. But though the new colonialists are the glue holding society together in many weak states, their presence often deepens the dependency of these states on outsiders. They unquestionably fill vital roles, providing lifesaving healthcare, educating children, and distributing food in countries where the government can't or won't. But, as a consequence, many of these states are failing to develop the skills necessary to run their countries effectively, while others fall back on a global safety net to escape their own accountability. Have the new colonialists gone too far in attempting to manage responsibilities that should be those of governments alone? And given the dependency they have nurtured, can the world afford to let them one day walk away?

A Shift of Money and Power

Dependency is not a new phenomenon in the world's most destitute places. But as wealthy governments have lost their appetite for the development game, the new colonialists have filled the breach. In 1970, seven of every 10 dollars given by the United States to the developing world came from official development assistance (ODA). Today, ODA is a mere 15 percent of such flows, with the other 85 percent coming from private capital flows, remittances, and NGO contributions. Nor is this trend strictly an American phenomenon. In 2006, total aid to the developing world from countries of the Organisation for Economic Co-operation and Development (OECD) amounted to $325 billion. Just a third of that sum came from governments.

The expanding budgets of humanitarian NGOs are indicative of the power shift taking place. During the 1990s, the amount of aid flowing through NGOs in Africa, rather than governments, more than tripled. Spending by the international relief and development organization CARE has jumped 65 percent since 1999, to $607 million last year. Save the Children's budget has tripled since 1998; Doctors Without Borders' budget has doubled since 2001; and Mercy Corps' expenditures have risen nearly 700 percent in a decade.

The shift is equally apparent on the receiving end. When aid reaches developing countries, it increasingly bypasses the host governments altogether, often going straight into the coffers of the new colonialists on the ground. In 2003, the USAID Office of U.S. Foreign Disaster Assistance distributed two thirds of its budget through NGOs rather than affected governments. Between 1980 and 2003, the amount of aid from OECD countries channeled through NGOs grew from $47 million to more than $4 billion. One reason for the shift is the growing reluctance of rich countries to route aid through corrupt foreign officials. That has created an increasing reliance on new colonialists to deliver assistance—and produce results.

But the new colonialists are doing far more than simply carrying out the mandates of wealthy benefactors back home. They often tackle challenges that donors and developing-country governments either ignore or have failed to address properly. International Alert, a London-based peace-building organization, monitors corruption in natural-resource management in unstable countries such as the Democratic Republic of the Congo and serves as an early warning system to Western governments about impending conflicts. The Gates Foundation, which has spent more in the past decade on neglected-disease research than all the world's governments combined, has been so dissatisfied with existing international health indexes that it is funding the development of brand-new metrics for ranking developing-world health systems.

Seeing jobs that need to be done, the new colonialists simply roll up their sleeves and go to work, with or without the cooperation of states. That can be good for the family whose house needs rebuilding or the young mother who needs vaccinations for her child. But it can be a blow to the authority of an already weak government. And it may do nothing to ensure that a state will be able to provide for its citizens in the future.

The Power behind the Throne

The responsibilities the new colonialists assume are diverse—improving public health, implementing environmental initiatives, funding small businesses, providing military training, even promoting democracy. But whatever the task, the result is generally the same: the slow and steady erosion of the host state's responsibility and the empowerment of the new colonialists themselves.

The extent of the new colonialists' influence is perhaps best illustrated in Afghanistan. The government possesses only the most rudimentary control over its territory, and President Hamid Karzai has made little progress in combating corruption and narcotics trafficking. The result is a shell of a government, unable to provide basic services or assert its authority. Today, 80 percent of all Afghan services, such as healthcare and education, are delivered by international and local NGOs. According to its own estimates, the Afghan government administers only a third of the several billion dollars of aid flowing into the country each year. The rest is managed directly by private contractors, development agencies, and humanitarian aid groups. Major donors such as Britain only briefly include the Afghan government in their aid agendas: Although 80 percent of Britain's $200 million in annual aid to Afghanistan is dedicated to state ministries, as soon as the money arrives, it is swiftly handed over to NGOs like Oxfam or CARE for the actual construction of schools and hospitals. The transfers simply reflect many donors' lack of confidence in Afghan ministries to distribute funds competently and implement aid mandates on their own.

Many of the gains that Afghanistan has made since the fall of the Taliban can undoubtedly be attributed to the efforts and largesse of the many thousands of NGOs that have set up shop in Kabul. But not everyone is thankful for their labor. Karzai has derided the wasteful overlap, cronyism, and unaccountability among foreign NGOs in Afghanistan as "NGOism," just another "ism," after communism and Talibanism, in his country's unfortunate history. In 2005, Ramazan Bashardost, a parliamentary candidate in Kabul, sailed to electoral victory by running on an anti-NGO platform, threatening to expel nearly 2,000 NGOs that he claimed were corrupt, for-profit ventures providing little service to the country.

Many NGOs understandably resent such criticism, particularly as it lumps together a diverse lot—private contractors, international aid agencies, local NGOs—and ignores the important contributions some have made. But none of these groups is anxious to perform so well that it works itself out a job. No matter how well-intentioned, these new colonialists need weak states as much as weak states need them.

None of the new colonialists is anxious to perform so well that it works itself out of a job. They need weak states as much as weak states need them.

This kind of perverse dependency is on display in Georgia, where new colonialists have come to wield an inordinate amount of influence since the country emerged from Soviet rule. Today, its pro-Western president is supported by a steady dose of financial and political aid from abroad, and many state functions are financed or managed by outside help. In advance of the country's Rose Revolution, foreign political consultants advised the opposition's campaign strategy. The American consulting firm Booz Allen Hamilton has been hired to help rebuild state ministries from the ground up, recruiting new staff and retraining bureaucrats. These foreign technocrat-consultants participate in the day-to-day decision-making on critical national matters, such as political reform and intelligence sharing. But in Georgia, as well as other countries where these consultants operate, as they help mold state functions and prioritize development policies, they also write the complex grant applications that their home governments consider—grants that effectively extend their own positions of influence. The result is a vicious cycle of dependency as new colonialists vie for the contracts that will keep them in business.

That isn't to say that the new colonialists don't get results—many do. And in few areas are the efforts of the new colonialists more impressive than in the public-health arena. When Cambodia emerged from more than a decade of civil war in 1991, the public healthcare system was nonexistent. Since 1999, the government has outsourced much of the country's healthcare to international NGOs such as HealthNet and Save the Children. Today, it is estimated that 1 in 10 Cambodians receives Healthcare from such groups, which run hundreds of hospitals and clinics throughout the country and often provide far better care than government institutions. So reliable are these NGOs in providing quality care that it is difficult to imagine the government taking over responsibilities anytime soon—if ever.

Many aid organizations will say that their ultimate goal is to ensure their services are no longer needed. But aid organizations and humanitarian groups need dysfunction to maintain their relevance. Indeed, their institutional survival depends on it. Although aid groups occasionally have pulled out of countries because of security concerns or to protest the manipulation of aid, it is difficult to find examples where these groups have pulled up stakes because the needs they seek to address are no more. And as these groups deepen their presence in weak states, they often bleed the country of local talent. The salaries they offer are not only better and the work more effective, but there are often no comparable opportunities for well-educated locals in their country's civil service or private sector. The new colonialists may depend on this talent to ensure their legitimacy and local expertise, but it further weakens the host government's ability to attract their own best and brightest, ensuring that they remain reliant on new colonialists for know-how and results.

An Unbroken Cycle

There is no single global clearinghouse that coordinates, or even tracks, how these actors behave around the world. If new colonialists only pay lip service to local ownership and democracy, there is little to suggest that the cycle of mutual dependence will ever be broken. And if that is the case, the new-colonialist crutch may enable corrupt governments to continue to avoid their responsibilities in perpetuity.

Of course, there is another disturbing possibility that many observers do not like to countenance: Without the new colonialists, today's weak states could be tomorrow's basket cases. It speaks to the ubiquity of the new colonialists that this prospect seems remote. Nor can most weak states successfully resist their influence. When Cyclone Nargis struck Burma in May, the governing military junta initially resisted outside assistance. But state incapacity, corruption, and incompetence often make a defiant stance impossible. After several weeks, the regime's leaders had little choice but to accept the help of aid workers who were clamoring to gain access to the people in greatest need.

How then should the international community respond to the increasing influence of the new colonialists? Some observers argue that the market should take the lead in solving development challenges. Unfortunately, new investment often avoids failing states, and aid groups can rightly say that they do the work no one else is willing to do. Other observers think it is time to restore the centrality of the United Nations, at least as a coordinating force among these actors. But globalization resists the centralization of power, and the United Nations lacks the support of member states to take on such ambitious and expensive goals.

The fundamental challenge in this messy new landscape will be to establish a system of accountability. To earn a place at the table of global governance, the new colonialists will have to keep their promises not only to their donors and benefactors but to the citizens of failing states themselves. Competition among aid groups might actually serve to improve this accountability in the future. In many ways, the new colonialists are building a genuine global constituency, and, for better or worse, they may be the first—and last—line of defense for states sliding toward failure.

Want to Know More?

In *Global Development 2.0: Can Philanthropists, the Public, and the Poor Make Poverty History?* (Washington: Brookings Institution Press, 2008), economists and NGO experts debate whether the incredible proliferation of development players can work together to improve life for the world's poor. Ann Florini argues that only collective action by civil society, national governments, and private enterprise can tackle the challenges of the 21st century in *The Coming Democracy: New Rules for Running a New World* (Washington: Island Press, 2003). For an influential analysis of the rise of global civil society, see Jessica T. Mathews's "**Power Shift**" (*Foreign Affairs,* January/February 1997).

Several organizations produce rankings on the performance of global development players. The Hudson Institute's **Index of Global Philanthropy** tracks the scale of private giving to the developing world with case studies of its effectiveness. The One World Trust, established by a group of British parliamentarians, assesses the operations of some of the world's most powerful NGOs in the **2007 Global Accountability Report.**

Sebastian Mallaby exposes the often contentious relations between NGOs and international aid agencies—and the poor who get lost in the shuffle—in "**NGOs: Fighting Poverty, Hurting the Poor**" (*Foreign Policy*, September/October 2004). Erika Check reports on the fight to get lifesaving medicines to the world's poor and the growing influence of the Gates Foundation on global publichealth priorities in "**Quest for the Cure**" (*Foreign Policy*, July/August 2006).

For links to relevant websites, access to the *FP* Archive, and a comprehensive index of related *Foreign Policy* articles, go to ForeignPolicy.com.

Assess Your Progress

1. Who are the "new colonialists?"
2. What roles do these actors play?
3. What impact might they have on the state?
4. How do aid agencies come to depend on dysfunction and how does this affect weak states?
5. What is the challenge in dealing with aid agencies?

Michael A. Cohen, Maria Figueroa Küpçü, and **Parag Khanna** are senior research fellows at the New America Foundation.

A Few Dollars at a Time

How to Tap Consumers for Development

PHILIPPE DOUSTE-BLAZY AND DANIEL ALTMAN

Starting in this quarter, hundreds of millions of people will have an unprecedented opportunity to help the world's most unfortunate inhabitants. When purchasing airline tickets through most major reservation websites or through a travel agent, consumers will be asked if they want to make a direct contribution to the fight against the world's three deadliest epidemics: HIV/AIDS, malaria, and tuberculosis. Part of a movement called innovative financing, the project is a new kind of aid that could fundamentally change the relationship between the rich and the poor throughout the world, a few dollars at a time.

Awareness about the epidemics that rage throughout the developing world occasionally crests in the international media when there is an outbreak, as there was of the Ebola virus in the 1990s and of dengue fever in the first years of this century. These periodic outbreaks usually subside within a year or two, or at least are contained before they become pandemics. The HIV/AIDS, malaria, and tuberculosis epidemics have shown more staying power, however, and even now, after years of attention and treatment, each of these diseases still causes more deaths in developing countries than any other single disease, according to the World Health Organization. In 2004, the last year for which statistics were available at the time of this writing, together these three diseases caused one in eight deaths in low-income countries.

Part of the reason these diseases are so harmful is that they reinforce one another. Hundreds of millions of people around the world have latent tuberculosis infections. In most cases, tuberculosis never becomes active, but the disease is much more likely to explode into a full-blown infection, and the infection tends to be much more severe, in people who also have HIV/AIDS. Even those without latent tuberculosis are more susceptible to getting the disease if they already have HIV/AIDS. This is partly because HIV/AIDS suppresses the immune system—which also means that it is harder for people with HIV/AIDS to fight off malaria. And completing the vicious circle, malaria seems to make HIV/AIDS worse: studies by researchers at the Centers for Disease Control suggest that the body encourages HIV to replicate when it creates antigens to fight malaria. Not surprisingly, patients in the developing world—especially in the tropical zones of Latin America, the Caribbean, Africa, and Southeast Asia—are often diagnosed with two or three of these diseases. It makes sense, then, to fight all three together.

Why make them a priority? Worldwide, the mortality rate for heart disease and cancer combined is five times as high as the mortality rate for HIV/AIDS, malaria, and tuberculosis combined. But unlike HIV/AIDS and tuberculosis, heart disease and cancer are not contagious. Heart disease and cancer also tend to prey on the aged, whereas HIV/AIDS, malaria, and tuberculosis kill millions of young adults, children, and babies every year. The World Health Organization estimates that HIV/AIDS and malaria together kill more children under the age of five than all forms of cancer and heart disease combined. By contrast, the American Heart Association reports that 83 percent of people who die from coronary heart disease in the United States are 65 or older. Tuberculosis kills across all ages, but the average age at death is dropping in many countries because of the disease's association with HIV/AIDS.

Stopping HIV/AIDS, malaria, and tuberculosis does not just add a few years to someone's life; it adds a lifetime. Moreover, these lifetimes add real value to the world, and not just in moral terms. Every life lost to infectious disease represents lost economic activity and lost economic development. For example, the death of all the world's poorest people—those destined to earn just $2 a day for 30 working years (with weekends off)—would mean a loss to the world's future economic output of more than $50 billion every year. And that is not counting the loss to overall economic development in poor countries ravaged by these infectious diseases.

There are economic costs to rich countries, too. Disease-stricken states cannot afford to import as much from wealthier ones as they otherwise would. In addition, the desperation caused by these diseases is a source of instability that can devolve into conflict, sometimes pulling neighboring countries and even global powers into difficult situations. As early as 1987, a CIA report discussed how HIV/AIDS could exacerbate conflict in sub-Saharan Africa. A 2006 study by the Institute for the Theory and Practice of International Relations at the College of William and Mary showed that the prevalence of HIV/AIDS in developing countries was strongly associated with higher levels of civil conflict and more human rights abuses. Recent research by Andrew Price-Smith of Colorado

College has suggested that epidemics can distort demographics by reducing the working-age population, weaken governments, and reduce the state's ability to take care of its people, all effects that in turn can breed conflict. If the world could better control these diseases, the benefits—economic, social, and otherwise—would be remarkable.

The good news is that HIV/AIDS, malaria, and tuberculosis are completely controllable diseases; successful treatments are available for all three. The hard part is purchasing and delivering the treatments. The United Nations took up this challenge when its members set the Millennium Development Goals and committed themselves to reversing the spread of these three diseases and to making treatments available to everyone who needed them by 2015. In 2002, the UN's members founded the Global Fund to Fight AIDS, Tuberculosis and Malaria as a central source of financing. The deadline is only five years away, however, and the effort is running tragically behind schedule.

This is largely for lack of money. In 2007, according to the Organization for Economic Cooperation and Development, 22 wealthy countries on its Development Assistance Committee gave $118 billion in direct aid to the developing world but earmarked only $5.3 billion of this for health programs. (Much greater sums went to education, infrastructure, industrial assistance, and debt restructuring.) At the beginning of 2007, according to the World Health Organization, more than five million HIV-positive people in developing countries needed antiretroviral treatment but were not receiving it. To treat all of them every day for a year with just the most basic regimen of drugs would have required raising global aid for health by 20–30 percent. To treat them with the latest generation of antiretroviral drugs would have required more than doubling health-related aid—and that would have been for just HIV/AIDS. There is an enormous gap in the funding for the fight against infectious diseases. The pressing question of how to close it is a matter of life or death for hundreds of thousands of people every year.

A Penny for Your Tickets

One of the most promising methods for closing the gap is innovative financing. The goal of this kind of development aid is to harness markets in an intense effort to quickly raise hundreds of millions, perhaps even billions, of dollars—the kind of money that can make a real difference in the development, purchasing, and delivery of life-saving treatments. Starting big and front-loading investments creates incentives for researchers to look for new treatments, encourages pharmaceutical companies to design the resulting drugs so that they are easy to distribute and administer in poor countries, and reduces the drugs' prices by guaranteeing bulk orders.

A handful of such programs have sprung up in the past several years. For example, the International Finance Facility for Immunization, a charitable corporation set up in 2006 under the auspices of the British government, issues bonds guaranteed by the governments of wealthy countries to raise hundreds of millions of dollars a year for vaccines. The governments repay the bonds over time. So far, the International Finance Facility for Immunization has collected $1.6 billion in up-front cash. Another initiative, (Red), collects donations from companies that sell goods and services under its (Product) Red brand, which is advertised to consumers as a charitable endeavor. Participating brands include household names such as American Express, Apple, Converse, Gap, and Hallmark. Together, they have raised $130 million in three years.

And then there is UNITAID. The program, under the auspices of the World Health Organization, stands apart for collecting money directly from consumers and businesses through the worldwide market for airline tickets. The idea is to share a tiny fraction of globalization's enormous economic gains with sick people in poor countries. UNITAID does not require consumers to buy any particular brand. In 13 countries, whenever consumers purchase an airline ticket, a small tax—sometimes as little as $1—is set aside for the fight against the three major epidemics. With this simple model, UNITAID raised $1.2 billion in the first three years of its existence. And it has begun to finance the antiretroviral treatments of three out of four children who receive treatment for HIV/AIDS, help treat over one million people for tuberculosis, buy 20 million bed nets to protect against malaria-carrying mosquitoes, and more.

Innovative financing sprang from the recognition by former French President Jacques Chirac, Brazilian President Luiz Inácio Lula da Silva, and former Chilean President Ricardo Lagos that the Millennium Development Goals could not be met with official aid alone. A commission of academics and policy experts established by Chirac to investigate other options released scores of ideas in late 2004. The one that grabbed Chirac's attention called for collecting revenue from a tiny tax on transactions in some major industry—currency exchange, carbon-emissions trading, cars, air travel—and committing it to one or more of the Millennium Development Goals.

The three leaders eventually settled on the idea of an airline-ticket tax, and one of us, Philippe Douste-Blazy, then the French foreign minister, proposed that he and his staff turn the idea into reality. The genius of the tax was not only that it would be a tiny levy on a very broad base but also that it would not significantly affect the flow of travelers to the countries that instituted it. If the French government implemented the tax, for example, it would apply only to tickets purchased in France. As a result, French people might be marginally discouraged from flying, but not foreigners traveling to France, unless they bought their tickets in countries that also had the tax. It would be the first time in modern history that countries would be levying a tax on their own citizens exclusively for the benefit of citizens of other countries.

The French and Chilean governments began collecting the tax within a year. South Korea and nine African countries soon followed suit. Before Chirac left office in 2007, the program was housed at the World Health Organization under the name UNITAID, derived from the French "tous unis pour aider" (everyone united to help). The board of UNITAID was composed of representatives from its founding countries—Brazil, Chile, France, Norway, and the United Kingdom—with additional seats for representatives from Africa, Asia, international health groups, and nongovernmental organizations, including patients' rights groups.

Soon, the organization began to receive direct contributions from a few European governments and from the Bill and Melinda Gates Foundation. These were motivated not just by UNITAID's pioneering role in innovative financing but also by its novel approach to spending. UNITAID's board remains committed to financing programs that will have a major impact on HIV/AIDS, malaria, and tuberculosis all at once: creating the first child-sized doses of antiretroviral medicines, lowering the prices of the most cutting-edge malaria treatments to match those of old-fashioned quinine pills, and commercializing the first child-specific drug for tuberculosis. It has also undertaken to finance these treatments as long as the patients need them, something that governments, which allot foreign aid on a yearly basis through an onerous political process, can rarely do. UNITAID can achieve these things because its immense spending power allows it to purchase hundreds of millions of dollars' worth of treatments. Pharmaceutical companies thus have an incentive to reformat medicines—creating, for example, pediatric doses and transforming difficult-to-measure syrups into pills—and to reprice them for underserved populations in the developing world.

One by one, countries began adopting the tax. By the end of 2007, 17 states had passed a law that would implement it and 17 more were considering doing so.

Good Travels

But there was limited enthusiasm in the world's biggest market for airline tickets, the United States. And so it seemed clear that if UNITAID was to become truly global, it would need a complementary approach: voluntary contributions. This idea was the brainchild of Jean-François Rial, a French entrepreneur who heads Voyageurs du Monde, France's leading tourism agency. Realizing that only three companies (Sabre, Amadeus, and Travelport) controlled the reservation systems for two billion plane tickets issued each year—roughly 80 percent of the world's total—he reasoned that if those three companies incorporated a voluntary-contribution mechanism into their reservation software, travelers around the world would have a chance to directly fund the fight against HIV/AIDS, malaria, and tuberculosis.

After two years of development, the mechanism is expected to launch on all three systems this quarter. Travelers from any country who book a trip with Expedia, Opodo, or Travelocity, among many other websites, will be asked during checkout whether they would like to contribute two dollars, two euros, or two pounds to save the lives of poor people. The prompt will be seamlessly integrated into the booking experience—a pop-up window on the computer screen, a box for the travel agent to check. Within weeks, it will become a routine part of life for millions of travelers around the globe—a routine with the potential to help save as many as three million lives every year and prevent the loss of tens of billions of dollars annually in new economic activity, increasing opportunities for growth in poor countries and limiting some of the causes of instability and conflict. The contributors will also have a chance to interact with one another and possibly with the people they are helping through an associated online social initiative called Massive Good. Such communication will enable participants to make the program even more effective: they will be able to encourage businesses where they live to opt for the voluntary contribution when those businesses book travel, and they will be able to check that the treatments arrived at their destinations.

A preliminary study conducted by McKinsey & Company in 2007 suggested that the new mechanism could raise $1 billion in its first four years, almost doubling UNITAID's budget from the airline-ticket tax and other contributions. With this money, UNITAID is now helping manufacturers of generic drugs roll the various medicines needed to treat an epidemic into a single pill. To achieve this, UNITAID is trying to persuade the pharmaceutical companies that developed those medicines to pool their intellectual property and offer it as a package to generic-drug manufacturers. Creating a single pill would greatly simplify the treatment of all three major epidemics—an unprecedented move in public health. UNITAID also hopes to launch a satellite tracking mechanism so that contributors can follow the journey of the treatments they purchase from the factories to the patients, thereby reinforcing solidarity between the world's rich and the world's poor.

Supplements, Not Replacements

Voluntary contributions come with some downsides, however. Most notably, if the program succeeds, the governments of wealthy countries might feel less obligated to send official aid overseas. This possibility could become especially likely during an economic downturn, when governments might be looking for excuses to cut foreign aid—even as they hand out hundreds of billions of dollars to save their troubled banks and insurance companies. Conversely, if the voluntary-contribution scheme were to founder, these governments might take that as a popular verdict against the Millennium Development Goals and use it as a pretext to reduce their official aid.

Some of the nongovernmental organizations that fight HIV/AIDS, malaria, and tuberculosis also might have reason for concern. These groups depend on official aid, in addition to private donations, for a large part of their funding, and they might resent seeing heads of state celebrate the launch of a voluntary-contribution scheme while they freeze or trim that support. Because UNITAID and the other innovative financing mechanisms channel most of their spending through a few big delivery organizations, such as UNICEF and the Clinton HIV/AIDS Initiative, they cannot replace the efforts of hundreds of smaller groups working on locally targeted programs.

This concern is of paramount importance for all innovative financing mechanisms, which were intended as supplements, not replacements, to help close the gap between official aid and the huge sums necessary to turn the tide against the three big epidemics once and for all. If governments invoke these financing schemes as substitutes for official aid, then those funds' very purpose will be defeated. To avoid this, the Millennium Foundation for Innovative Finance for Health, which is a UNITAID partner, and other independent or quasi-independent entities will have to hold governments to account, by shaming them publicly for cutting aid budgets when they do and by holding them to their promises that they will increase aid at least enough to keep up with inflation. The backers of innovative financing mechanisms, such as UNITAID, have two main responsibilities: to help fight diseases through novel ways of raising money and also to ensure that their success does not undermine the existing efforts they set out to strengthen.

Assess Your Progress

1. What is helping to finance the campaign against HIV/AIDS, malaria, and tuberculosis?
2. Why are these diseases so harmful? Why target them in particular?
3. What are the potential costs to the rich states of these diseases?
4. What is the goal of innovative financing?
5. What are the downsides of voluntary contributions?

Philippe Douste-Blazy, who served as France's Foreign Minister from 2005 to 2007, is currently the United Nations' Special Adviser for Innovative Financing for Development and Chair of UNITAID. **Daniel Altman** is President of North Yard Economics, a not-for-profit consulting firm serving developing countries. This article is adapted from their book on innovative financing, which will be published in January 2010 by PublicAffairs.

The Politics of Hunger

How Illusion and Greed Fan the Food Crisis

PAUL COLLIER

After many years of stability, world food prices have jumped 83 percent since 2005—prompting warnings of a food crisis throughout much of the world earlier this year. In the United States and Europe, the increase in food prices is already yesterday's news; consumers in the developed world now have more pressing concerns, such as the rising price of energy and the falling price of houses. But in the developing world, a food shock of this magnitude is a major political event. To the typical household in poor countries, food is the equivalent of energy in the United States, and people expect their government to do something when prices rise. Already, there have been food riots in some 30 countries; in Haiti, they brought down the prime minister. And for some consumers in the world's poorest countries, the true anguish of high food prices is only just beginning. If global food prices remain high, the consequences will be grim both ethically and politically.

Politicians and policymakers do, in fact, have it in their power to bring food prices down. But so far, their responses have been less than encouraging: beggar-thy-neighbor restrictions, pressure for yet larger farm subsidies, and a retreat into romanticism. In the first case, neighbors have been beggared by the imposition of export restrictions by the governments of food-exporting countries. This has had the immaculately dysfunctional consequence of further elevating world prices while reducing the incentives for the key producers to invest in the agricultural sector. In the second case, the subsidy hunters have, unsurprisingly, turned the crisis into an opportunity; for example, Michel Barnier, the French agricultural minister, took it as a chance to urge the European Commission to reverse its incipient subsidy-slashing reforms of the Common Agricultural Policy. And finally, the romantics have portrayed the food crisis as demonstrating the failure of scientific commercial agriculture, which they have long found distasteful. In its place they advocate the return to organic small-scale farming—counting on abandoned technologies to feed a prospective world population of nine billion.

The real challenge is not the technical difficulty of returning the world to cheap food but the political difficulty of confronting the lobbying interests and illusions on which current policies rest. Feeding the world will involve three politically challenging steps. First, contrary to the romantics, the world needs more commercial agriculture, not less. The Brazilian model of high-productivity large farms could readily be extended to areas where land is underused. Second, and again contrary to the romantics, the world needs more science: the European ban and the consequential African ban on genetically modified (GM) crops are slowing the pace of agricultural productivity growth in the face of accelerating growth in demand. Ending such restrictions could be part of a deal, a mutual de-escalation of folly, that would achieve the third step: in return for Europe's lifting its self-damaging ban on GM products, the United States should lift its self-damaging subsidies supporting domestic biofuel.

Supply-Side Solutions

Typically, in trying to find a solution to a problem, people look to its causes—or, yet more fatuously, to its "root" cause. But there need be no logical connection between the cause of a problem and appropriate or even just feasible solutions to it. Such is the case with the food crisis. The root cause of high food prices is the spectacular economic growth of Asia. Asia accounts for half the world's population, and because its people are still poor, they devote much of their budgets to food. As Asian incomes rise, the world demand for food increases. And not only are Asians eating more, but they are also eating better: carbohydrates are being replaced by protein. And because it takes six kilograms of grain to produce one kilogram of beef, the switch to a protein-heavy diet further drives up demand for grain.

The two key parameters in shaping demand are income elasticity and price elasticity. The income elasticity of demand for food is generally around 0.5, meaning that if income rises by, say, 20 percent, the demand for food rises by 10 percent. (The price elasticity of demand for food is only around 0.1: that is, people simply have to eat, and they do not eat much less in response to higher prices.) Thus, if the supply of food were fixed, in order to choke off an increase in demand of 10 percent after a 20 percent rise in income, the price of food would need to double. In other words, modest increases in global income will drive prices up alarmingly unless matched by increases in supply.

In recent years, the increase in demand resulting from gradually increasing incomes in Asia has instead been matched with several supply shocks, such as the prolonged drought in Australia. These shocks will only become more common with the climatic volatility that accompanies climate change. Accordingly, against a backdrop of relentlessly rising demand, supply will fluctuate more sharply as well.

Because food looms so large in the budgets of the poor, high world food prices have a severely regressive effect in their toll. Still, by no means are all of the world's poor adversely affected by expensive food. Most poor people who are farmers are largely self-sufficient. They may buy and sell food, but the rural markets in which they trade are often not well integrated into global markets and so are largely detached from the surge in prices. Where poor farmers are integrated into global markets, they are likely to benefit. But even the good news for farmers needs to be qualified. Although most poor farmers will gain most of the time, they will lose precisely when they are hardest hit: when their crops fail. The World Food Program is designed to act as the supplier of last resort to such localities. Yet its budget, set in dollars rather than bushels, buys much less when food prices surge. Paradoxically, then, the world's insurance program against localized famine is itself acutely vulnerable to global food shortages. Thus, high global food prices are good news for farmers but only in good times.

The unambiguous losers when it comes to high food prices are the urban poor. Most of the developing world's large cities are ports, and, barring government controls, the price of their food is set on the global market. Crowded in slums, the urban poor cannot grow their own food; they have no choice but to buy it. Being poor, they would inevitably be squeezed by an increase in prices, but by a cruel implication of the laws of necessity, poor people spend a far larger proportion of their budgets on food, typically around a half, in contrast to only around a tenth for high-income groups. (Hungry slum dwellers are unlikely to accept their fate quietly. For centuries, sudden hunger in slums has provoked the same response: riots. This is the classic political base for populist politics, such as Peronism in Argentina, and the food crisis may provoke its ugly resurgence.)

At the end of the food chain comes the real crunch: among the urban poor, those most likely to go hungry are children. If young children remain malnourished for more than two years, the consequence is stunted growth—and stunted growth is not merely a physical condition. Stunted people are not just shorter than they would have been; their mental potential is impaired as well. Stunted growth is irreversible. It lasts a lifetime, and indeed, some studies find that it is passed down through the generations. And so although high food prices are yesterday's news in most of the developed world, if they remain high for the next few years, their consequences will be tomorrow's nightmare for the developing world.

In short, global food prices must be brought down, and they must be brought down fast, because their adverse consequences are so persistent. The question is how. There is nothing to be done about the root cause of the crisis—the increasing demand for food. The solution must come from dramatically increasing world food supply. That supply has been growing for decades, more than keeping up with population growth, but it now must be accelerated, with production increasing much more rapidly than it has in recent decades. This must happen in the short term, to bring prices down from today's levels, and in the medium and long terms, since any immediate increase in supply will soon be overtaken by increased demand.

Fortunately, policymakers have the power to do all of this: by changing regulation, they can quickly generate an increase in supply; by encouraging organizational changes, they can raise the growth of production in the medium term; and by encouraging innovations in technology, they can sustain this higher growth indefinitely. But currently, each of these steps is blocked by a giant of romantic populism: all three must be confronted and slain.

The First Giant of Romantic Populism

The first giant that must be slain is the middle- and upper-class love affair with peasant agriculture. With the near-total urbanization of these classes in both the United States and Europe, rural simplicity has acquired a strange allure. Peasant life is prized as organic in both its literal and its metaphoric sense. (Prince Charles is one of its leading apostles.) In its literal sense, organic agricultural production is now a premium product, a luxury brand. (Indeed, Prince Charles has his own such brand, Duchy Originals.) In its metaphoric sense, it represents the antithesis of the large, hierarchical, pressured organizations in which the middle classes now work. (Prince Charles has built a model peasant village, in traditional architectural style.) Peasants, like pandas, are to be preserved.

Peasants, like pandas, show little inclination to reproduce themselves.

But distressingly, peasants, like pandas, show little inclination to reproduce themselves. Given the chance, peasants seek local wage jobs, and their offspring head to the cities. This is because at low-income levels, rural bliss is precarious, isolated, and tedious. The peasant life forces millions of ordinary people into the role of entrepreneur, a role for which most are ill suited. In successful economies, entrepreneurship is a minority pursuit; most people opt for wage employment so that others can have the worry and grind of running a business. And reluctant peasants are right: their mode of production is ill suited to modern agricultural production, in which scale is helpful. In modern agriculture, technology is fast-evolving, investment is lumpy, the private provision of transportation infrastructure is necessary to counter the lack of its public provision, consumer food fashions are fast-changing and best met by integrated marketing chains, and regulatory standards are rising toward the holy grail of the traceability of produce back to its source. Far from being the answer to global poverty, organic self-sufficiency is a luxury lifestyle. It is appropriate for burnt-out investment bankers, not for hungry families.

Large organizations are better suited to cope with investment, marketing chains, and regulation. Yet for years, global development agencies have been leery of commercial agriculture, basing their agricultural strategies instead on raising peasant production. This neglect is all the more striking given the standard account of how economic development started in Europe: the English enclosure movement, which was enabled by legislative changes, is commonly supposed to have launched development by permitting large farms that could achieve higher productivity. Although current research qualifies the conventional account, reducing the estimates of productivity gains to the range of 10–20 percent, to ignore commercial agriculture as a force for rural development and enhanced food supply is surely ideological.

Innovation, especially, is hard to generate through peasant farming. Innovators create benefits for the local economy, and to the extent that these benefits are not fully captured by the innovators, innovation will be too slow. Large organizations can internalize the effects that in peasant agriculture are localized externalities—that is, benefits of actions that are not reflected in costs or profits—and so not adequately taken into account in decision-making. In the European agricultural revolution, innovations occurred on small farms as well as large, and today many peasant farmers, especially those who are better off and better educated, are keen to innovate. But agricultural innovation is highly sensitive to local conditions, especially in Africa, where the soils are complex and variable. One solution is to have an extensive network of publicly funded research stations with advisers who reach out to small farmers. But in Africa, this model has largely broken down, an instance of more widespread malfunctioning of the public sector. In eighteenth-century Great Britain, the innovations in small-holder agriculture were often led by networks among the gentry, who corresponded with one another on the consequences of agricultural experimentation. But such processes are far from automatic (they did not occur, for example, in continental Europe). Commercial agriculture is the best way of making innovation quicker and easier.

Over time, African peasant agriculture has fallen further and further behind the advancing commercial productivity frontier, and based on present trends, the region's food imports are projected to double over the next quarter century. Indeed, even with prices as high as they currently are, the United Nations Food and Agriculture Organization is worried that African peasants are likely to reduce production because they cannot afford the increased cost of fertilizer inputs. There are partial solutions to such problems through subsidies and credit schemes, but it should be noted that large-scale commercial agriculture simply does not face this particular problem: if output prices rise by more than input prices, production will be expanded.

A model of successful commercial agriculture is, indeed, staring the world in the face. In Brazil, large, technologically sophisticated agricultural companies have demonstrated how successfully food can be mass-produced. To give one remarkable example, the time between harvesting one crop and planting the next—the downtime for land—has been reduced to an astounding 30 minutes. Some have criticized the Brazilian model for displacing peoples and destroying rain forest, which has indeed happened in places where commercialism has gone unregulated. But in much of the poor world, the land is not primal forest; it is just badly farmed. Another benefit of the Brazilian model is that it can bring innovation to small farmers as well. In the "out-growing," or "contract farming," model, small farmers supply a central business. Depending on the details of crop production, sometimes this can be more efficient than wage employment.

There are many areas of the world that have good land that could be used far more productively if properly managed by large companies. Indeed, large companies, some of them Brazilian, are queuing up to manage those lands. Yet over the past 40 years, African governments have worked to scale back large commercial agriculture. At the heart of the matter is a reluctance to let land rights be marketable, and the source of this reluctance is probably the lack of economic dynamism in Africa's cities. As a result, land is still the all-important asset (there has been little investment in others). In more successful economies, land has become a minor asset, and thus the rights of ownership, although initially assigned based on political considerations, are simply extensions of the rights over other assets; as a result, they can be acquired commercially. A further consequence of a lack of urban dynamism is that jobs are scarce, and so the prospect of mass landlessness evokes political fears: the poor are safer on the land, where they are less able to cause trouble.

Commercial agriculture is not perfect. Global agribusiness is probably overly concentrated, and a sudden switch to an unregulated land market would probably have ugly consequences. But allowing commercial organizations to replace peasant agriculture gradually would raise global food supply in the medium term.

The War on Science

The second giant of romantic populism is the European fear of scientific agriculture. This has been manipulated by the agricultural lobby in Europe into yet another form of protectionism: the ban on GM crops. GM crops were introduced globally in 1996 and already are grown on around ten percent of the world's crop area, some 300 million acres. But due to the ban, virtually none of this is in Europe or Africa.

Robert Paarlberg, of Wellesley College, brilliantly anatomizes the politics of the ban in his new book, *Starved for Science*. After their creation, GM foods, already so disastrously named, were described as "Frankenfoods"—sounding like a scientific experiment on consumers. Just as problematic was the fact that genetic modification had grown out of research conducted by American corporations and so provoked predictable and deep-seated hostility from the European left. Although Monsanto, the main innovator in GM-seed technology, has undertaken never to market a seed that is incapable of reproducing itself, skeptics propagated a widespread belief that farmers will be trapped into annual purchases of "terminator" seeds from a monopoly supplier. Thus were laid the political foundations for a winning coalition: onto the base of national agricultural protectionism was added the anti-Americanism of the left and the paranoia of health-conscious consumers who, in the wake of the mad cow disease outbreak in the United Kingdom in the 1990s, no longer trusted their governments' assurances. In the 12 years since the ban was introduced, in 1996, the scientific case for lifting it has become progressively more robust, but the political coalition against GM foods has only expanded.

The GM-crop ban has had three adverse effects. Most obviously, it has retarded productivity growth in European agriculture. Prior to 1996, grain yields in Europe tracked those in the United States. Since 1996, they have fallen behind by 1–2 percent a year. European grain production could be increased by around 15 percent were the ban lifted. Europe is a major cereal producer, so this is a large loss. More subtly, because Europe is out of the market for GM-crop technology, the pace of research has slowed. GM-crop research takes a very long time to come to fruition, and its core benefit, the permanent reduction in food prices, cannot fully be captured through patents. Hence, there is a strong case for supplementing private research with public money. European governments should be funding this research, but instead research is entirely reliant on the private sector. And since private money for research depends on the prospect of sales, the European ban has also reduced private research.

However, the worst consequence of the European GM-crop ban is that it has terrified African governments into themselves banning GM crops, the only exception being South Africa. They fear that if they chose to grow GM crops, they would be permanently shut out of European markets. Now, because most of Africa has banned GM crops, there has been no market for discoveries pertinent to the crops that Africa grows, and so little research—which in turn has led to the critique that GM crops are irrelevant for Africa.

Africa cannot afford this self-denial; it needs all the help it can possibly get from genetic modification. For the past four decades, African agricultural productivity per acre has stagnated; raising production has depended on expanding the area under cultivation. But with Africa's population still growing rapidly, this option is running out, especially in light of global warming. Climate forecasts suggest that in the coming years, most of Africa will get hotter, the semiarid parts will get drier, and rainfall variability on the continent will increase, leading to more droughts. It seems likely that in southern Africa, the staple food, maize, will at some point become nonviable. Whereas for other regions the challenge of climate change is primarily about mitigating carbon emissions, in Africa it is primarily about agricultural adaptation.

It has become commonplace to say that Africa needs a green revolution. Unfortunately, the reality is that the green revolution in the twentieth century was based on chemical fertilizers, and even when fertilizer was cheap, Africa did not adopt it. With the rise in fertilizer costs, as a byproduct of high-energy prices, any African green revolution will perforce not be chemical. To counter the effects of Africa's rising population and deteriorating climate, African agriculture needs a biological revolution. This is what GM crops offer, if only sufficient money is put into research. There has as yet been little work on the crops of key importance to the region, such as cassava and yams. GM-crop research is still in its infancy, still on the first generation: single-gene transfer. A gene that gives one crop an advantage is identified, isolated, and added to another crop. But even this stage offers the credible prospect of vital gains. In a new scientific review, Jennifer Thomson, of the Department of Molecular and Cell Biology at the University of Cape Town, considers the potential of GM technology for Africa. Maize, she reports, can be made more drought-resistant, buying Africa time in the struggle against climatic deterioration. Grain can be made radically more resistant to fungi, reducing the need for chemicals and cutting losses due to storage. For example, stem borer beetles cause storage losses in the range of 15–40 percent of the African maize crop; a new GM variety is resistant.

It is important to recognize that genetic modification, like commercialization, is not a magic fix for African agriculture: there is no such fix. But without it, the task of keeping Africa's food production abreast of its population growth looks daunting. Although Africa's coastal cities can be fed from global supplies, the vast African interior cannot be fed in this way other than in emergencies. Lifting the ban on GM crops, both in Africa and in Europe, is the policy that could hold down global food prices in the long term.

The final giant of romantic populism is the American fantasy that the United States can escape dependence on Arab oil by growing its own fuel—making ethanol or other biofuels, largely from corn. There is a good case for growing fuel. But there is not a good case for generating it from American grain: the conversion of grain into ethanol uses almost as much energy as it produces. This has not stopped the American agricultural lobby from gouging out grotesquely inefficient subsidies from the government; as a result, around a third of American grain has rapidly been diverted into energy. This switch demonstrates both the superb responsiveness of the market to price signals and the shameful power of subsidy-hunting lobbying groups. If the United States wants to run off of agrofuel instead of oil, then Brazilian sugar cane is the answer; it is a far more efficient source of energy than American grain. The killer evidence of political capture is the response of the U.S. government to this potential lifeline: it has actually restricted imports of Brazilian ethanol to protect American production. The sane goal of reducing dependence on Arab oil has been sacrificed to the self-serving goal of pumping yet more tax dollars into American agriculture.

Inevitably, the huge loss of grain for food caused by its diversion into ethanol has had an impact on world grain prices. Just how large an impact is controversial. An initial claim by the Bush administration was that it had raised prices by only three percent, but a study by the World Bank suggests that the effect has been much larger. If the subsidy were lifted, there would probably be a swift impact on prices: not only would the supply of grain for food increase, but the change would shift speculative expectations. This is the policy that could bring prices down in the short term.

Striking a Deal

The three policies—expanding large commercial farms, ending the GM-crop ban, and doing away with the U.S. subsidies on ethanol—fit together both economically and politically. Lifting the ethanol subsidies would probably puncture the present ballooning of prices. The expansion of commercial farms could, over the next decade, raise world output by a further few percentage points. Both measures would buy the time needed for GM crops to deliver on their potential (the time between starting research and the mass application of its results is around 15 years). Moreover, the expansion of commercial farming in Africa would encourage global GM-crop research on Africa-suited crops, and innovations would find a ready market not so sensitive to political interference. It would also facilitate the localized adaptation of new varieties. It is not by chance that the only African country in which GM crops have not been banned is South Africa, where the organization of agriculture is predominantly commercial.

Politically, the three policies are also complementary. Homegrown energy, keeping out "Frankenfoods," and preserving the peasant way of life are all classic populist programs: they sound instantly appealing but actually do harm. They must be countered by messages of equal potency.

One such message concerns the scope for international reciprocity. Although Americans are attracted to homegrown fuel, they are infuriated by the European ban on GM crops. They see the ban for what it is: a standard piece of anti-American protectionism. Europeans, for their part, cling to the illusory comfort of the ban on high-tech crops, but they are infuriated by the American subsidies on ethanol. They see the subsidies for what they are: a greedy deflection from the core task of reducing U.S. energy profligacy. Over the past half century, the United States and Europe have learned how to cooperate. The General Agreement on Tariffs and Trade was fundamentally a deal between the United States and Europe that virtually eliminated tariffs on manufactured goods. NATO is a partnership in security. The Organization for Economic Cooperation and Development is a partnership in economic governance. Compared to the difficulties of reaching agreement in these areas, the difficulties of reaching a deal on the mutual de-escalation of recent environmental follies is scarcely daunting: the United States would agree to scrap its ethanol subsidies in return for Europe's lifting the ban on GM crops. Each side can find this deal infuriating and yet attractive. It should be politically feasible to present this to voters as better than the status quo.

The romantic hostility to scientific and commercial agriculture must be countered.

How might the romantic hostility toward commercial and scientific agriculture be countered politically? The answer is to educate the vast community of concern for the poorest countries on the bitter realities of the food crisis. In both the United States and Europe, millions of decent citizens are appalled by global hunger. Each time a famine makes it to television screens, the popular response is overwhelming, and there is a large overlap between the constituency that responds to such crises and the constituency attracted by the idea of preserving organic peasant lifestyles. The cohabitation of these concerns needs to be challenged. Many people will need to agonize over their priorities. Some will decide that the vision articulated by Prince Charles is the more important one: a historical lifestyle must be preserved regardless of the consequences. But however attractive that vision, these people must come face-to-face with the prospect of mass malnutrition and stunted children and realize that the vital matter for public policy is to increase food supplies. Commercial agriculture may be irredeemably unromantic, but if it fills the stomachs of the poor, then it should be encouraged.

American environmentalists will also need to do some painful rethinking. The people most attracted to achieving energy self-sufficiency through the production of ethanol are potentially the constituency that could save the United States from its ruinous energy policies. The United States indeed needs to reduce its dependence on imported oil, but growing corn for biofuel is not the answer. Americans are quite simply too profligate when it comes to their use of energy; Europeans, themselves pretty profligate, use only half the energy per capita and yet sustain a high-income lifestyle. The U.S. tax system needs to be shifted from burdening work to discouraging energy consumption.

The mark of a good politician is the ability to guide citizens away from populism.

The mark of a good politician is the ability to guide citizens away from populism. Unless countered, populism will block the policies needed to address the food crisis. For the citizens of the United States and Europe, the continuation of high food prices will be an inconvenience, but not sufficiently so to slay the three giants on which the current strain of romantic populism rests. Properly informed, many citizens will rethink their priorities, but politicians will need to deliver these messages and forge new alliances. If food prices are not brought down fast and then kept down, slum children will go hungry, and their future lives will be impaired. Shattering a few romantic illusions is a small price to pay.

Assess Your Progress

1. What are the major challenges of meeting food demand?
2. What is the root cause of high food prices?
3. Who are the biggest losers with respect to higher food prices and why? What are the potential impacts of this problem?
4. How can policymakers help to increase food production?
5. How can the challenges that limit food production be overcome?

Paul Collier is Professor of Economics and Director of the Center for the Study of African Economies at Oxford University and the author of *The Bottom Billion: Why the Poorest Countries Are Failing and What Can Be Done About It.*

The Micromagic of Microcredit

KAROL BOUDREAUX AND TYLER COWEN

Microcredit has star power. In 2006, the Nobel Committee called it "an important liberating force" and awarded the Nobel Peace Prize to Muhammad Yunus, the "godfather of microcredit." The actress Natalie Portman is a believer too; she advocates support for the Village Banking Campaign on its MySpace page. The end of poverty is "just a mouse click away," she promises. A button on the site swiftly redirects you to paypal.com, where you can make a contribution to microcredit initiatives.

After decades of failure, the world's aid organizations seem to think they have at last found a winning idea. The United Nations declared 2005 the "International Year of Microcredit." Secretary-General Kofi Annan declared that providing microloans to help poor people launch small businesses recognizes that they "are the solution, not the problem. It is a way to build on their ideas, energy, and vision. It is a way to grow productive enterprises, and so allow communities to prosper."

Many investors agree. Hundreds of millions of dollars are flowing into microfinance from international financial institutions, foundations, governments, and, most important, private investors—who increasingly see microfinance as a potentially profitable business venture. Private investment through special "microfinance investment vehicles" alone nearly doubled in 2005, from $513 million to $981 million.

On the charitable side, part of microcredit's appeal lies in the fact that the lending institutions can fund themselves once they are launched. Pierre Omidyar, the founder of eBay, explains that you can begin by investing $60 billion in the world's poorest people, "and then you're done!"

But can microcredit achieve the massive changes its proponents claim? Is it the solution to poverty in the developing world, or something more modest—a way to empower the poor, particularly poor women, with some control over their lives and their assets?

On trips to Africa and India we have talked to lenders, borrowers, and other poor people to try to understand the role microcredit plays in their lives. We met people like Stadile Menthe in Botswana. Menthe is, in many ways, the classic borrower. A single mother with little formal education, she borrowed money to expand the small grocery store she runs on a dusty road on the outskirts of Botswana's capital city, Gaborone. Menthe's store has done well, and she has expanded into the lucrative business of selling phone cards. In fact, she's been successful enough that she has built two rental homes next to her store. She has diversified her income and made a better life for herself and her daughter. But how many borrowers are like Menthe? In our judgment, she is the exception, not the norm. Yes, microcredit is mostly a good thing. Very often it helps keep borrowers from even greater catastrophes, but only rarely does it enable them to climb out of poverty.

The modern story of microcredit began 30 years ago, when Yunus—then an economics professor at Chittagong University in southeastern Bangladesh—set out to apply his theories to improving the lives of the poor in the nearby village of Jobra. He began in 1976 by lending $27 to a group of 42 villagers, who used the money to develop informal businesses, such as making soap or weaving baskets to sell at the local market. After the success of the first experiment, Yunus founded Grameen Bank. Today, the bank claims more than five million "members" and a loan repayment rate of 98 percent. It has lent out some $6.5 billion.

At the outset, Yunus set a goal that half of the borrowers would be women. He explained, "The banking system not only rejects poor people, it rejects women. . . . Not even one percent of their borrowers are women." He soon discovered that women were good credit risks, and good at managing family finances. Today, more than 95 percent of Grameen Bank's borrowers are women. The UN estimates that women make up 76 percent of microcredit customers around the world, varying from nearly 90 percent in Asia to less than a third in the Middle East.

While 70 percent of microcredit borrowers are in Asia, the institution has spread around the world; Latin America and sub-Saharan Africa account for 14 and 10 percent of the number of borrowers, respectively. Some of the biggest microfinance institutions include Grameen Bank, ACCION International, and Pro Mujer of Bolivia.

The average loan size varies, usually in proportion to the income level of the home country. In Rwanda, a typical loan might be $50 to $200; in Romania, it is more likely to be $2,500 to $5,000. Often there is no explicit collateral. Instead, the banks lend to small groups of about five people, relying on peer pressure for repayment. At mandatory weekly meetings, if one borrower cannot make her payment, the rest of the group must come up with the cash.

The achievements of microcredit, however, are not quite what they seem. There is, for example, a puzzling fact at the heart of the enterprise. Most microcredit banks charge interest rates of 50 to 100 percent on an annualized basis (loans, typically, must be paid off within weeks or months). That's not as scandalous as it sounds—local moneylenders demand much higher rates. The puzzle is a matter of basic economics: How can people in new businesses growing at perhaps 20 percent annually afford to pay interest at rates as high as 100 percent?

The answer is that, for the most part, they can't. By and large, the loans serve more modest ends—laudable, but not world changing.

Microcredit does not always lead to the creation of small businesses. Many microlenders refuse to lend money for start-ups; they insist that a business already be in place. This suggests that the business was sustainable to begin with, without a micro-loan. Sometimes lenders help businesses to grow, but often what they really finance is spending and consumption.

That is not to say that the poor are out shopping for jewelry and fancy clothes. In Hyderabad, India, as in many other places, we saw that loans are often used to pay for a child's doctor visit. In the Tanzanian capital of Dar es Salaam, Joel Mwakitalu, who runs the Small Enterprise Foundation, a local microlender, told us that 60 percent of his loans are used to send kids to school; 40 percent are for investments. A study of microcredit in Indonesia found that 30 percent of the borrowed money was spent on some form of consumption.

Sometimes consumption and investment are one and the same, such as when parents send their children to school. Indian borrowers often buy mopeds and motorbikes—they are fun to ride but also a way of getting to work. Cell phones are used to call friends but also to run businesses.

For better or worse, microborrowing often entails a kind of bait and switch. The borrower claims that the money is for a business, but uses it for other purposes. In effect, the cash allows a poor entrepreneur to maintain her business without having to sacrifice the life or education of her child. In that sense, the money is for the business, but most of all it is for the child. Such lifesaving uses for the funds are obviously desirable, but it is also a sad reality that many microcredit loans help borrowers to survive or tread water more than they help them get ahead. This sounds unglamorous and even disappointing, but the alternative—such as no doctor's visit for a child or no school for a year—is much worse.

Commentators often seem to assume that the experience of borrowing and lending is completely new for the poor. But moneylenders have offered money to the world's poor for millennia, albeit at extortionate rates of interest. A typical moneylender is a single individual, well-known in his neighborhood or village, who borrows money from his wealthier connections and in turn lends those funds to individuals in need, typically people he knows personally. But that personal connection is rarely good for a break; a moneylender may charge 200 to 400 percent interest on an annualized basis. He will insist on collateral (a television, for instance), and resort to intimidation and sometimes violence if he is not repaid on time. The moneylender operates informally, off the books, and usually outside the law.

So compared to the alternative, microcredit is often a very good deal indeed. Microcredit critics often miss this point. For instance, Aneel Karnani, who teaches at the University of Michigan's business school, argues that microfinance "misses its mark." Karnani says that in some cases microcredit can make life for the planet's bottom billion even worse by reducing their cash flow. Karnani cites the high interest rates that microlenders charge and points out that "if poor clients cannot earn a greater return on their investment than the interest they must pay, they will become poorer as a result of microcredit, not wealthier." But the real question has never been credit vs. no credit; rather, it is moneylender vs. modern microcredit. Credit can bring some problems, but microcredit is easing debt burdens more than it is increasing them.

At microlender SERO Lease and Finance in Tanzania, borrower Margaret Makingi Marwa told us that she prefers working with a microfinance institution to working with a moneylender. Moneylenders demand quick repayment at high interest rates. At SERO, Marwa can take six months or a year to pay off her lease contract. Given that her income can vary and that she may not have money at hand every month, she prefers to have a longer-term loan.

Moneylenders do offer some advantages, especially in rural areas. Most important, they come up with cash on the spot. If your child needs to go to the doctor right now, the moneylender is usually only a short walk away. Even under the best of circumstances, a microcredit loan can take several days to process, and the recipient will be required to deal with many documents, not to mention weekly meetings.

There is, however, an upside to this "bureaucracy." In reality, it is the moneylender who is the "micro" operator. Microcredit is a more formal, institutionalized business relationship. It represents a move up toward a larger scale of trade and business organization. Microcredit borrowers gain valuable experience in working within a formal institution. They learn what to expect from lenders and fellow borrowers, and they learn what is expected of themselves. This experience will be a help should they ever graduate to commercial credit or have other dealings with the formal financial world.

The comparison to moneylending brings up another important feature of microcredit. Though its users avoid the kind of intimidation employed by moneylenders, microcredit could not work without similar incentives. The lender does not demand collateral, but if you can't pay your share of the group loan, your fellow borrowers will come and take your TV. That enforcement process can lead to abuses, but it is a gentler form of intimidation than is exercised by the moneylender. If nothing else, the group members know that at the next meeting any one of them might be the one unable to repay her share of the loan.

If borrowers are using microcredit for consumption and not only to improve a small business, how do they repay? Most borrowers are self-employed and work in the informal sector of the economy. Their incomes are often erratic; small, unexpected expenses can make repayment impossible in any given week or month. In the countryside, farmers have seasonal incomes and little cash for long periods of time.

Borrowers manage, at least in part, by relying on family members and friends to help out. In some cases, the help comes in the form of remittances from abroad. Remittances that cross national borders now total more than $300 billion yearly. A recent study in Tanzania found that microcredit borrowers get 34 percent of their income from friends and family, some of whom live abroad, but others of whom live in the city and have jobs in the formal sector. That's the most effective kind of foreign aid, targeted directly at the poor and provided by those who understand their needs.

Here again, microcredit does something that traditional banks do not. A commercial bank typically will not lend to people who work in the informal sector, precisely because their erratic incomes make them risky bets. The loan officer at a commercial bank does not care that your brother in Doha is sending money each month to help you out. But a microcredit institution cares only that you come to your weekly meeting with a small sum in hand for repayment. Because of microcredit, families can leverage one person's ability to find work elsewhere to benefit the entire group.

Sometimes microcredit leads to more savings rather than more debt. That sounds paradoxical, but borrowing in one asset can be a path toward (more efficient) saving in other assets.

To better understand this puzzle, we must set aside some of our preconceptions about how saving operates in poor countries, most of all in rural areas. Westerners typically save in the form of money or money-denominated assets such as stocks and bonds. But in poor communities, money is often an ineffective medium for savings; if you want to know how much net saving is going on, don't look at money. Banks may be a daylong bus ride away or may be plagued, as in Ghana, by fraud. A cash hoard kept at home can be lost, stolen, taken by the taxman, damaged by floods, or even eaten by rats. It creates other kinds of problems as well. Needy friends and relatives knock on the door and ask for aid. In small communities it is often very hard, even impossible, to say no, especially if you have the cash on hand.

People who have even extremely modest wealth are also asked to perform more community service, or to pay more to finance community rituals and festivals. In rural Guerrero State, in Mexico, for example, one of us (Cowen) found that most people who saved cash did not manage to hold on to it for more than a few weeks or even days. A dollar saved translates into perhaps a quarter of that wealth kept. It is as if cash savings faces an implicit "tax rate" of 75 percent.

Under these kinds of conditions, a cow (or a goat or pig) is a much better medium for saving. It is sturdier than paper money. Friends and relatives can't ask for small pieces of it. If you own a cow, it yields milk, it can plow the fields, it produces dung that can be used as fuel or fertilizer, and in a pinch it can be slaughtered and turned into saleable meat or simply eaten. With a small loan, people in rural areas can buy that cow and use cash that might otherwise be diverted to less useful purposes to pay back the microcredit institution. So even when microcredit looks like indebtedness, savings are going up rather than down.

Microcredit *is* making people's lives better around the world. But for the most part, it is not pulling them out of poverty. It is hard to find entrepreneurs who start with these tiny loans and graduate to run commercial empires. Bangladesh, where Grameen Bank was born, is still a desperately poor country. The more modest truth is that microcredit may help some people, perhaps earning $2 a day, to earn something like $2.50 a day. That may not sound dramatic, but when you are earning $2 a day it is a big step forward. And progress is not the natural state of humankind; microcredit is important even when it does nothing more than stave off decline.

With microcredit, life becomes more bearable and easier to manage. The improvements may not show up as an explicit return on investment, but the benefits are very real. If a poor family is able to keep a child in school, send someone to a clinic, or build up more secure savings, its well-being improves, if only marginally. This is a big part of the reason why poor people are demanding greater access to microcredit loans. And microcredit, unlike many charitable services, is capable of paying for itself—which explains why the private sector is increasingly involved. The future of microcredit lies in the commercial sector, not in unsustainable aid programs. Count this as another benefit.

If this portrait sounds a little underwhelming, don't blame microcredit. The real issue is that we so often underestimate the severity and inertia of global poverty. Natalie Portman may not be right when she says that an end to poverty is "just a mouse click away," but she's right to be supportive of a tool that helps soften some of poverty's worst blows for many millions of desperate people

Assess Your Progress

1. What has made microcredit programs so popular?
2. What are the origins of microcredit and who are its biggest beneficiaries?
3. What is a major drawback of microcredit?
4. With whom do microfinanciers now compete? What are each competitor's advantages and disadvantages?
5. How does microcredit contribute to bettering people's lives?

Karol Boudreaux is a senior research fellow at the Mercatus Center at George Mason University. **Tyler Cowen** is a professor of economies at George Mason University and author of *Discover Your Inner Economist: Use Incentives to Fall in Love, Survive Your Next Meeting, and Motivate Your Dentist* (2007).

Many Borrowers of Microloans Now Find the Price Is Too High

NEIL MACFARQUHAR

In recent years, the idea of giving small loans to poor people became the darling of the development world, hailed as the long elusive formula to propel even the most destitute into better lives.

Actors like Natalie Portman and Michael Douglas lent their boldface names to the cause. Muhammad Yunus, the economist who pioneered the practice by lending small amounts to basket weavers in Bangladesh, won a Nobel Peace Prize for it in 2006. The idea even got its very own United Nations year in 2005.

But the phenomenon has grown so popular that some of its biggest proponents are now wringing their hands over the direction it has taken. Drawn by the prospect of hefty profits from even the smallest of loans, a raft of banks and financial institutions now dominate the field, with some charging interest rates of 100 percent or more from their impoverished customers.

"We created microcredit to fight the loan sharks; we didn't create microcredit to encourage new loan sharks," Mr. Yunus recently said at a gathering of financial officials at the United Nations. "Microcredit should be seen as an opportunity to help people get out of poverty in a business way, but not as an opportunity to make money out of poor people."

The fracas over preserving the field's saintly aura centers on the question of how much interest and profit is acceptable, and what constitutes exploitation. The noisy interest rate fight has even attracted Congressional scrutiny, with the House Financial Services Committee holding hearings this year focused in part on whether some microcredit institutions are scamming the poor.

Rates vary widely across the globe, but the ones that draw the most concern tend to occur in countries like Nigeria and Mexico, where the demand for small loans from a large population cannot be met by existing lenders.

Unlike virtually every Web page trumpeting the accomplishments of microcredit institutions around the world, the page for Te Creemos, a Mexican lender, lacks even one testimonial from a thriving customer—no beaming woman earning her first income by growing a soap business out of her kitchen, for example. Te Creemos has some of the highest interest rates and fees in the world of microfinance, analysts say, a whopping 125 percent average annual rate.

The average in Mexico itself is around 70 percent, compared with a global average of about 37 percent in interest and fees, analysts say. Mexican microfinance institutions charge such high rates simply because they can get away with it, said Emmanuelle Javoy, the managing director of Planet Rating, an independent Paris-based firm that evaluates microlenders.

"They could do better; they could do a lot better," she said. "If the ones that are very big and have the margins don't set the pace, then the rest of the market follows."

Manuel Ramírez, director of risk and internal control at Te Creemos, reached by telephone in Mexico City, initially said there had been some unspecified "misunderstanding" about the numbers and asked for more time to clarify, but then stopped responding.

Unwitting individuals, who can make loans of $20 or more through websites like Kiva or Microplace, may also end up participating in practices some consider exploitative. These websites admit that they cannot guarantee every interest rate they quote. Indeed, the real rate can prove to be markedly higher.

Debating Microloans' Effects

Underlying the issue is a fierce debate over whether microloans actually lift people out of poverty, as their promoters so often claim. The recent conclusion of some researchers is that not every poor person is an entrepreneur waiting to be discovered, but that the loans do help cushion some of the worst blows of poverty.

"The lesson is simply that it didn't save the world," Dean S. Karlan, a professor of economics at Yale University, said about microlending. "It is not the single transformative tool that proponents have been selling it as, but there are positive benefits."

Still, its earliest proponents do not want its reputation tarnished by new investors seeking profits on the backs of the poor, though they recognize that the days of just earning enough to cover costs are over.

"They call it 'social investing,' but nobody has a definition for social investing, nobody is saying, for example, that you have to make less than 10 percent profit," said Chuck Waterfield, who runs mftransparency.org, a website that promotes transparency and is financed by big microfinance investors.

Making pots of money from microfinance is certainly not illegal. CARE, the Atlanta-based humanitarian organization, was the force behind a microfinance institution it started in Peru in 1997. The initial investment was around $3.5 million, including $450,000 of taxpayer money. But last fall, Banco de Credito, one of Peru's largest banks, bought the business for $96 million, of which CARE pocketed $74 million.

"Here was a sale that was good for Peru, that was good for our broad social mission and advertising the price of the sale wasn't the point of the announcement," Helene Gayle, CARE's president, said. Ms. Gayle described the new owners as committed to the same social mission of alleviating poverty and said CARE expected to use the money to extend its own reach in other countries.

The microfinance industry, with over $60 billion in assets, has unquestionably outgrown its charitable roots. Elisabeth Rhyne, who runs the Center for Financial Inclusion, said in Congressional testimony this year that banks and finance firms served 60 percent of all clients. Nongovernmental organizations served 35 percent of the clients, she said, while credit unions and rural banks had 5 percent of the clients.

Private capital first began entering the microfinance arena about a decade ago, but it was not until Compartamos, a Mexican firm that began life as a tiny nonprofit organization, generated $458 million through a public stock sale in 2007, that investors fully recognized the potential for a windfall, experts said.

Although the Compartamos founders pledged to plow the money back into development, analysts say the high interest rates and healthy profits of Compartamos, the largest microfinance institution in the Western Hemisphere with 1.2 million active borrowers, push up interest rates all across Mexico.

According to the Microfinance Information Exchange, a website known as the Mix, where more than 1,000 microfinance companies worldwide report their own numbers, Compartamos charges an average of nearly 82 percent in interest and fees. The site's global data comes from 2008.

But poor borrowers are often too inexperienced and too harried to understand what they are being charged, experts said. In Mexico City, Maria Vargas has borrowed larger and larger amounts from Compartamos over 20 years to expand her T-shirt factory to 25 sewing machines from 5. She is hazy about what interest rate she actually pays, though she considers it high.

"The interest rate is important, but to be honest, you can get so caught up in work that there is no time to go fill out paperwork in another place," she said. After several loans, now a simple phone call to Compartamos gets her a check the next day, she said. Occasionally, interest rates spur political intervention. In Nicaragua, President Daniel Ortega, outraged that interest rates there were hovering around 35 percent in 2008, announced that he would back a microfinance institution that would charge 8 to 10 percent, using Venezuelan money.

There were scattered episodes of setting aflame microfinance branches before a national "We're not paying" campaign erupted, which was widely believed to be mounted secretly by the Sandinista government. After the courts stopped forcing small borrowers to repay, making international financial institutions hesitant to work with Nicaragua, the campaign evaporated.

A Push for More Transparency

The microfinance industry is pushing for greater transparency among its members, but says that most microlenders are honest, with experts putting the number of dubious institutions anywhere from less than 1 percent to more than 10 percent. Given that competition has a pattern of lowering interest rates worldwide, the industry prefers that approach to government intervention. Part of the problem, however, is that all kinds of institutions making loans plaster them with the "microfinance" label because of its do-good reputation.

Damian von Stauffenberg, who founded an independent rating agency called Microrate, said that local conditions had to be taken into account, but that any firm charging 20 to 30 percent above the market was "unconscionable" and that profit rates above 30 percent should be considered high.

Mr. Yunus says interest rates should be 10 to 15 percent above the cost of raising the money, with anything beyond a "red zone" of loan sharking. "We need to draw a line between genuine and abuse," he said. "You will never see the situation of poor people if you look at it through the glasses of profit-making."

Yet by that measure, 75 percent of microfinance institutions would fall into Mr. Yunus's "red zone," according to a March analysis of 1,008 microlenders by Adrian Gonzalez, lead researcher at the Mix. His study found that much of the money from interest rates was used to cover operating expenses, and argued that tackling costs, as opposed to profits, could prove the most efficient way to lower interest rates.

Many experts label Mr. Yunus's formula overly simplistic and too low, a route to certain bankruptcy in countries with high operating expenses. Costs of doing business in Asia and the sheer size of the Grameen Bank he founded in Bangladesh allow for economies of scale that keep costs down, analysts say. "Globally interest rates have been going down as a general trend," said Ms. Javoy of Planet Rating.

Many companies say the highest rates reflect the costs of reaching the poorest, most inaccessible borrowers. It costs more to handle 10 loans of $100 than one loan of $1,000. Some analysts fear that a pronounced backlash against high interest rates will prompt lenders to retreat from the poorest customers.

But experts also acknowledge that banks and others who dominate the industry are slow to address problems.

Added Scrutiny for Lenders

Like Mexico, Nigeria attracts scrutiny for high interest rates. One firm, LAPO, Lift Above Poverty Organization, has raised questions, particularly since it was backed by prominent investors like Deutsche Bank and the Calvert Foundation.

LAPO, considered the leading microfinance institution in Nigeria, engages in a contentious industry practice sometimes referred to as "forced savings." Under it, the lender keeps a portion of the loan. Proponents argue that it helps the poor learn to save, while critics call it exploitation since borrowers do not get the entire amount up front but pay interest on the full loan.

LAPO collected these so-called savings from its borrowers without a legal permit to do so, according to a Planet Rating report. "It was known to everybody that they did not have the right license," Ms. Javoy said.

Under outside pressure, LAPO announced in 2009 that it was decreasing its monthly interest rate, Planet Rating noted, but at the same time compulsory savings were quietly raised to 20 percent of the loan from 10 percent. So, the effective interest rate for some clients actually leapt to nearly 126 percent annually from 114 percent, the report said. The average for all LAPO clients was nearly 74 percent in interest and fees, the report found.

Anita Edward says she has borrowed money three times from LAPO for her hair salon, Amazing Collections, in Benin City, Nigeria. The money comes cheaper than other microloans, and commercial banks are virtually impossible, she said, but she resents the fact that LAPO demanded that she keep $100 of her roughly $666 10-month loan in a savings account while she paid interest on the full amount.

"That is not O.K. by me," she said. "It is not fair. They should give you the full money."

The loans from LAPO helped her expand from one shop to two, but when she started she thought she would have more money to put into the business.

"It has improved my life, but not changed it," said Ms. Edward, 30.

Godwin Ehigiamusoe, LAPO's founding executive director, defended his company's high interest rates, saying they reflected the high cost of doing business in Nigeria. For example, he said, each of the company's more than 200 branches needed its own generator and fuel to run it.

Until recently, Microplace, which is part of eBay, was promoting LAPO to individual investors, even though the website says the lenders it features have interest rates between 18 and 60 percent, considerably less than what LAPO customers typically pay.

As recently as February, Microplace also said that LAPO had a strong rating from Microrate, yet the rating agency had suspended LAPO the previous August, six months earlier. Microplace then removed the rating after *The New York Times* called to inquire why it was still being used and has since taken LAPO investments off the website.

At Kiva, which promises on its website that it "will not partner with an organization that charges exorbitant interest rates," the interest rate and fees for LAPO was recently advertised as 57 percent, the average rate from 2007. After *The Times* called to inquire, Kiva changed it to 83 percent.

Premal Shah, Kiva's president, said it was a question of outdated information rather than deception. "I would argue that the information is stale as opposed to misleading," he said. "It could have been a tad better."

While analysts characterize such microfinance websites as well-meaning, they question whether the sites sufficiently vetted the organizations they promoted.

Questions had already been raised about Kiva because the website once promised that loans would go to specific borrowers identified on the site, but later backtracked, clarifying that the money went to organizations rather than individuals.

Promotion aside, the overriding question facing the industry, analysts say, remains how much money investors should make from lending to poor people, mostly women, often at interest rates that are hidden.

"You can make money from the poorest people in the world—is that a bad thing, or is that just a business?" asked Mr. Waterfield of mftransparency.org. "At what point do we say we have gone too far?"

Assess Your Progress

1. Why are advocates of microfinance concerned about the direction the practice has taken?
2. What accounts for high interest rates for many microfinance loans?
3. What is needed to avoid abuses in the microfinance industry?

Elisabeth Malkin contributed reporting from Mexico City.

Haiti: A Creditor, Not a Debtor

NAOMI KLEIN

If we are to believe the G-7 finance ministers, Haiti is on its way to getting something it has deserved for a very long time: full "forgiveness" of its foreign debt. In Port-au-Prince, Haitian economist Camille Chalmers has been watching these developments with cautious optimism. Debt cancellation is a good start, he told *Al Jazeera English,* but "It's time to go much further. We have to talk about reparations and restitution for the devastating consequences of debt." In this telling, the whole idea that Haiti is a debtor needs to be abandoned. Haiti, he argues, is a creditor—and it is we, in the West, who are deeply in arrears.

Our debt to Haiti stems from four main sources: slavery, the US occupation, dictatorship and climate change. These claims are not fantastical, nor are they merely rhetorical. They rest on multiple violations of legal norms and agreements. Here, far too briefly, are highlights of the Haiti case.

The Slavery Debt

When Haitians won their independence from France in 1804, they would have had every right to claim reparations from the powers that had profited from three centuries of stolen labor. France, however, was convinced that it was Haitians who had stolen the property of slave owners by refusing to work for free. So in 1825, with a flotilla of war ships stationed off the Haitian coast threatening to re-enslave the former colony, King Charles X came to collect: 90 million gold francs—ten times Haiti's annual revenue at the time. With no way to refuse, and no way to pay, the young nation was shackled to a debt that would take 122 years to pay off.

In 2003, Haitian President Jean-Bertrand Aristide, facing a crippling economic embargo, announced that Haiti would sue the French government over that long-ago heist. "Our argument," Aristide's former lawyer Ira Kurzban told me, "was that the contract was an invalid agreement because it was based on the threat of re-enslavement at a time when the international community regarded slavery as an evil." The French government was sufficiently concerned that it sent a mediator to Port-au-Prince to keep the case out of court. In the end, however, its problem was eliminated: while trial preparations were under way, Aristide was toppled from power. The lawsuit disappeared, but for many Haitians the reparations claim lives on.

The Dictatorship Debt

From 1957 to 1986, Haiti was ruled by the defiantly kleptocratic Duvalier regime. Unlike the French debt, the case against the Duvaliers made it into several courts, which traced Haitian funds to an elaborate network of Swiss bank accounts and lavish properties. In 1988 Kurzban won a landmark suit against Jean-Claude "Baby Doc" Duvalier when a US District Court in Miami found that the deposed ruler had "misappropriated more than $504,000,000 from public monies."

Haitians, of course, are still waiting for their payback—but that was only the beginning of their losses. For more than two decades, the country's creditors insisted that Haitians honor the huge debts incurred by the Duvaliers, estimated at $844 million, much of it owed to institutions like the IMF and the World Bank. In debt service alone, Haitians have paid out tens of millions every year.

Was it legal for foreign lenders to collect on the Duvalier debts when so much of it was never spent in Haiti? Very likely not. As Cephas Lumina, the United Nations Independent Expert on foreign debt, put it to me, "the case of Haiti is one of the best examples of odious debt in the world. On that basis alone the debt should be unconditionally canceled."

But even if Haiti does see full debt cancellation (a big if), that does not extinguish its right to be compensated for illegal debts already collected.

The Climate Debt

Championed by several developing countries at the climate summit in Copenhagen, the case for climate debt is straightforward. Wealthy countries that have so spectacularly failed to address the climate crisis they caused owe a debt to the developing countries that have done little to cause the crisis but are disproportionately facing its effects. In short: the polluter pays. Haiti has a particularly compelling claim. Its contribution to climate change has been negligible; Haiti's per capita CO_2 emissions are just 1 percent of US emissions. Yet Haiti is among the hardest hit countries—according to one index, only Somalia is more vulnerable to climate change.

Haiti's vulnerability to climate change is not only—or even mostly—because of geography. Yes, it faces increasingly heavy storms. But it is Haiti's weak infrastructure that turns challenges into disasters and disasters into full-fledged catastrophes.

The earthquake, though not linked to climate change, is a prime example. And this is where all those illegal debt payments may yet extract their most devastating cost. Each payment to a foreign creditor was money not spent on a road, a school, an electrical line. And that same illegitimate debt empowered the IMF and World Bank to attach onerous conditions to each new loan, requiring Haiti to deregulate its economy and slash its public sector still further. Failure to comply was met with a punishing aid embargo from 2001 to '04, the death knell to Haiti's public sphere.

This history needs to be confronted now, because it threatens to repeat itself. Haiti's creditors are already using the desperate need for earthquake aid to push for a fivefold increase in garment-sector production, some of the most exploitative jobs in the country. Haitians have no status in these talks, because they are regarded as passive recipients of aid, not full and dignified participants in a process of redress and restitution.

A reckoning with the debts the world owes to Haiti would radically change this poisonous dynamic. This is where the real road to repair begins: by recognizing the right of Haitians to reparations.

Assess Your Progress

1. What is the case for reparations for Haiti?
2. How did dictatorship contribute to Haiti's debt burden?
3. What increases Haiti's vulnerability to climate change?

UNIT 3

Conflict and Instability

Unit Selections

Learning Outcomes

After reading this unit you should be able to:

- Identify the sources of conflict and instability in the developing world.
- Recognize the complexity of conflict and instability in developing countries.
- Explain the connection between state weakness and conflict.
- Discuss the implications of the emergence of a new type of war in Africa.
- Analyze the connections between drug trafficking and violence in Mexico.
- Outline the challenges of effective peacekeeping.

Student Website

www.mhhe.com/cls

Internet References

The Carter Center
www.cartercenter.org

Center for Strategic and International Studies (CSIS)
www.csis.org

Conflict Research Consortium
http://conflict.colorado.edu

Institute for Security Studies
www.iss.co.za

International Crisis Group
www.crisisgroup.org

PeaceNet
www.igc.org/peacenet

Refugees International
www.refintl.org

Conflict and instability in the developing world remain major threats to international peace and security. Conflict stems from a combination of sources including ethnic and religious diversity, nationalism, the struggle for state control, and competition for resources. In some cases, colonial boundaries either encompass diverse groups or separate people from their ethnic kin, creating the circumstances that can lead to conflict. A state's diversity can increase tension among groups competing for scarce resources and opportunities. When some groups benefit or are perceived as enjoying privileges at the expense of others, ethnicity can offer a convenient vehicle for mobilization. Moreover, ethnic politics lends itself to manipulation both by regimes that are seeking to protect privileges, maintain order, or retain power and those that are challenging existing governments. In an atmosphere charged with ethnic and political tension, conflict and instability often arise as groups vie to gain control of the state apparatus in order to extract resources and allocate benefits. While ethnicity has played a role in many conflicts, competition over power and resources may sometimes be mistaken for ethnic warfare. Ethnic diversity and competition for resources combined with other factors, resulted in the war that raged in the Democratic Republic of Congo between 1998 and 2004. This was a prime example of the complex causes of conflicts. The war generated economic disruption, population migration, massive casualties, environmental degradation, and drew several other countries into the fighting. This murderous competition provides evidence of the emergence of a new type of warfare in Africa, one in which profit trumps ideology and politics. Weak and failing states also contribute to conflict. States with limited capacity are unable to adequately address the poverty and deprivation that often leads to instability and conflict. Failed states also encourage warlord behavior and may also offer a haven for terrorists and criminals. The spill-over from the conflict in these states can cause wider instability.

There is no shortage of conflict around the world, although the causes may differ from region to region. The Taliban poses a continuing security threat in Afghanistan as well as an increasingly dangerous challenge to the fragile government in Pakistan. Yemen has become a serious concern because of its increasing association with international terrorism. Efforts to combat this development have been complicated by deteriorating economic and political conditions. Iran's nuclear program and the unrest since the June 2009 elections have produced a volatile set of circumstances. Parts of Africa continue to be conflict prone. Somalia remains the world's most prominent example of a failed state, and the chaos in the region continues. The killing in Darfur has declined but Sudan's 2011 referendum on independence in the south threatens to spark renewed conflict in that region. Sudan highlights the difficulties of effective international peacekeeping. In Latin America, drug violence has also emerged as a serious threat to the Mexican government.

© Department of Defense/Airman 1st Class Kurt Gibbons III, U.S. Air Force

Threats to peace and stability in the developing world remain complicated, dangerous, and clearly have the potential to threaten international security.

Fixing a Broken World

The planet's most wretched places are not always the most dangerous.

In almost any discussion of world affairs, there is one thing on which doves and hawks invariably agree: much more needs to be done to shore up states that are failing, in a state of collapse, or so poor that they are heading in that direction.

For development-minded people, such benighted places are an obvious concern because of their desperate suffering; and for hard-nosed strategists, states that hardly work are places where terrorists could step into the vacuum. Indeed there is a certain convergence between these points of view: aid workers agree that security is essential to prosperity, and generals want economic development to boost security.

In America these days, defense planners say they worry more about weak states, even non-states, than about strong ones. "Ungoverned, undergoverned, misgoverned and contested areas" offer fertile grounds for terrorists and other nefarious groups, says the Pentagon's National Defense Strategy, issued last year. The penning of that document was overseen by the defense secretary, Robert Gates, who will remain in charge of defense policy under Barack Obama. Large chunks of its language could have been issued by bleeding-heart aid agencies or the United Nations: it speaks of the need to "build the capacity of fragile or vulnerable partners" and to address "local and regional conflicts" that exacerbate tensions and encourage drug-smuggling, gun-running and other illegality. To the chagrin of old-school sceptics, nation-building is now an integral part of American strategy.

Similarly, the European Union's declared security strategy sees state failure as an "alarming" phenomenon. It opines that: "Neighbours who are engaged in violent conflict, weak states where organised crime flourishes, dysfunctional societies or exploding population growth on its borders all pose problems for Europe."

A rather precise taxonomy is offered by Robert Cooper, a British diplomat and Eurocrat, in his book, "The Breaking of Nations". He splits the world into three zones: Hobbesian or "pre-modern" regions of chaos; areas ruled effectively by modern nation-states; and zones of "postmodern" co-operation where national sovereignty is being voluntarily dissolved, as in the European Union. In his view, chaos in critical parts of the world must be watched carefully. "It was not the well-organised Persian Empire that brought about the fall of Rome, but the barbarians," he writes.

Strategists have worried about failing states ever since the end of the cold war. At first, zones of war and chaos were seen primarily as threats to the people living within them, or not far away. But since the attacks on America in September 2001 such places have increasingly been seen as a threat to the entire world. Western intervention is now justified in the name of fighting terrorism, not just of altruism.

Take the case of Somalia: America sent troops there in 1992 to help the United Nations stave off a humanitarian catastrophe, but the armed chaos of Mogadishu soon drove it out. In recent years, America has again been active in that region, carrying out air strikes in Somalia against suspected jihadist camps. It supported Ethiopia's military invasion in 2006 to defeat the Islamist militias that had taken power in Mogadishu (arguably causing even more chaos) and is now backing an African peacekeeping mission for the same reasons. The waters off the Somali coast, moreover, have become one of the prime zones of piracy at sea, disrupting shipping through the Suez Canal. Even China has felt the need to send warships to the Gulf of Aden to protect its shipping.

Afghanistan, too, is often seen as a classic example of the perils of collapsing states: acute poverty and years of civil war led to the rise of the Taliban and allowed al-Qaeda to turn into a global menace. After the American-led intervention in 2001, both have rebated themselves across the border in Pakistan's lawless tribal regions, from where they wage a growing insurgency in southern Afghanistan, destabilise Pakistan and plot attacks against Western targets around the world.

Western intelligence agencies say that, with the recent improvement in security in Iraq (a totalitarian state that became a failed state only after the American-led invasion), the world's jihadists now prefer to head for Pakistan, Somalia or Yemen.

Misrule, violence, corruption, forced migration, poverty, illiteracy and disease can all reinforce each other. Conflict may impoverish populations, increase the availability of weapons and debilitate rulers. Weak governments, in turn, are less able to stop corruption and the production and smuggling of arms and drugs, which may in turn help finance warlords, insurgents and terrorists.

Instability breeds instability. The chronic weaknesses of civil institutions in Sierra Leone and Liberia contributed to the outbreak of devastating civil wars in both countries, fuelled by the profits from the illegal smuggling of "blood diamonds". Meanwhile war and genocide in Rwanda contributed to the collapse of the Democratic Republic of Congo in the 1990s. The chaos there, sustained in part by fighting over mineral resources, sucked in Rwanda, Burundi and Uganda. Chad and Sudan support rebels in each other's countries.

At the very least, there is evidence that economic growth in countries next to failing states can be badly damaged. And if a poorly functioning but important oil-producing state like Nigeria were to fall apart, the economic fallout would be global. Moreover, weak governments may lack the wherewithal to identify and contain a pandemic that could spread globally.

That said, the interplay of these factors is hard to describe, and the very definition of failed states and ungoverned spaces is anything but simple. Few states have completely failed, except perhaps for Somalia. And even here, the territory is not completely ungoverned. A part of the country, called Somaliland, is more or less autonomous and stable—and another bit, Puntland, is relatively calm, although it is the source of much piracy. The region to the south is dominated by warring clans, but even here some aspects of normal life, such as mobile telephone networks, manage to survive.

Lesser Breeds before the Law

One starting point in any analysis of failed countries is the theory of Max Weber, the father of social science. He defined the state as the agency which successfully monopolises the legitimate use of force. But what does legitimate mean? In some places, state power is exercised, brutally but effectively, by whoever is top dog in a perpetual contest between kleptocrats or warlords whose behaviour is lawless in every sense.

If definitions are elusive, what about degrees of state failure? Perhaps the most detailed study is the index of state weakness in developing countries drawn up by the Brookings Institution, a think-tank in Washington, DC. This synthesises 20 different indicators and identifies three "failed" states—Somalia, Afghanistan and the Democratic Republic of Congo—along with 24 other "critically weak" ones. One striking feature of such tables is that states fail in different ways. Among the ten worst performers, Iraq is comparatively wealthy and does well in social welfare, but is highly insecure; Zimbabwe is comparatively secure, but ruined economically and politically. The next ten-worst performers are even more mixed.

The collapse of states is as varied as the states themselves. Some were never functioning states at all, just lines drawn on maps by colonisers. Many African borders encompassed lots of ethnic groups and divided some of them. When the colonialists left, so did the bureaucracies that supported these entities, abandoning them to poverty, civil war or both. The cold war helped fuel many conflicts, for instance in Angola and Mozambique, where superpowers backed rival factions. Other parts of Africa, such as Somalia, fell apart after the withdrawal of superpower support.

The conflicts of Central America died down in the years following the end of the cold war. But the fighting in Colombia has dragged on, as the FARC guerrillas finance themselves through drugs and kidnapping. The end of Soviet communism freed or created many countries in Europe. Some prospered as they were absorbed into NATO and the European Union, while others fragmented bloodily, notably Yugoslavia. Enclaves of "frozen conflicts" remain on Russia's periphery—for example Abkhazia, South Ossetia and Transdniestria which survive as unrecognised statelets with the Kremlin's support.

Whichever way state collapse is assessed, it will always be an imperfect measure of priorities for policymakers. On a map of the world using the Brookings index of weak states, the epicentre is self-evidently sub-Saharan Africa, particularly around Congo, with blobs of red in Iraq, Afghanistan and Myanmar. But this overlaps only in part with, say, the ungoverned spaces that America's State Department regards as the nastiest havens for international terrorists, such as al-Qaeda.

On that list, Iraq and Afghanistan figure prominently—but in these countries, arguably, the problem is more one of national insurgencies than international terror. Once the tribes of western Iraq (whose grievances were local) had been induced to switch sides to the Americans, al-Qaeda was quickly evicted from that area. Al-Qaeda's senior leaders are sheltering in Pakistan, yet this ranks as only the 33rd-weakest state on the Brookings index.

One area of concern is the Sahel, a vast semi-arid area south of the Sahara desert. The Americans fear that in this region Islamist terrorists could begin co-operating with existing rebel outfits, such as the Tuareg, or with drug smugglers. The Pentagon has created a new Africa Command to help monitor the area more closely and train local government forces.

The State Department identifies other ungoverned spaces such as Yemen (30th on the Brookings index), parts of Colombia (47th), the seas between the Philippines (58th) and Indonesia (77th), bits of Lebanon (93rd) and the "tri-border area" between Brazil, Argentina and Paraguay (none ranked as particularly weak).

Conversely many of the most wretched places in the world—Congo, Burundi, Zimbabwe, Haiti, Myanmar and North Korea—are not known as havens for international terrorists. Attacks linked to al-Qaeda, moreover, have been conducted in well-run countries such as Britain and Spain. For American counter-terrorism officials, the biggest terrorist threat to the homeland is posed by European radicals who are able to travel to America more freely than, say, a Yemeni. Some scholars worry about social breakdown in poor mega-cities. But to regard the British Midlands and the *banlieues* of Paris as ungoverned spaces would be stretching a point.

The common denominator for al-Qaeda's activity is not state failure, but the fact that attacks are carried out by extremists claiming to act in the name of the world's Muslims. Their safe havens are not necessary geographical but social. Being based in a remote spot, far from government authorities, may be important for training, building *esprit de corps* and, in the view of intelligence agencies, trying to develop chemical and biological weapons.

But for al-Qaeda, remoteness alone is not enough. Terrorists need protection too, and that has to be secured from local populations as in Pakistan's tribal belt. International terrorists, moreover, need to be able to travel, communicate and transfer funds; they need to be within reach of functioning population centres. Stewart Patrick of the Council on Foreign Relations, an American think-tank, argues in a forthcoming book that international terrorists do not find the most failed states particularly attractive; they prefer "weak but moderately functional" states. The shell of state sovereignty protects them from outside intervention, but state weakness gives them space to operate autonomously.

Afghanistan's history is telling. Al-Qaeda was forged from the Arab volunteers who had fought with the Afghan *mujahideen* against the Soviet occupation of the country. With the end of the cold war and the fall of the communist government in Kabul, the country fell into civil war. Arab fighters largely pulled out in dismay.

Some went to Bosnia and Chechnya. Others intensified insurgencies back home in Egypt and Algeria. Osama bin Laden found shelter in Sudan under the protection of its Islamist regime. What took him back to Afghanistan was the rise of the Taliban. Afghanistan at that time was not an ungoverned space, but a state sponsor of terrorism; indeed, al-Qaeda arguably became a terrorist sponsor of a state.

Terrorism aside, what of other global plagues? Afghanistan is still the world's biggest source of the opium poppy, despite the presence of foreign troops. Next is Myanmar, also near the bottom of the pile. But Colombia, though not "critically" weak, is the biggest producer of cocaine. The cocaine routes pass through countries of all sorts; Mexico is among the top performers in the Brookings index, but is the main drugs highway to America. Similarly, piracy depends on geography. A nonexistent state may allow pirates to flourish, but without the proximity of a shipping route they have no targets to prey on.

Measures of corruption, such as Transparency International's Corruption Perceptions Index, correlate strongly with the index of state weakness. But here too there are anomalies: Russia is ranked as a middling country in terms of state weakness, but does worse in the corruption index; Italy scores below some African countries.

When it comes to pandemics, there is no simple correlation between disease and dysfunctional states. The countries suffering most from HIV/AIDS are in southern Africa: apart from Zimbabwe, most governments in that region are quite well run. The states that have seen the most cases of the deadly H5N1 strain of bird flu are Indonesia, Vietnam, China and Egypt, none of them among the worst cases of misrule or non-rule.

Everybody agrees that more effective government around the world is desirable, especially for those living in or near broken countries. Failed states always cause misery, but only sometimes are they a global threat. Given that failures come in so many varieties, fixing them is bound to be more of an art than a science.

Assess Your Progress

1. What types of states are susceptible to conflict and instability?
2. How do the factors that contribute to conflict and instability reinforce one another?
3. Why do terrorists prefer "weak but moderately functional" states?
4. Aside from conflict, what other global problems are associated with state weakness?

Afghanistan's Rocky Path to Peace

Even if all essential parties are interested in a negotiated settlement, getting to yes is no sure thing.

J. ALEXANDER THIER

It is a hallmark of intractable conflicts that the distance between the status quo and the conflict's inevitable resolution can appear unbridgeable. Such is the case with today's Afghanistan.

For the first time since 2001, when the US-led intervention in Afghanistan began, a serious prospect exists for political dialogue among the various combatants, aimed at the cessation of armed conflict. Over the past few months, and highlighted by a conference on Afghanistan held in London on January 28, 2010, signs have emerged of a concerted and comprehensive effort to engage elements of the insurgency in negotiations, reconciliation, and reintegration.

In London, Afghan President Hamid Karzai repeated a previous offer to negotiate with, and reintegrate, not only low-level foot soldiers and commanders of the Afghan insurgency, but also its leadership, including the Taliban chief Mullah Muhammad Omar. Karzai went further by announcing that he would in the spring convene a national peace *jirga,* a traditional Afghan assembly, to facilitate high-level talks with the insurgency. Karzai expressed hope that Saudi Arabia would play a key role in this process.

Eight and a half years after the invasion, amid rising insecurity across Afghanistan and with a continuously expanding international troop presence in the country, the prospect of a negotiated settlement with some or all elements of the insurgency is enticing. However, a successful path toward sustainable peace in Afghanistan remains far from obvious. Fundamental questions persist about the willingness and capability of key actors, inside and outside Afghanistan, to reach agreements and uphold them. Further, the content of an agreement or series of agreements, as well as the process by which any accord would be established, is uncertain. And even if all essential parties are interested in a negotiated settlement, getting to yes is no sure thing.

Peace—Who Wants It?

Winston Churchill said "to jaw-jaw is always better than to war-war," but jaw-jaw is not always easier. In Afghanistan, the process is not off to a promising start. Already, US Secretary of State Hillary Clinton has all but ruled out negotiating with the Taliban's senior leadership. She told National Public Radio in January that the United States is "not going to talk to the really bad guys because the really bad guys are not ever going to renounce Al Qaeda and renounce violence and agree to re-enter society. That is not going to happen with people like Mullah Omar and the like."

Meanwhile, President Barack Obama took full ownership of the war in a December 1, 2009, speech at the US Military Academy. The president, after having sent 21,000 additional troops to Afghanistan in the first months of his presidency, ordered another 30,000 soldiers into the theater—a place he called the "epicenter of violent extremism," where "our national security is at stake." By the summer of 2010, the international presence will amount to about 135,000 troops, with the United States contributing 100,000 of them.

Obama's announcement came nine days before he accepted the Nobel Peace Prize in Oslo, but it was no peacemaker's gambit. Rather, he sent the troops to undergird a robust new strategy aimed at displacing the insurgency from key population centers. While this surge of forces may eventually create more propitious conditions for a negotiated settlement, it may in the near term have the opposite effect.

Even so, it is time to take seriously the idea of political reconciliation in Afghanistan, to weigh the prospects for arriving at such an outcome, and to consider the obstacles in the way. If we cannot even imagine how reconciliation might be achieved, it will be impossible either to prepare the way or to determine whether the path is worth traveling in the first place.

Every war has its own logic—and its own economy.

Is the conflict in Afghanistan ripe for resolution? In a conflict, after all, reaching a settlement can be very difficult even when the key players have decided that they want it. Every war has its own logic—and its own economy.

Peace in Afghanistan will require the stars to align. Several constellations of actors will have to participate to secure a lasting peace. These include the "progovernment Afghans"—that is, along with the government itself, those opposition groups that are not fighting the government; the insurgents (themselves composed of at least three major groupings); the United States and its partners in the International Security Assistance Force (ISAF); and regional powers like Pakistan, Iran, India, and China. Also in the mix are several spoilers—groups that likely will never want stability. These include Al Qaeda, Pakistani radical groups in solidarity with the Afghan insurgents, and the drug traffickers who move 90 percent of the world's illicit opium.

In any case, do the progovernment forces want to reconcile with the Taliban? Karzai, who sees his future and his legacy hinging on a political settlement, has been a strong advocate for such efforts, and he is using his executive power and personal prestige in support of them. He is backed by large segments of an Afghan society that is bone-tired of war and is likely willing to accept significant compromises in exchange for stability.

Many, however, including some close to Karzai, may be much more ambivalent. Assume for a moment that a deal means conceding to the Taliban control over some part of southern Afghanistan. The people around Karzai who govern these provinces, who operate construction and road-building enterprises, and who profit from the drug trade would under such a settlement lose their power and their cash cows.

Two of the enterprises that generate the most profit are transport—essential for supplying international forces—and private security, in the form of companies that guard convoys, bases, and reconstruction projects. These multibillion-dollar industries would wither rapidly if stability were established and international forces withdrew. Other Karzai allies—such as his two warlord-cum vice presidents from the Northern Alliance, Muhammad Fahim and Karim Khalili—represent constituencies that have fought the Taliban since 1994 and are not keen to see them gain any power.

Other potential opponents of a peace deal include civil society organizations that have pushed for human and especially women's rights in the post-Taliban period. Allowing the return of Taliban-style gender apartheid policies, even in limited sections of the country, would be anathema to these groups and the vocal international constituency that supports them.

Men with Guns

And what about the insurgents? The three major groupings—Mullah Omar's Taliban, directed from sites in Pakistan; the Haqqani network; and Gulbuddin Hekmatyar's Hezb-e-Islami—are not a monolith, and may treat the prospect of negotiations differently. This differentiation is often seen as a good thing, because parts of the insurgency might split off from the rest. But recalcitrant actors might also try to sabotage the process. Also, even a successful settlement with one group will not under these circumstances end the insurgency.

The harder question, though, is why the insurgency would sue for peace if it believes it is winning and the Americans are preparing to leave. Considering the Karzai government's continued loss of moral authority, the insurgency's still largely safe haven in Pakistan, and an ongoing decline in public support for the war in NATO countries, the insurgents might easily decide to wait out the next few years, meanwhile waging a very effective guerrilla campaign.

But several factors could conspire to change their calculus. The first is the war itself. Obama's deployment decisions will essentially double the number of forces in the country this year. The Afghan security forces are also growing—and some are getting better at their jobs. The bigger force numbers, moreover, are accompanied by a new counterinsurgency strategy, one that looks likely to produce effects more lasting than those generated by the Bush administration's "economy of force" strategy, which involved too few troops to secure territory won through battle.

NATO also seems finally to have figured out how to reduce Afghan civilian casualties, depriving the insurgency of a key propaganda asset at a moment when militants are killing more civilians than ever. The United Nations estimates that in 2008 the Afghan and international military forces killed 828 civilians, and the insurgents killed 1,160. In 2009, the numbers were 596 and 1,630 respectively.

The war on the Pakistani side of the border, involving drone aircraft, has also been stepped up, and both the Pakistani Taliban's top leader and his replacement have been picked off in such strikes in recent months. It is unclear whether guided missile attacks have been used against Afghan insurgent targets in Pakistan as yet, but certainly the capability exists.

If all this adds up to a change in military momentum, popular attitudes might change, costing the Taliban support and increasing the number of people willing to inform or even fight against them.

Most Afghans have had little incentive to risk their necks for a government widely viewed as corrupt and ineffective.

Increased credibility of Afghan and international civilian efforts also could have an impact on public opinion. While most Afghans do not support the Taliban, they have had little incentive to risk their necks for a government widely viewed as corrupt and ineffective. If the Afghan government and its international partners can present a compelling, plausible alternative to the Taliban, backed by significant new investments in delivery of services and good governance, the environment will become less hospitable for the insurgents. The Afghan government and NATO have also launched a massive new reintegration effort intended to lure insurgent soldiers and low-level commanders off the battlefield. If this program succeeds in demobilizing combatants and safely reintegrating them into society, prospects for defeating the rebels would brighten.

The Pakistan Factor

And finally, the insurgency would be dealt a heavy blow if it lost its sanctuary in Pakistan. The Taliban recruit, train, fundraise, convalesce, and maintain their families there. For years, the Pakistani government has denied that the insurgent leadership was present in the country, but this has begun to change. In February, the government arrested Mullah Abdul Ghani Baradar, the operational commander of the Afghan Taliban. The Pakistanis also arrested Mullahs Abdul Salam and Mir Muhammad, the Taliban's "shadow governors" for two Afghan provinces.

Pakistan has come under increasing pressure from the Obama administration to confront the Afghan Taliban, with senior US officials reportedly telling the Pakistanis that if they do not act within their own territory, the United States will. Islamabad is also grappling with an internal struggle against militants who are determined to overthrow the state, and it has learned some hard lessons after getting burned by extremist fires that it has stoked in the past. That said, Pakistan is unlikely to abandon its longstanding patron-client relationships with groups that it still considers strategic assets. But it might use its leverage to help force a political outcome in Afghanistan.

The United States, despite some hedging, seems to view an Afghan political settlement that includes the Taliban as a possible element of its plan to draw down US forces. In early 2009, the Obama administration's focus was almost exclusively on "reintegration," or coaxing insurgents off the battlefield, rather than "reconciliation," which implies a broader political settlement with insurgent leaders. According to a March 2009 statement of Obama's new Afghanistan and Pakistan strategy: "Mullah Omar and the Taliban's hard core that have aligned themselves with Al Qaeda are not reconcilable and we cannot make a deal that includes them."

It appears that eight months of bad news from Afghanistan, along with declining support for the war among the US public and some soul-searching deliberations, softened the administration's stance toward the prospect of negotiations. In his December West Point address, Obama said, "We will support efforts by the Afghan government to open the door to those Taliban who abandon violence and respect the human rights of their fellow citizens." And in January of this year, just days before the London conference, General Stanley McChrystal, Obama's hand-picked commander of the ISAF, said, "I believe that a political solution to all conflicts is the inevitable outcome."

Afghanistan's neighbors and other regional powers also have a say in the process—or at least a veto. Pakistan, Iran, India, Russia, and Saudi Arabia have all contributed to Afghan instability over the past three decades, supporting various warring factions (while also at times supporting peaceful development). Afghanistan is a poor, mountainous, landlocked country with a weak central government, and while it is difficult to control, it has always been too easily destabilized by the predations and manipulations of larger powers. An agreement among regional actors to promote mutual noninterference in Afghanistan's internal affairs would be necessary to secure the peace.

Efforts to reach such an agreement are hampered by regional and international rivalries that drive the desire to intervene. Pakistan, the most significant of the regional players, backed the Taliban in the 1990s in order to end Afghanistan's civil war, open trade routes to the newly independent states in Central Asia, and secure a friendly government in Kabul. This strategy worked for a while, but the Taliban regime proved so odious and extreme that Pakistan found itself, on September 11, 2001, on the wrong side of a great conflict engulfing the region.

The Pakistani security establishment, though it cooperated with the US invasion of Afghanistan, has found it difficult to completely break with its former clients, and has allowed the Taliban sanctuary in Pakistan. Thus Pakistan serves simultaneously as the primary supply route for the ISAF and as the base for the insurgent leadership.

The Indian Presence

Why this untenable balancing act? The Pakistani military and its intelligence apparatus still feel surrounded by India. Pakistan has lost three or four wars to India (depending on how you count them). India's superiority in economic and conventional military strength, combined with Pakistan's unresolved border issues with both India (Kashmir) and Afghanistan (the Durand Line), keeps Pakistan's guard up. Islamabad is also facing a severe domestic militancy crisis that has cost thousands of lives—and, in Baluchistan, a simmering separatist insurgency that, Pakistan charges, receives Afghan-Indo support.

India for its part maintains strong relations with the Karzai government and is training Afghan civil servants and providing hundreds of millions in aid to Kabul—despite itself having the highest number of poverty-stricken people in the world. Pakistan feels threatened by India's relationship with Afghanistan, and so continues to maintain a hedge in the Taliban.

Pakistan's attitude toward the use of militants as a strategic asset in Kashmir and Afghanistan is changing.

Many believe, as a consequence, that the road to peace in Afghanistan runs through Delhi. Yet, if Afghan stability is held hostage to a comprehensive accord between Pakistan and India, we can forget about it. In the near term, ways must be found to mitigate Pakistan's concerns about India and Afghanistan. The resumption of comprehensive talks between Pakistan and India—which were tabled after a Pakistan-based extremist group carried out a November 2008 massacre in Mumbai—could provide a critical outlet. Also, because of brutality and overreaching by the Pakistani Taliban and other groups in the past few years, Pakistan's attitude toward the use of militants as a strategic asset in Kashmir and Afghanistan is changing.

Iran's potential role also remains ambiguous. Tehran has supported the Karzai government, provided some development assistance near western Afghanistan's border with Iran, and was a strong foe of the Taliban. It has also acted consistently to combat the opium trade, which has helped create an estimated 4 to 5 million Iranian addicts—a massive public health crisis.

On the other hand, Iran is encircled by US forces in Iraq and Afghanistan, and it faces continuing confrontation with the United States over its nuclear program. A settlement in Afghanistan would allow the United States to concentrate more on dealing with Iran, and would free up US military assets as well. Tehran might prefer to see America bogged down in a costly conflict.

Art of the Deal

Prevailing on key parties to agree to a peace deal will depend heavily on the shape of the deal itself. Last year some starting positions were aired, but both sides effectively demanded the other's capitulation. The Afghan and US governments called on insurgents to reject Al Qaeda, lay down their arms, and accept the Afghan constitution. The insurgents demanded withdrawal of foreign forces, removal of the Karzai government, and revision of the Afghan constitution to create a "true" Islamic republic.

Each of the three primary parties—the Afghan government, the Taliban, and the United States—would enter negotiations with their political survival depending on one condition. For Kabul, the condition for survival is just that—survival. In other words, the Karzai government will not make a deal requiring it to step down or hand over power. Such a prospect appears to Kabul far worse than the status quo; in addition, the likelihood of the government's catastrophic collapse seems distant enough to ignore.

For the Taliban leadership, the condition is the withdrawal of foreign forces. The Taliban's success today relies not on ideology, but rather on resistance to foreign occupation and Karzai's corrupt puppet regime. It would be hard for the Taliban, perhaps impossible, to accept some sort of accommodation with Karzai—but it is nearly unimaginable that the Taliban would accept any agreement that does not include the fairly quick withdrawal of foreign forces from the Taliban heartland, and their timeline-based withdrawal from the entire country. Between this Taliban demand and the US desire to withdraw, a pleasing symmetry exists. But Afghanistan's fragility and that of neighboring Pakistan—a country that to the United States represents an even greater national security concern—will make pulling out entirely a risky endeavor.

For the Obama administration, the one completely sacrosanct condition for a peace deal with insurgents is a firm, verifiable break with Al Qaeda. Al Qaeda was the reason for going into Afghanistan to begin with, and this issue will prevent US withdrawal until it is addressed. But *can* the Taliban break with Al Qaeda? The two entities grew up together, and so did their leaders—fighting the Soviets, ruling Afghanistan from 1996 to 2001, and since 2001 returning to the fight, against the Americans. They have shared foxholes, and reportedly have established family ties through marriages.

The Taliban have made an effort to suggest they would rule without Al Qaeda. In November 2009, they released a statement claiming that the "Islamic Emirate of Afghanistan wants to take constructive measures together with all countries for mutual cooperation, economic development, and [a] good future on the basis of mutual respect." But would a ban on Al Qaeda in Taliban-controlled territory be verifiable? After all, international terrorist cells continue to operate in Pakistan, where the United States has resorted to an all-but-official drone war because of the lack of local cooperation and the inaccessibility of the territory.

Up for Discussion

Aside from these core conditions, everything is to some extent negotiable. Some groups in the "progovernment" camp have for years supported changes to the 2004 constitution and to Afghan law that would increase power sharing, decentralization, and strengthening of Islamic strictures. Many conservative political leaders, mostly former mujahideen figures, would love to see an increased role for Islamic law, or sharia. A political and legal map that allows for regional variation might make sense in such an ethnically and geographically segmented country.

Meanwhile, a process of political reconciliation with the Taliban could be used not only to mollify the insurgents, but also to address tensions still lingering from the civil war, as well as perceived inequities among Afghanistan's regions and ethnicities, which continue to cause conflict. Addressing these tensions and inequities should be a key focus of the upcoming peace jirga.

The United States, its Western allies, and the UN would come under serious political fire if a deal with the Taliban meant abandoning Afghan women—whose privations under the Taliban have served to rally international support for the intervention since 2001. But any legal changes that threatened Afghanistan's gains in human rights would likely be limited and subtle, at least on paper. Since we are not talking about a deal that would put the Taliban in charge of the national government—in the near term, at any rate—little danger exists that the constitution would be changed to ban outright girls' education or women's access to employment.

To be sure, an accommodation with the Taliban might accelerate the steady erosion of rights that Afghan women have experienced in recent years. Indeed, the democratically elected parliament passed a family law last year—signed by President Karzai—that sanctioned, among other things, marital rape under certain circumstances. And if, after the ink dried on an agreement, the Taliban imposed an unofficial ban on female employment in provinces that they controlled, no ISAF offensive would likely be triggered, even if such a ban were in contravention of the constitution or the terms of the peace agreement.

There is also a real possibility that combatants on all sides of the conflict who have committed war crimes and atrocities will not be brought to justice. Evidence from many conflicts suggests a sustainable peace is unlikely without such reckoning.

Even so, the real issue in negotiations is not likely to be the rules themselves, but rather who makes and enforces them. Power sharing is the firmament of all peace processes, and changing the Afghan political system will have to involve sharing power. What exactly would a power sharing arrangement look like? Would the Taliban (and other groups) be given control over certain provinces? Would they help fill out the ranks of the Afghan national security forces? Would they be guaranteed a number of ministries or seats in the parliament? Or would they simply be allowed to compete for such things in a (quasi) democratic process?

Peace accords that have been reached in Bosnia, Burundi, and Northern Ireland, to name a few examples, spell out such arrangements in great detail. In the end, it is even more difficult to implement such complex provisions than to agree on them.

Neighboring countries will also be looking for certain guarantees. Pakistan wants its allies to succeed, and wants to be a key player in the peace process itself. Afghans, including perhaps the Taliban, will resent a strong Pakistani role in the process, but no process will take place without Pakistan. And unless Pakistan nudges the Taliban to the table by denying them sanctuary, the insurgents can always, if the pressure gets too high in Afghanistan, retreat into Pakistan, where they can go to ground and wait out the United States for a few more years.

Iran, Russia, and the Central Asian states for their part will want guarantees that the Taliban and other groups will not harbor or export militancy. All the neighbors are likely to agree on one thing—that Afghanistan should be neutral, eschewing alliances with any of the regional powers.

Can It Happen Here?

Even if all the parties are willing to negotiate, and sufficient space exists to reach a viable agreement despite all the red lines, achieving resolution will still be enormously challenging. Between and among the various actors there is a fundamental lack of trust, and talks this year will occur amid an intense military campaign. It is unclear whether either the Karzai government or the insurgent leaders have the wherewithal to discipline their own constituencies. Strong leadership will be needed on all sides both to craft an agreement and to achieve buy-in for unpopular concessions.

The profusion of players, motivations, conditions, and potential spoilers seems to cast serious doubt on prospects for a negotiated peace. But the status quo cannot hold either. Obama has already signaled that the Afghan mission has the full support of his government until July 2011. At that point, if the trajectory of the war has not changed appreciably, US strategy will. Nobody knows what that means. It could mean abandonment of the counterinsurgency strategy, with increased focus given instead to the sort of counterterrorism strategy reportedly advocated by Vice President Joseph Biden in 2009, with few troops on the ground and heavy reliance on drones and special forces to strike at terrorist targets. A new strategy could entail the replacement of the Karzai government.

Perhaps the most important issue affecting chances for a negotiated outcome is whether, to the various players, such an outcome looks more attractive than the alternatives. If the Taliban think they can run out the American clock without losing the war, they will do so. If the Karzai government and the Americans think they can beat the Taliban and stabilize Afghanistan without a deal, they will try. If the Pakistanis think that a weak, unstable Afghanistan that brings billions into their coffers is better, they will undermine a deal. So will the Iranians, if they decide the better alternative is a weak and unstable Afghanistan that pins down American forces.

But all of these factors might cut in more than one direction. Paradoxically, it is conceivable that the prospect of a US surge and departure could make a negotiated outcome more attractive to all parties—that is, negotiations might appear preferable to the risk of collapse and failure.

Do the Afghan people get a say? After 30 years of war they are among the poorest and most traumatized people on earth. But they are possessed of endurance and an indomitable spirit. If the indigenous, neutral leadership that supports a just peace could find its voice, that might spur a movement that presses the parties to reconcile.

Assess Your Progress

1. What factors influence prospects for negotiations in Afghanistan?
2. Who are the important actors in any effort to achieve a settlement in Afghanistan?
3. What are the obstacles to such an agreement?
4. What role do Pakistan and India play in the Afghan conflict?

J. Alexander Thier is the director for Afghanistan and Pakistan at the US Institute of Peace. He is the editor and coauthor of *The Future of Afghanistan* (USIP, 2009).

Civil Conflict Flares
In northern Yemen, the government has spent five years battling some 10,000 Zayidi Shiite rebels, known as Houthis. Since last August, government troops have been waging a bloody offensive called Operation Scorched Earth, with little success.

A Refugee Crisis
Some 250,000 Yemenis have fled the fighting and crowded into overwhelmed refugee camps that are rife with disease and malnutrition.

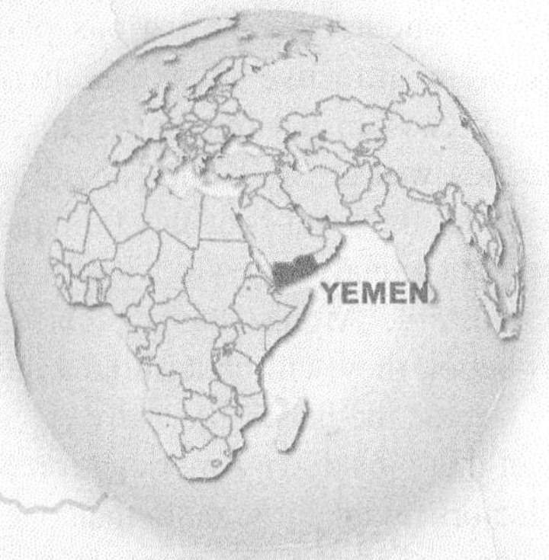

A Wider War?
Saudi Arabia entered the civil war in November, when Houthi rebels crossed into its territory. More than 100 Saudi soldiers have since been killed, and though a fragile cease-fire now holds, many fear that the war will soon expand. The Saudis have accused Iran of arming the Houthis, suggesting that the rebellion could turn into a proxy fight between the two regional powers.

A Nation on the Brink

It's not Just Al-Qaeda. Water Shortages, Collapsing Oil Supplies, War, Refugees, Pirates, Poverty—Why Yemen is Failing.

CHRISTOPHER BOUCEK AND DAVID DONADIO

Yemen—once known to Americans mainly as the site of the suicide attack on the U.S.S. *Cole* in 2000—has recently reentered the public imagination as a central front in the war on terror. An alarming number of would-be jihadists—like Nidal Malik Hasan, the Fort Hood shooter; and Umar Farouk Abdulmutallab, the Christmas Day bomber—have sought spiritual direction or logistical support there, and American security officials now consider Yemen a counterterrorism priority second only to South Asia.

But as the map at right shows, Yemen faces an astonishing confluence of other challenges that make fighting terrorism even harder. Among them: a civil war in the north, a secessionist movement in the south, dangerously depleted natural resources, rampant corruption and unemployment, and the fearsome possibility that Yemen will become the first country in modern history to run out of water.

It's also now clear that Yemen's government lacks the capacity to exert full control over much of its territory. This has created a refuge from which alQaeda can mount terrorist attacks across the country—and increasingly across the wider world.

At the heart of all these problems is Yemen's looming economic collapse. Already the poorest country in the Arab world, Yemen is rapidly depleting its oil reserves and lacks any options for creating a sustainable post-oil economy. Unemployment is estimated at 35 percent, higher than what the U.S. faced during the Great Depression.

Accelerating the economic decline is a protracted civil war in the north between Shia insurgents and the Sana'a-based government. The war has caused a refugee crisis and extensive damage to infrastructure, and its costs will result in a major budget deficit next year. (The government is already burning through roughly $200 million in foreign-currency reserves per month.) Even if that war subsides, the worsening economy will likely inflame a roiling secessionist movement in the south. Yemen has often teetered on the brink of collapse, but it has never faced so many interconnected challenges at once. And the stakes have never been greater.

Al-Qaeda's New Home
By some estimates, as many as 300 al-Qaeda fighters are active in Yemen, especially in the southern tribal areas of Ma'rib and Shabwah, where the government has little authority. The group's local branch, al-Qaeda in the Arabian Peninsula, has deep connections with Yemeni tribes and plenty of potential recruits among the country's jobless young men.

Assess Your Progress

1. Why is Yemen a counter-terrorism priority?
2. How do economic and political factors affect Yemen's ability to cope with its adversity?
3. What accounts for Yemen's internal divisions?

Christopher Boucek is an associate in the Middle East Program at the Carnegie Endowment for International Peace, where **David Donadio** is a writer and editor.

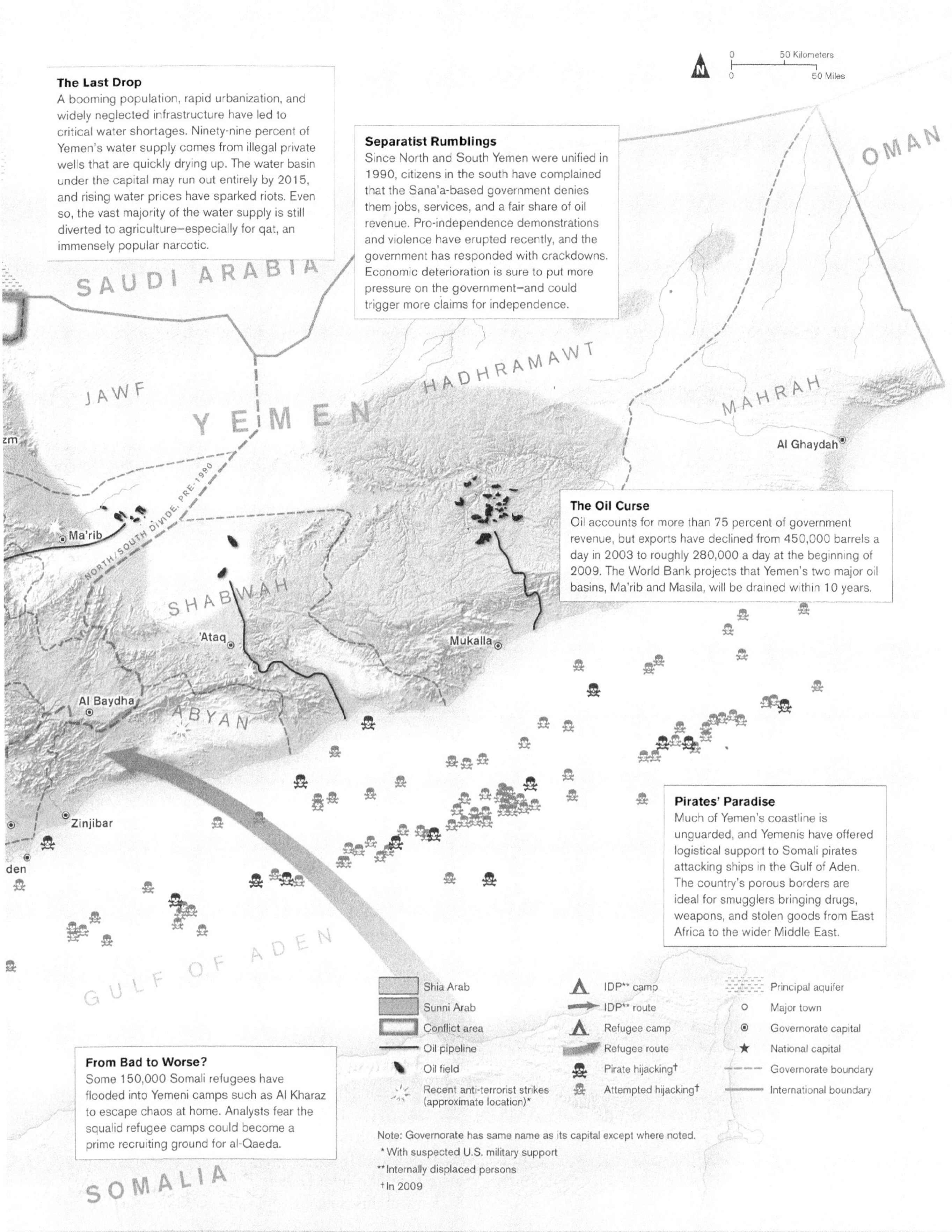

 Map Sources: Adelphi Energy, Atlantic Research, Carnegie Endowment for International Peace, Central Intelligence Agency, International Chamber of Commerce, Relief Web, United Nations, World Bank.

Africa's Forever Wars

JEFFREY GETTLEMAN

There is a very simple reason why some of Africa's bloodiest, most brutal wars never seem to end: They are not really wars. Not in the traditional sense, at least. The combatants don't have much of an ideology; they don't have clear goals. They couldn't care less about taking over capitals or major cities—in fact, they prefer the deep bush, where it is far easier to commit crimes. Today's rebels seem especially uninterested in winning converts, content instead to steal other people's children, stick Kalashnikovs or axes in their hands, and make them do the killing. Look closely at some of the continent's most intractable conflicts, from the rebel-laden creeks of the Niger Delta to the inferno in the Democratic Republic of the Congo, and this is what you will find.

What we are seeing is the decline of the classic African liberation movement and the proliferation of something else—something wilder, messier, more violent, and harder to wrap our heads around. If you'd like to call this war, fine. But what is spreading across Africa like a viral pandemic is actually just opportunistic, heavily armed banditry. My job as the *New York Times*' East Africa bureau chief is to cover news and feature stories in 12 countries. But most of my time is spent immersed in these un-wars.

I've witnessed up close—often way too close—how combat has morphed from soldier vs. soldier (now a rarity in Africa) to soldier vs. civilian. Most of today's African fighters are not rebels with a cause; they're predators. That's why we see stunning atrocities like eastern Congo's rape epidemic, where armed groups in recent years have sexually assaulted hundreds of thousands of women, often so sadistically that the victims are left incontinent for life. What is the military or political objective of ramming an assault rifle inside a woman and pulling the trigger? Terror has become an end, not just a means.

This is the story across much of Africa, where nearly half of the continent's 53 countries are home to an active conflict or a recently ended one. Quiet places such as Tanzania are the lonely exceptions; even user-friendly, tourist-filled Kenya blew up in 2008. Add together the casualties in just the dozen countries that I cover, and you have a death toll of tens of thousands of civilians each year. More than 5 million have died in Congo alone since 1998, the International Rescue Committee has estimated.

Of course, many of the last generation's independence struggles were bloody, too. South Sudan's decades-long rebellion is thought to have cost more than 2 million lives. But this is not about numbers. This is about methods and objectives, and the leaders driving them. Uganda's top guerrilla of the 1980s, Yoweri Museveni, used to fire up his rebels by telling them they were on the ground floor of a national people's army. Museveni became president in 1986, and he's still in office (another problem, another story). But his words seem downright noble compared with the best-known rebel leader from his country today, Joseph Kony, who just gives orders to burn.

Even if you could coax these men out of their jungle lairs and get them to the negotiating table, there is very little to offer them. They don't want ministries or tracts of land to govern. Their armies are often traumatized children, with experience and skills (if you can call them that) totally unsuited for civilian life. All they want is cash, guns, and a license to rampage. And they've already got all three. How do you negotiate with that?

The short answer is you don't. The only way to stop today's rebels for real is to capture or kill their leaders. Many are uniquely devious characters whose organizations would likely disappear as soon as they do. That's what happened in Angola when the diamond-smuggling rebel leader Jonas Savimbi was shot, bringing a sudden end to one of the Cold War's most intense conflicts. In Liberia, the moment that warlord-turned-president Charles Taylor was arrested in 2006 was the same moment that the curtain dropped on the gruesome circus of 10-year-old killers wearing Halloween masks. Countless dollars, hours, and lives have been wasted on fruitless rounds of talks that will never culminate in such clear-cut results. The same could be said of indictments of rebel leaders for crimes against humanity by the International Criminal Court. With the prospect of prosecution looming, those fighting are sure never to give up.

How did we get here? Maybe it's pure nostalgia, but it seems that yesteryear's African rebels had a bit more class. They were fighting against colonialism, tyranny, or apartheid. The winning insurgencies often came with a charming, intelligent leader wielding persuasive rhetoric. These were men like John Garang, who led the rebellion in southern Sudan with his Sudan People's Liberation Army. He pulled off what few guerrilla leaders anywhere have done: winning his people their own country. Thanks in part to his tenacity, South

Sudan will hold a referendum next year to secede from the North. Garang died in a 2005 helicopter crash, but people still talk about him like a god. Unfortunately, the region without him looks pretty godforsaken. I traveled to southern Sudan in November to report on how ethnic militias, formed in the new power vacuum, have taken to mowing down civilians by the thousands.

Even Robert Mugabe, Zimbabwe's dictator, was once a guerrilla with a plan. After transforming minority white-run Rhodesia into majority black-run Zimbabwe, he turned his country into one of the fastest-growing and most diversified economies south of the Sahara—for the first decade and a half of his rule. His status as a true war hero, and the aid he lent other African liberation movements in the 1980s, account for many African leaders' reluctance to criticize him today, even as he has led Zimbabwe down a path straight to hell.

These men are living relics of a past that has been essentially obliterated. Put the well-educated Garang and the old Mugabe in a room with today's visionless rebel leaders, and they would have just about nothing in common. What changed in one generation was in part the world itself. The Cold War's end bred state collapse and chaos. Where meddling great powers once found dominoes that needed to be kept from falling, they suddenly saw no national interest at all. (The exceptions, of course, were natural resources, which could be bought just as easily—and often at a nice discount—from various armed groups.) Suddenly, all you needed to be powerful was a gun, and as it turned out, there were plenty to go around. AK-47s and cheap ammunition bled out of the collapsed Eastern Bloc and into the farthest corners of Africa. It was the perfect opportunity for the charismatic and morally challenged.

In Congo, there have been dozens of such men since 1996, when rebels rose up against the leopard skin-capped dictator Mobutu Sese Seko, probably the most corrupt man in the history of this most corrupt continent. After Mobutu's state collapsed, no one really rebuilt it. In the anarchy that flourished, rebel leaders carved out fiefdoms ludicrously rich in gold, diamonds, copper, tin, and other minerals. Among them were Laurent Nkunda, Bosco Ntaganda, Thomas Lubanga, a toxic hodgepodge of Mai Mai commanders, Rwandan genocidaires, and the madman leaders of a flamboyantly cruel group called the Rastas.

I met Nkunda in his mountain hideout in late 2008 after slogging hours up a muddy road lined with baby-faced soldiers. The chopstick-thin general waxed eloquent about the oppression of the minority Tutsi people he claimed to represent, but he bristled when I asked him about the warlord-like taxes he was imposing and all the women his soldiers have raped. The questions didn't seem to trouble him too much, though, and he cheered up soon. His farmhouse had plenty of space for guests, so why didn't I spend the night?

Nkunda is not totally wrong about Congo's mess. Ethnic tensions are a real piece of the conflict, together with disputes over land, refugees, and meddling neighbor countries. But what I've come to understand is how quickly legitimate grievances in these failed or failing African states deteriorate into rapacious, profit-oriented bloodshed. Congo today is home to a resource rebellion in which vague anti-government feelings become an excuse to steal public property. Congo's embarrassment of riches belongs to the 70 million Congolese, but in the past 10 to 15 years, that treasure has been hijacked by a couple dozen rebel commanders who use it to buy even more guns and wreak more havoc.

Probably the most disturbing example of an African un-war comes from the Lord's Resistance Army (LRA), begun as a rebel movement in northern Uganda during the lawless 1980s. Like the gangs in the oil-polluted Niger Delta, the LRA at first had some legitimate grievances—namely, the poverty and marginalization of the country's ethnic Acholi areas. The movement's leader, Joseph Kony, was a young, wig-wearing, gibberish-speaking, so-called prophet who espoused the Ten Commandments. Soon, he broke every one. He used his supposed magic powers (and drugs) to whip his followers into a frenzy and unleashed them on the very Acholi people he was supposed to be protecting.

The LRA literally carved their way across the region, leaving a trail of hacked-off limbs and sawed-off ears. They don't talk about the Ten Commandments anymore, and some of those left in their wake can barely talk at all. I'll never forget visiting northern Uganda a few years ago and meeting a whole group of

Africa Heats Up

Scientists have long warned that warming global temperatures and the resource scarcities that result will bring more violent conflicts. The U.S. government even directed its intelligence community to study the potential national security implications of climate change. But the evidence showing that rising temperatures cause armed conflict has been sketchy at best—until now.

In a recent study published in *Proceedings of the National Academy of Sciences,* a team of economists compared variations in temperature with the incidence of conflict in sub-Saharan Africa between 1981 and 2002 and found startling results: Just a 1 degree Celsius increase in temperature resulted in a 49 percent increase in the incidence of civil war. The situation looks even bleaker in coming decades. Given projected increases in global temperatures, the authors see a 54 percent increase in civil conflict across the region. If these conflicts are as deadly as the wars during the study period, Africa could suffer an additional 393,000 battle deaths by 2030.

The main reason for the projected violence is global warming's impact on agriculture, but there could be other factors as well. For instance, violent crime tends to increase when temperatures are high, while economic productivity decreases. In an especially depressing aside, the authors note that even under the "optimistic scenario" for economic growth and political reform in the coming decades, "neither is able to overcome the large effects of temperature increase on civil war incidence."

—Joshua E. Keating

women whose lips were sheared off by Kony's maniacs. Their mouths were always open, and you could always see their teeth. When Uganda finally got its act together in the late 1990s and cracked down, Kony and his men simply marched on. Today, their scourge has spread to one of the world's most lawless regions: the borderland where Sudan, Congo, and the Central African Republic meet.

Child soldiers are an inextricable part of these movements. The LRA, for example, never seized territory; it seized children. Its ranks are filled with brainwashed boys and girls who ransack villages and pound newborn babies to death in wooden mortars. In Congo, as many as one-third of all combatants are under 18. Since the new predatory style of African warfare is motivated and financed by crime, popular support is irrelevant to these rebels. The downside to not caring about winning hearts and minds, though, is that you don't win many recruits. So abducting and manipulating children becomes the only way to sustain the organized banditry. And children have turned out to be ideal weapons: easily brainwashed, intensely loyal, fearless, and, most importantly, in endless supply.

In this new age of forever wars, even Somalia looks different. That country certainly evokes the image of Africa's most chaotic state—exceptional even in its neighborhood for unending conflict. But what if Somalia is less of an outlier than a terrifying forecast of what war in Africa is moving toward? On the surface, Somalia seems wracked by a religiously themed civil conflict between the internationally backed but feckless transitional government and the Islamist militia al-Shabab. Yet the fighting is being nourished by the same old Somali problem that has dogged this desperately poor country since 1991: warlordism. Many of the men who command or fund militias in Somalia today are the same ones who tore the place apart over the past 20 years in a scramble for the few resources left—the port, airport, telephone poles, and grazing pastures.

Somalis are getting sick of the Shabab and its draconian rules—no music, no gold teeth, even no bras. But what has kept locals in Somalia from rising up against foreign terrorists is Somalia's deeply ingrained culture of war profiteering. The world has let Somalia fester too long without a permanent government. Now, many powerful Somalis have a vested interest in the status quo chaos. One olive oil exporter in Mogadishu told me that he and some trader friends bought a crate of missiles to shoot at government soldiers because "taxes are annoying."

Most frightening is how many sick states like Congo are now showing Somalia-like symptoms. Whenever a potential leader emerges to reimpose order in Mogadishu, criminal networks rise up to finance his opponent, no matter who that may be. The longer these areas are stateless, the harder it is to go back to the necessary evil of government.

All this might seem a gross simplification, and indeed, not all of Africa's conflicts fit this new paradigm. The old steady—the military coup—is still a common form of political upheaval, as Guinea found out in 2008 and Madagascar not too long thereafter. I have also come across a few non-hoodlum rebels who seem legitimately motivated, like some of the Darfurian commanders in Sudan. But though their political grievances are well defined, the organizations they "lead" are not. Old-style African rebels spent years in the bush honing their leadership skills, polishing their ideology, and learning to deliver services before they ever met a Western diplomat or sat for a television interview. Now rebels are hoisted out of obscurity after they have little more than a website and a "press office" (read: a satellite telephone). When I went to a Darfur peace conference in Sirte, Libya, in 2007, I quickly realized that the main draw for many of these rebel "leaders" was not the negotiating sessions, but the all-you-can-eat buffet.

For the rest, there are the un-wars, these ceaseless conflicts I spend my days cataloging as they grind on, mincing lives and spitting out bodies. Recently, I was in southern Sudan working on a piece about the Ugandan Army's hunt for Kony, and I met a young woman named Flo. She had been a slave in the LRA for 15 years and had recently escaped. She had scarred shins and stony eyes, and often there were long pauses after my questions, when Flo would stare at the horizon. "I am just thinking of the road home," she said. It was never clear to her why the LRA was fighting. To her, it seemed like they had been aimlessly tramping through the jungle, marching in circles.

This is what many conflicts in Africa have become—circles of violence in the bush, with no end in sight.

Assess Your Progress

1. Why are many of Africa's wars non-traditional?
2. What are the implications of this development for peaceful settlement of these conflicts?
3. How do the current rebel groups differ from past conflicts?
4. How did the end of the cold war contribute to the emergence of this non-traditional warfare?
5. Why has the emergence of this type of conflict contributed to the use of child soldiers?

Jeffrey Gettleman is East Africa bureau chief for the New York Times.

The Most Dangerous Place in the World

Somalia is a state governed only by anarchy. A graveyard of foreign-policy failures, it has known just six months of peace in the past two decades. Now, as the country's endless chaos threatens to engulf an entire region, the world again simply watches it burn.

JEFFREY GETTLEMAN

When you land at Mogadishu's international airport, the first form you fill out asks for name, address, and caliber of weapon. Believe it or not, this disaster of a city, the capital of Somalia, still gets a few commercial flights. Some haven't fared so well. The wreckage of a Russian cargo plane shot down in 2007 still lies crumpled at the end of the runway.

Beyond the airport is one of the world's most stunning monuments to conflict: block after block, mile after mile, of scorched, gutted-out buildings. Mogadishu's Italianate architecture, once a gem along the Indian Ocean, has been reduced to a pile of machine-gun-chewed bricks. Somalia has been ripped apart by violence since the central government imploded in 1991. Eighteen years and 14 failed attempts at a government later, the killing goes on and on and on—suicide bombs, white phosphorus bombs, beheadings, medieval-style stonings, teenage troops high on the local drug called *khat* blasting away at each other and anything in between. Even U.S. cruise missiles occasionally slam down from the sky. It's the same violent free-for-all on the seas. Somalia's pirates are threatening to choke off one of the most strategic waterways in the world, the Gulf of Aden, which 20,000 ships pass through every year. These heavily armed buccaneers hijacked more than 40 vessels in 2008, netting as much as $100 million in ransom. It's the greatest piracy epidemic of modern times.

In more than a dozen trips to Somalia over the past two and a half years, I've come to rewrite my own definition of chaos. I've felt the incandescent fury of the Iraqi insurgency raging in Fallujah. I've spent freezing-cold, eerily quiet nights in an Afghan cave. But nowhere was I more afraid than in today's Somalia, where you can get kidnapped or shot in the head faster than you can wipe the sweat off your brow. From the thick, ambush-perfect swamps around Kismayo in the south to the lethal labyrinth of Mogadishu to the pirate den of Boosaaso on the Gulf of Aden, Somalia is quite simply the most dangerous place in the world.

I've felt the incandescent fury of the Iraqi insurgency. I've spent freezing-cold nights in an Afghan cave. But nowhere was I more afraid than in today's Somalia.

The whole country has become a breeding ground for warlords, pirates, kidnappers, bomb makers, fanatical Islamist insurgents, freelance gunmen, and idle, angry youth with no education and way too many bullets. There is no Green Zone here, by the way—no fortified place of last resort to run to if, God forbid, you get hurt or in trouble. In Somalia, you're on your own. The local hospitals barely have enough gauze to treat all the wounds.

The mayhem is now spilling across Somalia's borders, stirring up tensions and violence in Kenya, Ethiopia, and Eritrea, not to mention Somalia's pirateinfested seas. The export of trouble may just be beginning. Islamist insurgents with al Qaeda connections are sweeping across the country, turning Somalia into an Afghanistan-like magnet for militant Islam and drawing in hard-core fighters from around the world. These men will eventually go home (if they survive) and spread the killer ethos. Somalia's transitional government, a U.N.-santioned creation that was deathly ill from the moment it was born four years ago, is about to flatline, perhaps spawning yet another doomed international rescue mission. Abdullahi Yusuf Ahmed, the old war horse of a president backed by the United States, finally resigned in December after a long, bitter dispute with the prime minister, Nur Hassan Hussein. Ostensibly, their conflict was about a peace deal with the Islamists and a few cabinet posts. In truth, it may be purely academic. By early this year, the government's zone of control was down to a couple of city blocks. The country is nearly as big as Texas.

Just when things seem as though they can't get any worse in Somalia, they do. Beyond the political crisis, all the elements for a full-blown famine—war, displacement, drought, skyrocketing food prices, and an exodus of aid workers—are lining up again, just as they did in the early 1990s when hundreds of thousands of Somalis starved to death. Last May, I stood in the doorway of a hut in the bone-dry central part of the country watching a sick little boy curl up next to his dying mother. Her clothes were damp. Her breaths were shallow. She hadn't eaten for days. "She will most likely die," an elder told me and walked away.

Just when things seem they can't get any worse in Somalia, they do. Beyond the political crisis, all the elements for a full-blown famine are lining up again.

It's crunch time for Somalia, but the world is like me, standing in the doorway, looking in at two decades of unbridled anarchy, unsure what to do. Past interventions have been so cursed that no one wants to get burned again. The United States has been among the worst of the meddlers: U.S. forces fought predacious warlords at the wrong time, backed some of the same predacious warlords at the wrong time, and consistently failed to appreciate the twin pulls of clan and religion. As a result, Somalia has become a graveyard of foreign-policy blunders that have radicalized the population, deepened insecurity, and pushed millions to the brink of starvation.

Somalia is a political paradox—unified on the surface, poisonously divided beneath. It is one of the world's most homogeneous nation-states, with nearly all of its estimated 9 to 10 million people sharing the same language (Somali), the same religion (Sunni Islam), the same culture, and the same ethnicity. But in Somalia, it's all about clan. Somalis divide themselves into a dizzying number of clans, subclans, sub-subclans, and so on, with shifting allegiances and knotty backstories that have bedeviled outsiders for years.

At the end of the 19th century, the Italians and the British divvied up most of Somalia, but their efforts to impose Western laws never really worked. Disputes tended to be resolved by clan elders. Deterrence was key: "Kill me and you will suffer the wrath of my entire clan." The places where the local ways were disturbed the least, such as British-ruled Somaliland, seem to have done better in the long run than those where the Italian colonial administration supplanted the role of clan elders, as in Mogadishu.

Somalia won independence in 1960, but it quickly became a Cold War pawn, prized for its strategic location in the Horn of Africa, where Africa and Asia nearly touch. First it was the Soviets who pumped in weapons, then the United States. A poor, mostly illiterate, mainly nomadic country became a towering ammunition dump primed to explode. The central government was hardly able to hold the place together. Even in the 1980s, Maj. Gen. Mohamed Siad Barre, the capricious dictator who ruled from 1969 to 1991, was derisively referred to as "the mayor of Mogadishu" because so much of the country had already spun out of his control.

When clan warlords finally ousted him in 1991, it wasn't much of a surprise what happened next. The warlords unleashed all that military-grade weaponry on each other, and every port, airstrip, fishing pier, telephone pole—anything that could turn a profit—was fought over. People were killed for a few pennies. Women were raped with impunity. The chaos gave rise to a new class of parasitic war profiteers—gunrunners, drug smugglers, importers of expired (and often sickening) baby formula—people with a vested interest in the chaos continuing. Somalia became the modern world's closest approximation of Hobbes's state of nature, where life was indeed nasty, brutish, and short. To call it even a failed state was generous. The Democratic Republic of the Congo is a failed state. So is Zimbabwe. But those places at least have national armies and national bureaucracies, however corrupt. Since 1991, Somalia has not been a state so much as a lawless, ungoverned space on the map between its neighbors and the sea.

In 1992, U.S. President George H.W. Bush tried to help, sending in thousands of Marines to protect shipments of food. It was the beginning of the post-Cold War "new world order," when many believed that the United States, without a rival superpower, could steer world events in a new and morally righteous way. Somalia proved to be a very bad start. President Bush and his advisors misread the clan landscape and didn't understand how fiercely loyal Somalis could be to their clan leaders. Somali society often divides and subdivides when faced with internal disputes, but it quickly bands together when confronted by an external enemy. The United States learned this the hard way when its forces tried to apprehend the warlord of the day, Mohammed Farah Aidid. The result was the infamous "Black Hawk Down" episode in October 1993. Thousands of Somali militiamen poured into the streets, carrying rocket-propelled grenades and wearing flip-flops. They shot down two American Black Hawk helicopters, killing 18 U.S. soldiers and dragging the corpses triumphantly through the streets. This would be Strike One for the United States in Somalia.

Humiliated, the Americans pulled out and Somalia was left to its own dystopian devices. For the next decade, the Western world mostly stayed away. But Arab organizations, many from Saudi Arabia and followers of the strict Wahhabi branch of Sunni Islam, quietly stepped in. They built mosques, Koranic schools, and social service organizations, encouraging an Islamic revival. By the early 2000s, Mogadishu's clan elders set up a loose network of neighborhood-based courts to deliver a modicum of order in a city desperate for it. They rounded up thieves and killers, put them in iron cages, and held trials. Islamic law, or *sharia,* was the one set of principles that different clans could agree on; the Somali elders called their network the Islamic Courts Union.

Mogadishu's business community spotted an opportunity. In Mogadishu, there are warlords and moneylords. While the warlords were ripping the country apart, the moneylords, Somalia's big-business owners, were holding the place together, delivering many of the same services—for a tidy profit, of course—that a government usually provides, such as healthcare, schools, power plants, and even privatized mail. The moneylords went as far as helping to regulate Somalia's monetary policy, and the Somali shilling was more stable in the 1990s—without a functioning central bank—than in the 1980s when there was a government. But with their profits came very high risks, such as chronic insecurity and extortion. The Islamists were a solution. They provided security without taxes, administration without a government. The moneylords began buying them guns.

By 2005, the CIA saw what was happening, and again misread the cues. This ended up being Strike Two.

In a post-September 11 world, Somalia had become a major terrorism worry. The fear was that Somalia could blossom into a jihad factory like Afghanistan, where al Qaeda in the 1990s plotted its global war on the West. It didn't seem to matter that at this point there was scant evidence to justify this fear. Some Western military analysts told policymakers that Somalia was too chaotic for even al Qaeda, because it was impossible for anyone—including terrorists—to know whom to trust. Nonetheless, the administration of George W. Bush devised a strategy to stamp out the Islamists on the cheap. CIA agents deputized the warlords, the same thugs who had been preying upon Somalia's population for years, to fight the Islamists. According to one Somali warlord I spoke with in March 2008, an American agent named James and another one named David showed up in Mogadishu with briefcases stuffed with cash. Use this to buy guns, the agents said. Drop us an e-mail if you have any questions. The warlord showed me the address: no_email_today@yahoo.com.

The plan backfired. Somalis like to talk; the country, ironically, has some of the best and cheapest cellular phone service in Africa. Word quickly spread that the same warlords no one liked anymore were now doing the Americans' bidding, which just made the Islamists even more popular. By June 2006, the Islamists had run the last warlords out of Mogadishu. Then something unbelievable happened: The Islamists seemed to tame the place.

I saw it with my own eyes. I flew into Mogadishu in September 2006 and saw work crews picking up trash and kids swimming at the beach. For the first time in years, no gunshots rang out at night. Under the banner of Islam, the Islamists had united rival clans and disarmed much of the populace, with clan support of course. They even cracked down on piracy by using their clan connections to dissuade coastal towns from supporting the pirates. When that didn't work, the Islamists stormed hijacked ships. According to the International Maritime Bureau in London, there were 10 pirate attacks off Somalia's coast in 2006, which is tied for the lowest number of attacks this decade.

The Islamists' brief reign of peace was to be the only six months of calm Somalia has tasted since 1991. But it was one thing to rally together to overthrow the warlords and another to decide what to do next. A rift quickly opened between the moderate Islamists and the extremists, who were bent on waging jihad. One of the most radical factions has been the Shabab, a multiclan military wing with a strict Wahhabi interpretation of Islam. The Shabab drove around Mogadishu in big, black pickup trucks and beat women whose ankles were showing. Even the other Islamist gunmen were scared of them. By December 2006, some of the population began to chafe against the Shabab for taking away their beloved khat, the mildly stimulating leaf that Somalis chew like bubble gum. Shabab leaders were widely rumored to be working with foreign jihadists, including wanted al Qaeda terrorists, and the U.S. State Department later designated the Shabab a terrorist organization. American officials have said that the Shabab are sheltering men who masterminded the bombings of the U.S. embassies in Kenya and Tanzania in 1998.

Somalia may indeed have sheltered a few unsavory characters, but the country was far from the terrorist hotbed many worry it has now become. In 2006, there was a narrow window of opportunity to peel off the moderate Islamists from the likes of the Shabab, and some U.S. officials, such as Democratic Rep. Donald M. Payne, the chairman of the House subcommittee on Africa, were trying to do exactly that. Payne and others met with the moderate Islamists and encouraged them to negotiate a powersharing deal with the transitional government.

But the Bush administration again reached for the gunpowder. The United States would not do much of the fighting itself, since sending large numbers of ground troops into Somalia with Iraq and Afghanistan raging would have been deemed insane. Instead, the United States anointed a proxy: the Ethiopian Army. This move would be Strike Three.

Ethiopia is one of the United States' best friends in Africa, its government having carefully cultivated an image as a Christian bulwark in a region seething with Islamist extremism. The Ethiopian leadership savvily told the Bush administration what it wanted to hear: The Islamists were terrorists and, unchecked, they would threaten the entire region and maybe even attack American safarigoers in Kenya next door.

Of course, the Ethiopians had their own agenda. Ethiopia is a country with a mostly Christian leadership but a population that is nearly half Muslim. It seems only a matter of time before there is an Islamic awakening in Ethiopia. On top of that, the Ethiopian government is fighting several rebel groups, including a powerful one that is ethnically Somali. The government feared that an Islamist Somalia could become a rebel beachhead next door. The Ethiopians were also scared that Somalia's Islamists would team up with Eritrea, Ethiopia's archenemy, which is exactly what ended up happening.

Not everyone in Washington swallowed the Ethiopian line. The country has a horrendous human rights record, and the Ethiopian military (which receives aid for human rights training from the United States) is widely accused of brutalizing its own people. But in December 2006, the Bush administration shared prized intelligence with the Ethiopians and gave them the green light to invade Somalia. Thousands of Ethiopian troops rolled across the border (many had secretly been in the country for months), and they routed the Islamist troops within a week. There were even some U.S. Special Forces with the Ethiopian units. The United States also launched several airstrikes in an attempt to take out Islamist leaders, and it continued with intermittent cruise missiles targeting suspected terrorists. Most have failed, killing civilians and adding to the boiling anti-American sentiment.

The Islamists went underground, and the transitional government arrived in Mogadishu. There was some cheering, a lot of jeering, and the insurgency revved up within days. The transitional government was widely reviled as a coterie of ex-warlords, which it mostly was. It was the 14th attempt since 1991 to stand up a central government. None of the previous attempts had worked. True, some detractors have simply been war profiteers hell-bent on derailing any government. But a lot of blame falls on what this transitional government has done—or not done. From the start, leaders seemed much more interested in who got what post than living up to the corresponding job descriptions. The government quickly lost the support of key clans in Mogadishu by its harsh (and unsuccessful) tactics in trying to wipe out the insurgents, and by its reliance on Ethiopian troops. Ethiopia and Somalia have fought several wars against each other over the contested Ogaden region that Ethiopia now claims. That region is mostly ethnically Somali, so teaming up with Ethiopia was seen as tantamount to treason.

The Islamists tapped into this sentiment, positioning themselves as the true Somali nationalists, and gaining widespread support again. The results were intense street battles between Islamist insurgents and Ethiopian troops in which thousands of civilians have been killed. Ethiopian forces have indiscriminately shelled entire neighborhoods (which precipitated a European Union investigation into war crimes), and have even used white phosphorous bombs that literally melt people, according to the United Nations. Hundreds of thousands of people have emptied out of Mogadishu and settled in camps that have become breeding grounds for disease and resentment. Death comes more frequently and randomly than ever before. I met one man in Mogadishu who was chatting with his wife on her cellphone when she was cut in half by a stray mortar shell. Another man I spoke to went out for a walk, got shot in the leg during a crossfire, and had to spend seven days eating grass before the fighting ended and he could crawl away.

Death comes more frequently and randomly than ever before. I met one man in Mogadishu who was chatting with his wife on her cellphone when she was cut in half by a stray mortar shell.

It's incredibly dangerous for us journalists, too. Few foreign journalists travel to Somalia anymore. Kidnapping is the threat du jour. Friends of mine who work for the United Nations in Kenya told me I had about a 100 percent chance of being stuffed into the back of a Toyota or shot (or both) if I didn't hire a private militia. Nowadays, as soon as I land, I take 10 gunmen under my employ.

By late January, the only territory the transitional government controlled was a shrinking federal enclave in Mogadishu guarded by a small contingent of African Union peacekeepers. As soon as the Ethiopians pulled out of the capital vicious fighting broke out between the various Islamist factions scrambling to fill the power gap. It took only days for the Islamists to recapture the third-largest town, Baidoa, from the government and install sharia law. The Shabab are not wildly popular, but they are formidable; for the time being they have a motivated, disciplined militia with hundreds of hard-core fighters and probably thousands of gunmen allied with them. The violence has shown no signs of halting, even with the election of a new, moderate Islamist president—one who had, ironically, been a leader of the Islamic Courts Union in 2006.

If the Shabab do seize control of the country, they might not stop there. They could send their battle-hardened fighters in battered four-wheel-drive pickup trucks into Ethiopia, Kenya, and maybe even Djibouti to try to snatch back the Somali-speaking parts of those countries. This scenario has long been part of an ethereal pan-Somali dream. Pursuit of that goal would internationalize the conflict and surely drag in neighboring countries and their allies.

The Shabab could also wage an asymmetric war, unleashing terrorists on Somalia's secular neighbors and their secular backers—most prominently, the United States. This would upend an already combustible dynamic in the Horn of Africa, catalyzing other conflicts. For instance, Ethiopia and Eritrea fought a nasty border war in the late 1990s, which killed as many as 100,000 people, and both countries are still heavily militarized along the border. If the Shabab, which boasts Eritrean support, took over Somalia, we might indeed see round two of Ethiopia versus Eritrea. The worst-case scenario could mean millions of people displaced across the entire region, crippled food production, and violence-induced breaches in the aid pipeline. In short, a famine in one of the most perennially needy parts of the world—again.

The hardest challenge of all might be simply preventing the worst-case scenario. Among the best suggestions I've heard is to play to Somalia's strengths as a fluid, decentralized society with local mechanisms to resolve conflicts. The foundation of order would be clan-based governments in villages, towns, and neighborhoods. These tiny fiefdoms could stack together to form district and regional governments. The last step would be uniting the regional governments in a loose national federation that coordinated, say, currency issues or antipiracy efforts, but did not sideline local leaders.

Western powers should do whatever they can to bring moderate Islamists into the transitional government while the transitional government still exists. Whether people like it or not, many Somalis see Islamic law as the answer. Maybe they're not fond of the harsh form imposed by the Shabab, who have, on at least one occasion, stoned to death a teenage girl who had been raped (an Islamic court found her guilty of adultery). Still, there is an appetite for a certain degree of Islamic governance. That desire should not be confused with support for terrorism.

A more radical idea is to have the United Nations take over the government and administer Somalia with an East Timor-style mandate. Because Somalia has already been an independent country, this option might be too much for Somalis to stomach. To make it work, the United Nations would need to delegate authority to clan leaders who have measurable clout on the ground. Either way, the diplomats should be working with the moneylords more and the warlords less.

But the problem with Somalia is that after 18 years of chaos, with so many people killed, with so many guntoting men rising up and then getting cut down, it is exceedingly difficult to identify who the country's real leaders are, if they exist at all. It's not just Mogadishu's wasteland of blown-up buildings that must be reconstructed; it's the entire national psyche. The whole country is suffering from an acute case of post-traumatic stress disorder. Somalis will have to move beyond the narrow interests of clans, where they have withdrawn for protection, and embrace the idea of a Somali nation.

If that happens, the work will just be beginning. Nearly an entire generation of Somalis has absolutely no idea what a government is or how it functions. I've seen this glassy-eyed generation all across the country, lounging on bullet-pocked street corners and spaced out in the back of pickup trucks, Kalashnikovs in their hands and nowhere to go. To them, law and order are thoroughly abstract concepts. To them, the only law in the land is the business end of a machine gun.

Assess Your Progress

1. What is the most dangerous place in the world?
2. Why does it have this reputation?
3. How does the ongoing chaos affect neighboring states?
4. What effect has U.S. involvement had on the conflict?
5. What are some suggested responses to this situation?

Jeffrey Gettleman is East Africa bureau chief for the *New York Times*.

Article 23

Africa's New Horror

J. Peter Pham

Think the only Sudan crisis is in Darfur, or that the horror there is winding down? You're wrong.

There's a new Sudan calamity in the making, and it may well come in 2010 with a unilateral declaration of independence by the enclave of South Sudan. If it does, the resulting conflict stands to be more painful, militarized, and devastating than Sudan has ever known. Imagine Darfur with a lot more guns, not to mention Chinese fighter jets.

The clock for this latest crisis started ticking ominously in 2005. A North-South civil war that left some 2 million dead and millions more displaced had finally ended. But that year's Comprehensive Peace Agreement pushed the touchiest issue of all—the independence of the South, a France-sized area of just under 10 million people that won its autonomy in that 2005 deal—six years into the future. The clock runs out in January 2011, but the crisis will likely come sooner.

Unfortunately, the "comprehensive strategy" on Sudan unveiled by U.S. President Barack Obama's administration in October depends almost entirely on the deluded notion that implementation of the 2005 peace agreement will go as planned. Obama's team said it hopes South Sudan's likely secession will be an "orderly transition to two separate and viable states at peace with each other."

But this is Sudan we're talking about, not Belgium. The actual scenario—if Sudan's recent history is any guide—is likely to be anything but orderly. A national census slated to happen before July 2007 was repeatedly delayed until finally taking place amid violence and gaping errors. Nonetheless, Khartoum has insisted that the count's doctored results be used to draw up parliamentary districts that favor the North. Voter registration, which also depends on the flawed census data, has just barely begun. So any expectation that April's general elections, a key test ahead of the January 2011 deadline, will be legitimate is surreal at best. The vote is likely to be marred by bloodshed, as most of the contenders will either be backed or opposed—and usually both—by heavily armed groups.

If the elections proceed but their results lack legitimacy, South Sudan's rulers will be under tremendous public pressure to unilaterally declare independence without a referendum. After all, the outcome of such a vote is not in doubt; you would be hard-pressed to find many southerners who prefer to remain under Khartoum's thumb.

There's also a tactical reason why South Sudan might go for broke: The North is acquiring an insuperable military advantage, and Khartoum is unlikely to relinquish its hold on the oil-rich South without a fight. In fact, for the last decade, Khartoum has been busy using revenue from that same oil to modernize its armed forces in preparation for conflict. In Darfur, the northern regime has used its primitive air force to deadly effect. When the Shenyang J-8 and Chengdu F-7 supersonic fighter-bombers recently acquired from China, the largest customer for Sudanese oil, are put to use, the results will be devastating. Chinese companies have also helped establish at least three weapons factories outside the Sudanese capital, including one that manufactures ammunition, effectively immunizing the regime against the effects of any future arms embargo.

Even if the South moves to secede before Khartoum's military might grows, the ensuing conflict will be messy. Skirmishes along the North-South border left at least 2,000 people dead and more than 250,000 displaced in 2009. The South's coming declaration of independence will undoubtedly provoke not only large-scale violence in the country formerly known as Sudan, but also the destabilization of the entire region as neighboring countries find themselves drawn in. Will Obama let it happen on his watch?

Assess Your Progress

1. What new crisis does Sudan face?
2. Why do prospects for a successful independence referendum seem bleak?
3. How might a new crisis in Sudan affect regional stability?

J. Peter Pham is senior fellow and Africa Project director at the National Committee on American Foreign Policy.

Reprinted in entirety by McGraw-Hill with permission from *Foreign Policy*, January/February 2010, p. 68. www.foreignpolicy.com.

Behind Iran's Crackdown, an Economic Coup

A dramatic shift of economic power has taken place—away from traditional private sector groupings and toward select religious foundations and Revolutionary Guards entities.

FARIBORZ GHADAR

Iran's election fraud last June, the civil unrest that followed, and the regime's continuing crackdown against dissenters have their roots in the country's poor economic condition. They are also rooted in efforts by President Mahmoud Ahmadinejad and his allies in the Islamic Revolutionary Guards Corps to grab control over large swaths of the economy. Although the government has subdued street demonstrations by brute force—including violent clashes in Tehran and elsewhere in November—the underlying economic problems and factional rivalries remain, and the flames of discontent may well flare up again soon.

Iran's economy is dominated by oil exports and the public sector. In 2008, oil accounted for 50 percent to 70 percent of government revenues and 80 percent of export earnings. The public sector (that is, activities directed or centrally controlled by the government) constitutes an estimated 60 percent of Iran's economy. Historically, the private sector—dominated by the merchant class in the bazaar—has handled most supply chain–related matters in the economy. This includes warehousing, distribution, sales, financing, and the management of logistics related to both imports and local production. Many agricultural producers and light industries have also relied on the bazaar to handle their logistical and financial requirements.

In recent decades, however, elements in the government have increasingly undermined the role of the private sector and the bazaar. One major change since the 1979 Islamic Revolution has been the expanding role of religious foundations, or *bonyads.* Their combined budgets are said to equal half the government sector's budget. Much of the funding for the bonyads originates with the state, via assets and businesses that the bonyads have been authorized to manage, or in the form of direct government subsidies. The bonyads are actively involved in the transportation and distribution sectors; before the revolution, these logistical activities traditionally fell within the bazaar's economic sphere.

More recently, the private sector and the bazaar have been further undermined by the imposition of stricter international sanctions in response to the Iranian government's nuclear activities—and also by administrative and price controls, smuggling, contraband, and widespread corruption, along with other rigidities in the economy. Much of the smuggling and contraband are controlled by the Revolutionary Guards, and this is a trend that has accelerated since Ahmadinejad assumed the presidency in 2005.

In addition, the regime has awarded numerous large contracts—for example, for a major gas pipeline to the Pakistani border, for the South Pars natural gas field, and for an expansion of the Tehran metro transportation system—to members of the Revolutionary Guards and their companies. The Revolutionary Guards, of which Ahmadinejad was once a member, form a large branch of the Iranian military. They are believed to number as many as 120,000. They control a paramilitary militia, the Basij. And in recent years they have built a sprawling business empire.

In essence, a dramatic shift of economic power has taken place—away from traditional private sector groupings and toward select religious foundations and Revolutionary Guards entities. To be sure, the bazaar remains a major force in Iran's economic landscape. This was plainly evident in October 2008, when the regime made too obvious an effort to reduce the role of the bazaar by imposing a value-added tax. The government's action met with stiff resistance, violent protest, and the closing of markets, which brought the national economy to a standstill. Officials quickly rescinded the value-added tax. Still, the Ahmadinejad administration continues in other ways to shift economic power toward the Revolutionary Guards and other friends of the regime.

At the same time, the government has massively mismanaged the economy, thereby creating high inflation and unemployment. It is important to understand that the protests in the streets of Tehran and other Iranian cities in the summer and fall of 2009 had as much to do with economic mismanagement as with election improprieties.

Losing at Monopoly

Petroleum is a key factor in assessing the Iranian economy. Oil production before the Islamic Revolution hovered around 5 million to 6 million barrels a day, of which 5 million were exported. Strikes, civil unrest, and a loss of technical and managerial experts (both domestic and foreign) reduced oil production to about 3.3 million barrels in 1979. Oil production in 1980 further declined—to less than 1.5 million barrels per day—because of continued technical difficulties and the beginning of the Iran-Iraq War. Production gradually increased to a level of 4 million barrels a day by 2008.

In the meantime, however, domestic consumption has risen rapidly, and crude exports have declined gradually to between 2 million and 2.5 million barrels a day. Thus, since the Islamic Revolution, the volume of oil exports has declined by more than 50 percent while the population has doubled. This year's street protests had no appreciable impact on oil production. However, given the reduced exports and increased local consumption, a protest strike aimed at the oil and gas sector would have a much more crippling effect on the economy than did strikes during the Islamic Revolution in 1979.

Iran's natural gas production has increased rapidly since 1979, but it primarily serves the domestic market. The country exports some natural gas to Turkey and it imports some from Turkmenistan. However, because the prices that Turkey pays are below the prices that Iran pays to Turkmenistan, the gas sector may in fact be a foreign exchange drain on Iran's economy. Gas exports, because of sanctions and US policy, have not risen. The Nabucco gas pipeline, planned for construction through Turkey, has been delayed. An Iran-Pakistan-India pipeline is unlikely to be constructed in the near future. And Iran lacks the necessary technologies to embark on a significant liquefied natural gas operation, thus further limiting its export capacity.

Despite these difficulties, the growth rate for Iran's gross domestic product (GDP) has ranged between 4.5 percent and 7.8 percent in recent years. This has much to do with the rising price of crude oil. In fact, 2008 was a record year for revenue generated by oil exports. As oil prices hit a record $147 per barrel, Iran managed to generate an estimated $85 billion in oil exports.

And yet, in spite of this massive increase in oil revenue, GDP growth declined sharply to 4.5 percent in 2008 from 7.8 percent in 2007. This was Iran's lowest growth rate in the past few years, and it is directly related to the economic mismanagement that has spawned rising subsidies and the monopolistic nature of much of the industrial economy (increasingly under the control of the Revolutionary Guards and preferred bonyads).

The result has been rising inflation. Housing prices in Tehran, for instance, quadrupled from 2004 to 2008. Last year the inflation rate soared to 26 percent, according to central bank figures. The rate this year may have dropped to 15 percent because of a decline in oil prices and a downturn in the global economy, but that number is still very high.

Meanwhile, the government's excessive subsidies and handouts have made Iran dependent on agricultural imports. Wheat imports rose from near zero years ago to more than 6 million tons in 2008. The growth rate in manufacturing and agricultural value-added has also declined from 2002 levels. And low levels of investment by the private sector, along with a surge in the number of young people, have brought about high unemployment.

Armies of the Jobless

Iran's official jobless rate is in the teens, but given the very large portion of the population that is in the 15- to 30-year-old range, it is very likely that true unemployment hovers at about twice the official rate. I estimate it to be above 30 percent. (There are 25 million Iranians employed, of whom a third are women. The working-age population is estimated at 45 to 50 million. Therefore, even assuming that all women who want jobs are employed, the unemployment rate is about 30 percent.)

The government's current statement of economic policy—the Fourth Development Plan—calls for the creation of 700,000 jobs per year. This goal is unlikely to be achieved. In any case, given Iran's population growth, an estimated 1 million jobs must be created each year to prevent unemployment from rising.

Some of us will remember the "misery index"—the sum of the unemployment and inflation rates—which was widely discussed during the Carter/Reagan era in the United States. The US misery index of that time, at its worst, was around 25 percent; today the number is about 13 percent. Those numbers pale against Iran's misery index, which ranges between 40 percent and 50 percent.

Thus we should not be surprised that, despite threats, intimidation, and beatings, many citizens have been willing to demonstrate in the streets of Iran's cities. The general public has seen its purchasing power decline even as members of the Basij and Revolutionary Guards benefit from subsidies and government-awarded business opportunities.

Defending the Revolution

Indeed, this may help explain why the Revolutionary Guards and Basij were so ruthless in handling the demonstrations that followed the June presidential election—in which widespread fraud helped secure Ahmadinejad's reelection—and the protests that broke out in early November. The Revolutionary Guards and the militiamen on motorcycles were not just protecting the Islamic revolution. They were protecting their incomes and economic position, as Ahmadinejad's tenure in office has seen rapid growth in the economic power of the paramilitary groups (both the Revolutionary Guards and the Basij).

Major General Muhammad Ali Jafari, the commander of the elite military branch of the Revolutionary Guards, has suggested that his group's suppression of the protests gives it a new, more central role in the country: "Because the Revolutionary Guards were assigned the task of controlling the situation, [they] took the initiative to quell a spiraling unrest. This event pushed [the Guards] into a new phase of the revolution and political struggles and we have to understand all its dimensions."

Iran's other hard-line forces have also been emboldened. Ahmadinejad's spiritual guide, Ayatollah Mohammad Yazdi, has said that "elected institutions are anathema to a religious government and should be no more than window dressing." However, in the face of lower oil revenues, if the Ahmadinejad administration, the Basij, and the Revolutionary Guards continue to feed at the trough without consideration for the general public, unrest will almost certainly return and accelerate.

The Ticking Bomb

Many of the "old guard" leadership associated with traditional business interests and the bazaar view this trend with serious concern. At the same time, many influential religious leaders have kept silent or offered only faint criticism of Ahmadinejad's election. It is clear to them that the regime and its allies are seriously challenging the role of traditional political leaders vis-à-vis business activities.

The past year has witnessed the escalation of a power struggle in Iran's political elite, a struggle that pits the old guard—led by two former presidents, Ali Akbar Hashemi Rafsanjani and Mohammad Khatami; a prominent cleric, Mehdi Karroubi; and Ahmadinejad's principal opponent in the election, Mir Hussein Moussavi—against Ahmadinejad, Yazdi, Ayatollah Ahmad Jannati, and the Revolutionary Guards.

The decision by Iran's supreme leader, Ayatollah Ali Khamenei, to back the latter group causes one to wonder if he has already lost control to the Revolutionary Guards and the conservative clerics who support them, or if he is simply in their camp. Leaders of the old guard understand that another four years of Ahmadinejad and his pro–Revolutionary Guard policies will diminish their own role to such an extent that they will in fact be at risk of losing their livelihoods and even their lives.

The question thus posed is whether a compromise between the two factions is possible. Can such disparate forces reach an understanding? What sort of compromise would make the faction of reformist, bazaar-connected, moderate clerics trust the faction of Ahmadinejad, the Revolutionary Guards, Yazdi, and Khamenei? Yet, if no compromise is achieved, Iran's economic time bomb will continue to tick.

Iran could evolve into a dictatorship of paramilitary thugs and oligarchs controlling a corrupt and monopolistic system.

Time is running short. If Ahmadinejad and the Revolutionary Guards are not reined in, Iran's economic and political structure could evolve into a dictatorship of paramilitary thugs and oligarchs controlling a monopolistic and corrupt system. Would that be acceptable to the majority of Iranians, rising numbers of whom will lack employment?

Assess Your Progress

1. What are the roots of Iran's unrest?
2. What economic shifts have occurred in recent decades?
3. Describe Iran's trends in oil and gas production.
4. How have inflation and unemployment contributed to the unrest? What has been the government's response?
5. The current circumstances pits what two political factions against one another?

Fariborz Ghadar, a senior scholar at the Center for Strategic and International Studies, is a professor at Pennsylvania State University and the founding director of its Center for Global Business Studies.

Mexico's Drug Wars Get Brutal

Given the rising tide of violence and the mounting evidence of drug-related corruption at all levels of government, it is probably fair to say that, so far, the cartels have managed to take the lead in a psychological war against the Mexican state.

FRANCISCO E. GONZÁLEZ

Narco-violence has intensified in Mexico since the early 2000s as a consequence of the Mexican government's crackdown on drug cartels. The spiral of violence has included shootouts on the public squares of big cities in broad daylight. A grenade attack on September 15, 2008, left eight dead and more than one hundred injured on the central square in Morelia (the capital of the state of Michoacán), on a night Mexicans were celebrating the 198th anniversary of their country's independence. The mayhem has included a proliferation of mass executions discovered on isolated ranches in remote areas, as well as in homes in crowded neighborhoods of cities as different and distant as Tijuana, on the border with California, and Mérida, on the Yucatán peninsula.

For most Mexicans, rich and poor, a psychological leap into a state of generalized fear and a perception of acute vulnerability coincided with an increase in gruesome displays of barbarism since the spring of 2006. These acts have included public displays of battered human heads, some thrown into plazas or placed on car rooftops, some thrown outside schools; mutilated torsos hanging from meat hooks; threats and taunts to rival cartels written on walls with the blood of butchered adversaries; and video-postings of torture and beheadings on YouTube.

How did Mexico spiral into this horrific wave of violence? The export of illegal substances to the United States became big business during the Prohibition years (1917–1933), but the seeds for the long-term growth and astounding profitability of the Mexico-US illegal drug trade were sown much earlier. Opiates (morphine and heroin) became a growing business in the United States in the wake of the American Civil War (1861–1865) and the two world wars (1914–1918 and 1939–1945). Since the nineteenth century, farmers in northwest Mexico had grown the opium poppies that satisfied part of this demand.

Mexico also became one of the ports of entry for cocaine. It was sold commercially and developed a mass market in the United States in the 1880s as a cure-all for everything from discolored teeth to flatulence. Smugglers from the Andean countries and their US networks used Mexico and the Caribbean as gateways to supply the illegal market that served Hollywood's and New York's glamorous sets in the 1950s and 1960s. Cocaine remained a luxury item that only the well-to-do could afford until the early 1980s, when crack cocaine invaded the streets of America's large cities, wreaking havoc particularly in poor African-American and Hispanic neighborhoods.

Mexican seasonal migrant workers in the 1920s introduced to Americans the smoking of cannabis leaves. A mass market for cannabis consumption did not develop, however, until the rise of the counterculture of the 1960s and 1970s. Lastly, a mass market for synthetic drugs such as methamphetamines developed in the 1990s in the United States, and Mexican drug cartels became dominant suppliers of these too.

For decades Mexico and the United States have pursued very different antidrug strategies. The United States launched the original "war on drugs" under President Richard Nixon in the early 1970s. This policy contained both domestic and very prominent international components, explicitly targeting Mexico as a key site for the eradication of opium crops and marijuana, as well as the Andean countries for the eradication of coca. Successive Mexican governments, on the other hand, pursued what analysts have dubbed a "live and let live" approach. This system, characterized by a working relationship between some Mexican authorities and drug lords, prevailed between the 1940s and the 1990s.

This does not mean that Mexican presidents or most high-ranking bureaucrats, governors, and military high commanders were involved in the illegal drug trade. It does mean, however, that given Mexico's complex and fragmented territorial politics, the country's governors, mayors, military officers, and police chiefs retained some autonomy to advance their interests and those of their allies, including drug traffickers.

The kingpins bought access to the Mexico-US border, and this access allowed them to expand their production and smuggling activities. The authorities in turn stuffed their pockets with cash— but also, crucially, kept relative public peace and a semblance of law and order through the containment (rather than the destruction) of drug syndicates. Direct confrontation meant risking public disorder and violence, and indeed whenever authorities went after traffickers, bloody shootouts ensued. But such confrontations were the exceptions rather than the rule. For those involved on both sides of the game, mutually understood rules and practices prevailed. Authorities did not tolerate open turf wars among competing cartels, and they prohibited them from harming innocent civilians through extortion, kidnappings, or assassinations.

Rising Violence

Mexican authorities came under increased pressure from the United States to clamp down on drug cartels after the 1985 murder of an American Drug Enforcement Administration (DEA) officer. Enrique Camarena, a DEA agent working under-cover in Mexico, had exposed big ranches in the state of Chihuahua where traffickers cultivated cannabis with the full knowledge of some federal authorities, military officers, and state and local officials. The traffickers captured and killed Camarena, and the discovery of his tortured, decomposing body created a furor in US public opinion. Footdragging by the authorities investigating the case convinced Americans that highly placed individuals in the government of President Miguel de la Madrid were involved with the traffickers.

By the time a new president, Carlos Salinas, expressed eagerness to join the United States in a free trade agreement in 1989, the Mexican government had to show that it was doing all it could to clean house. Salinas allowed DEA agents to return to work in Mexico and his government spent resources strengthening military and police operations against traffickers. In parallel, changes enacted under the administration of George H.W. Bush altered the long-standing equilibrium of the Mexico-US illegal drug trade. In 1989–90, Washington committed large-scale material resources, military training, and intelligence to try to bust the Andean cocaine trade. After years of engagement, the United States contributed to the demise of Colombia's main syndicates, the Medellín and Cali cartels, and to largely shutting down the Caribbean–Gulf of Mexico cocaine route. By the late 1990s, the battle lines had been redrawn and Mexico had ended up in the eye of the storm.

The demise of the Colombian cartels allowed the Mexican syndicates, which formerly had worked for the Colombians, to take over. The virtual closure of the Caribbean route strengthened the Central America–Mexico route by land and the Pacific Ocean route toward Mexico's western coast. Despite official efforts by Salinas's successor, President Ernesto Zedillo, drug traffic increased in the late 1990s and some Mexican authorities continued to be on the drug lords' payroll. The most embarrassing instance was revealed in 1997, when Zedillo's drug czar, General Jesús Gutiérrez Rebollo, was exposed as a beneficiary of the top leader of the Juárez cartel. The confluence of higher spending by Mexican governments to combat drug trafficking and higher illegal drug flows through the country's territory set the stage for a serious increase in narco-violence in the late 1990s.

This increase in drug-related violence coincided in 2000 with the loss of the presidency by the Institutional Revolutionary Party (PRI) for the first time in Mexico's history. Vicente Fox, of the center-right National Action Party (PAN), assumed the presidency promising many changes, among them the defeat of the drug cartels. Some analysts think that even before Fox became president, PAN governments at the state and local levels in the early 1990s had pursued a more principled approach to combating drug trafficking, which had resulted in higher levels of drug-related violence in border states such as Baja California and Chihuahua. Fox purged and reorganized the federal police forces and tried to extradite captured drug lords to the United States.

This policy, though effective at raising the number of individuals arrested and drug shipments confiscated, fell far short of the government's objective of defeating the cartels. Moreover, the capture of some cartel leaders was tantamount to kicking hornets' nests without having the means to spray the rattled insects. The capture of Benjamín Arellano Félix, head of the Tijuana cartel, in 2002, and of Osiél Cárdenas Guillén, head of the Gulf cartel, in 2003, led to a vicious war within and among the criminal organizations, as upcoming drug leaders battled to assert or reassert control over territory, resources, and manpower. The change in the balance of power among the cartels led to new alliances. The Gulf, Tijuana, and Juárez cartels struck deals to take on another bloc made up of the Sinaloa, Milenio, Jalisco, and Colima cartels.

Likewise, the reorganized police forces soon succumbed to the bribes and threats of the criminal syndicates. Government infiltration continued to such an extent that a spy for a drug cartel was discovered working in the president's office in 2005. Violence had gotten so out of control by 2004–05 that Fox implemented an operation involving 1,500 army and federal police officers in Mexico-US border cities. In this context, the conflict intensified and started mutating into the bloody spectacle that Mexicans witness today.

Calderón's War

Felipe Calderón, also from the PAN, took over the presidency from Fox on December 1, 2006. Calderón won a fiercely contested and extremely close election against the candidate of the center-left Party of the Democratic Revolution (PRD), Andrés Manuel López Obrador. Throughout the campaign, public opinion surveys had shown that Mexican citizens' top concerns were lack of economic opportunities, and crime and general insecurity. Shortly after assuming office, Calderón declared a war on drugs by deploying the Mexican military in a series of large-scale operations that by the end of 2008 had involved close to 40,000 troops and 5,000 federal police.

The decision to bring the armed forces into the fray was controversial, and observers disagreed about the reasons the president raised the stakes in this way, investing his political capital in the war on drugs. During the presidential campaign Calderón had not hinted that this policy would come to define his government.

Some analysts highlighted a political explanation, according to which weak incoming presidents in contemporary Mexico have to carry out spectacular acts early on to establish their authority, boost their standing with the public, and help gain some autonomy over groups within the Mexican political class that try to limit their scope of action. From this perspective, Calderón may have ordered the military surge against the drug cartels to "turn the page" on the then- raging postelectoral conflict with the PRD candidate. Given the contentious electoral results, López Obrador had declared himself the "legitimate" president. Calderón's decisive action showed in effect who was the real commander-in-chief.

Other analysts have argued that the political explanation sounds like a conspiracy theory. The main reason behind the military surge, they suggest, was the incoming adminstration's realization that the cartels were dominating more territory and public spaces and that if this process were left unchecked, it could lead to a situation of state failure similar to the one that Colombia had to endure. Also, according to this view, a war on drugs had existed in all but name during Fox's term. Given the ineffectiveness of police forces in combating the syndicates, Calderón was left without any option but to involve the military.

In fact these two explanations are not mutually exclusive. Calderón might have decided to pursue a war on drugs given, first, genuine concern regarding the uncontrolled violence in parts of the country, including his home state of Michoacán; and, second, his wish to make the armed forces key allies in the context of the postelectoral conflict with López Obrador and the PRD. Regardless of the mix of motivations for launching the surge against traffickers, in the short term Calderón has reaped higher political than operational benefits. Opinion polls show that a majority of the Mexican public supports the president's stance against the cartels. By mid-2007, the postelectoral conflict and López Obrador's continuing maneuvers to discredit Calderón had disappeared from the headlines. But dominating the news instead has been a brutal intensification of drug-related violence.

The Corruption Conundrum

Operationally, Calderón's war against drugs has already resulted in the arrests of more than a dozen top drug lords and record seizures of arms, cash, and drugs. Yet the campaign started as, and it remains, a steep uphill battle. The main conundrum is still the ineffectiveness of law enforcement in Mexico. Aside from questions of jurisdiction (Mexico's federal structure means that approximately 3,800 law enforcement institutions exist throughout the country), the root cause of the problem is the drug cartels' extensive penetration of government agencies and co-optation of government officials. This is a hurdle that is almost impossible to overcome without somehow depriving the drug lords of the astounding profits they currently make.

Indeed, the paradox of tougher enforcement is that, as the cost of doing business in the illegal drug trade rises, the street price of drugs goes up too, thereby raising profit margins. The result is that some drug traffickers and would-be traffickers may decide that pursuing this line of business is becoming prohibitively risky, but as long as profits from the trade remain so out of line compared with any other economic activity, there will always be individuals ready to risk their lives.

Studies of drug gang members in cities like Chicago have shown that only the "top dogs" make stratospheric profits, while most of the rank and file make so little that they have second and third jobs, while still living with their mothers! Yet, no matter how low the probability of making it to the top, individuals will take a chance on the dangers of the drug trade if their social conditions are precarious enough and their opportunities for advancement are negligible. And it goes without saying that conditions of hopelessness and extreme life choices abound in developing countries such as Mexico. As long as these conditions persist, and as long as the system put in place to counter the narcotics trade leads to the generation of exceptional profits, there will continue to be individuals willing to play this lottery.

The generation of exceptional profits, moreover, also provides the plentiful cash that drug lords use to buy into the system. Only now are we realizing the extent to which top Mexican authorities are in the pay of the drug lords. Since at least the Camarena affair, and probably for much longer, Mexicans had assumed that the cartels had bought off some among the political elite. But never before have so many top ranking law enforcers been exposed as under Calderón. They have been exposed at the local, state, and federal levels, and have ranged from the lowliest privates among the ranks to the head of Mexico's Interpol office and the federal government's drug czar.

Only now are we realizing the extent to which top Mexican authorities are in the pay of the drug lords.

Even though many officials might refuse to collaborate with the drug cartels irrespective of the pecuniary gains on offer, the criminal syndicates also compel cooperation by issuing threats and sometimes carrying them out. The assassination in May 2008 of Edgar Millán Gómez, the acting chief of Mexico's federal police, allegedly in retribution for the arrest in January of one of the top leaders of the Sinaloa cartel, increased the sense of vulnerability even for those who go about their daily lives surrounded by bodyguards.

Fate did not help the government's cause when a small jet carrying Mexico's top law enforcement officials—including the interior secretary and Calderón's closest political ally, Juan Camilo Mouriño, as well as the country's antidrug prosecutor, José Luis Santiago Vasconcelos—crashed in downtown Mexico City on November 4, 2008, killing all on board. Even though official evidence has suggested that turbulence caused the accident, conspiracy theories have spread around Mexico, fueling the sense that the government has suffered another blow, this time at its core.

In the two years since the start of Calderón's war on drugs, the government has raised the stakes for the cartels by hitting them with full military force. The cartels have responded with an intensification of both their turf wars and their war against the

Mexican state. As a result, drug-related violence has spread from states where it has been endemic for years into states that had not seen drug-related violence before. The number of dead almost doubled in just one year—from 2,700 in 2007 to more than 5,300 in 2008. Given the rising tide of violence and the mounting evidence of drug-related corruption at all levels of government, it is probably fair to say that, so far, the cartels have managed to take the lead in a psychological war against the Mexican state.

I noted earlier that Calderón's drug war has yielded higher short-term political than operational benefits. However, some political implications of the war could have a big impact on the operational capacity for waging it. The most important of these political implications has been Calderón's ability to get the US government to accept that the war on drugs is a matter of co-responsibility. In effect, Calderón has managed to bring the United States into the eye of the storm.

Calderón has managed to bring the United States into the eye of the storm.

Washington Lends a Hand

Colombia receives the lion's share of US anti-narcotics aid in Latin America—this has been the case for several decades. But Calderón's declaration of a war on drugs in Mexico got the attention of President George W. Bush and the US Congress in 2007. As a result, a $1.4 billion, three-year program, the Mérida Initiative, started operating in December 2008. The aim is to assist the Mexican government wage the war against drugs by helping it with technology and training.

There is no doubt that, in the case of Colombia, the agreement between Presidents Andrés Pastrana and Bill Clinton, which led to the creation of Plan Colombia in 2000, has proved a game changer. In the late 1990s, analysts and policy makers talked about Colombia as a potential failed state. Although the US Government Accountability Office has shown that Plan Colombia has not been a great success in terms of curbing the production of coca and the transportation of cocaine, it has undoubtedly strengthened the Colombian state and its capacity to strike against non-state actors, notably guerrillas and paramilitary groups. Colombia, which until recently possessed an underdeveloped military, has come a long way in eight years, and the central government's presence around the country's territory is stronger than ever.

These benefits have been very costly in some regards. Aerial fumigation to eradicate coca plants has damaged legal crops and produced adverse health effects in those exposed to the herbicides. The number of dead and displaced as a result of the intensification of the conflict since the early 2000s has grown enormously. News of extensive human rights violations has made headlines around the world. And yet, the plan's contribution to strengthening the state—and thereby to reestablishing a still precarious but nonetheless basic sense of security for many Colombians, particularly in big cities—has meant that a substantial majority of that country's public favors the continuation of President Alvaro Uribe's policies, and of Colombia's cooperation with the United States.

What then for Mexico? There is danger in carrying the Colombia-Mexico analogy too far. After all, the United States does not share a border with Colombia, let alone a 2,000-mile one as it does with Mexico. For Mexico, the danger of an escalating war on drugs, with the United States helping to strengthen Mexican authorities' firepower, is that some of the extreme conditions created in Colombia since 2000 could be repeated. For the United States, the danger from such an escalation is potentially far greater than in its engagement with Colombia. An escalation of the war on drugs in Mexico could spill over into US territory. Indeed, an April 2008 report by the US National Drug Intelligence Center, part of the Department of Justice, found evidence of Mexican smuggling operations in all but two states (Vermont and West Virginia) of the union. Drug-related violence connected with the Mexican cartels has been increasingly reported in cities of the American southwest, from San Diego to Phoenix, Las Vegas, and Dallas.

Some analysts have gone so far as to start calling this a borderless war. This is no doubt an exaggeration. But there is also no doubt that unless US authorities can control the massive trafficking of weapons, cash, and chemical precursors of drugs that originate in the United States and are shipped into Mexico, America risks exposing its "soft underbelly," a term now often used to describe its southern border. As it is, some 90 percent of armaments confiscated from the cartels comes from the more than 7,000 gun outlets situated on US soil within 50 miles of the Mexican border.

The stakes for the United States in Mexico, thus, are much higher than they could ever be in Colombia. Supplying the Mexican government with technology and training to help prop up its fighting capabilities is an important first step, but it is not enough. Without seriously denting the demand for illegal drugs and preventing the southbound flow of weapons, cash, and drug-making chemicals, the United States will keep feeding the flames that threaten to consume the basis for civilized life in Mexico.

Assess Your Progress

1. What are the origins of Mexico's involvement in the drug trade?
2. Why has drug violence increased?
3. Why is tougher enforcement of drug laws a challenge?
4. What might the consequences be for Mexico and the United States of escalating the efforts against drug trafficking?

Francisco E. González is an associate professor of politics and Latin American studies at Johns Hopkins University's School of Advanced International Studies. He is the author of *Dual Transitions from Authoritarian Rule: Institutionalized Regimes in Chile and Mexico, 1970–2000* (Johns Hopkins University Press, 2008).

Call in the Blue Helmets

Peacekeeping: Can the UN cope with increasing demands for its soldiers?

Call it peacekeeping, peace-enforcement, stabilisation or anything else, but one thing is clear: the world's soldiers are busier than ever operating in the wide grey zone between war and peace.

The United Nations has seen a sixfold increase since 1998 in the number of soldiers and military observers it deploys around the world. About 74,000 military personnel (nearly 100,000 people including police and civilians, and increasing fast) are currently involved in 18 different operations—more than any country apart from the United States. And it is not just the UN that is in high demand. NATO, the European Union and the African Union (AU), as well as other coalitions of the willing, have some 74,000 soldiers trying to restore peace and stability in troubled countries. Added to their number come the more than 160,000 American, British and other troops in Iraq.

The "war on terror" is one cause of this military hyperactivity. But Jean-Marie Guéhenno, the UN's under-secretary for peacekeeping, also sees more hopeful reasons. The growing demand for blue helmets, he says, is a good sign that a number of conflicts are ending.

This is only partly true. In Congo, southern Sudan and Liberia—the UN's three biggest operations—the blue helmets are shoring up peace agreements. But in countries such as Lebanon or Côte d'Ivoire, they are at best holding the line between parties still in conflict.

One reason for the surge in UN peacekeeping is that Africa, the region most in need of peacekeepers, is least able to provide for itself. The AU is trying to improve its peacekeeping capacity, but is desperately short of resources. It has handed over its operation in Burundi to the UN. Now it wants the blue helmets to help relieve its 7,000 hard-pressed AU peacekeepers in Sudan's troubled region of Darfur.

The Sudanese government has long resisted such a deployment, accusing the UN of being an agent of the West. But under sustained international pressure to halt what Washington regards as genocide, it has grudgingly agreed to allow in a "hybrid" UN and AU force. An advance party of 24 police advisers and 43 military officers, wearing blue berets and AU armbands, has started to arrive in Darfur to test Sudan's co-operation. According to a three-phase plan, the force will be built up into a contingent of 17,000 soldiers and 3,000 police officers.

Can the UN take on another onerous peacekeeping operation? Mr Guéhenno says the world already faces two kinds of "overstretch": the military sort, in which many armed forces of many leading countries are badly strained by foreign operations; and "political overstretch", in which the world's political energies are focused on just a few acute problems while the UN is left to deal as best it can with many chronic or less visible conflicts.

Mr Guéhenno is cautious about what he can achieve in Darfur. He says he may get the soldiers, given the right political conditions, but is worried about getting enough "enablers"—the crucial specialised units and equipment that enhance the ability of a force to move and operate. These include army engineers and logisticians, field hospitals and nurses, heavy-lift aircraft and transport helicopters, as well as proper command-and-control and intelligence-gathering: in other words, the wherewithal of modern Western expeditionary forces. These capabilities are in short supply and are expensive; the few countries that have them are using them, and the others can't afford them.

In a region as vast as Darfur, an effective UN force would need to be highly mobile, and make use both of unmanned surveillance drones and special forces. It would need to sustain itself in a harsh environment, some 1,400km (870 miles) from the nearest harbour and with few airfields. Engineers could drill for water, but would be under pressure to share it with local populations and with refugees. And then there is the problem of time. On current plans it would take six to nine months to build up to full strength in Darfur. Having to merge with the AU adds further complications to the command structure.

Finding a Fire Engine

Apart from military capability, or lack of it, there is the question of political will. Who will risk their soldiers' lives, and their valuable military assets, in a faraway conflict? NATO, the world's foremost military alliance, has struggled for months to find a few thousand additional soldiers—and a few extra helicopters—to back up its troops fighting in southern Afghanistan.

By contrast, European countries moved with unusual speed when the UN appealed for its hapless mission in Lebanon to be reinforced last summer in order to end the war between Israel and Hizbullah. Within weeks of a ceasefire being called in August, French and Italian peacekeepers were coming ashore. It was the first time that sizeable Western forces had donned blue helmets since the unhappy days of the war in Bosnia.

But there were particular reasons for this. Lebanon, of course, is more easily accessible than Afghanistan or Darfur. But it is also less dangerous than southern Afghanistan, and European governments regard the Israeli-Arab conflict as much closer to their interests than the effort to pacify rebellious Pashtun tribesmen.

Kofi Annan, the former UN secretary-general, liked to say that the UN is the only fire brigade that must go out and buy a fire engine before it can respond to an emergency. The Security Council must first authorise an operation and pass a budget, and then the secretariat beseeches governments to contribute forces and arranges the means to transport them. This system has created a two-tier structure: powerful countries decide the missions (and pay for them)

Current UN Peacekeeping Missions

Location	Mission Name	Year of Deployment	Number of Personnel*
Congo	MONUC	1999	22,167
Liberia	UNMIL	2003	18,382
Southern Sudan	UNMIS	2005	13,021
Lebanon	UNIFIL	1978	11,431
Côte d'Ivoire	UNOCI	2004	11,150
Haiti	MINUSTAH	2004	3,142
Kosovo	UNMIK	1999	4,631
Burundi	ONUB	2004	3,142
Ethiopia and Eritrea	UNMEE	2000	2,687
Timor-Leste	UNMIT	2006	1,340
Golan Heights (Israel/Syria)	UNDOF	1974	1,247
Cyprus	UNFICYP	1964	1,069
Afghanistan[a]	UNAMA	2002	850
Western Sahara	MINURSO	1991	459
Georgia	UNOMIG	1993	419
Middle East[b]	UNTSO	1948	374
Sierra Leone[a]	UNIOSIL	2006	298
India and Pakistan	UNMOGIP	1949	113

*Includes military, police and civilians
[a]Political or peace-building missions
[b]Egypt, Jordan, Israel, Lebanon and Syria
Source: United Nations

while poor countries such as India, Pakistan, Bangladesh, Nepal and Jordan supply the soldiers. They receive a payment for doing so; this becomes for some a subsidy for their own armed forces, while the deployment also provides their troops with training.

Idealists such as Sir Brian Urquhart, a former UN under secretary-general, believe it is high time the UN had its own "fire engine": a permanent force that could deploy quickly to stop conflicts before they spin out of control. The UN's founding fathers envisioned some kind of international army, but all proposals for a standing UN force have foundered—partly because of political objections to giving the UN too much power, partly because of the practical difficulties of recruiting, training and paying for such a force.

After the failure of the UN in the mid-1990s to stop blood-letting in Somalia, Rwanda and the Balkans, many argued it would be better for those who are properly equipped to deal with putting out the fires of conflict. In 1999, it was NATO that stopped the killing of ethnic Albanians in Kosovo, while a force led by Australia halted the conflict in East Timor. A year later, in Sierra Leone, the quick deployment of about 1,000 British soldiers helped save what was then the UN's largest peace-keeping mission from collapsing under attack by rebels of the Revolutionary United Front.

All this seemed to confirm that the UN could take on only soft peacekeeping and "observer" missions with co-operation from the warring sides. But in 2000 a panel headed by Lakhdar Brahimi recommended a complete rethink of UN peacekeeping. The United Nations, it acknowledged, "does not wage war"; but its operations nevertheless had to "project credible force" and be ready to distinguish between victim and aggressor.

Mr Brahimi's central recommendation was the creation of multinational brigades around the world ready to deploy at short notice. This idea of pre-assembling bits of the fire engine has made only fitful progress. But other proposals have been acted on. They include the creation of a more powerful headquarters to oversee the UN effort; stockpiling of equipment; compilation of lists of military officers, police and other experts who will be on *call* to join UN missions; and the meshing of peacekeeping with ordinary policing, government reform and economic development.

New missions are now much more likely to be given robust mandates authorising them to use "all necessary means" under Chapter VII of the UN Charter: in other words, aggressive military force. In places such as Congo and Haiti, the UN has even been accused of using too much force.

Since the world is likely to need large numbers of peacekeepers for the foreseeable future, a further option is being explored: "leasing" the fire engine by hiring private security companies to do more of the work. Don't expect anything to happen quickly, though. The world, and especially the Americans, has moved a long way towards the privatisation of war. But for many, the privatisation of peacekeeping is still a step too far.

Assess Your Progress

1. What accounts for the surge in UN peacekeeping?
2. What is the process for deploying UN peacekeepers?
3. In what ways has the UN increased peacekeeping capability?

UNIT 4

Political Change in the Developing World

Unit Selections

Learning Outcomes

After reading this unit you should be able to:

- Describe the recent trends in the progress of human rights and democracy worldwide.
- Suggest ways in which post-conflict settlements may fall short of democracy.
- Outline challenges that face even successful transitions to democracy like South Africa.
- Analyze the prospects for peace in the Middle East.
- Evaluate the prospects for democracy in Latin America.

Student Website

www.mhhe.com/cls

Internet References

Center for Research on Inequality, Human Security, and Ethnicity
www.crise.ox.ac.uk

Latin American Network Information Center—LANIC
www.lanic.utexas.edu

ReliefWeb
www.reliefweb.int/w/rwb.nsf

A recent assessment of democracy and human rights found a decline in both for the fourth consecutive year. The history of authoritarian colonial rule and the failure to prepare colonies adequately for democracy at independence helps to account for the present situation in many cases. Even when there was an attempt to foster parliamentary government, the experiment failed frequently, largely due to the lack of a democratic tradition and a reliance on political expediency. Independence-era leaders frequently resorted to centralization of power and authoritarianism, either to pursue ambitious development programs or more often simply to retain power. In some cases, leaders experimented with socialist development schemes that emphasized ideology and the role of party elites. The promise of rapid, equitable development proved elusive, and the collapse of the Soviet Union further discredited this strategy. Other countries had the misfortune to come under the rule of tyrannical leaders who were concerned only with enriching themselves and who brutally repressed anyone with the temerity to challenge their rule. Although there are a few notable exceptions, the developing world's experiences with democracy since independence have been uneven.

The results of democracy's "third wave" have been mixed so far. While democracy has increased across the world, the pace of democratic change has slowed recently; and in some instances democratic reform has regressed. There has been a backlash against democracy in some parts of Asia, particularly illustrated by the forces' intervention into the politics of some countries. The end of the civil war in Sri Lanka and the re-election of the incumbent president resulted in a crackdown against the opposition and an indication of a turn away from democracy. Although Latin America has been the developing world's most successful region in establishing democracy, widespread dissatisfaction due to corruption, inequitable distribution of wealth, and the threats to civil rights have produced a left wing, populist trend in the region's politics recently. Several countries have decided to either extend presidential terms or abolish term limits.

Africa's experience with democracy has also been varied since the third wave of democratization swept over the continent beginning in 1990. Although early efforts resulted in the ouster of many leaders, some of whom had held power for decades, and international pressure forced several countries to hold multiparty elections, the political landscape in Africa includes consolidating democracies and states still mired in conflict. Among the success stories is Ghana, which held elections in late 2008 that resulted in the opposition leader defeating the ruling party's candidate. South Africa, the continent's biggest success story, held its fourth round of democratic elections in April 2009. The elections took place amid allegations of corruption against the new president, Jacob Zuma, and featured a nasty split in the ruling African National Congress. Although South Africa continues to face major challenges, its democracy remains vibrant. Ghana and South Africa stand in sharp contrast to the circumstances in some other parts of Africa. Congo's 2006 elections brought a state of tenuous peace to most of the country although the threat of fighting continues in the eastern part of the country. Nigeria's 2007 elections were flawed, and the country also continues to face widespread corruption and political unrest, especially in the Niger Delta region. The situation could become even more complicated with the recent death of President Yar'Adua.

© 2003 Thomas Hartwell/USAID (U.S. Agency for International Development)

Political change has begun in some parts of the Middle East, but it will be a long-term challenge. Iraq continues to face the task of reconciling its Sunni, Shiite, and Kurdish communities, and the threat of sectarian violence remains. The role of Islam in the region and its incompatibility with democracy continues to be a major issue. There is some evidence that Islamic political parties have moderated their message and that those that have not do not fare well in elections. Prospects for broader democratic reform in the region will depend on the success of efforts to reframe the political debate.

While there has been significant progress toward democratic reform around the world, as the recent trend suggests there is no guarantee that these efforts will be sustained. Although there has been an increase in the percentage of the world's population living under democracy, nondemocratic regimes still exist. Furthermore, some semidemocracies hold elections but citizens lack full civil and political rights. International efforts to promote democracy often tend to focus on elections rather than on the long-term requirements of democratic consolidation. More effective ways of promoting and sustaining democracy must be found in order to expand freedom further in the developing world.

Crying for Freedom

A disturbing decline in global liberty prompts some hard thinking about what is needed for democracy to prevail.

More than at any time since the cold war, liberal democracy needs defending. That warning was issued recently by Arch Puddington, a veteran American campaigner for civil and political rights around the world.

This week the reasons for his concern became clearer. Freedom House, a lobby group based in Washington, DC (where Mr Puddington is research director), found in its latest annual assessment that liberty and human rights had retreated globally for the fourth consecutive year. It said this marked the longest period of decline in freedom since the organisation began its reports nearly 40 years ago.

Freedom House classifies countries as "free", "partly free" or "not free" by a range of indicators that reflect its belief that political liberty and human rights are interlinked. As well as the fairness of their electoral systems, countries are assessed for things like the integrity of judges and the independence of trade unions. Among the latest findings are that authoritarian regimes are not just more numerous; they are more confident and influential.

In its report entitled "Freedom in the World 2010: Global Erosion of Freedom", the American lobby group found that declines in liberty occurred last year in 40 countries (in Africa, Latin America, the Middle East and the ex-Soviet Union) while gains were recorded in 16. The number of electoral democracies went down by three, to 116, with Honduras, Madagascar, Mozambique and Niger dropping off the list while the Maldives were reinstated. This leaves the total at its lowest since 1995, although it is still comfortably above the 1990 figure of 69.

Taken as a whole, the findings suggest a huge turn for the worse since the bubbly mood of 20 years ago, when the collapse of Soviet communism, plus the fall of apartheid, convinced people that liberal democracy had prevailed for good. To thinkers like America's Francis Fukuyama, this was the time when it became evident that political freedom, underpinned by economic freedom, marked the ultimate stage in human society's development: the "end of history", at least in a moral sense.

In the very early days after the Soviet collapse, Russia and some of its neighbours swarmed with Western advisers, disseminating not only the basics of market economics but also the mechanics of multi-party democracy. And for a short time, these pundits found willing listeners.

Today, the idea that politicians in ex-communist countries would take humble lessons from Western counterparts seems laughable. There is more evidence of authoritarians swapping tips. In October, for example, the pro-Kremlin United Russia party held its latest closed-door meeting with the Chinese Communist party. Despite big contrasts between the two countries—not many people in Russia think there is a Chinese model they could easily apply—the Russians were interested by the Chinese "experience in building a political system dominated by one political party," according to one report of the meeting.

For freedom-watchers in the West, the worrying thing is that the cause of liberal democracy is not merely suffering political reverses, it is also in intellectual retreat. Semi-free countries, uncertain which direction to take, seem less convinced that the liberal path is the way of the future. And in the West, opinion-makers are quicker to acknowledge democracy's drawbacks—and the apparent fact that contested elections do more harm than good when other preconditions for a well-functioning system are absent. It is a sign of the times that a British reporter, Humphrey Hawksley, has written a book with the title: "Democracy Kills: What's So Good About the Vote?".

A more nuanced argument, against the promotion of electoral democracy at the expense of other goals, has been made by other observers. Paul Collier, an Oxford professor, has asserted that democracy in the absence of other desirables, like the rule of law, can hobble a country's progress. Mark Malloch-Brown, a former head of the UN Development Programme, is still a believer in democracy as a driver of economic advancement, but he thinks that in countries like Afghanistan, the West has focused too much on procedures—like multi-party elections—and is not open enough to the idea that other kinds of consensus might exist. At the University of California, Randall Peerenboom defends the "East Asian model", according to which economic development naturally precedes democracy.

Whatever the eggheads may be saying, there are some obvious reasons why Western governments' zeal to promote democracy, and the willingness of other countries to listen, have ebbed. In many quarters (including Western ones), the assault on Saddam Hussein's Iraq, and its bloody aftermath, seemed to confirm people's suspicion that promoting democracy as an American foreign-policy aim was ill-conceived or plain cynical.

In Afghanistan, the other country where an American-led coalition has been waging war in democracy's name, the corruption and deviousness of the local political elite, and the flaws of last year's election, have been an embarrassment. In the Middle East, America's enthusiasm for promoting democracy took a dip after the Palestinian elections of 2006, which brought Hamas to office. The European Union's "soft power" on its eastern rim has waned as enlargement fatigue has grown.

But perhaps the biggest reason why democracy's magnetic power has waned is the rise of China—and the belief of its would-be imitators that they too can create a dynamic economy without easing their grip on political power. In the political rhetoric of many authoritarian governments, fascination with copying China's trick can clearly be discerned.

For example, Syria's ruling Baath party talks of a "socialist market economy" that will fuel growth while keeping stability. Communist Vietnam has emulated China's economic reforms, but it was one of the states scolded by Freedom House this year for curbing liberty. Iran has called in Chinese legal experts and economists. There are limits to how much an Islamic republic and a communist state can have in common, but they seem to agree on what to avoid: Western-style freedom.

Even Cuba, while clinging to Marxist ideas, has shown an interest in China's economic reforms. And from the viewpoint of many poor countries, especially in Africa, co-operating with China—both economically and politically—has many advantages: not least the fact that China refrains from delivering lectures on political and human freedom. The global economic downturn—and China's ability to survive it—has clearly added to that country's appeal. The power of China (and a consequent lessening of official concern over human rights) is palpable in Central Asia. But as dissidents in the region note, it is not just Chinese influence that makes life hard for them; it is also the dithering of Western governments which often temper their moral concerns with commercial ones.

The Argument for Open Argument

Given that democracy is unlikely to advance, these days, through the military or economic preponderance of the West, its best hope lies in winning a genuinely open debate. In other words, wavering countries, and sceptical societies, must be convinced that political freedom works best.

So how does the case in defence of democracy stand up these days? As many a philosopher has noted, the strongest points to be made in favour of a free political contest are negative. Democracy may not yield perfect policies, but it ought to guard against all manner of ills, ranging from outright tyranny (towards which a "mild" authoritarian can always slide) to larceny at the public expense.

Transparency International, a corruption watchdog, says that all but two of the 30 least corrupt countries in the world are democracies (the exceptions are Singapore and Hong Kong, and they are considered semi-democratic). Autocracies tend to occupy much higher rankings on the corruption scale (China is somewhere in the middle) and it is easy to see why. Entrenched political elites, untroubled by free and fair elections, can get away more easily with stuffing their pockets. And strongmen often try to maintain their hold on power by relying on public funds to reward their supporters and to buy off their enemies, leading to a huge misallocation of resources.

Yet it is easy to find corrupt democracies—indeed, in a ramshackle place like Afghanistan elections sometimes seem to make things worse. Or take the biggest of the ex-Soviet republics. Russia is authoritarian and has a massive problem with corruption; Ukraine is more democratic—the forthcoming elections are a genuine contest for power, with uncertain results—but it too has quite a big corruption problem. Ukraine has no "Kremlin", wielding authority over all-comers, but that does not make it clean or well-governed.

What about the argument that economic development, at least in its early stages, is best pursued under a benign despot? Lee Kuan Yew, an ex-prime minister of Singapore, once asserted that democracy leads to "disorderly conduct", disrupting material progress. But there is no evidence that autocracies, on average, grow faster than democracies. For every economically successful East Asian (former) autocracy like Taiwan or South Korea, there is an Egypt or a Cameroon (or indeed a North Korea or a Myanmar) which is both harsh and sluggish.

The link between political systems and growth is hard to establish. Yet there is some evidence that, on average, democracies do better. A study by Morton Halperin, Joseph Siegle and Michael Weinstein for the Council of Foreign Relations (CFR), using World Bank data between 1960 and 2001, found that the average annual economic growth rate was 2.3% for democracies and 1.6% for autocracies. Other studies, though, are less clear.

Believers in democracy as an engine of progress often make the point that a climate of freedom is most needed in a knowledge-based economy, where independent thinking and innovation are vital. It is surely no accident that every economy in the top 25 of the Global Innovation Index is a democracy, except semi-democratic Singapore and Hong Kong.

China, which comes 27th in this table, is often cited as a vast exception to this rule. Chinese brainpower has made big strides in fields like computing, green technology and space flight. The determination of China's authorities to impose their own terms on the information revolution was highlighted this week when Google, the search engine, said it might pull out of China after a cyber-attack that targeted human-rights activists. Since entering the Chinese market in 2006, Google had agreed to the censorship of some search results, at the authorities' insistence.

Admirers of China's iron hand may conclude that it can manage well without the likes of Google, which was being trounced in the local market by Baidu, a Chinese rival. But in the medium term, the mentality that insists on hobbling search engines will surely act as a break on creative endeavour. And no country should imagine that by becoming as autocratic as China, it will automatically become as dynamic as China is.

What about the argument that autocracy creates a modicum of stability without which growth is impossible? In fact, it is not evident that authoritarian countries are more stable than democracies.

Quite the contrary. Although democratic politicians spend a lot of time vacillating, arguing and being loud and disagreeable, this can reinforce stability in the medium term; it allows the interests and viewpoints of more people to be heard before action is taken. On the State Fragility Index, which is produced annually by George Mason University and studies variables such as "political effectiveness" and security, democracies tend to do much better than autocracies. Tito's Yugoslavia was stable, as was Saddam Hussein's Iraq—but once the straitjacket that held their systems together came off, the result was a release of pent-up pressure, and a golden opportunity for demagogues bent on mayhem.

At the very least, a culture of compromise—coupled with greater accountability and limits on state power—means that democracies are better able to avoid catastrophic mistakes, or criminal cruelty. Bloody nightmares that cost tens of millions of lives, like China's Great Leap Forward or the Soviet Union's forced collectivisation programme, were made possible by the concentration of power in a small group of people who faced no restraint.

Liberal democratic governments can make all manner of blunders, but they are less likely to commit mass murder. Amartya Sen, a Nobel prize-winning economist, has famously argued that no country with a free press and fair elections has ever had a large famine. And research by those three CFR scholars found that poor autocracies were at least twice as likely as democracies to suffer an economic disaster (defined as a decline of 10% or more in GDP in a year). With no noisy legislatures or robust courts to hold things up, autocracies may be faster and bolder. They are also more accident-prone.

For all its frustrations, open and accountable government tends in the long run to produce better policies. This is because no group of mandarins, no matter how enlightened or well-meaning, can claim to be sure what is best for a complex society. Autocracies tend to be too heavy at the top: although decisions may be more easily taken, the ethos of autocracies—their secrecy and paranoia—makes it harder for alternative views to emerge. Above all, elections make the transfer of power legitimate and smooth. Tyrannies may look stable under one strongman; but they can slide into instability, even bloody chaos, if a transition goes awry. Free elections also mean that policy mistakes, even bad ones, are more quickly corrected. Fresh ideas can be brought in and politicians thrown out before they grow too arrogant.

But if something has been learnt from the recent backlash against democratic enthusiasm, it is that ballot boxes alone are nothing like enough. Unless solid laws protect individual and minority rights, and government power is limited by clear checks, such as tough courts, an electoral contest can simply lead to a "tyranny of the majority", as Alexis de Tocqueville, a French philosopher, called it. That point has particular force in countries where some variety of political Islam seems likely to prevail in any open contest. In such places, minorities include dissident Muslims who often prefer to remain under the relative safety offered by a despot.

Another caveat is that democracy has never endured in countries with mainly non-market economies. The existence of an overweening state machine that meddles in everything can tempt leaders to use it against their political foes. Total control of the economy also sucks the air away from what Istvan Bibo, a Hungarian political thinker, called "the little circles of freedom"—the free associations and independent power centres that a free economy allows. Free-market economies help create a middle class that is less susceptible to state pressure and political patronage.

Perhaps most important, democracy needs leaders with an inclination and ability to compromise: what Walter Bagehot, a 19th-century editor of *The Economist,* called a "disposition rather to give up something than to take the uttermost farthing". Without a propensity for tolerating and managing differences, rival groups can easily reduce democracy to a ruthless struggle for power that ultimately wears down liberal institutions.

Democracy, this suggests, is more likely to succeed in countries with a shared feeling of belonging together, without strong cultural or ethnic fissures that can easily turn political conflict into the armed sort. Better positioned are "people so fundamentally at one that they can safely afford to bicker," as Lord Balfour, a 19th-century British politician, said. Such was not the case in Yugoslavia in the 1990s or in Lebanon in the 1970s.

Even where all the right conditions are in place, democracy will not prevail unless its proponents show success at governing. No constitution can, in itself, guarantee good governance. The success of any political system ultimately depends on whether it can provide basic things like security, wealth and justice. And in countries where experiments in democracy are in full swing, daily reality is more complex than either zealous democracy-promoters or authoritarian sceptics will allow.

In Kabul a 26-year-old handyman called Jamshed speaks for many compatriots when he lists the pros and cons of the new Western-imposed order. Compared with life under the Taliban, he appreciates the new "freedom to listen to music, to go out with your wife, to study or do whatever you want." But he cannot help remembering that "under the Taliban, you could leave your shop to pray and nobody would steal anything... now the government is corrupt, they take all your money."

Jamshed has never read John Stuart Mill or Ayn Rand. But whether he is ruled by theocrats or Western-backed election winners, he knows what he doesn't like.

Assess Your Progress

1. What trends are evident in the latest Freedom House survey?
2. What questions have arisen about promoting democracy worldwide?
3. How have U.S. actions contributed to skepticism about the promotion of democracy?
4. What effect has China's rise had on the promotion of democracy?
5. What advantages do democracies have in producing economic growth and good public policy?
6. What is needed to strengthen democracy's attraction?

In Sri Lanka, the Triumph of Vulgar Patriotism

Rajapaksa's patriotism merges nation and state, and it promotes a love of country based on a particular reading of the Sinhalese people's foundation myth, a reading in which all other groups . . . are present only as shadows.

NIRA WICKRAMASINGHE

On January 27, 2010, incumbent President Mahinda Rajapaksa was declared the winner of Sri Lanka's sixth presidential election. He triumphed over his main challenger, former army commander Sarath Fonseka, with a comfortable tally of 58 percent to 40 percent. The opposition immediately launched demonstrations to protest alleged election fraud.

According to a report by an independent monitoring group, the Commonwealth Expert Team, the presidential polling did not fully meet benchmarks for democratic elections. Yet most observers acknowledge that the outcome was affected not by vote rigging so much as by large-scale propaganda in the media in favor of Rajapaksa in weeks preceding the polls. State television, for example, repeatedly screened images of Uganda's notorious Idi Amin to instill fear of military dictatorship among Sinhalese voters.

A crackdown on the losers followed the release of the election results. Members of an elite army commando unit and army deserters who had supported Fonseka were arrested. Fonseka's office in Colombo was raided. On February 8, the former general himself was arrested under suspicion of conspiring to topple the government and assassinate Rajapaksa. Parliament was dissolved ahead of parliamentary elections scheduled for April.

For the longer term, the incumbent president is said to entertain hopes of consolidating family rule. His youthful son ran for parliament from Hambantota, Rajapaksa's hometown, and is expected to be groomed to become prime minister.

Sri Lanka's opposition parties have not remained silent in the face of these provocations. A number of demonstrations calling for Fonseka's release peppered the country and were violently suppressed. But as the government castigates as treason virtually any form of political opposition or criticism of official abuses, and as fears of reprisals grow, much of the public has been silenced and depoliticized.

A Result Foretold

The massive support that Rajapaksa mustered in the January election was strongest in the Sinhalese-dominated rural south, the area from where the president hails. He received more than 60 percent of the vote in that region. Tamils, especially in the north and in urban areas, along with Muslims in the east, paradoxically cast their lot with Fonseka, a well-known Sinhalese supremacist and the architect of last May's brutal military victory over the rebel Tamil Tigers.

They voted for him because, in ethnically and religiously divided Sri Lanka, the former general had become the nominal leader of the opposition, and was supported by the Tamil National Alliance, the main Tamil party in parliament. Moreover, in the Eastern Province where paramilitary Tamil armed groups, aided and abetted by the government, have been a law unto themselves since the demise of the Tamil Tigers, Tamils and Muslims saw in Fonseka the only candidate capable of restoring some degree of security for the people.

Even so, votes from urban areas, and from Tamils—who make up only 12 percent of the country's population of 21.3 million—proved not nearly sufficient for Fonseka to overcome Rajapaksa. The reason is that the incumbent regime succeeded where all others failed: It ended a debilitating, three-decades-long civil war.

Although many people in the south maintain serious concerns about Rajapaksa's government—which they recognize as grotesquely nepotistic, openly corrupt, and slow to deliver an expected peace dividend—this did not, at the crucial hour, outweigh their immense gratitude for being secure at last in their everyday lives.

When Rajapaksa decided last November to hold the presidential election two years earlier than previously scheduled, it seemed that the opposition parties would mount no real challenge. His victory appeared a certainty, a fait accompli. But Fonseka, disgruntled by the regime's dismissive attitude toward him, disturbed this scenario. Rallying around him all of Rajapaksa's political foes, the former army chief emerged as the consensus opposition candidate.

Fonseka's campaign hinged on criticizing the Rajapaksa administration for failing to carry out reconstruction, build the economy, and tackle corruption and mismanagement. Fonseka also deplored the deterioration of freedoms and rights in a country where, in recent years, a prominent editor was murdered and many others offering critical voices have been beaten up, kidnapped in notorious white vans, or detained under questionable charges. Fonseka even openly accused the secretary of defense, the president's brother, of committing war crimes during the last phase of the battle against the Tamil Tigers.

To voters, however, the anti-Rajapaksa alliance appeared fragile and divided. The Tamil National Alliance, the main Tamil party backing Fonseka, called for a merger of the Northern and Eastern provinces, the Tamils' traditional homelands, an idea that Fonseka rejected. The Marxist-nationalist Janata Vimukti Peramuna (the People's Liberation Front, or JVP) and the United National Party (UNP), the biggest opposition party, held conflicting views on the issue of granting more administrative power to the Tamils. The JVP opposed the idea of a Tamil homeland, while the UNP was more receptive to the idea of some form of self-determination for the Tamils.

In any case, in a country where the media had been beaten into submission and all state institutions had been blatantly misused over the previous two years to bolster Rajapaksa's image, it would have taken a miracle for this makeshift coalition to achieve a whirlwind victory. No miracle occurred.

The 30 Years' War

Each of the presidential candidates presented himself as the force behind the government's victory over Tamil "terrorism"—a victory that was dramatically achieved in the spring of 2009 with the death of Tamil Tiger leader Velupillai Prabhakaran and the destruction of the military edifice that he had constructed over 30 years.

Each of the presidential candidates presented himself as the force behind the government's victory over "Tamil terrorism."

The Tamil Tigers (formed in 1972 as the New Tamil Tigers, and renamed in 1976 as the Liberation Tigers of Tamil Eelam) had been fighting for a separate Tamil state (or "*eelam*") in Sri Lanka's north and east since 1977. They argued that Tamils had been victims of discrimination under successive majority Buddhist Sinhalese governments. Legislation granting primacy to the Sinhalese language and to Buddhism, together with fears of Sinhalese colonization of their lands, was invoked to justify assassinations, massacres, and countless suicide bombings on civilian as well as military targets in the south.

After the repeated failure of talks between the government and the Tigers—partly due to the Sinhalese parties' unwillingness to work together to broker a devolution deal that would be acceptable to the Tamil people—the Tigers and government forces renewed the military conflict in 2006. Rajapaksa's "war to eliminate terrorism" gained considerable international support and was provided the armament required for sustained military operations.

After liberating the Eastern Province in 2008, the Sri Lankan army headed by General Fonseka broke through rebel lines and drove the Tigers from areas in the north that they had controlled for decades. Thousands of civilians were held hostage by the Tigers in their final retreat. Eventually, after the fall of the Tigers' de facto capital, Kilinochchi, and the death of the Tamil leader, the 30-year war came to an end.

While the military phase of the conflict ended last May, the human costs of the war's conclusion will never be known. No independent media were allowed in the war zone during the final battle, but the United Nations estimates that 7,000 people died in early May and many more in the final two weeks of the fighting.

With the end of the war, another ordeal began for the quarter-million displaced Tamils who were interned in barbed-wired camps, where little access was provided to independent journalists and international agencies. The material conditions in the camps were monitored by the UN, which ensured that basic needs were provided for, but (unverifiable) stories of rape, other violence, and extortion reached the media. However, the Sinhalese people in the south appeared indifferent to the plight of their countrymen—the result of longtime exposure to government media that portrayed all Tamils as potential terrorists.

The Postwar State

Events since the end of the war have confirmed observers' fears that Sri Lanka is moving toward becoming a nepotistic state dominated by a coterie of sycophants seemingly intent on draining the coffers of state institutions. Meanwhile, the country is confronting serious economic challenges: The economy continues to totter despite a $2.8 billion bailout package from the International Monetary Fund.

According to IMF guidelines, the government is supposed to operate with a budget deficit of no more than 7 percent of GDP. But the deficit has already reached 8.5 percent of GDP and is likely to rise further. The government's claims notwithstanding, there is little foreign direct investment—the regime is spending heavily on borrowed funds.

Exports have contracted sharply, though US demand has started to pick up again. The European Union decided to suspend preferential tariff benefits for Sri Lanka following an investigation by the European Commission that concluded that the country fell short in implementing UN human rights conventions relevant to the trade benefits. Corruption and cronyism continue to depress investment.

At the same time the government, even though it no longer faces a civil war, is expanding the military, whose troop strength is already larger than that of the Israeli army. Emergency regulations remain in place, giving the regime's security forces special powers of search, arrest, and seizure of property.

And in the wake of the government's triumph over the Tamil Tigers, an insidious chauvinism has taken hold over much of the country. A few months ago the government issued a new thousand rupee note to commemorate its victory. On one side of the note is Rajapaksa's image; on the other is an Iwo Jima–like representation of Sri Lankan soldiers hoisting a flag, presumably after the fall of the Tamil stronghold of Kilinochchi. The new bill reflects the nature of the state in Sri Lanka today—patrimonial, nepotistic, nationalistic, and militarized.

To be sure, Fonseka's arrest has emboldened the previously feeble opposition. The United National Party now has a rallying cry, a cause célèbre that has resonance inside the country as well as outside. Arresting a war hero appears to have been a major miscalculation on Rajapaksa's part. Not only did it damage the country's image even further, it has elicited angry reactions from erstwhile allies such as the Buddhist clergy. The head priests of the major Buddhist sects, in a stern message to the president, called for the immediate release of Fonseka and other army personnel who had been taken into custody.

Protests immediately followed Fonseka's arrest. Hundreds of lawyers carrying placards demonstrated peacefully in front of the court complex in Colombo. Other supporters of the retired general gathered outside the supreme court, where a petition against his detention was heard. The opposition parties were gathering strength in advance of the parliamentary elections scheduled for April.

But whatever happens in current clashes between the government and the opposition, the centralized nature of Sri Lanka's state is not likely to change soon. Indeed, the regime's ideology—a form of vulgar civic patriotism that does not recognize any special rights for minorities—demands a strong centralized government along the lines of the one inherited from the colonial era.

The New Patriotism

This new patriotism has little in common with the "postnational" or "constitutional" patriotism that has been proposed as an alternative form of loyalty that is distinct from nationalism and is compatible with universal values. To the contrary, Rajapaksa's patriotism merges nation and state, and it promotes a love of country based on a particular reading of the Sinhalese people's foundation myth, a reading in which all other groups—those formally known as minorities—are present only as shadows.

Even expressions of banal nationalism can, in some cases, alienate cultural minorities. The regime and especially the president are constantly flagging Sinhalese Buddhist nationhood in public life, as well as policing the private lives of citizens. For instance, when Rajapaksa visited the sacred city of Anuradhapura last May to attend religious observances, he is reported to have offered hereditary gold ornaments to the sacred Bo tree, a ritual that ancient kings used to perform and that later was entrusted to high Buddhist officials. The president has allowed, if not encouraged, the media to portray him as another King Dutugemunu, another son of southern Sri Lanka who succeeded in seizing Anuradhapura from the Tamil king Elara.

Apart from such symbolic acts, the patriotic state is acting on society itself. Not only has it begun to monitor a long-forgotten excise law that forbids women from buying alcoholic drinks, it has also decreed that women are not permitted to enter government school premises unless clad in a sari (predominantly worn by Sinhalese women), and that liquor cannot be bought or consumed during the entire week surrounding the Buddhist Vesak festival. Being patriotic now means agreeing to abide by these rules, whether you are from the Sinhalese, Tamil, Muslim, or any other community.

The world in general appears to be moving away from the belief that pluralism and diversity are in themselves a panacea for societies' problems. But even if we accept citizenship and equality as higher values, only a principled regime can strive to protect the neutrality of the public sphere and ensure that majoritarianism and discrimination do not set in. Rajapaksa's regime has yet to display such principle.

Whatever the flaws of multiculturalism, they are still lesser evils than those faced today by Sri Lanka's minorities.

Whatever the flaws of multiculturalism and its avatar, the devolution of power—flaws that include essentializing the fragment, promoting the formation of ethnic enclaves, and denying the hybridity of communities and the possibility of multiple belongings—they are still lesser evils than those faced today by Sri Lanka's minorities, as well as by opponents of the Rajapaksa regime, as they encounter the administration's crude civic patriotism and ruthless repression.

The war is over, but journalists are still disappearing. Critics of the regime are vilified, attacked, or arrested on flimsy charges. Sri Lanka's government—which has close ties with Myanmar, Iran, Russia, China, and Pakistan—displays the type of defiant hubris that comes with the perception of being treated unfairly by the international community. But the chauvinist Sri Lankan state that is taking shape is founded on a grotesque travesty of the values it claims to champion in its critique of Western hypocrisy.

Assess Your Progress

1. What has followed in the aftermath of Sri Lanka's 2010 elections?
2. What accounted for the incumbent president's reelection?
3. Who was the opposition candidate and what was his platform?
4. What challenges does Sri Lanka face?
5. What are the prospects for a multicultural society in Sri Lanka?

NIRA WICKRAMASINGHE is a professor of modern South Asian studies at Leiden University.

Bring Me My Machine Gun

Scott Johnson and Karen MacGregor

South Africa has never had a president like Jacob Zuma. For one thing, the 67-year-old self-educated "farm boy" (his own words) has five wives and at least 20 children. On special occasions like weddings and funerals he decks himself out in traditional Zulu finery: leopard skin, headdress and spear. "A leader is a person who doesn't sit back," he tells NEWSWEEK. "Who will do things and make mistakes and be corrected. Who is not reserved." In contrast to the statesmanly lawyer Nelson Mandela and Thabo Mbeki, Mandela's Latin-quoting successor, Zuma revels in his tribal roots. "In a sense, he is our first real African president," says his close friend Jeremy Gordin, author of "Zuma: A Biography." "Mandela . . . came from Xhosa royalty. Mbeki was [educated] in England. But Zuma is a real African, and this real Africanness and lack of sophistication, combined with a real shrewdness, is very compelling."

But also troubling. The continent is littered with the wreckage of countries that were driven into the ground by similarly charismatic postcolonial leaders in the name of revolutionary justice. Africans call them Big Men—demagogues who rose to power promising a better share of the wealth for their followers and railing against anyone who stood in the way. Zuma practically invites the comparison, even down to his choice of a theme song: the Zulu antiapartheid anthem "Lethu Mshini Wami"—"Bring Me My Machine Gun." As head of the ruling African National Congress, however, he's facing only token opposition in this week's South African presidential election. Zuma is extraordinarily intelligent, despite his lack of formal schooling. But he's inheriting some vast challenges: crime-ravaged cities, a reeling economy and the country's ongoing AIDS crisis, among other things. Unemployment among black youth is hovering around 50 percent. Even so, Zuma seems confident he's up to his new job.

For good or ill, the next president is a lot different from his predecessors.

His critics ask just what he's up to. Three years ago he was acquitted of rape charges brought against him by a family friend. The judge ruled that the sex had been consensual, but Zuma's cavalier remarks offended many observers—he even argued that the woman had invited his attention by wearing a short dress. And on April 6, barely two weeks before Election Day, the attorney general's office dropped the last 14 outstanding charges of fraud, racketeering and corruption against the candidate, eliminating the last obstacle to his rise. "The majority of the people in this country are very happy," Zuma told NEWSWEEK after the decision, vehemently denying any wrongdoing. "They think justice has been done." Still, roughly half the likely voters in one recent poll said they believed he was guilty—and many said they would vote for him anyway. Opposition politicians have begun legal proceedings to keep the case alive. "I have never been corrupt, and I'm fighting corruption within my organization," says Zuma. "So that is not going to be a problem."

Questions of integrity aside, Zuma has shared something else with many of Africa's Big Men: a hardscrabble childhood. He was 4 when his father died. His mother found work as a domestic in the city of Durban, but she couldn't afford to send the boy to school. Instead he herded cattle in the countryside. He was still in his teens when a relative recruited him for the ANC in 1959. Four years later he was arrested and sentenced to 10 years in prison for conspiring against the apartheid regime. He was jailed with Mandela on Robben Island.

The experience only reinforced Zuma's commitment to the revolution after his release. He eventually rose to be the ANC's intelligence chief, based in Zambia at the party's headquarters in exile. When one of his best operatives was compromised on a mission inside South Africa in 1985, Zuma instructed a member of an ANC cell in Durban to take the heat instead, so the operative could escape. The cell member, a young man named Mo Shaik, was arrested along with two of his brothers. Their father was detained and suffered a stroke; his mother died of a heart attack. Mo and his brother Yunis were tortured and spent a year in solitary confinement. "Zuma later apologized to my father for all that had happened, and he ensured that everything would be OK with my family," says Mo. "Zuma knows the difference between those who made sacrifices and those who seek to take advantage now."

Zuma and the Shaiks grew even closer after he returned home in 1990, when the ANC was unbanned. Zuma allegedly received nearly $600,000 in financial help from another of the brothers, Schabir Shaik, a successful businessman. Both men insist it was only a loan, and according to Zuma it has been repaid. But Schabir was subsequently convicted of corruption and fraud. He was released this March for undisclosed health reasons after serving two years and four months of a 15-year sentence.

But Zuma kept fighting until the charges against him were dropped—not because the case was weak, the prosecutor announced, but merely because the filing of charges had come to appear politically motivated. "I've got no ill feelings," Zuma says now. "I'm not going for revenge." But some of his allies have vowed to go after the "witches," "snakes" and "mischievous forces of darkness" responsible for the charges against him. And the candidate himself has filed a libel suit against one South African cartoonist who depicted him as a thug about to rape a woman labeled "Justice."

But in some ways Zuma offers new hope for a unified South Africa. He demurs at being called the country's first Zulu president. "The Zuluness is not the big issue," he says. "I've always looked at myself first as a South African—a black South African who always fought for the interests of the oppressed."

His allies have vowed to go after the 'witches' and 'snakes' responsible for the charges.

In fact, he has a strong record as a man who transcends ethnic and even racial barriers. He had a vital role 10 years ago in ending the virtual civil war between the ANC and armed followers of Zulu political leader Mangosuthu Buthelezi, a conflict that left thousands dead. In the past couple of years Zuma has reached out to the country's white-minority Afrikaners, calling them "the white tribe of Africa." One problem: many English-speaking South Africans now feel left out. Recently the president-to-be met for three hours with a delegation from the country's second-largest labor union, Solidarity, with 130,000 mostly Afrikaner members. (He speaks at least a little Afrikaans himself.) "He doesn't always take up your concerns and be a Mr. Fix-It, but he does listen," says Dirk Hermann, the union's head. "And that's hugely important for us. He's like a Zulu king, sitting under his tree, listening to his tribe." Zuma's challenge now is to make sure his tribe includes everyone in South Africa.

Assess Your Progress

1. Describe Jacob Zuma's path to the South African presidency.
2. How is South African president Jacob Zuma different from his predecessors?
3. Despite its success, what challenges does South Africa still face?
4. What are Zuma's strengths and weaknesses as president of South Africa?

Free at Last?

BERNARD LEWIS

The Arab World in the Twenty-First Century

As the twentieth century drew to an end, it became clear that a major change was taking place in the countries of the Arab world. For almost 200 years, those lands had been ruled and dominated by European powers and before that by non-Arab Muslim regimes—chiefly the Ottoman Empire. After the departure of the last imperial rulers, the Arab world became a political battleground between the United States and the Soviet Union during the Cold War. That, too, ended with the collapse of the Soviet Union in 1991. Arab governments and Arab dynasties (royal or presidential) began taking over. Arab governments and, to a limited but growing extent, the Arab peoples were at last able to confront their own problems and compelled to accept responsibility for dealing with them.

Europe, long the primary source of interference and domination, no longer plays any significant role in the affairs of the Arab world. Given the enormous oil wealth enjoyed by some Arab rulers and the large and growing Arab and Muslim population in Europe, the key question today is, what role will Arabs play in European affairs? With the breakup of the Soviet Union, Russia ceased to be a major factor in the Arab world. But because of its proximity, its resources, and its large Muslim population, Russia cannot afford to disregard the Middle East. Nor can the Middle East afford to disregard Russia.

The United States, unlike Europe, has continued to play a central role in the Arab world. During the Cold War, the United States' interest in the region lay chiefly in countering the growing Soviet influence, such as in Egypt and Syria. Since the end of the Cold War, U.S. troops have appeared occasionally in the region, either as part of joint peace missions (as in Lebanon in 1982-83) or to rescue or protect Arab governments from their neighboring enemies (as in Kuwait and Saudi Arabia in 1990–91). But many in the Arab world—and in the broader Islamic world—have seen these activities as blatant U.S. imperialism. According to this perception, the United States is simply the successor to the now-defunct French, British, and Soviet empires and their various Christian predecessors, carrying out yet another infidel effort to dominate the Islamic world.

Increasing U.S. involvement in the Middle East led to a series of attacks on U.S. government installations during the 1980s and 1990s. At first, Washington's response to the attacks was to withdraw. After the attacks on the U.S. marine barracks in Beirut in 1983 and on the U.S. component of a United Nations mission in Mogadishu in 1993, Washington pulled out its troops, made angry but vague declarations, and then launched missiles into remote and uninhabited places. Even the 1993 attack on the World Trade Center, in New York City, brought no serious rejoinder. These responses were seen by many as an expression of fear and weakness rather than moderation, and they encouraged hope among Islamist militants that they would eventually triumph. It was not until 9/11 that Washington felt compelled to respond with force, first in Afghanistan and then in Iraq, which were perceived as the sources of these attacks.

Other powers, both external and within the region, are playing increasingly active roles. Two neighboring non-Arab but predominantly Muslim countries, Iran and Turkey, have a long history of involvement in Arab affairs. Although the Turks, no doubt because of their past experience, have remained cautious and defensive, mainly concerned with a possible threat from Kurdish northern Iraq, the Iranians have become more active, especially since Iran's Islamic Revolution entered a new militant and expansionist phase. The broader Islamic world, free from outside control for the first time in centuries, is also naturally interested in events in the heartland of Islam. China and India, which will share or compete for primacy in Asia and elsewhere in the twenty-first century are also taking an interest in the region.

The Challenge of Peace

The political landscape within the Arab world has also changed dramatically since the end of the Cold War. Pan-Arabism, which once played a central role in the region, has effectively come to an end. Of the many attempts to unite different Arab countries, all but one, the unification of North and South Yemen after they were briefly separated by an imperial intrusion, have failed. Since the death of Egyptian President Gamal Abdel Nasser, in 1970, no Arab leader has enjoyed much support outside his own country. Nor has any Arab head of state dared to submit his attainment or retention of power to the genuinely free choice of his own people.

At the same time, issues of national identity are becoming more significant. Non-Arab ethnic minorities—such as the Kurds in Iran, Iraq, and Turkey and the Berbers in North

Africa—historically posed no major threat to central governments, and relations were generally good between Arabs and their non-Arab Muslim compatriots. But a new situation arose after the defeat of Saddam Hussein in the Persian Gulf War. The U.S. invasion of Iraq in 1991 had a strictly limited purpose: to liberate Kuwait. When this was accomplished, U.S. forces withdrew, leaving Saddam in control of his armed forces and free to massacre those of his subjects, notably Kurds and Shiites, who had responded to the United States' appeal for rebellion. Saddam was left in power, but his control did not extend to a significant part of northern Iraq, where a local Kurdish regime in effect became an autonomous government. This region was largely, although not entirely, Kurdish and included most of the Kurdish regions of Iraq. For the first time in modern history, there was a Kurdish country with a Kurdish government—at least in practice, if not in theory. This posed problems not only for the government of Iraq but also for those of some neighboring countries with significant Kurdish populations, notably Turkey. (Because of the strong opposition of these neighbors, the creation of an independent Kurdish state in the future seems unlikely. But a Kurdish component of a federal Iraq is a serious possibility.)

Another major problem for the region is the Palestinian issue. The current situation is the direct result of the policy, endorsed by the League of Nations and later by the United Nations, to create a Jewish national home in Palestine. With rare exceptions, the Arabs of Palestine and the leading Arab regimes resisted this policy from the start. A succession of offers for a Palestinian state in Palestine were made—by the British mandate government in 1937, by the United Nations in 1947—but each time Palestinian leaders and Arab regimes refused the offer because it would have meant recognizing the existence of a Jewish state next door. The struggle between the new state of Israel and the Palestinians has continued for over six decades, sometimes in the form of battles between armies (as in 1948, 1956, 1967, and 1973) and more recently between Israeli citizens and groups that are variously described as freedom fighters or terrorists.

The modern peace process began when President Anwar al-Sadat, of Egypt, fearing that the growing Soviet presence in the region was a greater threat to Arab independence than Israel could ever constitute, made peace with Israel in 1979. He was followed in 1994 by King Hussein of Jordan and, less formally, by other Arab states that developed some commercial and quasi-diplomatic contacts with Israel. Dialogue between Israel and the Palestine Liberation Organization led to some measure of formal mutual recognition and, more significant, to a withdrawal of Israeli forces from parts of the West Bank and the Gaza Strip and the establishment of more or less autonomous Palestinian authorities in these places.

But the conflict continues. Important sections of the Palestinian movement have refused to recognize the negotiations or any agreements and are continuing the armed struggle. Even some of those who have signed agreements—notably Yasir Arafat—have later shown a curious ambivalence toward their implementation. From the international discourse in English and other European languages, it would seem that most of the Arab states and some members of the Palestinian leadership have resigned themselves to accepting Israel as a state. But the discourse in Arabic—in broadcasts, sermons, speeches, and school textbooks—is far less conciliatory, portraying Israel as an illegitimate invader that must be destroyed. If the conflict is about the size of Israel, then long and difficult negotiations can eventually resolve the problem. But if the conflict is about the existence of Israel, then serious negotiation is impossible. There is no compromise position between existence and nonexistence.

Running on Empty

The state of the region's economy, and the resulting social and political situation, is a source of increasing concern in the Arab world. For the time being, oil continues to provide enormous wealth, directly to some countries in the region and indirectly to others. But these vast sums of money are creating problems as well as benefits. For one thing, oil wealth has strengthened autocratic governments and inhibited democratic development. Oil-rich rulers have no need to levy taxes and therefore no need to satisfy elected representatives. (In the Arab world, the converse of a familiar dictum is true: No representation without taxation.)

In addition to strengthening autocracy, oil wealth has also inhibited economic development. Sooner or later, oil will be either exhausted or replaced as an energy source, and the wealth and power that it provides will come to an end. Some more far-sighted Arab governments, aware of this eventuality, have begun to encourage and foster other kinds of economic development. Some of the Persian Gulf states are showing impressive expansion, especially in tourism and international finance. But the returns accruing from these sectors are still limited compared to the enormous wealth derived from oil.

Oil wealth has also led to the neglect or abandonment of other forms of gainful economic activity. From 2002 to 2006, a committee of Arab intellectuals, working under the auspices of the United Nations, produced a series of reports on human development in the Arab world. With devastating frankness, they reviewed the economic, social, and cultural conditions in the Arab world and compared them with those of other regions. Some of these comparisons—reinforced by data from other international sources—revealed an appalling pattern of neglect and underdevelopment.

Over the last quarter of a century, real gdp per capita has fallen throughout the Arab world. In 1999, the gdp of all the Arab countries combined stood at $531.2 billion, less than that of Spain. Today, the total non-oil exports of the entire Arab world (which has a population of approximately 300 million people) amount to less than those of Finland (a country of only five million inhabitants). Throughout the 1990s, exports from the region, 70 percent of which are oil or oil-related products, grew at a rate of 1.5 percent, far below the average global rate of six percent. The number of books translated every year into Arabic in the entire Arab world is one-fifth the number translated into Greek in Greece. And the number of books, both those in their original language and those translated, published per million people in the Arab world is very low compared with the figures for other regions. (Sub-Saharan Africa has a lower figure, but just barely.)

The situation regarding science and technology is as bad or worse. A striking example is the number of patents registered in the United States between 1980 and 2000: from Saudi Arabia, there were 171; from Egypt, 77; from Kuwait, 52; from the United Arab Emirates, 32; from Syria, 20; and from Jordan, 15—compared with 16,328 from South Korea and 7,652 from Israel. Out of six world regions, that comprising the Middle East and North Africa received the lowest freedom rating from Freedom House. The Arab countries also have the highest illiteracy rates and one of the lowest numbers of active research scientists with frequently cited articles. Only sub-Saharan Africa has a lower average standard of living.

Another shock came with the 2003 publication in China of a list of the 500 best universities in the world. The list did not include a single one of the more than 200 universities in the Arab countries. Since then, new rankings have appeared every year. The Arab universities remain absent, even from the relatively short list for the Asia-Pacific region. In an era of total and untrammeled independence for the Arab world, these failings can no longer be attributed to imperial oppressors or other foreign malefactors.

One of the most important social problems in the Arab world, as elsewhere in the Islamic world, is the condition of women. Women constitute slightly more than half the population, but in most Arab countries they have no political power. Some Muslim observers have seen in the depressed and downtrodden status of the female Arab population one of the main reasons for the underdevelopment of their society as compared with the advanced West and the rapidly developing East. Modern communications and travel are making these contrasts ever more visible. Some countries, such as Iraq and Tunisia, have made significant progress toward the emancipation of women by increasing opportunities for them. In Iraq, women have gained access to higher education and, consequently, to an ever-widening range of professions. In Tunisia, equal rights for women were guaranteed in the 1959 constitution. The results have been almost universal education for women and a significant number of women among the ranks of doctors, journalists, lawyers, magistrates, and teachers, as well as in the worlds of business and politics. This is perhaps the most hopeful single factor for the future of freedom and progress in these countries.

Another social problem is immigrant communities in the Arab world, which have received far less attention than Arab immigrant communities in Europe. These immigrants are attracted by oil wealth and the opportunities that it provides, and they undertake tasks that local people are either unwilling or unable to perform. This is giving rise to new and growing alien communities in several Arab countries, such as South Asians in the United Arab. The assimilation of immigrants from one Arab country into another has often proved difficult, and the acceptance of non-Arab and non-Muslim immigrants from remoter lands poses a more serious problem.

All these problems are aggravated by the communications revolution, which is having an enormous impact on the Arab population across all social classes. Even in premodern times, government control of news and ideas in the Islamic countries was limited—the mosque, the pulpit, and, above all, the pilgrimage—provided opportunities for the circulation of both information and ideas without parallel in the Western world. To some extent, modern Middle Eastern governments had learned how to manipulate information, but that control is rapidly diminishing as modern communications technology, such as satellite television and the Internet, has made people in the Arab countries, as elsewhere, keenly aware of the contrasts between different groups in their own countries and, more important, of the striking differences between the situations in their countries and those in other parts of the world. This has led to a great deal of anger and resentment, often directed against the West, as well as a countercurrent striving for democratic reform.

The Rise of the Radicals

Most westerners saw the defeat and collapse of the Soviet Union as a victory in the Cold War. For many Muslims, it was nothing of the sort. In some parts of the Islamic world, the collapse of the Soviet Union represented the devastating loss of a patron that was difficult or impossible to replace. In others, it symbolized the defeat of an enemy and a victory for the Muslim warriors who forced the Soviets to withdraw from Afghanistan. As this latter group saw it, the millennial struggle between the true believers and the unbelievers had gone through many phases, during which the Muslims were led by various lines of caliphs and the unbelievers by various infidel empires. During the Cold War, the leadership of the unbelievers was contested between two rival superpowers, the United States and the Soviet Union. Since they—the Muslim holy warriors in Afghanistan—had disposed of the larger, fiercer, and more dangerous of the two in the 1980s, dealing with the other, they believed, would be comparatively easy.

That task was given a new urgency by the two U.S. interventions in Iraq: that during the brief Persian Gulf War of 1990–91 and the 2003 invasion that resulted in the overthrow of Saddam and the attempt to create a new and more democratic political and social order. Opinions differ on the measure of the United States' achievements so far, but even its limited success has been sufficient to cause serious alarm, both to regimes with a vested interest in the survival of the existing order and, more important, to groups with their own radical plans for overthrowing it.

In the eyes of Islamist radicals, both of these wars have constituted humiliating defeats for Islam at the hands of the surviving infidel superpower. This point has been made with particular emphasis by Osama bin Laden, a Saudi who played a significant role in the war against the Soviets in Afghanistan and subsequently emerged as a very articulate leader in the Islamic world and as the head of al Qaeda, a new Islamist radical group. He has repeatedly made his case against the United States, most notably in his declaration of jihad of February 1998, in which he elaborated three grievances against the infidel enemies of Islam. The first was the presence of U.S. troops in Saudi Arabia, the holy land of Islam. The second was the use of Saudi bases for an attack on Iraq, the seat of the longest and most glorious period of classical Islamic history. The third was U.S. support for the seizure of Jerusalem by what he contemptuously called "the statelet" of the Jews.

Another claimant for the mantle of Islamic leadership is the Islamic Republic of Iran. The 1979 Iranian Revolution constituted a major shift in power, with a major ideological basis, and had a profound impact across the Muslim world. Its influence was by no means limited to Shiite communities. It was also very extensive and powerful in countries where there is little or no Shiite presence and where Sunni-Shiite differences therefore have little political or emotional significance. The impact of the Iranian Revolution in the Arab countries was somewhat delayed because of the long and bitter Iran-Iraq War (1980–88), but from the end of the war onward, Iran's influence began to grow, particularly among Shiites in neighboring Arab countries. These populations, even in those places where they are numerous, had for centuries lived under what might be described as a Sunni ascendancy. The Iranian Revolution, followed by the regime change in Iraq in 2003, gave them new hope; the Shiite struggle has once again, for the first time in centuries, become a major theme of Arab politics. This struggle is very important where Shiites constitute a majority of the population (as in Iraq) or a significant proportion of the population (as in Lebanon, Syria, and parts of the eastern and southern Arabian Peninsula). For some time now, the eastern Arab world has seen the odd spectacle of Sunni and Shiite extremists occasionally cooperating in the struggle against the infidels while continuing their internal struggle against one another. (One example of this is Iran's support for both the strongly Sunni Hamas in Gaza and the strongly Shiite Hezbollah in Lebanon.)

The increasing involvement of Iran in the affairs of the Arab world has brought about major changes. First, Iran has developed into a major regional power, its influence extending to Lebanon and the Palestinian territories. Second, although the rift between the Sunnis and the Shiites is significant, Iran's involvement has rendered it less important than the divide between both of them and their non-Arab, non-Muslim enemies. Third, just as the perceived Soviet threat induced Sadat to make peace with Israel in 1979, today some Arab leaders see the threat from Iran as more dangerous than that posed by Israel and therefore are quietly seeking accommodation with the Jewish state. During the 2006 war between Israeli forces and Hezbollah, the usual pan-Arab support for the Arab side was replaced by a cautious, even expectant, neutrality. This realignment may raise some hope for Arab-Israeli peace.

The Struggle for the Future

For much of the twentieth century, two imported Western ideologies dominated in the Arab world: socialism and nationalism. By the beginning of the twenty-first century, these worldviews had become discredited. Both had, in effect, accomplished the reverse of their declared aims. Socialist plans and projects were put in place, but they did not bring prosperity. National independence was achieved, but it did not bring freedom; rather, it allowed foreign overlords to be replaced with domestic tyrants, who were less inhibited and more intimate in their tyranny. Another imported European model, the one-party ideological dictatorship, brought neither prosperity nor dignity—only tyranny sustained by indoctrination and repression.

Today, most Arab regimes belong to one of two categories: those that depend on the people's loyalty and those that depend on their obedience. Loyalty may be ethnic, tribal, regional, or some combination of these; the most obvious examples of systems that rely on loyalty are the older monarchies, such as those of Morocco and the Arabian Peninsula. The regimes that depend on obedience are European-style dictatorships that use techniques of control and enforcement derived from the fascist and communist models. These regimes have little or no claim to the loyalty of their people and depend for survival on diversion and repression: directing the anger of their people toward some external enemy—such as Israel, whose misdeeds are a universally sanctioned public grievance—and suppressing discontent with ruthless police methods. In those Arab countries where the government depends on force rather than loyalty, there is clear evidence of deep and widespread discontent, directed primarily against the regime and then inevitably against those who are seen to support it. This leads to a paradox—namely, that countries with pro-Western regimes usually have anti-Western populations, whereas the populations of countries with anti-Western regimes tend to look to the West for liberation.

Both of these models are becoming less effective; there are groups, increasing in number and importance, that seek a new form of government based not primarily on loyalty, and still less on repression, but on consent and participation. These groups are still small and, of necessity, quiet, but the fact that they have appeared at all is a remarkable development. Some Arab states have even begun to experiment, cautiously, with elected assemblies formed after authentically contested elections, notably Iraq after its 2005 election.

In some countries, democratic opposition forces are growing, but they are often vehemently anti-Western. The recent successes of Hamas and Hezbollah demonstrate that opposition parties can fare very well when their critiques are cast in religious, rather than political, terms. The religious opposition parties have several obvious advantages. They express both their critiques and their aspirations in terms that are culturally familiar and easily accepted, unlike those of Western-style democrats. In the mosques, they have access to a communications network—and therefore tools to disseminate propaganda—unparalleled in any other sector of the community. They are relatively free from corruption and have a record of helping the suffering urban masses. A further advantage, compared with secular democratic opposition groups, is that whereas the latter are required by their own ideologies to tolerate the propaganda of their opponents, the religious parties have no such obligation. Rather, it is their sacred duty to suppress and crush what they see as antireligious, anti-Islamic movements. Defenders of the existing regimes argue, not implausibly, that loosening the reins of authority would lead to a takeover by radical Islamist forces.

Lebanon is the one country in the entire region with a significant experience of democratic political life. It has suffered not for its faults but for its merits—the freedom and openness that others have exploited with devastating effect. More recently, there have been some hopeful signs that the outside exploitation and manipulation of Lebanon might at last be diminishing.

The Palestinian leadership has been gone for decades; Syria was finally induced to withdraw its forces in 2005, leaving the Lebanese, for the first time in decades, relatively free to conduct their own affairs. Indeed, the Cedar Revolution of 2005 was seen as the beginning of a new era for Lebanon. But Lebanese democracy is far from secure. Syria retains a strong interest in the country, and Hezbollah—trained, armed, and financed by Iran—has become increasingly powerful. There have been some signs of a restoration of Lebanese stability and democracy, but the battle is not yet over, nor will it be, until the struggle for democracy spreads beyond the borders of Lebanon.

Today, there are two competing diagnoses of the ills of the region, each with its own appropriate prescription. According to one, the trouble is all due to infidels and their local dupes and imitators. The remedy is to resume the millennial struggle against the infidels in the West and return to God-given laws and traditions. According to the other diagnosis, it is the old ways, now degenerate and corrupt, that are crippling the Arab world. The cure is openness and freedom in the economy, society, and the state—in a word, genuine democracy. But the road to democracy—and to freedom—is long and difficult, with many obstacles along the way. It is there, however, and there are some visionary leaders who are trying to follow it. At the moment, both Islamic theocracy and liberal democracy are represented in the region. The future place of the Arab world in history will depend, in no small measure, on the outcome of the struggle between them.

Assess Your Progress

1. What changes have taken place in the Arab world?
2. What is the range of opinion among Palestinians regarding a settlement with Israel?
3. How has oil affected the region's economy? Is this effect likely to last?
4. What are the origins of Islamic radicalism in the region?
5. What are the two models of rule in the Arab world?
6. What are the prospects for challenges to existing regimes?

"Moderates" Redefined: How to Deal with Political Islam

It is imperative for the United States to engage mainstream Islamic political parties that are committed to gradual change through the ballot box.

EMILE NAKHLEH

Political Islam has been part of the modern Middle East landscape for several decades, but until recently the United States has rarely perceived a need to engage it. After the attacks against New York and Washington on September 11, 2001, the administration of George W. Bush painted political Islam in the Middle East, as in the rest of the Muslim world, with the broad brush of terrorism. The administration saw no meaningful differences between the minority of Islamic activists who support violence and terrorism and the majority of activists who reject the radical message of Osama bin Laden and his Al Qaeda organization.

Partly as a result, Muslims worldwide perceived Bush's global war on terror as a war on Islam, which they rejected outright. Middle East Islamic activists in particular viewed the invasions of Iraq and Afghanistan, along with Washington's continuing strong support for Israel, as amounting to an American attack on Muslim lands. Islamic activists and mainstream Islamic political parties and movements identified, as other examples of Washington's anti-Islamic posture, the tacit US support for Israel's Lebanon war in 2006 and Gaza war in 2008–9, the abuses of prisoners at Guantánamo Bay and Abu Ghraib, and the detention of thousands of Muslims in Iraq, Afghanistan, and elsewhere.

Islamic activists also viewed the cozy relationship between the United States and Arab authoritarian regimes, as well as Washington's refusal to accept Hamas's electoral victory in Gaza in 2006, as indications of America's lack of commitment to democracy and human rights, and its lack of interest in reaching out to civil society institutions in the region.

Middle Eastern regimes, for their part, were suspicious of the Bush administration's call for democracy. Elites in the region—both Islamic and secular—viewed as hypocritical the contradiction between Washington's rhetoric of democracy and its continued coddling of dictatorial regimes. The United States was seen as uninterested in engaging Arab civil society to promote civil rights, political reform, and democratization. According to opinion polls, Arab publics perceived the United States from 2003 to 2008 as advocating regime change in any country whose policies contradicted American interests in the region. Washington's bellicose rhetoric against Iran and Syria following the fall of Saddam Hussein's regime in 2003, and its undermining of the freely elected Hamas government in the Palestinians' Gaza territory, were cited as reasons for low favorability ratings accorded the United States and Bush's policies in the region.

Some academics, think tanks, and intelligence analysts in recent years have urged US policy makers to engage credible civil society institutions in the Middle East—despite the objections of entrenched authoritarian regimes—in order to encourage political and educational reforms in these societies and spur governments to open up public space for mainstream groups to participate in the political process. They have pointed out that regimes' repressive measures to curtail civil rights and freedoms of speech, assembly, and political organization have created, in many countries, a political landscape featuring just two paradigms—the authoritarian paradigm imposed by the regimes, and a radical paradigm promulgated by Al Qaeda, bin Laden, and his deputy, Ayman al-Zawahiri.

Consequently, these experts have argued that, in order to achieve the strategic objective of political reform and democratization in the region, it is imperative for the United States to engage mainstream Islamic political parties that are committed to gradual change through the ballot box. Examples of such parties and movements include the Muslim Brotherhood in Egypt, the Islamic Action Front in Jordan, the Islamic Constitutional Movement in Kuwait, Al Wifaq in Bahrain, Hamas in Palestine, Hezbollah in Lebanon, and the Justice and Development Party in Morocco.

In opposition to this idea, other analysts have contended that engaging Islamic groups would undercut the stability of pro-US authoritarian regimes and would embolden Islamic movements to contest—and win—elections, thereby paving the way for potentially anti-American Islamic regimes to emerge. Furthermore, Islamic regimes might impose Islamic law (*sharia*), which would restrict civil rights and personal freedoms and undermine the ability of liberal, secular organizations to participate in the political process. According to this argument, the "resistance" (*muqawama*) ideology of some of the Islamic parties would determine their behavior in government, thereby exacerbating conflicts and inviting more tension between regimes and societies.

The key belief underpinning opposition to engagement is that the United States should abandon the strategic policy goal of promoting democracy and continue to manage its bilateral relations with friendly Middle Eastern regimes based on the dictates of America's traditional national interests in the region—economic, political, and strategic. But in fact, political and social realities on the ground raise serious doubts about the validity of this view. And, fortunately for US-Muslim relations in the Middle East and elsewhere, the Barack Obama administration has adopted a more nuanced, sensible, and pragmatic approach.

Obama Extends a Hand

President Obama's post-inauguration statements on political Islam, along with two major speeches—in April 2009 in Ankara, and in June in Cairo—have resonated well in the Muslim world. The speeches reflected a willingness to move beyond the confrontational policy of the previous administration and toward a new era of "smart diplomacy." The bounce from Obama's conciliatory rhetoric among Arabs and Muslims will be long-lasting if it is followed by significant policy shifts—on human rights, political reform, democracy, war crimes, the closing of the Guantánamo prison—and by renewed efforts at the highest level to resolve the Israeli-Palestinian conflict.

The administration's recent direct contacts with Iranian officials—despite Tehran's heavy-handed silencing of dissent over the June presidential election—again signals Obama's commitment to engaging the Muslim world and moving from confrontation to diplomacy. Efforts to decouple elements of the Afghan Taliban (many of whom are just fighting the presence of foreign troops in their country) from the more globally dangerous Al Qaeda and the Pakistani Taliban are another affirmation by the Obama administration that it seeks simultaneously to fight terrorism and extend a peaceful hand to the wider Muslim world.

The bad news about Afghanistan is that the fire-fight is becoming much bloodier and the Taliban are emboldened. Still, Obama's historic Cairo speech, in which he detailed a vision of future relations with the Muslim world, helped put to rest the perception among many Muslims that the war on terror is a war on Islam. Also, in addressing "Muslim communities," not Muslim regimes, the president in Cairo seemed to signal that engagement will be broad-based, will not be funneled only through regimes, and will focus on economic and educational opportunities that will help improve quality of life in these societies and provide youth with more hope for the future.

Obama's approach to engaging the Muslim world seems to reflect several core themes. First, America is not at war with Islam. Second, all religions share certain "noble" ideas, including justice, tolerance, fairness, and a desire to make choices freely. Likewise, people worldwide aspire for dignity, respect, equality, economic opportunity, progress, and security. Third, people in different societies, regardless of race, religion, and color, should be able to select their governments freely, and these governments should be transparent, accountable, just, and committed to the rule of law.

Fourth, the United States is committed to engaging Muslim communities to help foster a tolerant and creative vision of Islam—but Muslims themselves, not America, must drive the debate. Fifth, the United States is committed to working with Muslim communities to settle regional conflicts on the basis of justice, fairness, and equity. And in the pursuit of these objectives, Washington will partner with American Muslims, who can act as a bridge between the United States and the Muslim world.

John Brennan, the assistant to the president for homeland security and counterterrorism, in an August 6, 2009, speech at the Center for Strategic and International Studies in Washington, elaborated further on the administration's approach. Brennan emphasized two points from the Cairo speech. One is that America's values and its commitment to justice, respect, fairness, and peace are the most effective weapons in its arsenal to fight the forces of radicalism and terrorism. The other is that bringing hope, educational promise, and economic opportunity to the youth in Muslim societies offers the best defense against the false promises and death and destruction promoted by Al Qaeda and its affiliates.

An engagement strategy can succeed in the long term only if it is accompanied by tangible policies that would reflect a change of direction in America's posture toward the Arab Muslim world. Examples of such policies include withdrawal from Iraq, ending the war in Afghanistan, and a serious push to halt expansion of Israeli settlements in the West Bank and to resolve the Israeli-Palestinian conflict. One Muslim interlocutor in the region once told me, "You can't sell hot air—engagement without substance will not succeed."

It is equally critical, however, that engagement include a concerted effort to communicate with Muslim society and civil society organizations by promoting economic, educational, and women's rights initiatives—and by dealing directly with Islamic political groups. In this respect, the Obama administration continues to engage regimes bilaterally in the service of national interests, but it is also exploring avenues to engage Islamic political parties and civil society religious groups. Key administration officials apparently believe that engaging these communities will help empower them to effect political reform from within.

Engaging these groups—sensibly, pragmatically, and openly—would make strategic sense for the West.

And with good reason. An examination of the recent legislative record of mainstream Islamic groups, their support within their own communities, and their opposition to the rising neo-Salafi extremist trend, clearly shows that engaging these groups—sensibly, pragmatically, and openly—would make strategic sense for the West. It would also improve America's standing among Muslims worldwide, and help foster an atmosphere of mutual trust and respect between the United States and the Muslim world.

Engaging Arguments

Several trends in political Islam support the argument for a robust engagement policy. First, the Islamization of Middle East politics has changed qualitatively and quantitatively since 9/11, as we have seen growing demands for economic, educational, political, and social justice in Muslim societies. Numerous Islamic political parties and movements have become more engaged in the political process through elections. Meanwhile, authoritarian regimes have used the specter of terrorism to thwart efforts to democratize and to still all demands for political reform, regardless of whether these demands are voiced by secular opposition groups or by Islamic parties.

Second, religious-nationalist ideology is driving Islamic politics at the state level in most Muslim states, but particularly in the greater Middle East. In fact, religion has become an ideological force motivating action by, and defining the interests of, both states and non-state actors. Because of regime corruption and repression—along with the bankruptcy and marginalization of traditional secular elites, largely due to their association with regimes—Islamic political parties have gained legitimacy as agents of reform and as advocates of transparent, accountable government and of the rule of law.

Third, the relationship between religion and politics is changing, largely because of demographic and economic stresses, globalization, the communications revolution, entrenched authoritarianism in many Muslim countries, a weak identification with the state, and the general failure of secular nationalist ideologies. Religions and religious affiliation have become drivers of the political process across the globe—from Russia to India, from Ankara to Kuala Lumpur.

Fourth, because of regimes' diminishing legitimacy and the weakening of public identification with the state, Islam has become an identity anchor for millions of Muslims. Religious programs broadcast on global satellite television networks are able to carry the "sacred word" from Mecca and other centers of Islam to the remotest villages in West Africa, Central Asia, the Indus Valley, and western China—and of course throughout the Middle East.

Fifth, Islamic political activism in the Middle East, as in the rest of the Muslim world, has become more diverse and complex. Such diversity—cultural, economic, historical, political, religious, and demographic—dictates that, before Washington engages these groups, US policy makers must understand the varied historical narratives to which different Islamic groups cling, the reasons why entrenched authoritarian regimes oppose political participation by Islamic activists, the indigenous and country-specific agendas of Islamic groups, and their legislative behavior in national assemblies.

An Energized Debate

Sixth, political ideology has become embedded in an energized debate among Muslim activists on Islamic blogs and in the media, both print and electronic. The debate has focused on at least three themes. One is the future vision of Islam that Muslims should pursue, and whether such a vision should be limited to the moral dictates of the faith or should expand to the political and social realms. Another topic is whether Islamic political parties should continue to participate in the political process through elections even under regimes that actively undermine the democratic process, or whether they should instead reject politics and return to their core mission of proselytization (*da'wa*). Still another issue is whether Islamic political parties, which have traditionally been committed to the implementation of sharia, can equally maintain a long-term commitment to democracy and pluralism as these terms are understood in the West.

Seventh, Middle Eastern Islamic political parties remain territorially focused and committed to indigenous agendas. They do not share the global jihadist ideology of Al Qaeda and its affiliates. The strategic goal of these parties' struggles and activism is to liberate their territories from occupation and safeguard the political, economic, and security status of their people. In fact, Al Qaeda's second-in-command, Zawahiri, in 2006 severely criticized Islamic political parties in the region—including the Egyptian Muslim Brotherhood, the Palestinian Hamas, and the Moroccan Justice and Development Party—for participating in national elections. The parties in turn openly and forcefully rejected Al Qaeda's criticism.

Eighth, Islamic parties' disagreements with the United States and other Western powers in recent years have been driven by specific policies, not by disputes over governance issues. Public opinion polls—administered by organizations including Pew, Gallup, the BBC, and Zogby—have clearly shown that majorities of Muslims, including in the Middle East, endorse fair and free elections, transparent and accountable government, a free press, an independent judiciary, and the rule of law. Their disagreements with the United States, according to these polls, have been driven by specific policies, such as the Iraq War and US support for Israeli actions, which they consider aggressive, a threat to world peace, and anti-Islamic.

Ninth, mainstream Islamic political parties have fought the rise of the new Salafi ideology because of its conservative, intolerant, and exclusivist bent. The Salafi ideology, which in some cases has been supported by regimes as an antidote to mainstream Islamic activism, is grounded in a narrow reading of religious texts. It preaches an extremist version of Wahhabi Islam (which insists on a return to an original, purer form of the faith). It calls for the establishment of a strict version of Islamic law that imposes a rigid moral code on society, separates the sexes, and restricts women's participation in education, culture, and business.

A bloody conflict in August 2009 between Hamas and the Salafi Jund Ansar Allah group in Gaza, which featured an attack on a mosque in Rafah and the killing of the Salafi leader Shaykh Abu Mousa, illustrates the threat that mainstream Islamic parties across the Middle East are facing from the Salafi trend. Engaging mainstream Islamic political parties could help empower them to fight the Salafi movement in Middle Eastern societies, including Palestine, Egypt, Lebanon, Yemen, Morocco, Sudan, and Kuwait.

Islam and Potholes

Debate about Islamic political parties' participation in politics has focused on the question of whether their commitment to the electoral process is a tactical maneuver to get them into power, or whether they have made a strategic decision to pursue gradual political change through politics. One could ask: If these parties have espoused sharia as the basis for their existence, how strong or sustainable can their commitment to democracy and pluralism be? In fact, interviews with many Muslim activists over the years, and an examination of the electoral campaign platforms and legislative agendas of some Islamic political parties, reveal that their commitment to nationalist causes or social justice often supersedes their commitment to Islamic law.

Islamic parties in general have undergone a transformation in their religious ideology. They have moved away from their original "charters"—which usually espouse a strong commitment to sharia—and now focus instead on social, economic, and political practices. Once in a legislature, they have worked with other political parties to pass legislation dealing with roads, public utilities, and other bread-and-butter issues.

Hamas's charter, for example, which was written in the 1980s before the group's leaders even decided to form a political party, embodied the movement's religious commitment, its vision of Palestinian society and territory, and its opposition to participating in the political process. Although Lebanon's Hezbollah was launched with significant Iranian support, it has built an impressive political constituency in a community marked by impoverishment, deprivation, and dispossession.

A review of the political programs of Hamas and Hezbollah, two of the Middle East's most active political parties, shows that, although both parties initially scorned electoral politics, they subsequently became avid players in the political game and participated successfully in national elections. Hamas won Legislative Council elections in 2006, and Hezbollah has successfully competed in Lebanese parliamentary elections since 1992, including the spring 2009 elections.

The national political programs of Hamas and Hezbollah share two characteristics: a deep commitment to social justice and community development; and the embodiment of "resistance." The religious identity that each espouses is wedded to conceptions of resistance through community service and armed opposition to occupation. While they strongly draw on their Sunni (Hamas) and Shiite (Hezbollah) religious cultural heritages, neither group has made the imposition of sharia or the creation of an Islamic state its dominant objective. Hamas has not advocated reestablishment of the "caliphate." While Hezbollah officially advocates the *Vilayet-e Faqih,* or rule of Islamic judges, for many years it has accepted that the creation of such a system in religiously mixed Lebanon is infeasible and very unlikely.

Hezbollah and Hamas have been able to face down Israeli military assaults—a feat that conventional Arab armies have failed to accomplish since the creation of the state of Israel. As a result, both groups at times have enjoyed widespread popularity in the Arab world, even in more secular segments of society. According to public opinion polls, Hamas and Hezbollah symbolize for many Arabs a successful Islamic engagement in politics, a strong commitment to social justice, and a rejection of corruption and authoritarianism. Not surprisingly, Arab regimes, including the corruption-ridden Palestinian Authority in Ramallah under Mahmoud Abbas, have become wary of the success of Hamas and Hezbollah and have often opposed their rise, influence, and activities, and even turned a blind eye to Israel's recent military attempts to defeat them.

Thus Islamic parties—even beyond Hamas and Hezbollah—have over time changed their political ideologies and tempered their commitment to sharia in the face of the practical demands of electoral and legislative politics. In the early 1990s, some of these parties refused to participate in the electoral process because of the "un-Islamic" behavior of regimes; by the late 1990s, most had decided to take part in national elections and play the game of politics regardless of the nature of the government.

While Islamic parties still evince a commitment to Islamic law, sharia is so diverse and multifaceted that dedication to it need not imply a conservative Wahhabi-like or retrograde Taliban-like agenda. Political pragmatism, rather than purist religious ideology, has become the guiding principle of the Islamization of politics in Muslim-majority countries, including in the Middle East.

The Radical Element

Terrorists both in the Middle East and globally generally follow the radical paradigm of bin Laden and Al Qaeda, which claims that Islam—faith and territory—is under attack and that the "enemy" consists of the Christian Crusaders headed by the United States, the Zionists represented by Israel, and pro-Western Arab and Muslim regimes. Bin Laden further maintains that in the face of this attack, jihad by whatever means is a duty for all Muslims, and that the killing of innocent civilians and the use of weapons of mass destruction are justified.

Providing a religious justification for terrorism has been an effective recruiting strategy, especially among alienated youth with limited education and poor economic prospects. In justifying terrorism, bin Laden has presented violent jihad as a struggle between good and evil. The struggle, he argues, will continue until the "final days."

On this last point there is a disagreement between Al Qaeda, as an advocate of global jihad, and country-specific Islamist organizations such as Hamas and Hezbollah, which aspire to achieve territorial autonomy or independence. These parties do not share Al Qaeda's millenarian ideology and focus instead on their own objectives.

Although in the past decade the vast majority of Muslims worldwide has not renounced terrorism forcefully and openly, more and more Muslims in the last three years have been speaking out against terrorism and the wanton killing of innocent civilians. Moderate Muslim thinkers have argued that relations between Muslims and non-Muslims need not be full of conflict, as bin Laden has postulated. They also suggest that the Koran, revealed to the prophet Muhammad in seventh-century Arabia, must be transformed to fit Muslim life in a twenty-first–century globalized world.

Muslim thinkers in both Western and Muslim countries have argued that certain aspects of Western political culture, including parliamentary democracy, political and social pluralism, women's rights, civil society, and human rights, are compatible with Islamic scripture and traditions. As noted, according to many public opinion polls, most Muslims believe in these values. Mainstream Islamic political parties in the Middle East also endorse this view of democracy.

The radical paradigm promulgated by Al Qaeda appears to be on the wane because of its opposition to ideas that mainstream Islamic parties are promoting.

Thus, the radical paradigm promulgated by Al Qaeda appears to be on the wane today precisely because of its opposition to the ideas of tolerance, inclusion, and political participation that the mainstream Islamic parties are promoting. More and more Muslims are denouncing the killing of innocent civilians—Muslim and non-Muslim—and are beginning to question openly and publicly the logic of violence. More and more Islamic activists are choosing local and national causes over global jihad. And despite Al Qaeda's strong and persistent opposition to "man-made" democracy and elections, more and more Islamic political parties are participating in national elections and in the mundane activities of electoral politics and pragmatic governance. It is no coincidence that the radical political paradigm is declining at a time when Islamic parties have increasingly entered the political fray.

A Fraught Task

Regardless of Al Qaeda's fortunes, religious extremism and political radicalism will persist in the Middle East for years to come. This is the case because of factors having little or nothing to do with Islamic ideology—factors such as entrenched authoritarianism, weak state legitimacy, continuing disregard for civil and human rights, the rise of non-state actors and sub-state loyalties, systemic state corruption, economic stagnation, and the failure so far to find a solution to the Israeli-Palestinian conflict.

Several Arab regimes have used the fight against terrorism as an excuse to deny their peoples the right to participate in the political process freely, openly, and without harassment. Yet the record of Islamic political parties' participation in electoral politics, over several national elections, does not support the regimes' argument that such participation destabilizes society or undermines national security.

Indeed, it may be time for senior policy makers in Western countries to revisit their use of the term "moderate" when dealing with the Middle East. Policy makers have tended to bestow the "moderate" moniker on pro-Western governments despite their autocratic nature, while grouping Islamic activists generically into the "radical" category. But equating authoritarian regimes with "moderation" has resulted in a perception of hypocrisy and has helped drive the very radicalization that the West has sought to counter. Meanwhile, the effort to counter radicalization, when paired with a refusal to deal with Islamic groups, has yielded poor results. It might be more prudent, as well as honest, to describe such regimes as "friendly" or "pro-US" rather than "moderate."

Policy makers have tended to bestow the "moderate" moniker on pro-Western governments while grouping Islamic activists generically into the "radical" category.

Reaching out to the vast majority of Muslims will require a long-term commitment in time, resources, and personnel. It will require a thorough knowledge of the cultures involved, sophisticated influence operations, strategically developed public diplomacy campaigns, a coherent and carefully crafted message, and utilization of credible indigenous Muslim voices.

Engaging Islamic political parties is likewise a process fraught with challenges, especially since most "friendly" regimes in the Middle East are opposed to such engagement. Some Islamic parties will pose particularly thorny dilemmas for the United States. Hamas and Hezbollah, for example, are considered terrorist organizations under US law. Some Iraqi Islamic parties are closely aligned with Iran. And a few Shiite movements in Iraq and Bahrain advocate sectarian autonomy.

As the Obama administration proceeds with implementing principles that the president enunciated in his Cairo speech, policy makers will have to find ways to convince regimes that engaging civil society institutions and non-state actors in their societies will not necessarily undermine those regimes. Policy makers must continually point out that, if the people in a particular country have the right to choose their government freely, they will be more invested in social peace and political stability, which in the long run will minimize tensions between state and society.

This amounts to a daunting task, to be sure. But in the final analysis, engagement with Muslim societies must include the Islamic parties and movements in those societies. To believe otherwise is damaging both to regional stability and to America's strategic interests and standing in the Muslim world.

Assess Your Progress

1. How do many Muslims regard U.S. involvement in the Islamic world?
2. What are the arguments for and against engaging mainstream Islamic movements?
3. How has President Obama's outreach been received in the Middle East?
4. What themes does Obama's policy reflect?
5. What trends in political Islam suggest some support for this engagement effort?

Emile Nakhleh is a former senior intelligence officer with the US Central Intelligence Agency, where he served as director of the Political Islam Strategic Analysis program and chief of regional analysis for the Near East and South Asia. He is the author of *A Necessary Engagement: Reinventing America's Relations with the Muslim World* (Princeton University Press, 2008).

The Islamists Are Not Coming

Religious parties in the Muslim world are hardly the juggernauts they've been made out to be.

CHARLES KURZMAN AND IJLAL NAQVI

Do Muslims automatically vote Islamic? That's the concern conjured up by strongmen from Tunis to Tashkent, and plenty of Western experts agree. They point to the political victories of Islamic parties in Egypt, Palestine, and Turkey in recent years and warn that more elections across the Islamic world could turn power over to anti-democratic fundamentalists.

But these victories turn out to be exceptions, not the political rule. When we examined results from parliamentary elections in all Muslim societies, we found a very different pattern: Given the choice, voters tend to go with secular parties, not religious ones. Over the past 40 years, 86 parliamentary elections in 20 countries have included one or more Islamic parties, according to annual reports from the Inter-Parliamentary Union. Voters in these places have overwhelmingly turned up their noses at such parties. Eighty percent of these Islamic parties earned less than 20 percent of the vote, and a majority got less than 10 percent—hardly landslide victories. The same is true even over the last few years, with numbers barely changing since 2001.

80% Share of islamic parties that earned 20% or less of the vote over the last 40 years.

True, Islamic parties have won a few well-publicized breakthrough victories, such as in Algeria in 1991 and Palestine in 2006. But far more often, Islamic parties tend to do very poorly. What's more, the more free and fair an election is, the worse the Islamic parties do. By our calculations, the average percentage of seats won by Islamic parties in relatively free elections is 10 points lower than in less free ones.

Even if they don't win, Islamic parties often find themselves liberalized by the electoral process. We found that Islamic party platforms are less likely to focus on sharia law or armed jihad in freer elections and more likely to uphold democracy and women's rights. And even in more authoritarian countries, Islamic party platforms have shifted over the course of multiple elections toward more liberal positions: Morocco's Justice and Development Party and Jordan's Islamic Action Front both stripped sharia law from their platforms over the last several years.

These are still culturally conservative parties, by any standard, but their decision to run for office places them at odds with Islamic revolutionaries. In many cases, they're actually risking their lives. Almost two decades ago, even before his alliance with Osama bin Laden, Egyptian jihadist Ayman al-Zawahiri wrote a tract condemning the Muslim Brotherhood's abandonment of revolutionary methods in favor of electoral politics. "Whoever labels himself as a Muslim democrat, or a Muslim who calls for democracy, is like saying he is a Jewish Muslim or a Christian Muslim," he wrote. In Iraq, Sunni Islamic revolutionaries recently renewed their campaign "to start killing all those participating in the political process," according to a warning received by a Sunni politician who was subsequently assassinated in Mosul.

What enrages Zawahiri and his ilk is that Islamists keep ignoring demands to stay out of parliamentary politics. Despite threats from terrorists and a cold shoulder from voters, more and more Islamic parties are entering the electoral process. A quarter-century ago, many of these movements were trying to overthrow the state and create an Islamic society, inspired by the Iranian Revolution. Now, disillusioned with revolution, they are working within the secular system.

But today's problems for Islamic parties may recall an earlier historical moment, the watershed period of the early 20th century when demands for democracy and human rights first gained mass support in Muslim societies from the Russian Empire to the Ottoman Empire. Then as now, violent Islamic movements such as the Ottoman-era Islamic Unity Society objected to electoral politics. But that was not what ultimately undermined democracy in Muslim societies. Instead, secular autocrats, such as Mustafa Kemal Ataturk in Turkey and Reza Shah in Iran, suppressed pro-democratic Islamic movements, driving Islamists underground and helping to radicalize them.

Today, too, dictators and terrorists are conspiring to keep Islamic political parties from competing freely for votes. Government repression has been successful in one sense—Islamic parties have won few elections. In a broader sense, however, it is failing: According to the World Values Survey, which has polled cultural attitudes around the world, support for sharia is one-third lower in countries with relatively free elections than in other Muslim societies. In other words, suppressing Islamic movements has only made them more popular. Perhaps democratization is not such a gift to Islamists after all.

Assess Your Progress

1. How have Islamic parties fared in terms of voter support?
2. Under what circumstances do these parties fare the worst?
3. What impact do free elections seem to have on Islamic parties?
4. What effect does suppressing Islamic party participation have?

Charles Kurzman is professor of sociology and **Ijlal Naqvi** is a sociology graduate student at the University of North Carolina at Chapel Hill.

The Transformation of Hamas

Palestine's Islamic movement has subtly changed its uncompromising posture on Israel.

FAWAZ A. GERGES

Something is stirring within the Hamas body politic, a moderating trend that, if nourished and engaged, could transform Palestinian politics and the Arab-Israeli peace process. There are unmistakable signs that the religiously based radical movement has subtly changed its uncompromising posture on Israel. Although low-key and restrained, those shifts indicate that the movement is searching for a formula that addresses the concerns of Western powers yet avoids alienating its social base.

Far from impulsive and unexpected, Hamas's shift reflects a gradual evolution occurring over the past five years. The big strategic turn occurred in 2005, when Hamas decided to participate in the January 2006 legislative elections and thus tacitly accepted the governing rules of the Palestinian Authority (PA), one of which includes recognition of Israel. Ever since, top Hamas leaders have repeatedly declared they will accept a resolution of the conflict along the 1967 borders. The Damascus-based Khaled Meshal, head of Hamas's political bureau and considered a hardliner, acknowledged as much in 2008. "We are realists," he said, who recognize that there is "an entity called Israel." Pressed by an Australian journalist on policy changes Hamas might make, Meshal asserted that the organization has shifted on several key points: "Hamas has already changed—we accepted the national accords for a Palestinian state based on the 1967 borders, and we took part in the 2006 Palestinian elections."

Another senior Hamas leader, Ghazi Hamad, was more specific than Meshal, telling journalists in January 2009 that Hamas would be satisfied with ending Israeli control over the Palestinian areas occupied in the 1967 war—the West Bank, Gaza and East Jerusalem. In other words, Hamas would not hold out for liberation of the land that currently includes Israel.

Previously Hamas moderates had called at times for a *tahdia* (a minor truce, or "calm") or *hudna* (a longer-term truce, lasting as long as fifty years), which implies some measure of recognition, if only tacit. The moderates justified their policy shift by using Islamic terms (in Islamic history *hudnas* sometimes develop into permanent truces). Now leaders appear to be going further; they have made a concerted effort to re-educate the rank and file about the necessity of living side by side with their Jewish neighbors, and in so doing mentally prepare them for a permanent settlement. In Gaza's mosques pro-Hamas clerics have begun to cite the example of the famed twelfth-century Muslim military commander and statesman Saladin, who after liberating Jerusalem from the Crusaders allowed them to retain a coastal state in the Levant. The point is that if Saladin could tolerate the warring, bloodthirsty Crusaders, then today's Palestinians should be willing to live peacefully with a Jewish state in their midst.

The Saladin story is important because it provides Hamas with religious legitimacy and allows it to justify the change of direction to followers. Hamas's raison d'être rests on religious legitimation; its leaders understand that they neglect this at their peril. Western leaders and students of international politics should acknowledge that Hamas can no more abandon its commitment to Islamism than the United States can abandon its commitment to liberal democracy. That does not mean Hamas is incapable of change or compromise but simply that its political identity is strongly constituted by its religious legitimation.

It should be emphasized as well that Hamas is not monolithic on the issue of peace. There are multiple, clashing viewpoints and constituencies within the movement. Over the years I have interviewed more than a dozen leaders inside and outside the occupied territories. Although on the whole Hamas's public rhetoric calls for the liberation of all of historic Palestine, not only the territories occupied in 1967, a healthy debate has grown both within and without.

Several factors have played a role in the transformation. They include the burden of governing a war-torn Gaza and the devastation from Israel's 2008–09 attack, which has caused incalculable human suffering and increasing public dissatisfaction in Gaza with Hamas rule.

Before the 2006 parliamentary elections, Hamas was known for its suicide bombers, not its bureaucrats, even though between 2002 and 2006 the organization moved from rejectionism toward participation in a political framework that is a direct product of the Oslo peace process of the 1990s. After the elections, the shift continued. "It is much more difficult to run a government than to oppose and resist Israeli occupation," a senior Hamas leader told me while on official business in Egypt in 2007. "If we do not provide the goods to our people, they'll disown us." Hamas is not just a political party. It's a social movement, and as such it has a long record of concern about and close attention to public opinion. Given the gravity of deteriorating conditions in Gaza and Hamas's weak performance during last year's fighting, it should be no surprise that the organization has undergone a period of fairly intense soul-searching and reassessment of strategic options.

Ironically, despite the West's refusal to regard the Hamas government as legitimate and despite the continuing brutal siege of Gaza, demands for democratic governance within Gaza are driving change. Yet Hamas leaders are fully aware of the danger of alienating more-hardline factions if they show weakness or water down their position and move toward de facto recognition of Israel without getting something substantive in return. Hamas's strategic predicament lies in striking a balance between, on the one hand, a new moderating and maturing sensibility and, on the other, insistence on the right and imperative of armed resistance. This difficult balance often explains the tensions and contradictions in Hamas's public and private pronouncements.

What is striking about Hamas's shift toward the peace process is that it has come at a time of critical challenges from Al Qaeda–like jihadist groups; a low-intensity civil war with rival Fatah, the ruling party of the PA; and a deteriorating humanitarian situation in Gaza.

Last summer a militant group called Jund Ansar Allah, or the Warriors of God, one of a handful of Al Qaeda–inspired factions, declared the establishment of an Islamic emirate in Gaza—a flagrant rejection of Hamas's authority. Hamas security forces struck instantly and mercilessly at the Warriors, killing more than twenty members, including the group's leader, Abdel-Latif Moussa. In one stroke, the Hamas leadership sent a message to foes and friends alike that it will not tolerate global jihadist groups like Al Qaeda, which want to turn Gaza into a theater of transnational jihad.

Despite the crushing of Moussa's outfit, the extremist challenge persists. The Israeli siege, in place since 2006, along with the suffering and despair it has caused among Gaza's 1.4 million inhabitants, has driven hundreds of young Palestinians into the arms of small Salafist extremist factions that accuse Hamas of forfeiting the armed struggle and failing to implement Shariah law. Hamas leaders appear to be worried about the proliferation of these factions and have instructed clerics to warn worshipers against joining such bands.

Compared with these puritanical and nihilistic groups, Hamas is well within the mainstream of Islamist politics. Operationally and ideologically, there are huge differences between Hamas and jihadi extremists such as Al Qaeda—and there's a lot of bad blood. Hamas is a broad-based religious/nationalist resistance whose focus and violence is limited to Palestine/Israel, while Al Qaeda is a small, transnational terrorist network that has carried out attacks worldwide. Al Qaeda leaders Osama bin Laden and Ayman al-Zawahiri have vehemently criticized Hamas for its willingness to play politics and negotiate with Israel. Hamas leaders have responded that they know what is good for their people, and they have made it crystal clear they have no interest in transnational militancy. Their overriding goal is political and nationalist rather than ideological and global: to empower Palestinians and liberate the occupied Palestinian territories.

Unlike Al Qaeda and other fringe factions, Hamas is a viable social movement with an extensive social network and a large popular base that has been estimated at several hundred thousand. Given its tradition of sensitivity and responsiveness to Palestinian public opinion, a convincing argument could be made that the recent changes in the organization's conduct can be attributed to the high levels of poverty, unemployment and isolation of Palestinians in Gaza, who fear an even greater deterioration of conditions there.

A further example of Hamas's political and social priorities is its decision to agree in principle to an Egyptian-brokered deal that sketches out a path to peace with Fatah. After two years of bitter and violent division, the warring parties came very close to agreement in October. The deal collapsed at the last moment, but talks continue. There are two points to make about the Egyptian role: first, Hamas leaders say they feel somewhat betrayed by the Egyptians because after pressure from the Americans, Cairo unilaterally revised the final agreed-upon text without consulting the Hamas negotiating team. Second, many Palestinian and Arab observers think Egypt is in no hurry to conclude the Fatah-Hamas talks. They contend that faced with regional challenges and rivals (Iran, Turkey, Syria and Saudi Arabia), the Mubarak regime views its brokering process in the Palestinian-Israeli theater as an important regional asset and a way to solidify its relationship with Washington.

Despite its frequently reactionary rhetoric, Hamas is a rational actor, a conclusion reached by former Mossad chief Ephraim Halevy, who also served as Ariel Sharon's national security adviser and who is certainly not a peacenik. The Hamas leadership has undergone a transformation "right under our very noses" by recognizing that "its ideological goal is not attainable and will not be in the foreseeable future," Halevy wrote in the Israeli daily *Yediot Ahronot* just before the 2008 attack on Gaza. He believes Hamas is ready and willing to accept the establishment of a Palestinian state within the 1967 borders. The US Army Strategic Studies Institute published a similar analysis just before the Israeli offensive, concluding that Hamas was considering a shift of its position and that "Israel's stance toward [Hamas] . . . has been a major obstacle to substantive peacemaking."

Indeed, it could be argued that Hamas has moved closer to a vision of peace consistent with international law and consensus (two separate states in historic Palestine, divided more or less along the '67 borders with East Jerusalem as the capital of Palestine, and recognition of all states in the region) than the current Israeli governing coalition. Prime Minister Benjamin Netanyahu vehemently opposes the establishment of a genuinely viable Palestinian state in the West Bank and Gaza, and is opposed to giving up any part of Jerusalem—and

Netanyahu's governing coalition is more right wing and pro-settlement than he is.

Hamas's political evolution and deepening moderation stand in stark contrast to the rejectionism of the Netanyahu government and call into question which parties are "hardline" and which are "extremist." And at the regional level, a sea change has occurred in the official Arab position toward the Jewish state (the Arab League's 2002 Beirut Declaration, subsequently reiterated, offers full recognition and diplomatic relations if Israel accepts the international consensus regarding a two-state solution), while the attitudes of the Israeli ruling elite have hardened. This marks a transformation of regional politics and a reversal of roles.

Observers might ask, if Hamas is so eager to accept a two-state solution, why doesn't it simply accept the three conditions for engagement required by the so-called diplomatic Quartet (the United States, Russia, the European Union and the United Nations): recognition of Israel, renunciation of violence and acceptance of all previous agreements (primarily, the Oslo Accords)? In my interviews with Hamas officials, they stress that while they have made significant concessions to the Quartet, it has not lifted the punishing sanctions against Hamas, nor has it pressed Israel to end its siege, which has caused a dire humanitarian crisis. In addition, Hamas leaders believe that recognition of Israel is the last card in their hand and are reluctant to play it before talks even begin. Their diplomatic starting point will be to demand that Israel recognize the national rights of the Palestinians and withdraw from the occupied territories—but it will not be their final position.

There can be no viable, lasting peace between Israel and the Palestinians if Hamas is not consulted and if the Palestinians remain divided, with two warring authorities in the West Bank and Gaza. Hamas has the means and public support to undermine any agreement that does not address the legitimate rights and claims of the Palestinian people. Its Fatah/PA rival lacks a popular mandate and the legitimacy needed to implement a resolution of the conflict. PA President Mahmoud Abbas has been weakened by a series of blunders of his own making, and with his moral authority compromised in the eyes of a sizable Palestinian constituency, Abbas is yesterday's man—no matter how long he remains in power as a lame duck, and whether or not he competes in the upcoming presidential elections.

If the United States and Europe engaged Hamas, encouraging it to continue moderating its views instead of ignoring it or, worse yet, seeking its overthrow, the West could test the extent of Hamas's evolution. So far the strategy of isolation and military confrontation—pursued in tandem by Israel and the United States—has not appeared to weaken Hamas significantly. If anything, it has radicalized hundreds of young Palestinians, who have joined extremist factions and reinforced the culture of martyrdom and nihilism. All the while, the siege of Gaza has left a trail of untold pain and suffering.

If the Western powers don't engage Hamas, they will never know if it can evolve into an open, tolerant and peaceful social movement. The jury is still out on whether the Islamist movement can make that painful and ideologically costly transition. But the claim that engaging Hamas legitimizes it does not carry much weight; the organization derives its legitimacy from the Palestinian people, a mandate resoundingly confirmed in the free and fair elections of 2006.

To break the impasse and prevent gains by more extremist factions, the Obama administration and Congress should support a unified Palestinian government that could negotiate peace with Israel. Whatever they think of its ideology, US officials should acknowledge that Hamas is a legitimately elected representative of the Palestinian people, and that any treaty signed by a rump Fatah/PA will not withstand the test of time. And instead of twisting Cairo's arms in a rejectionist direction, Washington should encourage its Egyptian ally to broker a truce between Hamas and Fatah and thus repair the badly frayed Palestinian governing institutions. If the Obama administration continues to shun engagement with Hamas, Europe ought to take the lead in establishing an official connection. European governments have already dealt with Lebanon's Hezbollah, a group similar to Hamas in some respects, and they possess the skills, experience and political weight to help broker a viable peace settlement.

Like it or not, Hamas is the most powerful organization in the occupied territories. It is deeply entrenched in Palestinian society. Neither Israel nor the Western powers can wish it away. The good news, if my reading is correct, is that Hamas has changed, is willing to meet some of the Quartet's conditions and is making domestic political preparations for further changes. But if Hamas is not engaged, and if the siege of Gaza and Palestinian suffering continue without hope of ending the political impasse, there is a real danger of a regional war.

Assess Your Progress

1. How has Hamas shifted its stance on Israel?
2. To what can this shift be attributed?
3. What is striking about this shift in attitude?
4. What are the differences between the views of Hamas and those of Islamic radicals?
5. What should be done to take advantage of this change in attitude?

Fawaz A. Gerges is a professor of Middle Eastern politics and international relations at the London School of Economics and Political Science at the University of London. His most recent book is *Journey of the Jihadist Inside Muslim Militancy* (Harcourt).

Adios, Monroe Doctrine

When the Yanquis Go Home

JORGE G. CASTAÑEDA

The ouster of Honduran President Manuel Zelaya has provided Latin America with a revelatory moment. Beginning with the Monroe Doctrine—and extending through countless invasions, occupations, and covert operations—Washington has considered the region its backyard. So where was this superpower these past few months, as Honduras hung in the balance? More or less sitting on its hands. The fact is that the United States is no longer willing, or perhaps even able, to select who governs from Tegucigalpa, or anywhere else in the region for that matter. Looking back at the history of the hemisphere, this fact is remarkable—and certainly transformative. For the first time in centuries, the United States doesn't seem to care much what happens in Latin America.

The roots of the diminishing U.S. presence can be found in the end of the cold war. It's not that the rivalry with the Soviets was the only factor driving U.S. involvement in Latin America. Clearly, James Monroe and Teddy Roosevelt didn't plunge their country deep into the hemisphere out of an anticommunist impulse. But the conclusion of the long struggle with the Soviets sharpened a question that may have long lurked in Washington's subconscious: What national interests, exactly, did the United States have in Latin America?

Of course, it is tempting to view this possible retreat from the region as further evidence of Barack Obama's realist foreign policy. But consider the approach of Bill Clinton and George W. Bush. During their administrations, America's grandest policy moves in the hemisphere were in the realm of economic policy—NAFTA, the Mexican bailout of 1995, CAFTA. And, when the United States did exert itself militarily, it did so in concert with regional allies—as was the case in Haiti and with Plan Colombia. But since George H.W. Bush's invasion of Panama, there have been no unilateral military interventions, no coup plots or new embargoes, not even the propping up of decaying regimes.

To understand this new passivity, we can examine the two events that have most riled the old critics of imperialism: the Bush administration's alleged complicity in the botched military coup against Hugo Chávez in 2002 and the plans to build a wall along the Mexican border. Both of these events are partly real and largely idle. Even if the coup plotters in Caracas had the tacit approval of the United States, they were almost certainly acting on their own, and sloppily. Meanwhile, the fence has yet to be completed. Recession has abated the human flow northward—and policymakers surely know that a wall will be futile once the economy eventually recovers.

At first, in the case of the Clinton years, this attitude of benign neglect made Washington popular. But then, for reasons having more to do with Iraq and Afghanistan, that popularity evaporated. And, in the end, the rise of anti-Americanism in the region didn't make much of a difference. Chávez has not stopped selling oil to the United States; Ecuadorean President Rafael Correa rants against imperialism but maintains the dollar as his country's national currency, with the Fed's quiet acquiescence.

Of course, the United States still has its critics. Some—the left, mainly—would prefer that it play even less of a role: a unilateral end to the Cuban embargo, immigration reform, voiding the military basing agreement with Colombia. Others—the right, chiefly—have called for further confrontation with Chávez. But, by and large, a strange and centrist hemispheric consensus has emerged in support of U.S. indifference. Therefore, this policy will persist, unless things get nasty.

With the rise of Chavismo, it isn't always possible to see the salutary benefits from this new U.S. policy. But they are tangible. It has grown increasingly difficult for certain regimes to blame Washington for their failures. From Venezuela to Argentina to Bolivia, populist governments have pursued economic and social policies, as well as geopolitical alliances, that can scarcely help their people. When these policies inevitably fail, these governments won't be able to replicate the rhetorical trickery of the Cubans or the Sandinistas. They cannot hold Washington responsible for their setbacks. At best, they can argue that the peasants in the Andes are still hungry because of the presence of U.S. troops in Afghanistan, but that is not an easy sell.

And the change in regional dynamics is even more profound than that. The past decade has seen the rise of governments—like those of Lula in Brazil, Michelle Bachelet and Ricardo Lagos in Chile, and Tabaré Vázquez in Uruguay—that have ideological differences with Washington but a strong desire for a good working relationship with it. These governments can fend off the most radical segments of their left-wing constituencies, who frown on any relationship with Washington, by citing the end of U.S. imperialism in the hemisphere. When the so-called "Shiite" faction of Lula's Workers' Party protests against hosting George W. Bush for lunch, he can reply that, whatever one may think of Iraq, Bush did not inflict any harm on Brazil; when Chávez rails against the U.S.-Colombian military agreement, Chile and Uruguay can reasonably respond that, while they may not like the deal, it does not affect them.

This U.S. stance is also a positive development for symbolic reasons. Too much is made about the imperative for U.S. atonement or humility; they are both overrated. Nonetheless, the United States does carry baggage in the region, and the history of its engagement with Latin America is not a proud one. Breaking with that past, at least by not repeating it, is a good idea and wins points in most quarters of the hemisphere. There is a legitimate debate about the motivations for U.S. intervention in Latin America, as well as its consequences. But placing that history behind us allows for a relationship stripped of the rhetorically strident and often vapid atmospherics of the past.

Unfortunately, this new strategic environment is precarious. Over the long run, the U.S. policy of benign neglect stands a good chance of isolating Hugo Chávez. But such policy depends on turning the other cheek—and perseverance in turning the other cheek depends largely on the intensity and frequency of the slaps one receives.

The least-dangerous threat posed by Venezuela and its allies is economic: that companies will be nationalized without compensation; that a gradual drop in Venezuelan oil exports to the U.S. Gulf Coast will turn precipitous; that defaulting debt will trigger a regional financial crisis. None of these scenarios would be the end of the world, but Barack Obama could hardly pursue his jocular attitude toward Chávez if they materialized. Another danger lies in the Caracas caudillo's domestic policies. If he goes too far in muzzling the press, intimidating the opposition, and tampering with the electoral process or the courts, Washington will find itself unable to ignore his authoritarian crackdown.

But it's Chávez's foreign activities that could prove most menacing. For now, his partnership with Mahmoud Ahmadinejad is more bluster than substance. The idea that the two dictators' countries can truly help each other, given their economic similarities, is far-fetched. But it is possible to imagine situations in which Chávez would lend Iran a truly destabilizing hand. If Tehran faces trade sanctions, especially an embargo on gasoline sales, Venezuela could help mitigate the damage with exports. Venezuela could also serve as a base for transshipment of Russian arms sales to Iran, with the hope that Israel would not detect them until it is too late. Finally, Iran could farm out sensitive stages of its nuclear program to Venezuela, where it would hope to avoid the watchful eye of inspectors. Any of these scenarios could provoke the United States to abandon its deliberate passivity.

Chávez has already shown a penchant for mischief, particularly within Latin America. So far, he has meddled successfully in the electoral processes of smaller countries—Bolivia, Nicaragua, Ecuador, Paraguay, El Salvador, Honduras—and much less successfully in larger nations—Mexico, Peru, and Colombia. His flops have permitted a certain tolerance for his triumphs. At the end of the day, who governs in Managua is no longer a matter of huge preoccupation in most foreign ministries.

But the larger countries are a different kettle of fish. Two, in particular, stand out as tempting targets for Venezuelan adventurism. Colombia is Chávez's ongoing obsession. He cannot bring this country into his orbit electorally, but he could conceivably try to move it into his column through other means—revolution, insurrection, pressure from across the border. Peru, the more likely candidate for his meddling, will hold elections in 2011 under highly adverse circumstances, with its (unjustly) unpopular ruling party and no viable centrist alternative to the Chavista, Ollanta Humala. In either case, successful Venezuelan involvement would in all likelihood trigger a U.S. response of one type or another. These countries are simply too large, with too many U.S. investments and a central role in the drug trade.

While the region has reason to cheer this turn in U.S. policy, it simply can't afford for the United States to disappear. On matters such as immigration, free trade, and the battle against corruption, almost nothing can be done without U.S. cooperation or leadership. Or take the steps toward drug decriminalization made by California, Nevada, and Oregon. These shifts in policy could be more important for the hemisphere than the 40-year-old "war on drugs" or the Mérida Initiative or Plan Colombia. The producer countries of the drug trade will not advance toward decriminalization unless the consumer country *par excellence* moves in that direction first.

Economic development in Mexico, the Caribbean, and Central America is hardly conceivable, let alone possible, without a significant U.S. contribution, both monetary and conceptual. Building up infrastructure, stabilizing currencies, and establishing effective and transparent antitrust institutions are tasks that countries cannot carry out alone, given their integration with the U.S. economy.

Many of the region's traditionally anti-interventionist nations—Mexico, Brazil, Argentina—are coming to understand the need to anchor Latin America's democracy in a strong, intrusive, and detailed legal framework, the same way that free-trade agreements, as well as World Bank and IMF programs, have solidified economic policies that are finally yielding results. The United States must be part of this framework, to coax these countries along and to bestow credibility upon whatever is built. Many of the institutions that enshrine this emerging consensus—the American Convention on Human Rights, the Inter-American Democratic Charter, the Inter-American Commission on Human Rights, and the Inter-American Court of Human Rights—would be meaningless, like the League of Nations, if Washington were not a part of them.

These new structures are filled with potential. But, to deal with crises both ongoing and looming, they will need to devise answers to knotty questions: How will they address the subtle and innovative threats to electoral fairness, an impartial judiciary, and freedom of the press posed by Chávez's authoritarian drift? When does the legitimacy of a democratically elected president transform itself into the illegitimacy of undemocratic governance? When should free-trade privileges be suspended—when labor rights and environmental rule are threatened, or when democracy is interrupted?

Whatever policies emerge from these discussions would be meaningless without the United States. This is why the South American attempts at replacing the Organization of American States with a new organization that excludes the United States, Canada, and perhaps Mexico are futile at best, counterproductive at worst. The void left by U.S. retrenchment would be occupied by someone—and the alternatives are not attractive. Mexico is consumed by domestic tribulations, and Brazil is bound by an anti-interventionist diplomacy; only Caracas and Havana (the former with money, the latter with skill and experience) can fill the vacuum.

The end of the era of intervention should be hailed by the region. Washington's less intrusive presence will broaden the leeway certain governments have and force others to assume their responsibilities. But world events do not seem likely to permit an indefinite U.S. disengagement from the region, nor would that be desirable.

Washington has drifted into its current position with little forethought. But, to avoid the worst-case scenarios, it will need to actively manage its relations. The challenge presented by the Latin hard left must be confronted in a new fashion. Obama will need an actual doctrine—or, at least, coherent policy—to guide his decisions: a calculus that distinguishes between matters that are properly part of a country's domestic policy and those that entail violations of freely consented international agreements. By making this distinction, the United States could shed its history and get off the defensive, shifting the onus to Chávez. James Monroe's doctrine would officially be retired. A new era could truly begin.

Assess Your Progress

1. What accounts for the diminished U.S. role in Latin America?
2. What is the effect of this reduced role for regimes that have been critical of U.S. policy in the past?
3. What factors could prompt a more interventionist U.S. policy?
4. Why can't the region afford too much U.S. neglect?

Jorge G. Castañeda, the Global Distinguished Professor of Politics and Latin American and Caribbean Studies at New York University, was foreign minister of Mexico from 2000–2003.

The Return of *Continuismo?*

Latin America is witnessing an all-too-familiar pattern of presidents' manipulating the constitutional framework to seek additional terms in office.

SHELLEY A. MCCONNELL

Political struggles concerning presidential term limits have reemerged over the past year in Latin America. These struggles show that the region's institutional rules of democracy are still in flux. They also are raising fears that Latin America may witness a return to "*continuismo*"—a past tendency of some presidents to extend their stay in office through constitutional change, electoral fraud, or force.

In the 1980s and 1990s, Latin American countries undergoing transitions to democracy after two decades of authoritarian rule designed their constitutions to prevent a return to dictatorship. The central aim was to assure military subordination to elected civilian leaders and prevent armed overthrow of still-fragile democratic governments. However, Latin Americans were also conscious of the region's history of continuismo.

Countries returning to democracy therefore revived constitutional constraints on presidential reelection that had been developed under prior periods of democratic governance. These provisions either limited presidents to a single term in office or prohibited consecutive election, obliging presidents to step down for one or two terms before seeking office again. Countries without past democratic experience adopted similar precautions, and longstanding democracies already had them.

In subsequent years, such limits were in some cases loosened and immediate reelection to a second presidential term became common. This seemed like good news. Publics rewarded presidents who governed well by allowing them to continue serving. Argentina, Brazil, Colombia, the Dominican Republic, Peru, and Venezuela—and more recently Bolivia and Ecuador—all amended their constitutions to allow presidents to seek immediate reelection to one additional term. Chile, Costa Rica, El Salvador, Nicaragua, Panama, and Uruguay required an interval of at least one presidential term before a leader could seek reelection, and in some cases also imposed a two-term limit. Guatemala, Honduras, Mexico, and Paraguay retained prohibitions on reelection.

Some presidents tried to evade the limits, but these efforts generally failed. In 2000, the Peruvian legislature interpreted President Alberto Fujimori's bid for a third term as legal because it was to be only his second term under the 1993 constitution, but soon afterwards his government's bribery of legislators was exposed and he was forced to resign anyway. In Argentina, two-term president Carlos Menem wanted to run for an immediate third term, but the courts ruled his proposed candidacy unconstitutional.

In 2009, however, wrangling over presidential term limits resumed. In Venezuela, President Hugo Chávez championed a referendum that erased the term limits his own government had enacted. In Nicaragua, the Constitutional Chamber of the Supreme Court of Justice struck down limits on presidential reelection, allowing Daniel Ortega to seek an additional term in 2011 immediately following his current term; it would be his third term overall.

The trend is not confined to leftist leaders. The Colombian legislature last year authorized a referendum to decide whether to amend the constitution to permit immediate reelection of a president serving his second term. If the judiciary allows the referendum to be held, its passage would permit President Álvaro Uribe to run for a third term in 2010. In addition, Dominican Republic President Leonel Fernández, already in his third term overall, negotiated a constitutional amendment allowing him to run again, albeit only after he spends a term out of office.

It is not immediately obvious whether the relaxation of presidential term limits will spread, but Latin American countries historically have looked to one another for political precedents. The Organization of American States (OAS), which since 1990 has taken a leading role in protecting democratic governance in the Western Hemisphere, has raised no objection to the constitutional changes. In any case, to understand the possible consequences for democracy, one needs to distinguish among the ways that these constitutional amendments have proceeded in different countries.

Venezuelans Vote—Again

After Chávez's initial victory at the polls in 1998, Venezuela held an almost continuous series of referendums and elections, centering politics around the president's relationship with the electorate. His government moved quickly to bring promised change, enacting a new constitution through an elected constituent assembly dominated by Chávez's supporters. In a break with Venezuela's past practice of allowing presidents reelection only after a 10-year period out of office, the 1999 constitution permitted immediate reelection to a second term and simultaneously lengthened the presidential term to six years.

New elections were held in 2000 and Chávez won his first six-year term. After surviving a coup attempt and a recall referendum, the president rode high oil prices to a 63 percent reelection victory in 2006.

The following year, Venezuela held a referendum on a broad set of constitutional changes proposed by the president and authorized by the legislature. These included lifting all limits on presidential reelection. In what seemed like a public rebuke of Chávez's charismatic authority and transformational agenda, some 3 million of his past supporters stayed away from the polls and the referendum lost by a margin of 1.4 percent.

Yet just 14 months later, in February 2009, Chávez put forward another proposal for indefinite reelection, and this time it passed. Analysis of this referendum suggests that it succeeded in part because of lavish public spending in advance of the vote and government dominance of the media, and also because the referendum question had been restructured so that governors and mayors as well as the president would win expanded reelection rights. This change garnered support for the measure from politicians across the country. They in turn helped mobilize the "yes" vote.

The legality of the referendum's timing was contested. Opponents argued that the proposition was not substantively different from the one rejected in 2007, and so could not legally have been brought before the public again within the same presidential term. However, because opposition parties had boycotted the 2005 legislative elections, claiming the campaign conditions were not fair, they held no seats in the National Assembly and could not block the proposed change. Legislators from Chávez's party predictably authorized the referendum. Voters approved it by a comfortable margin, with 6.3 million in favor and 5.2 million against.

Critics of Chávez's "twenty-first-century socialism" equate indefinite reelection with the end of democracy.

This public process imbued the outcome with substantial legitimacy, but deep political polarization has meant that critics of Chávez's "twenty-first-century socialism" equate indefinite reelection with the end of democracy. Proponents respond that the public retains the right to vote Chávez out; indefinite reelection is not dictatorship as long as Venezuela's elections are free and fair, with a secret ballot and an honest count. This binds the question of democracy's future firmly to the quality of elections, which already have been a matter of concern because of Chávez's dominance of the electoral branch of the government.

Nicaragua's "Judicial Coup"

Ortega governed Nicaragua from 1979 to 1990, first as the leader of a revolutionary junta, and after 1984 as the elected president. He was defeated at the polls in 1990, and again in 1996 and 2001, but his party consistently won about 40 percent of the vote. In 2000, Ortega was able to negotiate an interparty agreement to reform the constitution so that presidents could be elected with just 35 percent of the vote if the candidate had a 5 percent lead over all others. Using this rule, he regained the presidency with a 38 percent plurality in 2006.

Two years into his second term, Ortega's Sandinista National Liberation Front (FSLN) party began sounding out the legislature about removing limits on presidential reelection. A 1995 constitutional amendment had set a two-term limit for the presidency and prohibited immediate reelection. Lawmakers could undertake constitutional changes only with a 60 percent vote, which meant the FSLN would need 56 of the 92 votes in the legislature to alter the reelection rules. However, the party had only 38 seats, and it was unable to muster support from opposition parties.

In the fall of 2009, Ortega and a group of 109 mayors challenged the legality of the two-term limit and the prohibition on immediate reelection of the president, together with electoral limits on the vice president and mayors. They first took their complaint to Nicaragua's Supreme Electoral Council, a fourth branch of government coequal to the Supreme Court, with the authority to decide electoral matters. That body promptly demurred, ruling that it was not empowered to decide the issue. The president and mayors then sought an injunction in the courts, claiming that the limits on reelection violated the constitutional principle of nondiscrimination before the law.

Justice proved unusually speedy in this affair. Within three days, the injunction passed through the Managua Court of Appeals, was accepted for consideration by the Supreme Court's Constitutional Chamber, and was ruled upon. The Constitutional Chamber ruling found in favor of the complaint, arguing that constitutional Article 147, limiting reelection based on one's job, was void because it contradicted the principle of nondiscrimination in the constitution's preamble and the guarantee of equality before the law in Article 27.

The ruling prepared an anticipatory defense against foreign criticism by citing international human rights covenants that uphold the right to seek office. However, that right has never been absolute, and the Chamber left intact language within Nicaragua's constitution that limits presidential candidacy on the basis of age, familial relationship to the president, and criminal record.

The problems with this process were legion. Since 2000, the Supreme Court had been composed of 16 members, half appointed from the FSLN and the other half from the Liberal party. Its Constitutional Chamber is composed of six Supreme Court justices, including both Sandinistas and Liberals. Oddly, the Liberal members did not attend the off-hours session to decide this case, and later claimed they were not notified of it. To fill the empty seats, the FSLN appointees called up substitute justices from their own party. As a result, the ruling was issued entirely by Sandinista supporters.

The Liberal justices then filed a communiqué rejecting the ruling. They claimed that the session of the Constitutional Chamber had been improperly formed, and that the Sandinista justices had usurped the role of the National Assembly and legislated from the bench. They denounced the ruling as the product of a conspiracy, calling it a "judicial coup" against the constitution. But they were powerless to overturn it. By contrast, the Supreme Electoral Council quickly accepted the ruling and announced it was "etched in stone."

The constitutional change was firmly rejected in the court of public opinion. Nicaragua had had a revolution in 1979 to overthrow a president who practiced continuismo, and there was bitter irony in seeing the revolutionary party head down that path. The Constitutional Chamber's ruling was particularly disturbing in light of allegations of widespread fraud in the 2008 municipal elections, which generated public uncertainty concerning the governing party's willingness to hold a fraud-free presidential election in 2011. In a rare display of unity, all four opposition parties, the two most influential business associations, the Catholic Church, and a score of civil society organizations denounced the constitutional change.

Colombia's Tailored Tinkering

Colombia represents a case of constitutional amendment by legislative acquiescence. As Uribe in 2009 began the final year of his second term as Colombia's president, he enjoyed stunning approval ratings from a public grateful for the tangible improvements his policies had made in personal security. A Gallup poll conducted in July 2009 showed 68 percent of respondents approving of Uribe's performance, and 58 percent said they thought Uribe should be allowed to run for a third term in 2010.

A drive by Uribe's supporters to collect signatures initiated legislative consideration of a referendum on whether to permit second-term presidents to seek consecutive reelection. This would not be the first constitutional change tailor-made to facilitate Uribe's career; in 2005, the Colombian legislature amended the constitution to allow him to seek reelection to a consecutive term.

In May 2009, the Colombian Senate approved the proposal. The lower house followed suit, but with a different version, creating a delay while a special committee reconciled the two texts. In August, the Senate approved the amendment with 56 votes in favor, and in early November the House passed it with 85 votes in favor to just 5 against. However, an opposition boycott of the vote in the Senate and 76 abstentions in the House showed that the issue was politically divisive. Given Uribe's popularity, congressmen who voted against the third term risked offending their constituents and losing their seats in legislative elections scheduled for March 2010. As a result, many absented themselves or abstained rather than directly opposing the amendment.

The proposal was then sent to the Constitutional Court, which was not expected to complete its review until February 2010. There would then be only a narrow window in which to hold the referendum before the May presidential election. As 2009 came to an end, time was against Uribe; a worsening economy and a corruption scandal were slowly sapping his support. Meanwhile, election authorities found that donors to the signature drive had exceeded allowed financial limits, putting the legality of the entire amendment process in doubt. The election authorities' judgment was not binding, but the Constitutional Court, known for its independence, was expected to take it into account. Speculation rose that the amendment might not survive judicial scrutiny.

If the referendum is held, one-quarter of registered voters will have to cast ballots for it to be considered valid. If turnout is low, Uribe might obtain a majority but still be unable to run for reelection. Colombia prides itself on being South America's oldest continually operating democracy, and even citizens who have supported Uribe might consider the amendment unwise. Should he win a third term, he would be positioned to make new high court appointments and dominate the judiciary. That would further erode checks and balances in a country where presidential powers are already considerable, and where the state has come under criticism for human rights violations.

Sizeable segments of the press and the intelligentsia in Colombia oppose the proposed change. For his part, Uribe has been cagey, refusing to be pinned down on whether he would run if doing so were legal. Certainly his government's staunch support for the referendum implies that he hopes to. Meanwhile, his refusal categorically to rule out another run has made it difficult for his supporters to rally around an alternative candidate.

The Dominican Party Pact

In October 2009, the Dominican Republic amended more than 40 articles of its constitution. Two issues—a prohibition on abortion and alteration of citizenship rights—dominated the media spotlight. The amendment of provisions for presidential reelection was less controversial because, while it removed term limits, it also prohibited consecutive election.

For much of the twentieth century, the Dominican Republic was governed by strongmen who held the presidency for extended periods. A crisis due to alleged electoral fraud in 1994 was resolved via an interparty agreement to amend the constitution. Under the new legal framework, presidents could be reelected to any number of four-year terms as long as they stepped aside for at least one term between their periods in office.

In 2002, the constitution was amended to allow a sitting president to seek immediate reelection one time. Whereas other Latin American presidents who changed constitutional rules to stand for reelection met with success at the polls, President Hipólito Mejía lost his 2004 reelection bid to Leonel Fernández, who had first served as president from 1996 to 2000. In 2008, Fernández was able to take advantage of Mejía's constitutional change to seek immediate reelection, and won a third term as president. He was then ineligible to run again.

The 2009 amendments drafted by President Fernández returned the Dominican Republic to the provisions of the 1994 constitution, which allowed an unlimited number of presidential terms as long as there was a pause between each one. This meant that, although Fernández would be obliged to step down as scheduled in 2012, he would be eligible to run for a fourth presidential term in 2016 or thereafter. The 2009 amendments underwent substantial legislative scrutiny before being passed in September.

Public concern was allayed because Fernández did not concoct an amendment that would permit him to seek immediate reelection to a fourth term, but instead returned the Dominican Republic to a prior presidential reelection rule that had enjoyed widespread legitimacy. Moreover, Fernández forged consensus on the 2009 draft with the main opposition leader, Miguel Vargas Maldonado, and consulted the island's third party as well. Legislative support was consequently strong, with 122 voting in favor to just 14 against.

The absence of a requirement for public ratification of constitutional amendments, while not unusual in Latin America, meant that the process was top-down, controlled from start to finish by those in power. Ordinary citizens had no opportunity to vote to retain term limits.

The interparty consensus-building behind the Dominican Republic's amendments should not be assumed to stem solely from a commitment to democratic principles and respect for the opposition. A less generous interpretation might construe the constitutional change as a pact meant to perpetuate the two leaders' dominance of their respective parties and give Fernández another shot at the presidency. Absent a cap on the total number of terms any one person may serve, former presidents have an incentive to block would-be successors and entrench themselves as their party's perennial candidate. Doing this impedes the entry of fresh faces and ideas into the political system, and reduces democracy within parties.

The Challenge to Democracy

The Venezuelan and Nicaraguan decisions to permit indefinite reelection of presidents, the Colombian legislature's approval of a referendum permitting a second-term president to seek immediate reelection, and the Dominican Republic's enabling of its president to seek a fourth term marked 2009 as the year in which prospects for continuismo reappeared on the region's horizon. Latin America is witnessing an all-too-familiar pattern of presidents' manipulating the constitutional framework to seek additional terms in office. Although the cases we have seen are not yet sufficient to establish a trend, precedents have been set that might serve as a rationale for other Latin American countries to soften reelection constraints.

Precedents have been set that might serve as a rationale for other countries to soften reelection constraints.

Such changes could easily exacerbate Latin America's hyper-presidentialism, in which the presidency tends to dominate other branches of government. Where institutional checks and balances are weak, elections could become the only means to hold presidents accountable, exposing election authorities to enormous political pressure. Indeed, the danger of such a slippery slope heightened concerns in Honduras about President Manuel Zelaya's alleged interest in relaxing constitutional limits on reelection, and these concerns helped trigger a military coup that suspended democracy there in June 2009. The Venezuelan referendum approving indefinite presidential reelection, held just four months earlier, loomed large as a precedent. It shaded interpretations of Zelaya's warm relations with Chávez and raised the perceived stakes of preserving Honduras's prohibition on reelection.

The recent constitutional changes to presidential reelection rules have occurred in a context of regional support for democracy, at a time when new instruments for the collective protection of democracy have been developed. The most comprehensive of these is the Inter-American Democratic Charter, which was signed in 2001 by all 34 countries in the OAS. This accord, which defines democracy and empowers the OAS to assist members whose democracy is eroding, was developed to prevent a repetition of Peruvian President Fujimori's "slow motion coup" in 2000, in which he dismantled the checks and balances in government to seek a third term as president. Nonetheless, the Democratic Charter has not deterred experimentation with third and fourth terms or even indefinite reelection, because these do not violate the definition of democracy articulated in the Democratic Charter's Articles 3 and 4.

Part of the dilemma may be that the OAS membership roster includes Canada and the English-speaking Caribbean states, which have parliamentary systems. In a parliamentary system there is no cap on the number of terms a prime minister can serve. If a political party holds the majority in the legislature, its leader becomes prime minister, so turnover in the executive branch depends more on internal party politics and voter support for political parties than on any constitutional limits. Thus, for example, Jamaican Prime Minister P.J. Patterson served from 1992 to 2006, inheriting the post that his party had won under Michael Manley and then winning three elections.

Such systems give the parliament the ability to hold a vote of no confidence that can force a prime minister to call new elections. But they draw on a democratic political culture, as much as checks and balances, to prevent abuse of power, since British colonialism inculcated different values and customs from those bequeathed by the Iberian colonial experience. Absent term limits of their own, Caribbean members of the OAS may be reluctant to criticize their Latin American counterparts whose presidents seek extended reelection; the inevitable comparisons might leave them vulnerable to accusations of hypocrisy.

While it might seem reasonable to consider Colombia's proposed three terms and the alternation model in the Dominican Republic as less troubling for democracy than the unlimited reelection now permitted in Venezuela and Nicaragua, any OAS evaluation of these amendments based on their content is a political non-starter. Member states rarely criticize one another on matters of internal politics. The principle of sovereignty grounds the organization's every move, a reaction to a long and difficult history of US intervention in the region.

Moreover, Washington's ongoing ideological confrontation with some leftist presidents in Latin America makes voicing bilateral objections to the recent constitutional changes in Venezuela and Nicaragua a prickly business. No Latin American leader wants to appear to back US meddling in a sister republic. For its part, the United States has criticized Chávez and Ortega for removing limits on reelection, and has discouraged Uribe from seeking a third term—but if Colombia passes the proposed referendum and Uribe wins reelection again, the United States will not likely cool relations with a right-wing president who is an ally in the fight against drugs and terrorism.

Applying the Democratic Charter

Meanwhile, the primary instrument for preventing democratic erosion in the hemisphere—the Inter-American Democratic Charter—is ill-suited to framing or even informing political struggles over institutional rules for presidential reelection. The specifications for democracy in the Charter call for periodic, free, and fair elections held with universal suffrage and a secret ballot. However, the document does not draw lessons from past experience with continuismo, nor is it intended to endorse any specific constitutional design or best practices. The Democratic Charter is therefore silent on whether lengthy presidencies would be likely to compromise elements of democracy it deems "essential," such as "the separation of powers and independence of the branches of government."

Even if it were advisable for the Democratic Charter to offer guidelines or to identify a range of appropriate democratic practices, amendment of the Charter to address this matter is unlikely. Indeed, opening the text for discussion would probably weaken rather than strengthen it—the regional consensus on liberal representative democracy is more fragile now than it was when the document was signed in 2001.

The Democratic Charter may nonetheless prove useful. No president's popularity lasts forever. Sooner or later, a president seeking to stay in office will face the choice of rigging the vote or stepping down. And the Charter allows for suspending the OAS membership of any state whose leaders do not come to power democratically. The organization's willingness to use this sanction was illustrated by its suspension of Honduras's membership in the wake of the June 2009 coup d'état.

The Democratic Charter also endorses the rule of law; therefore, distinguishing among countries in terms of the legality of their constitutional amendment processes is essential. The party collusion in the Dominican Republic may be viewed as thoughtful consensus-building or as an elite pact to provide President Fernández with a route to a fourth term in office. Either way, the constitutional change was made legally.

In Colombia, the path to constitutional change has followed pre-established procedures and allowed scrutiny from both the legislature and the Constitutional Court. The boycott of the vote in the Senate and mass abstentions in the lower house may have detracted from the amendment's perceived legitimacy, but they did not affect its legality. The signature collection process violated political finance regulations, but in Latin America such transgressions are rarely considered serious enough to void electoral outcomes or jeopardize a popular president.

With respect to the cases of indefinite reelection—cases that pose a more imminent prospect of empowering a president to govern for life—the constitutional changes in Venezuela and Nicaragua are markedly different. The Venezuelan process arguably violated restrictions on introducing a referendum proposal twice in the same presidential term, and it did so in a context where the president's willingness to be constrained by law was already questionable. However, the referendum was properly authorized by the legislature, and the public approved it in a clean vote with a decisive margin.

By contrast, Nicaragua's partisan manipulation of the Supreme Court was not accepted as legal by opposition justices. Indeed, they provided the OAS with possible grounds for launching an inquiry by proclaiming that the Constitutional Chamber's revocation of term limits represented a rupture of Nicaragua's democratic and institutional order. That language echoed Article 20 of the Inter-American Democratic Charter, which states that an unconstitutional rupture of the constitutional order in a member state is cause for OAS diplomatic action with or without an invitation from the government in question.

Despite Ortega's good record of accepting defeat in past presidential races, the partisan nature of the Constitutional Chamber's decision has given rise to concerns that the governing party may not be averse to distorting electoral rules to favor his reelection in 2011.

Will History Repeat?

Whether or not the erosion of presidential term limits will spread to additional countries is uncertain. The legislative vote in Colombia, the judicial process in Nicaragua, and the referendum in Venezuela have all revealed deep political divisions regarding the relaxation of term limits, and voters elsewhere may reject such changes if given the chance to do so through a ratification procedure. Leaders, too, may choose to retain electoral limits even when the leaders enjoy continuing public support—as in Brazil, where President Luiz Inácio Lula da Silva will leave office on January 1, 2011, when his second term expires. Judging by the current cases, reelection limits are more likely to be eased where presidents are relatively powerful and the institutions that constrain them are concomitantly weak.

Where sitting presidents are willing to bend the law to secure expanded reelection rights, they may not flinch at tampering with elections.

If similar initiatives arise elsewhere to extend the number of presidential terms allowed, whether they are consecutive or not, constitutional amendment processes will bear watching. Where sitting presidents are willing to bend the law to secure expanded reelection rights, they may not flinch at tampering with elections. There is a role for the OAS in reporting on deterioration of the rule of law and monitoring elections to prevent fraud. Ideally, such measures will not be needed; in and of itself, repeated reelection is not undemocratic. Nonetheless, for those conscious of Latin America's political history, there is understandable concern that the seeds of continuismo may have been replanted.

Assess Your Progress

1. What troubling trend has emerged in Latin American politics recently?
2. What is the impact of this trend likely to be?
3. What regional factors may have an effect on the emergence of this trend?
4. What is the primary regional means to prevent democratic decay?

Shelley A. McConnell, an assistant professor at St. Lawrence University, served for nine years as senior associate director of the Carter Center's Americas Program.

Perilous Times for Latin America

THEODORE J. PICCONE

Latin America has suffered more than its fair share of economic crises, but the global recession of 2008–2009 was supposed to be different. Because this crisis was triggered not by fiscal mismanagement in Latin America but by a combination of risky lending and lax regulation in the United States, some experts and politicians in the region proclaimed it a moment of "de-linkage" from the North. Yet early predictions of a soft landing—following a six-year economic bonanza for the region, which was largely driven by China's thirst for natural resources—proved incorrect.

Indeed, the prognosticators' pendulum has now swung in the opposite direction. We hear warnings about a long, slow, painful recovery in many of the region's nations. Reductions in poverty, unemployment, and inequality are not expected to be achieved until long after economic growth returns. Many expect to see populist, autocratic leaders once again pushing protectionism and resource nationalism.

Latin America is likely to muddle through the current economic turbulence. The bigger story in the region is an unfolding, longer-term crisis of democracy.

In reality, though, Latin America is likely to muddle through the current economic turbulence. The bigger story in the region is an unfolding, longer-term crisis of democracy.

First, the required caveat: Latin America and the Caribbean form a diverse region that is increasingly divided along a number of subregional and ideological lines. Mexico, Central America, and the Caribbean, with their higher dependence on the North American economy and on immigrant remittances, are experiencing more serious effects from the recession than are other areas. The volatile Andean region is torn between the Bolivarian ambitions of Venezuelan President Hugo Chávez and the democratic security message of Colombian President Álvaro Uribe. The Southern Cone, led by Brazil, is flexing its muscles in the Group of 20 and diversifying its trade and political relations with Asia, Europe, Africa, and even Iran.

Regional integration by most accounts is dead, notwithstanding Brazil's effort to establish a Union of South American Nations. Old tensions between neighbors are apparent again as talk of arms races gets louder.

Before the recession hit, different countries varied in their fiscal, trade, and debt situations. As a result, some will return to growth faster than others. States that before the crisis accumulated capital reserves and kept their spending in check, such as Chile and Brazil, have been able to carry out countercyclical spending policies. These policies include further investments in the social safety net, which will, at a minimum, soften the impact of the crisis on the poorest. States in a weaker fiscal position, such as Venezuela and Mexico, are in for a much tougher ride.

Politics Is Back

One direct political consequence of the global recession is that it has driven the final nail in the coffin of the neoliberal "Washington Consensus." What will take its place remains to be seen, but certainly Latin America's leaders are looking to reassert the state's role in regulating economic affairs.

As former Chilean President Ricardo Lagos put it at a recent Club of Madrid gathering on the political implications of the economic crisis, "Politics is back." And given the weakness of governments in the region, a consensus in favor of strengthening the state would on balance be a good thing. But will a stronger state be more or less democratic?

The answer depends largely on how leaders tackle longstanding structural challenges that have burdened the region with the world's highest rates of inequality and public insecurity. Latin America's persistent dependence on natural resource extraction and exports, reinforced by China's thirst for raw materials, means that the region will remain highly vulnerable to boom-and-bust cycles and external shocks. At the same time, continuing underinvestment in education, infrastructure, public services, and technology means that Latin America will fall further behind other regions in the global race for comparative advantage.

At the crux of these problems is that Latin America's economies are notoriously illicit and under-taxed, which leaves governments without the fiscal resources necessary to invest in a brighter future. Unless today's political leaders, and the special interests that support them, are willing to come to terms with the need to pay taxes, Latin America is doomed to remain a second-tier region.

A related economic and political challenge facing the region is respect for the rule of law. To attract private investment in today's competitive global market, states must maintain judicial systems and police institutions that are capable of protecting citizens and enterprises. While some progress in this arena has been made—witness the impressive prosecutions of former presidents and other senior officials on graft and human rights charges in Peru, Costa Rica, Chile, and Argentina—corruption remains a serious drag on the region's political economy. Trust in the social contract is frayed, and this leads small and large businesses alike to evade paying taxes whenever possible.

Short Term, Long Term

Every crisis has a silver lining—at least to the extent that crises can compel a fundamental rethinking of policy and facilitate progress toward achieving much-needed reforms. So perhaps the current crisis will prompt Latin American political leaders to make some hard decisions: Do they raise taxes, redistribute income, and invest in high-quality education and other public goods? Or do they borrow from the future by incurring new debt and relying on the usual export-led economic model, which seems only to reinforce chronic underdevelopment?

In essence, do they govern for short-term political gain, or with a long-term view toward putting their societies on a more sustainable and equitable growth path, even at the risk that they serve just one term? Does democracy, as it is now practiced in Latin America, allow a longer-term perspective? Or will the region's politicians be jarred into action only by another crisis?

While some of Latin America's democratization trends are positive—free elections, alternation of power, burgeoning civil society, and independent media are evident across the region—the underlying patterns of strong-man rule, elite control, corruption, and weak civic education still predominate.

To make matters worse, illicit networks such as those centered around drug trafficking are, in a vicious cycle of illegality, increasingly contaminating political and judicial systems in the region. These developments do not bode well for building consensus within nations around long-term goals.

The economic crisis if anything has exacerbated the difficulties involved in reaching such a consensus. Painful cuts in public services, and increasing crime and social tensions, have made coalition building all the more challenging. This in turn has increased the chances that populist and nationalist appeals to voters will succeed in a number of Latin American countries.

A proliferation of cross-border rivalries and of full-throated attacks against old enemies (Ecuador-Colombia, Peru-Chile, Venezuela-Colombia, Argentina-Uruguay, for example) demonstrates the tendency of politicans to change the subject when economic times turn sour.

The ongoing political crisis in Honduras following a military coup last summer demonstrates what can happen when key actors take matters into their own hands rather than pursuing some form of reconciliation.

Latin America's democrats, if they are to overcome their inherent tendency to govern for short-term gain, must build coalitions and undertake national dialogues to construct long-term visions for their countries. In this way they might establish some basic, common understandings about citizens' responsibility to honor the rule of law in exchange for their governments' delivery of public goods.

Crises Ahead?

Elections are one way to build consensus and hold incompetent leaders accountable—but, as Assistant Secretary of State for Western Hemisphere Affairs Arturo Valenzuela recently explained, they are insufficient by themselves to resolve a constitutional crisis.

We are likely to see more political crises in Latin America as leaders on both the left and the right, with support from key allies, continue to attempt to revise constitutions to extend their hold on power. The Organization of American States, riven by internal conflict, is proving itself incapable of resolving these emergencies, let alone preventing them.

So we are left with a rather downbeat forecast for democratic politics in the region. Even if the major economies continue to climb out of the recession and return to a path of growth in the short term, few benefits will accrue to the average person's economic status. This will raise social and political tensions for years to come.

Even as economic growth resumes, Latin America's great democratic experiment of the past two decades faces considerable peril unless the region's political and civic leaders invest themselves in constructing new forms of national dialogue and reconciliation and begin governing for the long haul.

Assess Your Progress

1. What were the effects of the 2008–2009 global recession for Latin America?
2. In what ways has the recession affected the politics of the region?
3. What are the short-and long-term governing options for Latin American political leaders?
4. What developments would reduce the tendency to govern for short term gains?

Theodore J. Piccone, a senior fellow and deputy director for foreign policy at the Brookings Institution, is an adviser to the Club of Madrid and has served on the staff of the National Security Council, the State Department, and the Pentagon.

UNIT 5

Population, Resources, Environment, and Health

Unit Selections

Learning Outcomes

After reading this unit you should be able to:

- Describe the environmental challenges facing the industrialized and developing countries.
- Discuss the implications of these challenges.
- Outline the connections between environment and security.
- Explain the threats associated with water insecurity.
- Evaluate the arguments for a right to water.
- List the environmental damages resulting from cook stoves in developing countries.
- Trace the links between population, resources, health, and environment.
- Comprehend the reasons why families slip back into poverty in developing countries.

Student Website

www.mhhe.com/cls

Internet References

Earth Pledge Foundation
www.earthpledge.org

EnviroLink
http://envirolink.org

Greenpeace
www.greenpeace.org

Linkages on Environmental Issues and Development
www.iisd.ca/linkages/

Population Action International
www.populationaction.org

World Health Organization (WHO)
www.who.ch

The Worldwatch Institute
www.worldwatch.org

The developing world's population continues to increase at an annual rate that exceeds the world average. The average fertility rate (the number of children a woman will have during her life) for all developing countries is 2.9, while for the least developed countries the figure is 4.9. Although growth has slowed considerably since the 1960s, world population is still growing at the rate of over 70 million per year, with most of this increase taking place in the developing world. Increasing population complicates development efforts, puts added stress on the ecosystem, and threatens food security. World population surpassed 6 billion toward the end of 1999 and, if current trends continue, could reach 9 billion or more by 2050. Even if, by some miracle, population growth was immediately reduced to the level found in industrialized countries, the developing world's population would continue to grow for decades.

Almost one-third of the population in the developing world is under the age of 15, with that proportion jumping to 40 percent in the least developed countries. The population momentum created by this age distribution means that it will be some time before the developing world's population growth slows substantially. Some developing countries have achieved progress in reducing fertility rates through family planning programs, but much remains to be done. At the same time, reduced life expectancy, especially related to the HIV/AIDS epidemic, is having a significant demographic impact especially in sub-Saharan Africa.

Over a billion people live in absolute poverty, as measured by a combination of economic and social indicators. Economic development has not only failed to eliminate poverty but has actually exacerbated it in some ways. Ill-conceived economic development plans have diverted resources from more productive uses and contributed to environmental degradation. Large-scale industrialization, sometimes unsuitable to local conditions, also increases pollution. If developing countries try to follow Western consumption patterns, sustainable development will be impossible. Furthermore, economic growth without effective environmental policies can lead to the need for more expensive clean-up efforts in the future. As population increases, it becomes more difficult to meet the basic human needs of the citizens of the developing world. Indeed, food scarcity looms as a major problem as the world struggles with a global food crisis, triggered by higher demand, skyrocketing oil prices, and the diversion of agricultural production to biofuels. Larger populations of poor people also places greater strains on scarce resources and fragile ecosystems. Trade disputes, resource scarcity, and the uncertainties of alternative energy supplies potentially make the world's efforts toward a greener environment a significant security challenge. Growing demand for water is rapidly depleting available supplies. Competition for scarce water resources not only affects agricultural production, but it also threatens to spark conflict. By some estimates, over the next 20 years, a gap of over 40% will exist between global demand and reliable water supplies. Greenhouse gas emissions are accelerating climate change; the adverse effects will be felt first by the developing world. Up until now, little has been done to prepare for the inevitable climate refugees that are certain to result from climate change.

Divisions between the North and the South on environmental issues became evident at the 1992 Rio Conference on Environment and Development. The conference highlighted the fundamental differences between the industrialized world and developing countries over the causes of, and the solutions to, global environmental problems. Developing countries pointed to consumption levels in the North as the main cause of environmental problems and called on the industrialized countries to pay most of the costs of environmental programs. Industrialized countries sought to convince developing countries to conserve their resources in their efforts to modernize and develop. These divisions have deepened on the issues of climate and greenhouse gas emissions. The Johannesburg Summit on Sustainable Development, a follow-up to the Rio conference, grappled with many of these issues, achieving some modest success in addressing water and sanitation needs. The recent Copenhagen Climate Conference aimed at establishing a new limit on greenhouse gases further demonstrated this rift between industrial and developing countries.

Rural-to-urban migration has caused an enormous influx of people to the cities, lured by the illusion of opportunity in cities and the attraction of urban life. As a result, urban areas in the developing world increasingly lack infrastructure to support this increased population and also have rising rates of pollution, crime, and disease. The fact that environmental factors account for about one-fifth of all diseases in developing countries illustrates the link between health and environmental issues. Environmental decline also makes citizens more vulnerable to natural disasters. Sustainable development is essential to reduce poverty and curtail the spread of diseases. Improving access to affordable health care in the poor countries would also contribute to reducing poverty. The HIV/AIDS epidemic in particular has forced attention on public health issues, especially in Africa. Africans account for 70 percent of the over 40 million AIDS cases worldwide. Besides the human tragedy that this epidemic creates, its implications for development are enormous. The loss of skilled and educated workers, the increase in the number of orphans, and the economic disruption that the disease causes will have a profound impact in the future. Evidence also suggests that sickness rapidly depletes family resources and contributes to backsliding into poverty and debt.

Is a Green World a Safer World?

Not Necessarily

A guide to the coming green geopolitical crises yet to come.

David J. Rothkopf

Greening the world will certainly eliminate some of the most serious risks we face, but it will also create new ones. A move to electric cars, for example, could set off a competition for lithium—another limited, geographically concentrated resource. The sheer amount of water needed to create some kinds of alternative energy could suck certain regions dry, upping the odds of resource-based conflict. And as the world builds scores more emissions-free nuclear power plants, the risk that terrorists get their hands on dangerous atomic materials—or that states launch nuclear-weapons programs—goes up.

The decades-long oil wars might be coming to an end as black gold says its long, long goodbye, but there will be new types of conflicts, controversies, and unwelcome surprises in our future (including perhaps a last wave of oil wars as some of the more fragile petrocracies decline). If anything, a look over the horizon suggests the instability produced by this massive and much-needed energy transition will force us to grapple with new forms of upheaval. Here's a guide to just a few of the possible green geopolitical tensions to come.

1. The Green Trade Wars

One source of international friction is far more certain to be a part of our energy future than many of the new technologies being touted as the next big thing. Consider the new U.S. approach in the energy and climate bill recently passed by the House of Representatives, which contains provisions for erecting trade barriers to countries that do not adopt measures to limit emissions. Proponents say these are necessary to reduce the chances of companies relocating to countries with lower emissions standards in order to get an unfair competitive edge. Such tariff regimes are also seen as keeping corporations from relocating to places where climate laws may be more lax, such as China.

Green protectionism is already a growth business. When the European Union considered restricting entry of biofuels based on a range of environmental standards, eight developing countries on three continents threatened legal action in the fall of 2008. In fact, there is a long tradition of such disputes (dolphin-safe tuna, anyone?), but the business community is worried that green protectionism could be a defining feature of international markets in the decades ahead. And of course, the prospect of green trade wars or even just opportunistic fiddling with trade laws to "protect" local jobs suggests a period of related international tensions, especially between developed countries and the emerging world.

2. The Rise and Fall of the Oil Powers

We're also going to witness the complex consequences of the simultaneous rise and decline of petrostates. First, the soaring price of oil—which could skyrocket to $250 a barrel, according to some recent Wall Street estimates—will fill their coffers. Sovereign wealth funds will grow fat again, and with the dollar likely to be weak for years to come, oil fat cats will be buying cheap U.S. assets and making American nationalists uncomfortable all the while.

Those fat cats still have a few good decades ahead of them. Twenty years from now, the world will still be getting at least three quarters of its energy from oil, coal, and natural gas. Today's energy infrastructure took years to develop, and even with revolutionary technological change, the energy mix can shift only marginally in the short term. So, as much as the West may wish to reduce its dependence on the likes of OPEC—because it's not good to be too dependent on anyone, because oil is dirty and killing the environment, because Providence has seen fit to identify the world's most dangerous regions by locating oil beneath them, and because oil is a drug that has corrupted the character of many of its producing nations—these countries will have considerable power for the foreseeable future.

But even as these states reach an apotheosis of power due to the price and scarcity of oil, the writing is on the wall. There is no return to oil once the supply peak has eventually been reached, and it is likely that the demand peak will come even before then. Burning oil at today's rate is just not a sustainable course unless you live inland or in far northern latitudes or own a company that manufactures hip waders.

So, the oil states will be rich, influential, and, paradoxically, in decline. The forward-looking among them might use the time they have to plan, to hedge their bets. But the slow death of the oil economy will undoubtedly lead to flare-ups as social pressures translate into political fractures and opportunistic politicians cling to wealth the old-fashioned way—by grabbing it from their neighbors.

Predicting just where these fractures will occur is difficult. But it doesn't take much imagination to conclude that a Russia dependent on oil exports but faced with declining demand, dwindling reserves, and an unprecedented demographic meltdown will feel diminished in ways that are likely to be dangerous for its neighbors. Or consider how oil's inevitable decline will impact the succession struggle in Saudi Arabia, and that's if the current structure hasn't already collapsed under the weight of the ruling family's mismanagement and neglect of its people. Economic powers with a geological death sentence on their heads are likely to be erratic. One way or another, they will make the rest of us feel their pain.

3. Aftershocks of the Coming Nuclear Boom

...[T]here is simply no way to reverse the effects of climate change without much more broadly embracing nuclear energy. Not only is it essentially emissions free, scalable, and comparatively energy efficient, but just 1 metric ton of uranium produces the same amount of energy as approximately 3,600 metric tons of oil (about 80,000 barrels). It is a far more sophisticated and proven technology than virtually all of the other emerging alternatives. These facts have already led to a very real renaissance in nuclear energy, one that is concentrated in the energy-hungry developing world (more than two thirds of announced projects are in developing countries).

Unfortunately, nuclear power is also fraught with real and perceived risks. Plant-safety hazards are pretty minimal, if history is any indicator. However, two real issues loom. One is how to safely dispose of spent fuel, a dilemma still hotly debated by environmentalists. And another is how to ensure the security of the fuel at every other stage of its life cycle, particularly in comparatively cash-strapped emerging countries, which are often in regions scarred by instability and home to terrorist organizations with their own nuclear ambitions.

With each new program, the chances of a security breach increase. Nor is the danger of a bad actor diverting fuel to produce an atomic bomb the only nuclear nightmare we're facing. Radioactive waste could be used to produce a dirty bomb with devastating impact. And fiddling with weapons programs behind closed doors might be the greatest security risk of all.

A nuclear event would have broad global aftershocks affecting areas as diverse as civil liberties and trade.

Nuclear-weapons expert Robert Gallucci once told me that, considering these growing risks, a deadly nuclear terrorist incident was "almost certain." Such an event would have broad global aftershocks affecting areas as diverse as civil liberties and trade. Imagine, for example, trying to ship anything anywhere in the world the day after. To give just one example, only 5 percent of shipping containers today are subject to visual inspection in the United States. Pressure to make inspection absolute in the wake of a nuclear event could easily lead to the buildup of millions of goods at U.S. ports, driving up consumer-goods prices as market supplies dwindle.

A new nuclear nonproliferation treaty is already on the drawing board, but even as U.S. President Barack Obama works to fulfill his dream of a world free of nuclear weapons, it is already clear that the risks posed by old-fashioned national stockpiles are being eclipsed by those associated with small groups exploiting cracks in an increasingly complex worldwide nuclear infrastructure.

4. Water Wars and Worse

Today, 1.1 billion people don't have ready access to clean water, and estimates suggest that within two decades as many as two thirds of the Earth's people will live in water-stressed regions. It has become a new conventional wisdom that water will become "the new oil," as Dow Chemical Chief Executive Andrew Liveris has said, both because of the new value it will have and the new conflicts it will generate.

Ironically, the hunt for energy alternatives to replace oil could make the water problem much worse. Some biofuels use significant amounts of water, including otherwise efficient sugar cane (unlike rain-soaked ethanol giant Brazil, most sugarcane producers have to irrigate). Similarly, the various technologies that are seen as essential to the clean use of coal are water hogs. Plug-in hybrid cars also increase water use because they draw electricity, and most types of power plants use water as a coolant. Even seemingly unrelated technologies, such as silicon chips (key to everything from smart-grid technologies to more efficient energy use) require a great deal of water to produce.

Many countries could begin to address this by working out schemes to charge for water, the single best way to grapple with this problem. Alternatively, they may build nuclear desalination plants that make saltwater drinkable. Neither course is perfect. A de facto privatization of water has occurred throughout the world, with low-income populations forced to purchase bottled water to avoid contamination, but even so, the ideal of the right to free water has held firm and governments have found it politically untenable to charge even nominal sums. And those nuclear desalination plants? As countries that have deployed this technology, such as India, Japan, and Kazakhstan, have found, they're bloody expensive, at hundreds of millions of dollars a pop.

5. The Great Lithium Game

In Asia, Europe, and the United States, people are getting excited about the electric car—and for good reason. Electric cars will enable greater independence from oil and could play a significant role in lowering carbon dioxide emissions. But the major fly in the ointment for the electric car is the battery.

Many solutions are being considered, including "air" batteries that produce electricity from the direct reaction of lithium metal with oxygen. The most likely option for now, though, is the lithium-ion battery used in cameras, computers, and cellphones. Lithium-ion batteries offer better storage and longer life than the older nickel-metal hydride models, making them ideal for a space-constrained, long-running vehicle.

All this means that lithium is likely to be a hot commodity in the years immediately ahead. It so happens that about three quarters of the world's known lithium reserves are concentrated in the southern cone of Latin America-to be precise, in the Atacama Desert, which is shared by two countries: Chile and Bolivia. Other than these reserves and the Spanish language, the one thing these two countries have in common is a historical animosity, cemented by their late 19th-century War of the Pacific. Chile was able to cut off Bolivia's access to the sea, a maneuver that rankles bitterly in La Paz to this day.

Bolivia's lack of coastline could become an issue again if the two lithium powerhouses start jostling to attract investors. Competition between Bolivian and Chilean lithium mines and, potentially, over domestic production of lithium batteries could very well bring about a second War of the Pacific—to say nothing of the huge environmental costs that lithium mining incurs. Any such tension could jeopardize U.S. efforts to adopt electric vehicles, as the United States already gets 61 percent of its lithium imports from Chile. China and Russia, which also hold significant reserves, would be poised to ride out and profit from such an event. Further, conflict between the two Latin American states would likely bolster the fortunes of batteries made from less efficient resources, such as those used in nickel-metal hydride batteries, or boost other technologies that use different substances with their own drawbacks. And in any event, the possibility of a regional lithium rush reminds us that whatever technologies take hold, demand will emerge for the scarce commodities on which they depend... and we know well where that can lead.

These are just a few, fleeting glimpses of the future, but many geopolitical ramifications of moving toward green energy are very much with us already. In India, anxiety among some in the business community is growing as the United States and China meet secretly and not-so-secretly to try to hammer out an agreement on climate change. It's fast dawning on some Indians that their government's tough stance (resisting mandated emissions caps and offering only to keep India's per capita emissions at or below the average emissions in developed countries) could effectively keep it from having a seat at the table when the core elements of a global deal are worked out in the conversation between the world's two leading emitters and a handful of others. Brazil has a very different view on where such talks should come out because it wants credit for its role as the world's largest absorber of carbon. Russia also has its particular stance, that of an energy provider, and, as with other countries in northern climes, global warming could increase Russia's tourism income, boost its agricultural output, and produce other economic benefits.

Add in the tensions associated with differing views on green protectionism, the shape of relevant international institutions, and the competition for resources, and you can easily see how this contentious climate conversation is going to increasingly reshape the world. And who knows which new technologies could make much of today's speculation moot?

The bottom line: A shift away from dirty old fuels is the only path toward reducing several of the greatest security threats the planet faces, but we must step carefully and avoid letting our optimism run away with us. By acknowledging that a greener world will hardly be devoid of geopolitical challenges and preparing accordingly, we may find a path to defusing our threats today, while largely avoiding the inadvertent drawbacks of desperately needed innovation.

Assess Your Progress

1. How might concern for the environment increase trade tensions?
2. What are the implications of continued dependence on oil?
3. What are the obstacles to greater reliance on nuclear power?
4. How might the search for alternative fuels worsen the water crisis?
5. How could the rising demand for lithium increase tensions?

David J. Rothkopf, a Foreign Policy blogger, is president and chief executive of **Garten Rothkopf,** a Washington-based advisor firm specializing in energy, climate, and global risk-related issues. He is a visiting scholar at the Carnegie Endowment for International Peace and author most recently of *Superclass: The Global Power Elite and the World They Are Making.*

Reprinted in entirety by McGraw-Hill with permission from *Foreign Policy,* September/October 2009, pp. 134–137. www.foreignpolicy.com.

The Last Straw

If you think these failed states look bad now, wait until the climate changes.

STEPHAN FARIS

Hopelessly overcrowded, crippled by poverty, teeming with Islamist militancy, careless with its nukes—it sometimes seems as if Pakistan can't get any more terrifying. But forget about the Taliban: The country's troubles today pale compared with what it might face 25 years from now. When it comes to the stability of one of the world's most volatile regions, it's the fate of the Himalayan glaciers that should be keeping us awake at night.

When it comes to the stability of one of the world's most volatile regions, it's the fate of the Himalayan glaciers that should be keeping us awake at night.

In the mountainous area of Kashmir along and around Pakistan's contested border with India lies what might become the epicenter of the problem. Since the separation of the two countries 62 years ago, the argument over whether Kashmir belongs to Muslim Pakistan or secular India has never ceased. Since 1998, when both countries tested nuclear weapons, the conflict has taken on the added risk of escalating into cataclysm. Another increasingly important factor will soon heighten the tension: Ninety percent of Pakistan's agricultural irrigation depends on rivers that originate in Kashmir. "This water issue between India and Pakistan is the key," Mohammad Yusuf Tarigami, a parliamentarian from Kashmir, told me. "Much more than any other political or religious concern."

Until now, the two sides had been able to relegate the water issue to the back burner. In 1960, India and Pakistan agreed to divide the six tributaries that form the Indus River. India claimed the three eastern branches, which flow through Punjab. The water in the other three, which pass through Jammu and Kashmir, became Pakistan's. The countries set a cap on how much land Kashmir could irrigate and agreed to strict regulations on how and where water could be stored. The resulting Indus Waters Treaty has survived three wars and nearly 50 years. It's often cited as an example of how resource scarcity can lead to cooperation rather than conflict.

But the treaty's success depends on the maintenance of a status quo that will be disrupted as the world warms. Traditionally, Kashmir's waters have been naturally regulated by the glaciers in the Himalayas. Precipitation freezes during the coldest months and then melts during the agricultural season. But if global warming continues at its current rate, the Intergovernmental Panel on Climate Change estimates, the glaciers could be mostly gone from the mountains by 2035. Water that once flowed for the planting will flush away in winter floods.

Research by the global NGO ActionAid has found that the effects are already starting to be felt within Kashmir. In the valley, snow rarely falls and almost never sticks. The summertime levels of streams, rivers, springs, and ponds have dropped. In February 2007, melting snow combined with unseasonably heavy rainfall to undermine the mountain slopes; landslides buried the national highway—the region's only land connection with the rest of India—for 12 days.

Normally, countries control such cyclical water flows with dams, as the United States does with runoff from the Rocky Mountains. For Pakistan, however, that solution is not an option. The best damming sites are in Kashmir, where the Islamabad government has vigorously opposed Indian efforts to tinker with the rivers. The worry is that in times of conflict, India's leaders could cut back on water supplies or unleash a torrent into the country's fields. "In a warlike situation, India could use the project like a bomb," one Kashmiri journalist told me.

Water is already undermining Pakistan's stability. In recent years, recurring shortages have led to grain shortfalls. In 2008, flour became so scarce it turned into an election issue; the government deployed thousands of troops to guard its wheat stores. As the glaciers melt and the rivers dry, this issue will only become more critical. Pakistan—unstable, facing dramatic drops in water supplies, caged in by India's vastly superior conventional forces—will be forced to make one of three choices. It can let its people starve. It can cooperate with India in building dams and reservoirs, handing over control of its waters to the country it regards as the enemy. Or it can ramp up support for the insurgency, gambling that violence can bleed India's resolve without degenerating into full-fledged war. "The idea of ceding territory to India is anathema," says Sumit Ganguly, a professor of political science at Indiana University. "Suffering, particularly for the elite, is unacceptable. So what's the other option? Escalate."

"It's very bad news," he adds, referring to the melting glaciers. "It's extremely grim."

The Kashmiri water conflict is just one of many climate-driven geopolitical crises on the horizon. These range from possible economic and treaty conflicts that will likely be resolved peacefully—the waters of the Rio Grande and Colorado River have long been a point of contention between the United States and Mexico, for instance—to possible outright wars. In 2007, the London-based

NGO International Alert compiled a list of countries with a high risk of armed conflict due to climate change. They cited no fewer than 46 countries, or one in every four, including some of the world's most gravely unstable countries, such as Somalia, Nigeria, Iran, Colombia, Bolivia, Israel, Indonesia, Bosnia, Algeria, and Peru. Already, climate change might be behind the deep drought that contributed to the conflict in the Darfur region of Sudan and hundreds of thousands of deaths.

Rising global temperatures are putting the whole world under stress, and the first countries to succumb will be those, such as Sudan, that are least able to adapt. Compare the Netherlands and Bangladesh: Both are vulnerable to rises in sea levels, with large parts of their territory near or under the level of the waves. But the wealthy Dutch are building state-of-the-art flood-control systems and experimenting with floating houses. All the impoverished Bangladeshis can do is prepare to head for higher ground. "It's best not to get too bogged down in the physics of climate," says Nils Gilman, an analyst at Monitor Group and the author of a 2006 report on climate change and national security. "Rather, you should look at the social, physical, and political geography of regions that are impacted."

Indeed, with a population half that of the United States crammed into an area a little smaller than Louisiana, Bangladesh might be among the most imperiled countries on Earth. In a normal decade, the country experiences one major flood. In the last 11 years, its rivers have leapt their banks three times, most recently in 2007. That winter, Cyclone Sidr, a Category 5 storm, tore into the country's coast, flattening tin shacks, ripping through paddies, and plunging the capital into darkness. As many as 10,000 people may have died.

Bangladesh's troubles are likely to ripple across the region, where immigration flows have been historically accompanied by rising tensions. In India's northeastern state of Assam, for instance, rapidly changing demographics have led to riots, massacres, and the rise of an insurgency. As global warming tightens its squeeze on Bangladesh, these pressures will mount. And in a worst-case scenario, in which the country is struck by sudden, cataclysmic flooding, the international community will have to cope with a humanitarian emergency in which tens of millions of waterlogged refugees suddenly flee toward India, Burma, China, and Pakistan.

Indeed, the U.S. military has come to recognize that weakened states—the Bangladeshes and Pakistans of the world—are often breeding grounds for extremism, terrorism, and potentially destabilizing conflict. And as it has done so, it has increasingly deployed in response to natural disasters. Such missions often require a warlike scale of forces, if not warlike duration. During the 2004 Indian Ocean tsunami, for instance, the United States sent 15,000 military personnel, 25 ships, and 94 aircraft. "The military brings a tremendous capacity of command-and-control and communications," says retired Gen. Anthony Zinni, the former head of U.S. Central Command. "You have tremendous logistics capability, transportation, engineering, the ability to purify water."

As the world warms, more years could start to look like 2007, when the U.N. Office for the Coordination of Humanitarian Affairs announced it had responded to a record number of droughts, floods, and storms. Of the 13 natural disasters it responded to, only one—an earthquake in Peru—was not related to the climate.

Worryingly, some analysts have suggested the United States might not fully grasp what it needs to respond to this challenge. The U.S. military has been required by law since 2008 to incorporate climate change into its planning, but though Pentagon strategic documents describe a climate-stressed future, there's little sign the Department of Defense is pivoting to meet it. "Most of the things that the military is requesting are still for a conventional war with a peer competitor," says Sharon Burke, an energy and climate change specialist at the Washington-based Center for a New American Security. "They say they're going to have more humanitarian missions, but there's no discussion at all of 'What do you need?'" The rate at which the war in Iraq has chewed through vehicles and equipment, for instance, has astonished military planners. "Is this a forewarning of what it's like to operate in harsher conditions?" Burke asks.

To be sure, some of the more severe consequences of climate change are expected to unfold over a relatively extended time frame. But so does military development, procurement, and planning. As global warming churns the world's weather, it's becoming increasingly clear that it's time to start thinking about the long term. In doing so, the West may need to adopt an even broader definition of what it takes to protect itself from danger. Dealing with the repercussions of its emissions might mean buttressing governments, deploying into disaster zones, or tamping down insurgencies. But the bulk of the West's effort might be better spent at home. If the rivers of Kashmir have the potential to plunge South Asia into chaos, the most effective response might be to do our best to ensure the glaciers never melt at all.

Life in a Failed State

Pakistan

"I remember being in high school when the Taliban took over in Afghanistan. I remember thinking to myself, 'Oh God, it's so close. Could that ever happen here?' and thinking that it wasn't possible. And now, 10 years later, I see the same thing happening in my own country."

— Fatima Bhutto Pakistani commentator

Assess Your Progress

1. How will climate change affect Pakistani-Indian relations over Kashmir?
2. What threats does climate change pose for Bangladesh?
3. How does climate change affect U.S. military missions and planning?

Stephan Faris is the author of *Forecast: The Consequences of Climate Change, from the Amazon to the Arctic, from Darfur to Napa Valley,* from which reporting for this article is drawn.

The World's Water Challenge

If oil is the key geopolitical resource of today, water will be as important—if not more so—in the not-so-distant future.

Erik R. Peterson and Rachel A. Posner

Historically, water has meant the difference between life and death, health and sickness, prosperity and poverty, environmental sustainability and degradation, progress and decay, stability and insecurity. Societies with the wherewithal and knowledge to control or "smooth" hydrological cycles have experienced more rapid economic progress, while populations without the capacity to manage water flows—especially in regions subject to pronounced flood-drought cycles—have found themselves confronting tremendous social and economic challenges in development.

Tragically, a substantial part of humanity continues to face acute water challenges. We now stand at a point at which an obscenely large portion of the world's population lacks regular access to fresh drinking water or adequate sanitation. Water-related diseases are a major burden in countries across the world. Water consumption patterns in many regions are no longer sustainable. The damaging environmental consequences of water practices are growing rapidly. And the complex and dynamic linkages between water and other key resources—especially food and energy—are inadequately understood. These factors suggest that even at current levels of global population, resource consumption, and economic activity, we may have already passed the threshold of water sustainability.

An obscenely large portion of the world's population lacks regular access to fresh drinking water or adequate sanitation.

A major report recently issued by the 2030 Water Resources Group (whose members include McKinsey & Company, the World Bank, and a consortium of business partners) estimated that, assuming average economic growth and no efficiency gains, the gap between global water demand and reliable supply could reach 40 percent over the next 20 years. As serious as this world supply-demand gap is, the study notes, the dislocations will be even more concentrated in developing regions that account for one-third of the global population, where the water deficit could rise to 50 percent.

It is thus inconceivable that, at this moment in history, no generally recognized "worth" has been established for water to help in its more efficient allocation. To the contrary, many current uses of water are skewed by historical and other legacy practices that perpetuate massive inefficiencies and unsustainable patterns.

The Missing Links

In addition, in the face of persistent population pressures and the higher consumption implicit in rapid economic development among large populations in the developing world, it is noteworthy that our understanding of resource linkages is so limited. Our failure to predict in the spring of 2008 a spike in food prices, a rise in energy prices, and serious droughts afflicting key regions of the world—all of which occurred simultaneously—reveals how little we know about these complex interrelationships.

Without significant, worldwide changes—including more innovation in and diffusion of water-related technologies; fundamental adjustments in consumption patterns; improvements in efficiencies; higher levels of public investment in water infrastructures; and an integrated approach to governance based on the complex relationships between water and food, water and economic development, and water and the environment—the global challenge of water resources could become even more severe.

Also, although global warming's potential effects on watersheds across the planet are still not precisely understood, there can be little doubt that climate change will in a number of regions generate serious dislocations in water supply. In a June 2008 technical paper, the Inter governmental Panel on Climate Change (IPCC) concluded that "globally, the negative impacts of climate change on freshwater systems are expected to outweigh the benefits." It noted that "higher water temperatures and changes in extremes, including droughts and floods, are projected to affect water quality and exacerbate many forms of water pollution."

Climate change will in a number of regions generate serious dislocations in water supply.

As a result, we may soon be entering unknown territory when it comes to addressing the challenges of water in all their dimensions, including public health, economic development, gender equity, humanitarian crises, environmental degradation, and global security. The geopolitical consequences alone could be profound.

Daunting Trends

Although water covers almost three-quarters of the earth's surface, only a fraction of it is suitable for human consumption. According to the United Nations, of the water that humans consume, approximately 70 percent is used in agricultural production, 22 percent in industry, and 8 percent in domestic use. This consumption—critical as it is for human health, economic development, political and social stability, and security—is unequal, inefficient, and unsustainable.

Indeed, an estimated 884 million people worldwide do not have access to clean drinking water, and 2.5 billion lack adequate sanitation. A staggering 1.8 million people, 90 percent of them children, lose their lives each year as a result of diarrheal diseases resulting from unsafe drinking water and poor hygiene. More generally, the World Health Organization (WHO) estimates that inadequate water, sanitation, and hygiene are responsible for roughly half the malnutrition in the world.

In addition, we are witnessing irreparable damage to ecosystems across the globe. Aquifers are being drawn down faster than they can naturally be recharged. Some great lakes are mere fractions of what they once were.

And water pollution is affecting millions of people's lives. China typifies this problem. More than 75 percent of its urban river water is unsuitable for drinking or fishing, and 90 percent of its urban groundwater is contaminated. On the global scale, according to a recent UN report on world water development, every day we dump some 2 million tons of industrial waste and chemicals, human waste, and agricultural waste (fertilizers, pesticides, and pesticide residues) into our water supply.

Over the past century, as the world's population rose from 1.7 billion people in 1900 to 6.1 billion in 2000, global fresh water consumption increased six-fold—more than double the rate of population growth over the same period. The latest "medium" projections from the UN's population experts suggest that we are on the way to 8 billion people by the year 2025 and 9.15 billion by the middle of the century.

The contours of our predicament are clear-cut: A finite amount of water is available to a rapidly increasing number of people whose activities require more water than ever before. The UN Commission on Sustainable Development has indicated that we may need to double the amount of freshwater available today to meet demand at the middle of the century—after which time demand for water will increase by 50 percent with each additional generation.

Why is demand for water rising so rapidly? It goes beyond population pressures. According to a recent report from the UN Food and Agriculture Organization, the world will require 70 percent more food production over the next 40 years to meet growing per capita demand. This rising agricultural consumption necessarily translates into higher demand for water. By 2025, according to the water expert Sandra Postel, meeting projected global agricultural demand will require additional irrigation totaling some 2,000 cubic kilometers—roughly the equivalent of the annual flow of 24 Nile Rivers or 110 Colorado Rivers.

Consumption patterns aside, climate change will accelerate and intensify stress on water systems. According to the IPCC, in coming decades the frequency of extreme droughts will double while the average length of droughts will increase six times. This low water flow, combined with higher temperatures, not only will create devastating shortages. It will also increase pollution of fresh water by sediments, nutrients, pesticides, pathogens, and salts. On the other hand, in some regions, wet seasons will be more intense (but shorter). In underdeveloped communities that lack capture and storage capacity, water will run off and will be unavailable when it is needed in dry seasons, thus perpetuating the cycle of poverty.

Climatic and demographic trends indicate that the regions of the world with the highest population growth rates are precisely those that are already the "driest" and that are expected to experience water stress in the future. The Organization for Economic Cooperation and Development has suggested that the number of people in water-stressed countries—where governments encounter serious constraints on their ability to meet household, industrial, and agricultural water demands—could rise to nearly 4 billion by the year 2030.

The Geopolitical Dimension

If oil is the key geopolitical resource of today, water will be as important—if not more so—in the not-so-distant future. A profound mismatch exists between the distribution of the human population and the availability of fresh water. At the water-rich extreme of the spectrum is the Amazon region, which has an estimated 15 percent of global runoff and less than 1 percent of the world's people. South America as a whole has only 6 percent of the world's population but more than a quarter of the world's runoff.

At the other end of the spectrum is Asia. Home to 60 percent of the global population, it has a freshwater endowment estimated at less than 36 percent of the world total. It is hardly surprising that some water-stressed countries in the region have pursued agricultural trade mechanisms to gain access to more water—in the form of food. Recently, this has taken the form of so-called "land grabs," in which governments and state companies have invested in farmland overseas to meet their countries' food security needs. *The Economist* has estimated that, to date, some 50 million acres have been remotely purchased or leased under these arrangements in Africa and Asia.

Although freshwater management has historically represented a means of preventing and mitigating conflict between countries with shared water resources, the growing scarcity of water will likely generate new levels of tension at the local, national, and even international levels. Many countries with limited water availability also depend on shared water, which increases the risk of friction, social tensions, and conflict.

The Euphrates, Jordan, and Nile Rivers are obvious examples of places where frictions already have occurred. But approximately 40 percent of the world's population lives in more than 260 international river basins of major social and economic importance, and 13 of these basins are shared by five or more countries. Interstate tensions have already escalated and could easily intensify as increasing water scarcity raises the stakes.

Within countries as well, governments in water-stressed regions must effectively and transparently mediate the concerns and demands of various constituencies. The interests of urban and rural populations, agriculture and industry, and commercial and domestic sectors often conflict. If allocation issues are handled inappropriately, subnational disputes and unrest linked to water scarcity and poor water quality could arise, as they already have in numerous cases.

Addressing the Challenge

Considering the scope and gravity of these water challenges, responses by governments and nongovernmental organizations have fallen short of what is needed. Despite obvious signs that we overuse water, we continue to perpetuate gross inefficiencies. We continue to skew consumption on the basis of politically charged subsidies or other supports. And we continue to pursue patently unsustainable practices whose costs will grow more onerous over time.

The Colorado River system, for example, is being overdrawn. It supplies water to Las Vegas, Los Angeles, San Diego, and other growing communities in the American Southwest. If demand on this river system is not curtailed, there is a 50 percent chance that Lake Mead will be dry by 2021, according to experts from the Scripps Institution of Oceanography.

Despite constant reminders of future challenges, we continue to be paralyzed by short-term thinking and practices. What is especially striking about water is the extent to which the world's nations are unprepared to manage such a vital resource sustainably. Six key opportunities for solutions stand out.

First, the global community needs to do substantially more to address the lack of safe drinking water and sanitation. Donor countries, by targeting water resources, can simultaneously address issues associated with health, poverty reduction, and environmental stewardship, as well as stability and security concerns. It should be stressed in this regard that rates of return on investment in water development—financial, political, and geopolitical—are all positive. The WHO estimates that the global return on every dollar invested in water and sanitation programs is $4 and $9, respectively.

Consider, for example, how water problems affect the earning power of women. Typically in poor countries, women and girls are kept at home to care for sick family members inflicted with water-related diseases. They also spend hours each day walking to collect water for daily drinking, cooking, and washing. According to the United Nations Children's Fund, water and sanitation issues explain why more than half the girls in sub-Saharan Africa drop out of primary school.

Second, more rigorous analyses of sustainability could help relevant governments and authorities begin to address the conspicuous mismanagement of water resources in regions across the world. This would include reviewing public subsidies—for water-intensive farming, for example—and other supports that tend to increase rather than remove existing inefficiencies.

Priced to Sell

Third, specialists, scholars, practitioners, and policy makers need to make substantial progress in assigning to water a market value against which more sustainable consumption decisions and policies can be made. According to the American Water Works Association, for example, the average price of water in the United States is $1.50 per 1,000 gallons—or less than a single penny per gallon. Yet, when it comes to the personal consumption market, many Americans do not hesitate to pay prices for bottled water that are higher than what they pay at the pump for a gallon of gasoline. What is clear, both inside and outside the United States, is that mechanisms for pricing water on the basis of sustainability have yet to be identified.

Fourth, rapid advances in technology can and should have a discernible effect on both the supply and demand sides of the global water equation. The technology landscape is breathtaking—from desalination, membrane, and water-reuse technologies to a range of cheaper and more efficient point-of-use applications (such as drip irrigation and rainwater harvesting). It remains to be seen, however, whether the acquisition and use of such technologies can be accelerated and dispersed so that they can have an appreciable effect in offsetting aggregate downside trends.

From a public policy perspective, taxation and regulatory policies can create incentives for the development and dissemination of such technologies, and foreign assistance projects can promote their use in developing countries. Also, stronger links with the private sector would help policy makers improve their understanding of technical possibilities, and public-private partnerships can be effective mechanisms for distributing technologies in the field.

Fifth, although our understanding of the relationship between climate change and water will continue to be shaped by new evidence, it is important that we incorporate into our approach to climate change our existing understanding of water management and climate adaptation issues.

Sixth, the complex links among water, agriculture, and energy must be identified with greater precision. An enormous amount of work remains to be done if we are to appreciate these linkages in the global, basin, and local contexts.

In the final analysis, our capacity to address the constellation of challenges that relate to water access, sanitation, ecosystems, infrastructure, adoption of technologies, and the mobilization of resources will mean the difference between rapid economic development and continued poverty, between healthier populations and continued high exposure to water-related diseases, between a more stable world and intensifying geopolitical tensions.

Assess Your Progress

1. What are the dimensions of the world's water crisis?
2. What changes are required to cope with the challenge of diminishing water resources?
3. What are the consequences of unequal, inefficient, and unsustainable water consumption?
4. What accounts for the rapid increase in water demand?
5. What steps should the international community take to address this crisis?

Erik R. Peterson is senior vice president of the Center for Strategic and International Studies and director of its Global Strategy Institute. **Rachel A. Posner** is assistant director of the CSIS Global Water Futures project.

Water Warriors

Declaring water a right, not a commodity, a global water justice movement is growing.

Maude Barlow

Thousands have lived without love, not one without water.

—W.H. Auden, *First Things First*

A fierce resistance to the corporate takeover of water has grown in every corner of the globe, giving rise to a coordinated and, given the powers it is up against, surprisingly successful water justice movement. "Water for all" is the rallying cry of local groups fighting for access to clean water and the life, health and dignity that it brings. Many of these groups have lived through years of abuse, poverty and hunger. Many have been left without public education and health programs when their governments were forced to abandon them under World Bank structural adjustment policies. But somehow, the assault on water has been the great standpoint for millions. Without water there is no life, and for thousands of communities around the world, the struggle over the right to their own local water sources has been politically galvanizing.

A mighty contest has grown between those (usually powerful) forces and institutions that see water as a commodity, to be put on the open market and sold to the highest bidder, and those who see water as a public trust, a common heritage of people and nature, and a fundamental human right. The origins of this movement, generally referred to as the global water justice movement, lie in the hundreds of communities around the world where people are fighting to protect their local water supplies from pollution, destruction by dams and theft—be it from other countries, their own governments or private corporations such as bottled water companies and private utilities backed by the World Bank. Until the late 1990s, however, most were operating in isolation, unaware of other struggles or the global nature of the water crisis.

Latin America was the site of the first experiments with water privatization in the developing world. The failure of these projects has been a major factor in the rejection of the neoliberal market model by so many Latin American countries that have said no to the extension of the North American Free Trade Agreement to the Southern Hemisphere and that have forced the big water companies to retreat. A number of Latin American countries are also opting out of some of the most egregious global institutions. This past May Bolivia, Venezuela and Nicaragua announced their decision to withdraw from the World Bank's arbitration court, the International Centre for the Settlement of Investment Disputes (ICSID), in no small measure because of the way the big water corporations have used the center to sue for compensation when the countries terminated private delivery contracts.

Latin America, with its water abundance, should have one of the highest per capita allocations of water in the world. Instead, it has one of the lowest. There are three reasons, all connected: polluted surface waters, deep class inequities and water privatization. In many parts of Latin America, only the rich can buy clean water. So it is not surprising that some of the most intense fights against corporate control of water have come out of this region of the world.

The first "water war" gained international attention when the indigenous peoples of Cochabamba, Bolivia, led by a five-foot, slightly built, unassuming shoemaker named Oscar Olivera, rose up against the privatization of their water services. In 1999, under World Bank supervision, the Bolivian government had passed a law privatizing Cochabamba's water system and gave the contract to US engineering giant Bechtel, which immediately tripled the price of water. In a country where the minimum wage is less than $60 a month, many users received water bills of $20 a month, which they simply could not afford. As a result, La Coordinadora de Defensa del Agua y de la Vida (Coalition in Defense of Water and Life), one of the first coalitions against water privatization in the world, was formed and organized a successful referendum demanding the government cancel its contract with Bechtel. When the government refused to listen, many thousands took to the streets in nonviolent protest and were met with army violence that wounded dozens and killed a 17-year-old boy. On April 10, 2000, the Bolivian government relented and told Bechtel to leave the country.

The Bolivian government had also bowed to pressure from the World Bank to privatize the water of La Paz and in 1997 gave Suez, a French-based multinational, a thirty-year contract to supply water services to it and El Alto, the hilly region surrounding the capital, where thousands of indigenous peoples live. From the beginning, there were problems. Aguas del Illimani, a Suez subsidiary, broke three key promises: it did not deliver to all the residents, poor as well as rich, leaving about 200,000 without water; it charged exorbitant rates for water hookups, about $450, equivalent to the food budget of a poor family for two years; and it did not invest in infrastructure repair or wastewater treatment, choosing instead to build a series of ditches and canals through poor areas of La Paz, which it used to send garbage, raw sewage and even the effluent from the city's abattoirs into Lake Titicaca, considered by UNESCO a World Heritage site. To add insult to injury, the company located its fortresslike plant under the beautiful Mount Illimani, where it captured the snowmelt off the mountain and, after rudimentary treatment, piped it into the homes of families and businesses in La Paz that could pay. The nearest community, Solidaridad, a slum of about 100 families with no electricity, heat or running water, had its only water supply cut off. Its school and health clinic, built with foreign-aid money, could not operate because of a lack of water. It was the same all through El Alto.

An intense resistance to Suez formed. FEJUVE, a network of local community councils and activists, led a series of strikes in January 2005, which crippled the cities and brought business to a halt. This resistance was a prime factor in the ousting of presidents Gonzalo Sánchez de Lozada and Carlos Mesa. Their replacement, Evo Morales, the first indigenous president in the country's history, negotiated Suez's departure. On January 3, 2007, he held a ceremony at the presidential palace celebrating the return of the water of La Paz and El Alto after a long and bitter confrontation. "Water cannot be turned over to private business," said Morales. "It must remain a basic service, with participation of the state, so that water service can be provided almost for free."

Although they have received less international attention, similar battles over privatized water have raged in Argentina. Río de la Plata (Silver River) separates Buenos Aires, the Argentine capital, from Montevideo, the capital of Uruguay. For 500 years, it has also been called Mar Dulce (Sweet Sea) because its size made people think it was a freshwater sea. Today, however, the river is famous for something else: it is one of the few rivers in the world whose pollution can be seen from space. On March 21, 2006, the Argentine government rescinded the thirty-year contract of Aguas Argentinas, the Suez subsidiary that had run the Buenos Aires water system since 1993, in no small part because the company broke its promise to treat wastewater, continuing to dump nearly 90 percent of the city's sewage into the river. In another broken promise, the company repeatedly raised tariffs, for a total increase of 88 percent in the first ten years of operation. Water quality was another issue; water in seven districts had nitrate levels so high it was unfit for human consumption. An April 2007 report by the city's ombudsman stated that most of the population of 150,000 in the southern district of the city lived with open-air sewers and contaminated drinking water.

Yet as Food and Water Watch reports, the Inter-American Development Bank continued to fund Suez as late as 1999, despite the mounting evidence that the company was pulling in 20 percent profit margins while refusing to invest in services or infrastructure. Outrageously, with the backing of the French government, Suez is trying to recoup $1.7 billion in "investments" and up to $33 million in unpaid water bills at the ICSID. Suez had just (in December 2005) been forced out of the province of Santa Fe, where it had a thirty-year contract to run the water systems of thirteen cities. The company is also suing the provincial government at the ICSID for $180 million. Close on the heels of the Buenos Aires announcement, Suez was forced to abandon its last stronghold in Argentina, the city of Córdoba, when water rates were raised 500 percent on one bill.

In all cases, strong civil society resistance was key to these retreats. A coalition of water users and residents of Santa Fe, led by Alberto Múñ oz and others, actually organized a huge and successful plebiscite, in which 256,000 people, about a twelfth of the population of the province, voted to rescind Suez's contract. They convened a Provincial Assembly on the Right to Water with 7,000 activists and citizens in November 2002, which set the stage for the political opposition to the company. The People's Commission for the Recovery of Water in Córdoba is a highly organized network of trade unions, neighborhood centers, social organizations and politicians with a clear goal of public water for all, and was instrumental in getting the government to break its contract with Suez. "What we want is a public company managed by workers, consumers and the provincial government, and monitored by university experts to guarantee water quality and prevent corruption," says Luis Bazán, the group's leader and a water worker who refused employment with Suez.

Mexico is a beachhead for privatization across the region, with its elites having access to all the water they need and also controlling governments at most levels of the country. Only 9 percent of the country's surface water is fit for drinking, and its aquifers are being drawn down mercilessly. According to the National Commission on Water, 12 million Mexicans have no access to potable water whatsoever and another 25 million live in villages and cities where the taps run as little as a few hours a week. Eighty-two percent of wastewater goes untreated. Mexico City has dried up, and its 22 million inhabitants live on the verge of crisis. Services are so poor in the slums and outskirts of the city that cockroaches run out when the tap is turned on. In many "colonias" in Mexico City and around the country, the only available water is sold from trucks that bring it in once a week, often by political parties that sell the water for votes.

In 1983 the federal government handed over responsibility for the water supply to the municipalities. Then in 1992 it passed a new national water bill that encouraged the municipalities to privatize water in order to receive funding. Privatization was supported by former President Vicente Fox, himself a former senior executive with Coca-Cola, and is also favored by the current president, Felipe Calderón. The World Bank and the Inter-American Development Bank are actively promoting water privatization in Mexico. In 2002 the World Bank provided $250 million for infrastructure repair with conditions that municipalities negotiate public-private partnerships. Suez is deeply entrenched in Mexico, running the water services for part of Mexico City, Cancún and about a dozen other cities. Its wastewater division, Degremont, has a large contract for San Luis Potosí and several other cities as well. The privatization of water has become a top priority for the Mexican water commission, Conagua. As in other countries, privatization in Mexico has brought exorbitant water rates, broken promises and cutoffs to those who cannot pay. The Water Users Association in Saltillo, where a consortium of Suez and the Spanish company Aguas de Barcelona run the city's water systems, reports that a 2004 audit by the state comptroller found evidence of contractual and state law violations.

A vibrant civil society movement has recently come together to fight for the right to clean water and resist the trend to corporate control in Mexico. In April 2005 the Mexican Center for Social Analysis, Information and Training (CASIFOP) brought together more than 400 activists, indigenous peoples, small farmers and students to launch a coordinated grassroots resistance to water privatization. The Coalition of Mexican Organizations for the Right to Water (COMDA) is a large collection of environmental, human rights, indigenous and cultural groups devoted not only to activism but also to community-based education on water, its place in Mexico's history and the need for legislation to protect the public's right to access. Their hopes for a government supportive of their perspective were dashed when conservative candidate Calderón won (many say stole) the 2006 presidential election over progressive candidate Andrés Manuel López Obrador. Calderón is working openly with the private water companies to cement private control of the country's water supplies.

Other Latin American cities or countries rejecting water privatization include Bogotá, Colombia (although other Colombian cities, including Cartagena, have adopted private water systems); Paraguay, whose lower house rejected a Senate proposal to privatize water in July 2005; Nicaragua, where a fierce struggle has been waged by civil society groups and where in January 2007 a court ruled against the privatization of the country's wastewater infrastructure; and Brazil, where strong public opinion has held back the forces of water privatization in most cities. Unfortunately, resistance in Peru, where increased rates, corruption and debt plague the system, has not yet reversed water privatization. Likewise, in Chile, resistance to water privatization is very difficult because of the entrenched commitment to market ideology of the ruling elites, although there is hope that the center-left government of Michelle Bachelet will be more open to arguments for public governance of Chile's water supplies.

From thousands of local struggles for the basic right to water—not just throughout Latin America but in Asia-Pacific countries, Africa and the United States and Canada—a highly organized international water justice movement has been forged and is shaping the future of the world's water. This movement has already had a profound effect on global water politics, forcing global institutions such as the World Bank and the United Nations to admit the failure of their model, and it has helped formulate water policy inside dozens of countries. The movement has forced open a debate over the control of water and challenged the "Lords of Water" who had set themselves up as the arbiters of this dwindling resource. The growth of a democratic global water justice movement is a critical and positive development that will bring needed accountability, transparency and public oversight to the water crisis as conflicts over water loom on the horizon.

Assess Your Progress

1. What are the two views of water as a resource?
2. What are the origins of the movement to make water a fundamental right?
3. Why does Latin America, with substantial water resources, have one of the worst per capita water allocations?

Maude Barlow is the author of *Blue Covenant: The Global Water Crisis and the Coming Battle for the Right to Water* (New Press), from which this article was adapted.

Soot from Third-World Stoves Is New Target in Climate Fight

ELISABETH ROSENTHAL

"It's hard to believe that this is what's melting the glaciers," said Dr. Veerabhadran Ramanathan, one of the world's leading climate scientists, as he weaved through a warren of mud brick huts, each containing a mud cookstove pouring soot into the atmosphere.

As women in ragged saris of a thousand hues bake bread and stew lentils in the early evening over fires fueled by twigs and dung, children cough from the dense smoke that fills their homes. Black grime coats the undersides of thatched roofs. At dawn, a brown cloud stretches over the landscape like a diaphanous dirty blanket.

In Kohlua, in central India, with no cars and little electricity, emissions of carbon dioxide, the main heat-trapping gas linked to global warming, are near zero. But soot—also known as black carbon—from tens of thousands of villages like this one in developing countries is emerging as a major and previously unappreciated source of global climate change.

While carbon dioxide may be the No. 1 contributor to rising global temperatures, scientists say, black carbon has emerged as an important No. 2, with recent studies estimating that it is responsible for 18 percent of the planet's warming, compared with 40 percent for carbon dioxide. Decreasing black carbon emissions would be a relatively cheap way to significantly rein in global warming—especially in the short term, climate experts say. Replacing primitive cooking stoves with modern versions that emit far less soot could provide a much-needed stopgap, while nations struggle with the more difficult task of enacting programs and developing technologies to curb carbon dioxide emissions from fossil fuels.

In fact, reducing black carbon is one of a number of relatively quick and simple climate fixes using existing technologies—often called "low hanging fruit"—that scientists say should be plucked immediately to avert the worst projected consequences of global warming. "It is clear to any person who cares about climate change that this will have a huge impact on the global environment," said Dr. Ramanathan, a professor of climate science at the Scripps Institute of Oceanography, who is working with the Energy and Resources Institute in New Delhi on a project to help poor families acquire new stoves.

"In terms of climate change we're driving fast toward a cliff, and this could buy us time," said Dr. Ramanathan, who left India 40 years ago but returned to his native land for the project.

Better still, decreasing soot could have a rapid effect. Unlike carbon dioxide, which lingers in the atmosphere for years, soot stays there for a few weeks. Converting to low-soot cookstoves would remove the warming effects of black carbon quickly, while shutting a coal plant takes years to substantially reduce global CO_2 concentrations.

But the awareness of black carbon's role in climate change has come so recently that it was not even mentioned as a warming agent in the 2007 summary report by the Intergovernmental Panel on Climate Change that pronounced the evidence for global warming to be "unequivocal." Mark Z. Jacobson, professor of environmental engineering at Stanford, said that the fact that black carbon was not included in international climate efforts was "bizarre," but "partly reflects how new the idea is." The United Nations is trying to figure out how to include black carbon in climate change programs, as is the federal government.

In Asia and Africa, cookstoves produce the bulk of black carbon, although it also emanates from diesel engines and coal plants there. In the United States and Europe, black carbon emissions have already been reduced significantly by filters and scrubbers.

Like tiny heat-absorbing black sweaters, soot particles warm the air and melt the ice by absorbing the sun's heat when they settle on glaciers. One recent study estimated that black carbon might account for as much as half of Arctic warming. While the particles tend to settle over time and do not have the global reach of greenhouse gases, they do travel, scientists now realize. Soot from India has been found in the Maldive Islands and on the Tibetan Plateau; from the United States, it travels to the Arctic. The environmental and geopolitical implications of soot emissions are enormous. Himalayan glaciers are expected to lose 75 percent of their ice by 2020, according to Prof. Syed Iqbal Hasnain, a glacier specialist from the Indian state of Sikkim.

These glaciers are the source of most of the major rivers in Asia. The short-term result of glacial melt is severe flooding in mountain communities. The number of floods from glacial lakes is already rising sharply, Professor Hasnain said. Once the glaciers shrink, Asia's big rivers will run low or dry for part of the year, and desperate battles over water are certain to ensue in a region already rife with conflict.

Doctors have long railed against black carbon for its devastating health effects in poor countries. The combination of health and environmental benefits means that reducing soot provides a "very big bang for your buck," said Erika Rosenthal, a senior lawyer at Earth Justice, a Washington organization. "Now it's in everybody's self-interest to deal with things like cookstoves—not just because hundreds of thousands of women and children far away are dying prematurely."

> **"Now it's in everybody's self-interest to deal with things like cookstoves—not just because hundreds of thousands of women and children far away are dying prematurely."**
>
> —Erika Rosenthal

In the United States, black carbon emissions are indirectly monitored and minimized through federal and state programs that limit small particulate emissions, a category of particles damaging to human health that includes black carbon. But in March, a bill was introduced in Congress that would require the Environmental Protection Agency to specifically regulate black carbon and direct aid to black carbon reduction projects abroad, including introducing cookstoves in 20 million homes. The new stoves cost about $20 and use solar power or are more efficient. Soot is reduced by more than 90 percent. The solar stoves do not use wood or dung. Other new stoves simply burn fuel more cleanly, generally by pulverizing the fuel first and adding a small fan that improves combustion.

That remote rural villages like Kohlua could play an integral role in tackling the warming crisis is hard to imagine. There are no cars—the village chief's ancient white Jeep sits highly polished but unused in front of his house, a museum piece. There is no running water and only intermittent electricity, which powers a few light bulbs.

The 1,500 residents here grow wheat, mustard and potatoes and work as day laborers in Agra, home of the Taj Majal, about two hours away by bus.

They earn about $2 a day and, for the most part, have not heard about climate change. But they have noticed frequent droughts in recent years that scientists say may be linked to global warming. Crops ripen earlier and rot more frequently than they did 10 years ago. The villagers are aware, too, that black carbon can corrode. In Agra, cookstoves and diesel engines are forbidden in the area around the Taj Majal, because soot damages the precious facade.

Still, replacing hundreds of millions of cookstoves—the source of heat, food and sterile water—is not a simple matter. "I'm sure they'd look nice, but I'd have to see them, to try them," said Chetram Jatrav, as she squatted by her cookstove making tea and a flatbread called roti. Her three children were coughing.

She would like a stove that "made less smoke and used less fuel" but cannot afford one, she said, pushing a dungcake bought for one rupee into the fire. She had just bought her first rolling pin so her flatbread could come out "nice and round," as her children had seen in elementary school. Equally important, the open fires of cookstoves give some of the traditional foods their taste. Urging these villagers to make roti in a solar cooker meets the same mix of rational and irrational resistance as telling an Italian that risotto tastes just fine if cooked in the microwave.

In March, the cookstove project, called Surya, began "market testing" six alternative cookers in villages, in part to quantify their benefits. Already, the researchers fret that the new stoves look like scientific instruments and are fragile; one broke when a villager pushed twigs in too hard.

But if black carbon is ever to be addressed on a large scale, acceptance of the new stoves is crucial. "I'm not going to go to the villagers and say CO_2 is rising, and in 50 years you might have floods," said Dr. Ibrahim Rehman, Dr. Ramanathan's collaborator at the Energy and Resources Institute. "I'll tell her about the lungs and her kids and I know it will help with climate change as well."

Assess Your Progress

1. How do cooking fires in developing countries contribute to climate change?
2. What are the health consequences to this method of cooking?
3. What are the obstacles to replacing these cook stoves?

Population, Human Resources, Health, and the Environment

Getting the Balance Right

ANTHONY J. MCMICHAEL

The UN's World Commission on Environment and Development (WCED)—the "Brundtland Commission," chaired by Gro Harlem Brundtland—released its seminal report *Our Common Future* in 1987.[1] Much has changed on the global environment front since then, only some of which was (or could have been) anticipated by that report. As human population continues to grow and as human societies, cultures, and economies become more interconnected against the background crescendo of "globalization" in recent decades, the collective human impact on the biosphere has increasingly assumed a global and systemic dimension. While issues like climate change, freshwater deficits, and degradation of food-producing systems and ocean fisheries were appearing on the horizon in 1987, they have now moved to the foreground. Today, it is evident that these momentous changes pose threats not only to economic systems, environmental assets, infrastructural integrity, tourism, and iconic nature, but also to the stability, health, and survival of human communities. This realization—along with the fact that human-induced global environmental changes impinge unequally on human groups—heightens the rationale for seeking sustainable development.

While the WCED report explored the rationale and the path toward sustainable development, the extent of subsequent large-scale environmental problems arising from the scale and the energy and materials intensity of prevailing modes of development could not have been fully anticipated in 1987. Indeed, paradoxically, concern over world population growth had temporarily receded in the mid-1980s, reflecting the prevailing mix of politics and optimism. The optimism derived from the apparent alleviation of hunger that had been achieved by the Green Revolution of the 1970s and 1980s in much of the developing world, and from the downturn in fertility rates in at least some developing regions. Today, however, the population issue is reemerging in public discussion, reflecting renewed recognition that population growth, along with rising consumption levels, is exacerbating climate change and other global environmental changes.[2]

If the commission's assessment were re-run this decade, its updated terms of reference would necessarily focus more attention on the social and health dimensions of the "development" process, both as inputs and, importantly, as outcomes. The charge to the commission, which focused on the often-conflicted relationship between economic activity and environmental sustainability, was framed at a time when the orthodox Rostovian view (that economic development occurs in five basic stages from "traditional society" to "age of high mass consumption") still remained influential.[3] Today, human capital and social capital—both of which were first properly understood and factored into the development calculus in the 1990s, along with the need for sound governance—are better recognized as prerequisites for environmentally sustainable development. At the same time, realization is growing that the attainment of positive human experience is the core objective of human societies.[4] In contrast, the commission's primary mandated focus was on how to reconcile environmental sustainability with social-economic development. That orientation afforded little stimulus to considering why, in human experiential terms, achieving such a balance is not an end in itself, but is a prerequisite for attaining human security, well-being, health, and survival. Why else do we seek sustainability?

People, Resources, Environment, and Development

The UN General Assembly Resolution A/38/161 of 1983 establishing the WCED specified that the commission would "take account of the interrelationships between people, resources, environment and development."[5] The full text of the resolution emphasized—as did the commission's name—the dual need for long-sighted environmental management strategies and greater cooperation among countries in seeking a sustainable development path to the common future. Two words in the quoted phrase are of particular interest: "people" and "resources."

Reference to "people," rather than to "populations," seems to emphasize the *human* dimension. However, it also distracts from issues of fertility and population size—a distraction that probably reflected two prevailing circumstances. In the 1980s—when world population growth was at its historic high—the United States's conservative Reagan Administration withheld international aid from family planning because of its perceived links with abortion counseling. This ill-informed and culturally high-handed approach, coming from a powerful country with great financial influence over UN policies, was complemented by the fact that many low-income countries considered that issues of fertility and population size were their own business. Nevertheless, and to its credit, the WCED report directly addressed the question of population size and its environmental consequences, urging lower fertility rates as a prerequisite for both poverty alleviation and environmental sustainability.

The word "resources" is ambiguous; it could be taken to refer to natural environmental resources or to human resources (human capital, including education and health status). To what extent did the WCED consider human well-being and health in relation to changing environmental conditions, population size, and resources? "Many such changes are accompanied by life-threatening hazards," stated the WCED in its overview of the report,[6] suggesting that the report would indeed explore how the state of the natural environment, our basic habitat, sets limits on human well-being, health, and survival, both now—and of particular relevance to sustainability—in future. Indeed, in launching the report in Oslo, on 20 March 1987, Chair Brundtland said:

> Our message is directed towards people, whose wellbeing is the ultimate goal of all environment and development policies. . . . If we do not succeed in putting our message of urgency through to today's parents and decision makers, we risk undermining our children's fundamental right to a healthy, life-enhancing environment.[7]

Despite these promising statements, the report itself gave only limited attention to considering how environmental degradation and ecological disruption affect the foundations of human population health. The report focused primarily on the prospects for achieving an "ecologically sustainable" form of social and economic development that conserves the natural environmental resource base for future human needs. It paid little attention to the fact that the conditions of the world's natural environment signify much more than assets for production, consumption, and economic development in general; the biosphere and its component ecosystems and biophysical processes provide the functions and flows that maintain life processes and therefore good health. Indeed, all extant forms of life have evolved via an exquisite dependency on environmental conditions.

This somewhat restricted vision on the part of the WCED is not surprising. Indeed, such a perspective has been reflected often in subsequent forays of UN agencies into the rationale and objectives of sustainable development—forays that have consistently overlooked or sometimes trivialized the role of sustainable development as a precondition to attaining well-being, health, and survival (see the box on for the example of the UN's Millennium Development Goals).[8] In defense of the report, however, it does state:

> It is misleading and an injustice to the human condition to see people merely as consumers. Their well-being and security—old age security, declining child mortality, health care, and so on—are the goal of development.[9]

In the 1980s and early 1990s, there was little evidence and understanding of the relationship between environmental conditions, ecological systems, and human health. For example, the First Assessment Report of the Intergovernmental Panel on Climate Change (IPCC), released in 1991, contained only passing reference to how global climate change would affect human health.[10] The IPCC report reviewed in detail the risks to farms, forests, fisheries, feathered and furry animals, to settlements, coastal zones, and energy generation systems. In contrast, it glossed cursorily over the risks to human health (and gave undue emphasis to solar ultraviolet exposure and skin cancer, which is very marginal to the climate change and health topic).

There was, then, only a rudimentary awareness that the profile and scale of environmental hazards to human health were undergoing a profound transformation. For instance, the human health risks due to stratospheric ozone depletion, first recognized during the late 1970s and early 1980s, had been easily understood. They belonged to the familiar category of direct-acting hazardous environmental exposures. An increase in ambient levels of ultraviolet radiation at Earth's surface would increase the risks of skin damage and skin cancer and would affect eye health (for example, cataract formation). Recognition of this straightforward risk to human biology facilitated the ready international adoption of the Montreal Protocol in 1987, requiring national governments to eliminate release of ozone-destroying gases (mostly chlorofluorocarbons, nitrous oxide, and methyl bromide).

In contrast, the great diversity of (mostly) less direct-acting but potentially more profound risks to human health from changes to Earth's climate system, agroecosystems, ocean fisheries, freshwater flows, and general ecosystem functioning (such as pollination, nutrient cycling, and soil formation) were only dimly perceived in the 1980s. Those health risks received relatively little attention in the WCED report, which focused instead on health hazards related to inadequate water supply and sanitation, malnutrition, drug addiction, and exposure to carcinogens and other toxins in homes and the workplace.

An Incomplete Model of Health Determinants

In discussing population health, the WCED report took a largely utilitarian view, discussing good health as an input to economic development and, specifically, as stimulus to the reduction of fertility and poverty. In this respect it was in good company: both the pioneering sanitary revolution of nineteenth-century England and World Health Organization's International Commission on Macroeconomics and Health, established in 2000, espoused the same rationale: good health fosters national wealth. To the extent that the WCED report addressed the determinants of population health, it focused mainly on the contributions of

Millennium Development Goals: How Much Progress Has Been Made?

By coincidence, the 20-year anniversary of the Brundtland report nearly coincides with the halfway mark of another UN project, the Millennium Development Goals (MDGs), 2000–2015.[1] The MDGs were launched in 2000 against a backdrop of increasing attention on what was termed "ecologically sustainable development" in large part stimulated by the WCED report. They encompass eight goals (each with associated targets): to eradicate extreme poverty and hunger; achieve universal primary education; promote gender equality and empower women; reduce child mortality; improve maternal health; combat HIV/AIDS, malaria, and other diseases; ensure environmental sustainability; and develop a global partnership for development.

Achievement of the MDGs is becoming increasingly improbable as time passes. Some headway has been made in relation to poverty reduction and child school enrollment. But there has been little alleviation of hunger and malnutrition, maternal mortality, and infant-child death rates (which have declined by around one sixth in poorer countries, well short of the two-thirds reduction target).

Inevitably, progress toward the goals has varied between regions and countries. China, for example, has made social and health advances on many fronts, albeit at the cost of increasingly serious environmental degradation. In contrast, in sub-Saharan Africa, no country is coming close to halving poverty, providing universal primary education, or stemming the devastating HIV/AIDS epidemic. More than 40 percent of persons in sub-Saharan Africa live in extreme poverty.

One quarter of the world's children aged less than 5 are underfed and underweight. This, as a proportion, is an improvement on the figure of one third in 1990. However, in sub-Saharan Africa and South Asia, nearly half the children remain underweight, and gains are minimal.

The total number of people living with AIDS has increased by nearly 7-million since 2001, to a total now of 40 million. Neither malaria nor tuberculosis is being effectively curtailed, with the attempt to reduce tuberculosis being threatened further by the recent emergence of strains with more extreme forms of antimicrobial resistance.

Perhaps this lack of progress is in part reflected in the UN's failure to explore and emphasize the primary interconnected role of Goal 7 for the achievement of the MDGs overall. Goal 7 seeks "environmental sustainability"—and achieving this particular goal is the bedrock for attaining most of the targets of the other seven goals. Without an intact and productive natural environment and its life-supporting global and regional systems and processes (such as climatic conditions, ocean vitality, ecosystem functioning, and freshwater circulation), the prospects are diminished for food production, safe drinking water adequate household and community energy sources, stability of infectious disease agents, and protection from natural environmental disasters.

The subsequent treatment by the UN of Goal 7 in relation to its health implications has been rather superficial, and mostly in relation to familiar, localized, environmental health hazards. For example, the UN's 2007 report on the MDGs focuses particularly on how Goal 7 relates to child diarrhoeal diseases. It states:

> *The health, economic and social repercussions of open defecation, poor hygiene and lack of safe drinking water are well documented. Together they contribute to about 88 per cent of the deaths due to diarrhoeal diseases—more than 1.5 million—in children under age five. Infestation of intestinal worms caused by open defecation affects hundreds of millions of predominantly school-aged children, resulting in reduced physical growth, weakened physical fitness and impaired cognitive functions. Poor nutrition contributes to these effects.*[2]

More encouraging is the recent, wider-visioned approach taken by the UN Millennium Project, undertaken for the Commission on Sustainable Development.[3] This project's definition of "environmental sustainability" refers explicitly to the health impacts of environmental changes, and states as follows:

> *Achieving environmental sustainability requires carefully balancing human development activities while maintaining a stable environment that predictably and regularly provides resources such as freshwater, food, clean air, wood, fisheries and productive soils and that protects people from floods, droughts, pest infestations and disease.*[4]

Notes

1. UN Secretary General, Millennium Development Goals (New York. United Nations, 2000), http://www.un.org/millenniumgoals/goals.html (accessed 23 August 2007).
2. United Nations, *The Millennium Development Goals Report 2007* (New York: United Nations, 2007).
3. J. Sachs and J. McArthur, "The Millennium Project: A Plan for Meeting the Millennium Development Goals," *Lancer* 365, no. 9456 (2005): 347–53.
4. Y. K. Nayarro, J. McNeely, D. Melnick, R. R. Sears, and G. Schmidt-Traub, *Environment and Human Wellbeing: A Practical Strategy* (New York: UN Millennium Project Task Force on Environmental Sustainability, 2005).

economic development, health care systems, and public health programs—and not on the fundamental health-supporting role of the natural environment and its ecosystem services.

The report noted the success of some relatively poor nations and provinces, such as China, Sri Lanka, and Kerala State in India, in lowering infant mortality and improving population health by investing in education (especially for girls), establishing primary health clinics, and enacting other health-care programs. The report extended this analysis, citing the history of the well-documented mortality decline in the industrial world—which preceded the advent of modern drugs and medical care, deriving instead from betterment of nutrition, housing, and hygiene. Progressive policies, strong social institutions, and innovative health care and public health protection (especially against infectious diseases), without generalized gains in national wealth, the report's authors said, can be sufficient to raise population health markedly.

This important insight, though, makes no explicit reference to the role of wider environmental conditions. While the control of mosquito populations with window-screens and insecticides certainly confers some health protection, for example, land-use practices, surface water management, biodiversity (frogs and birds eat mosquitoes), and climatic conditions can affect mosquito ecology and mosquito-borne disease transmission more profoundly. The issue must be tackled at both levels.

In fairness, understanding the patterns and determinants of human population health within a wider ecological frame has been impeded by strong cultural and intellectual undercurrents. The rise of modern western science and medicine, in concert with the contemporary ascendancy of neo-liberalism and individualism, has recast our views of health and disease in primarily personal terms. The Christian biblical notion from two thousand years ago of the Four Horsemen of the Apocalypse as the major scourges of population health and survival—war, conquest, famine, and pestilence—has been replaced by today's prevailing model of health and disease as predominantly a function of individual-level consumer behaviors, genetic susceptibility, and access to modern health care technologies.

In addition to this cultural misshaping of our understanding, our increasing technological sophistication has created the illusion that we no longer depend on nature's "goods and services" for life's basic necessities. In this first decade of the twenty-first century, however, we are being forcibly reminded of that fundamental dependence. Hence, a repeat WCED report, written now, would give much higher priority to the relationship between biosphere, environmental processes, human biological health, and survival.

Footprints, Environmental Conditions, and Human Well-being

It is interesting that the WCED report was being drafted at about the time when, according to recent assessments, the demands and pressures of the global human population were first over-reaching the planet's carrying capacity.[11]

In the time since the publication of the report, the "ecological footprint" has become a familiar concept. For any grouping of persons, it measures the amount of Earth's surface required to provide their materials and food and to absorb their wastes. Collectively, humankind reached a point in the mid-1980s when it began to exceed the limit of what Earth could supply and absorb on a sustainable basis. Since then, the human population has moved from having a precariously balanced environmental budget that left nothing in reserve to a situation today in which we are attempting to survive on a substantial, growing, overdraft: our global standard-of-living is estimated to be at the level that requires approximately 1.3 Earths (see Table).[12] We are therefore consuming and depleting natural environmental capital. This explains the accruing evidence of climate change, loss of fertile soil, freshwater shortages, declining fisheries, biodiversity losses and extinctions. This is not a sustainable trajectory, and it is what, generically, the WCED report exhorted the world to avoid.

In the 1980s, there was more ambivalence about the population component of the "footprint" concept. The absolute annual increments in human numbers were at a historical high, and many demographers and some enlightened policymakers were concerned that population growth needed constraining. That view faced an emergent western political ethos that eschewed family planning, abortion counseling, and governmental intervention. In the upshot, population growth has begun to slow in a majority of countries. Meanwhile, this is being offset by the rapid rise in wealth and consumption in many larger developing countries, including China, India, Brazil, and Mexico.

This planet simply cannot support a human population of 8 to 10 billion living at the level of today's high-income country citizens. Each of those citizens, depending on their particular country, needs 4 to 9 hectares of Earth's surface to provide materials for their lifestyle and to absorb their wastes. Meanwhile, India's population of 1.2 billion has to get by with less than 1 hectare per person. With an anticipated world population of 8 to 10 billion living within Earth's limits, there would be no more than about 1.5 hectares of ecological footprint per average-person—and this arithmetic would limit the resources available for other species. To comply equitably with this limit will necessitate radical changes in value systems and social institutions everywhere.

Global Environment: Emerging Evidence

The Brundtland Commission foresaw at least some of the impending serious erosion of large-scale environmental resources and systems. Indeed, the WCED report judged that by early in the twenty-first century, climate change might have increased average global temperatures sufficiently to displace agricultural production areas, raise sea levels (and perhaps flood coastal cities), and disrupt national economies. This apparently has not yet happened, although very recent scientific reports point strongly to an acceleration in the climate change process,[13] as the global emissions of carbon dioxide from fossil-fuel combustion and of other greenhouse gases from industrial and agricultural activities alter the global climate faster than previously expected.

Several other adverse environmental trends have emerged since 1987. Accessible oil stocks may now be declining—thereby stimulating an (ill-judged) scramble to divert food-grain production into biofuel production as an alternative source of liquid energy.[14] It has also become apparent that human actions are transforming the global cycles of various elements other than carbon, particularly nitrogen, phosphorus, and sulfur.[15] Human agricultural and industrial activity now generates as much biologically activated nitrogen (nitrogenous

Table 1 Changes in Key Global Indicators of Environment and Population Health (1987–2007)

	1987 (1985–1989)	2007 (2005–2009)	Comments
World population size	4.9 billion	6.7 billion	Slight reduction in absolute annual increment
Annual population growth rate	1.7%	1.2%	
Fertility rate (births/woman)	3.4	2.4	
Percent over age 65 years	6%	8%	Low-income countries have increased from 4% to 5.5%
Life expectancy, years	65	68	
Maternal mortality (per 100,000 births)	430	400	
Under 5 mortality, per 1,000 births	115	70	
Infant mortality, per 1,000 births	68	48	
Primary schooling	~60%	82%	See also Figure 1
Malnutrition prevalence	870 million	850 million	Recent increase, relative to the turn of century (~ 820 million)
Child stunting, less than age 5, prevalence	~ 30%	25%	Down from 35% circa 1950, but a persistent and serious problem in sub-Saharan Africa (highest prevalence) and South Asia
HIV/AIDS, prevalent cases	10 million	40 million	
AIDS deaths per year	~ 0.2 million	3.2 million	
Lack safe drinking water	1.3 billion (27%)	1.1 billion (15%)	Percent of world population shown in parenthesis
Lack sanitation	2.7 billion (54%)	2.6 billion (40%)	Percent of world population shown in parenthesis
CO_2 atmospheric concentration	325 parts per million	385 parts per million	Approx 0.5% rise per year, currently accelerating. (Pre-industrial concentration 275 parts per million)
Increase in average global temperature relative to 1961–1990 baseline	0.1 degrees Celsius	0.5 degrees Celsius	Warming faster at high latitude, especially in northern hemisphere
Global ecological footprint	1.0 planet Earths	1.3 planet Earths	Estimate of number of planet Earths needed to supply, sustainably, the world population's energy, materials and waste disposal needs

Source: Compiled from various international agency reports, databases, and scientific papers.

compounds such as ammonia) as do lightning, volcanic activity, and nitrogen-fixation on the roots of wild plants. Meanwhile, worldwide land degradation, freshwater shortages, and biodiversity losses are increasing. Those environmental problems were all becoming evident in the mid-1980s and were duly referred to in the WCED report, albeit without particular connection to considerations of human health.

Some other large-scale environmental stresses, however, were not evident in the 1980s. The scientific community had not anticipated the acidification of the world's oceans caused by absorption of increasingly abundant atmospheric carbon dioxide. This acidification—global average ocean pH has declined by a little over 0.1 points during the past several decades—endangers the calcification processes in the tiny creatures at the base of the marine food web. Nor was much attention paid to the prospect of loss of key species in ecosystems, such as pollinating insects (especially bees). Both those processes are now demonstrably happening, further jeopardizing human capital development, poverty alleviation, and good health.

During 2001–2006, the Millennium Eco-system Assessment (MA) was conducted as a comprehensive international scientific assessment with processes similar to those of IPCC. The MA documented the extent to which recent human pressures have accelerated the decline of stocks of many environmental assets, including changes to ecosystems.[15] The MA also projected likely future trends. This assessment documented how several other globally significant environmental graphs peaked in the mid-1980s. On land, the annual per capita production of cereal grains peaked and has subsequently drifted sideways and, recently, downwards. The harvest from the world's ocean fisheries also peaked at that time and has subsequently declined slowly—albeit with compensatory gains from aquaculture. These emergent negative trends in food-producing capacity jeopardize attempts to reduce hunger, malnutrition, and child stunting—a key target area of the Millennium Development Goals (see the box on next page).

The WCED report, if rewritten today, would presumably take a more integrative and systems-oriented approach to the topic of environmental sustainability and would incorporate greater awareness of the risks posed to human well-being and health.

Trends in Human Capital and Population Health

As discussed, the original UN resolution calling for the WCED report referred ambiguously to "resources." Within the overarching environmental context of the commission, the intended reference of that word may well have been to environmental resources (such as oil, strategic and precious metals, water supplies, etc.). Interestingly, the WCED treated the word as referring primarily to *human* resources in chapter 4, titled "Population and Human Resources."

The global population was 4.9 billion at the time the WCED report was published, and now exceeds 6.7 billion. It continues to increase by more than 70 million persons annually. Because overall fertility rates have declined a little faster than was previously expected, the current "medium" UN projection for population growth by 2050 is for a total of approximately 9.1 billion.[16] Most of that increase will occur in the low-income countries, predominantly in rapidly expanding cities.

Population growth necessarily increases demands on the local environment. But as the WCED report correctly argued, "the population issue is not solely about numbers."[17] Population size, density, and movement are part of a larger set of pressures on the environment. In some regions, resource degradation occurs because of the combination of poverty and the farming of thinly populated drylands and forests. Elsewhere, per-person levels of consumption and waste generation are the critical drivers of environmental stress. Extrapolation of current global economic trends foreshadows a potential five- to tenfold increase in economic activity by 2050. But this looks increasingly unachievable without radical changes in world technological choices and economic practices. The current experience of China is salutary in this regard: that country's rapid economic growth is engendering huge problems of freshwater supply, air quality, environmental toxins in food, desertification of western provinces—and, now, the world's largest national contribution to greenhouse gas emissions.

Is there an upside to population? "People," stated the WCED report, "are the ultimate resource. Improvements in education, health, and nutrition allow them to better use the resources they command, to stretch them further."[18] How have we progressed since 1987 in providing these improvements?

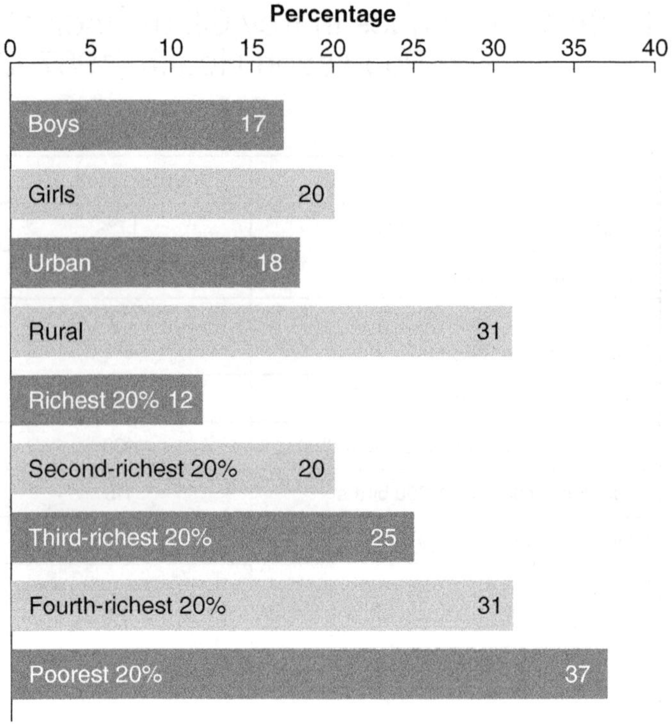

Figure 1 Children of primary school age not in school, by sex, place of residence, and household wealth, 2005

Source: United Nations, *Millennium Development Goals Report 2007* (New York: United Nations, 2007), http://www.un.org/millenniumgoals/goals.html (accessed 23 August, 2007).

Access to primary schooling has increased since 1987 (see Table 1). In particular, the proportion of young girls completing primary school has increased (starting from a lower base than for boys). Figure 1 on this page shows current proportions of the world's children not in primary schooling by key categories. Impediments persist in the form of poverty, parental illiteracy, civil war, and Islamic extremism (banning female education).

Beyond environmental stresses and deficits, the task of improving population health faces other, systemic difficulties. As my colleague C. D. Butler and I wrote last year:

> The gap between rich and poor, both domestically and internationally, has increased substantially in recent decades. Inequality between countries has weakened the United Nations and other global organisations and institutions. Foreign aid has declined, replaced by claims that market forces and the removal of trade-distorting subsidies will reduce poverty and provide public goods, including health care and environmental stability.[19]

Hunger and malnutrition persist at high levels (see box). Famines in Africa remain frequent, and 300 million people in India are undernourished. Further, the almost 50 percent prevalence of underweight children in sub-Saharan Africa and South Asia causes widespread stunting of growth, intellectual development, and energy levels. Yet elsewhere, hundreds of millions of people in all continents are overfed and, via obesity, at increased risk of diabetes and heart disease.

Over the past two decades, demographic and epidemiological transitions have become less orderly than was anticipated

Recent Trends in Population Health

Human health experienced unprecedented gains last century. Globally, average life expectancy approximately doubled from around 35 years to almost 70 years.[1] Rises in life expectancy have slowed a little in recent years in high-income countries. Meanwhile, rises are continuing (from a lower base) in much of the rest of the world. However, the regional picture is very uneven, and some divergence has occurred. The rise in life expectancy has stalled in much of sub-Saharan Africa, various ex-Soviet countries, North Korea, and Iraq (see the figure on the next page). Meanwhile, health inequalities persist both between and within countries and reflect, variously, differences in economic circumstance, literacy, social institutions, and political regimen.

Improved food supply is the likely cause of much of the health gain in modern western populations. The second agricultural revolution, which began in eighteenth-century Europe, brought mechanization, new cultivars, and, eventually, fossil fuel power. Consequently, the millennia-old pattern of subsistence crises diminished and then disappeared. The greater security and abundance of food apparently explains why adult males in northern European countries have grown around 10 centimeters taller and 20–30 kilograms heavier than their eighteenth-century predecessors.[2] Others have argued that improved food quality and safety raised the resistance of better-nourished persons to infectious diseases.[3]

Despite these gains, an estimated 850 million persons remain malnourished. In absolute terms, that figure has grown since the time of the WCED report, including over the past decade.[4] Meanwhile, it has become increasingly evident in both high-income and lower-income countries that an abundance of food energy, especially in the form of refined and selectively produced energy-dense (high fat, high sugar) foods, poses various serious risks to health.

In the 1980s, the general assumption was that these non-communicable diseases appear in the later stages of economic development and would increase with further gains in wealth and modernity. However it has become clear in the past two decades that these diseases, particularly heart disease, hypertensive stroke, and type 2 diabetes, are increasing markedly in lower-income populations as they undergo urbanization, and dietary change. The burden of cardiovascular disease—which accounts for around 30 percent of all deaths in today's world—will continue this shift to low- and middle-income countries. This, plus the persistent infectious disease burden, particularly in poorer subpopulations, will further increase global health inequalities.[5]

Notes

1. A. J. McMichael, M. McKee, V. Shkolnikov, and T. Vaikonen, "Mortality Trends and Setbacks: Global Convergence or Divergence?" *Lancet* 363, no. 9415, (2004): 1155–59.
2. R. W. Fogel, *The Escape from Hunger and Premature Death, 1700–2100: Europe, American and the Third World* (Cambridge: Cambridge University Press, 2004).
3. T. McKeown, R. G. Brown, and R. Record, "An Interpretation of the Modern Rise of Population in Europe," *Population Studies* 26 no. 3 (1972): 345–82.
4. Food and Agriculture Organization of the United Nations (FAO), *The State of Food Insecurity in the World 2004* (Rome: FAO, 2005).
5. M. Ezzati et al., "Rethinking the 'Diseases of Affluence' Paradigm: Global Patterns of Nutritional Risks in Relation to Economic Development." *PLoS Medicine* 2, no.5 (2005), e133.doi.10.1371/journal.pmed.0020133.

by conventional demographic models. There has been considerable divergence between countries in trends in death rates (life expectancy) and fertility rates. National health trends (see box), particularly in poor and vulnerable populations, are falling increasingly under the shadow of climate change and other adverse environmental trends.

In many, but not all low-income countries, fertility rates have declined faster than might have been predicted. However, in some countries (such as East Timor, Nigeria, and Pakistan) fertility remains high (4–7 children per woman). In some regions, the fertility decline has led to an economically and socially unbalanced age structure, especially in China, where in the wake of their "one-child policy," the impending dependency ratio is remarkably high—many fewer young adults will have to provide economic support for an older, longer-living generation.

In some other countries, population growth has declined substantially because of rapid falls in life expectancy.[20] Russia and parts of sub-Saharan Africa have very different demographic characteristics, and yet common elements may underlie their downward trends in life expectancy. Both regions lack public goods for health.[21] In Russia there is a lack of equality, safety, and public health services—and many men have lost status and authority following the collapse of the Communist party structure. Meanwhile, in a number of sub-Saharan African countries, there is serious corruption in government, deficient governance structures, food insecurity, and inadequate public health services.

The conventional assumption, also evident in the WCED report, has been that a health dividend will flow from poverty alleviation. However, it is becoming clear that those anticipated health gains are likely to be lower because of the now-world-wide rise of various non-communicable diseases, including those due to obesity, dietary imbalances, tobacco use, and urban air pollution.[22]

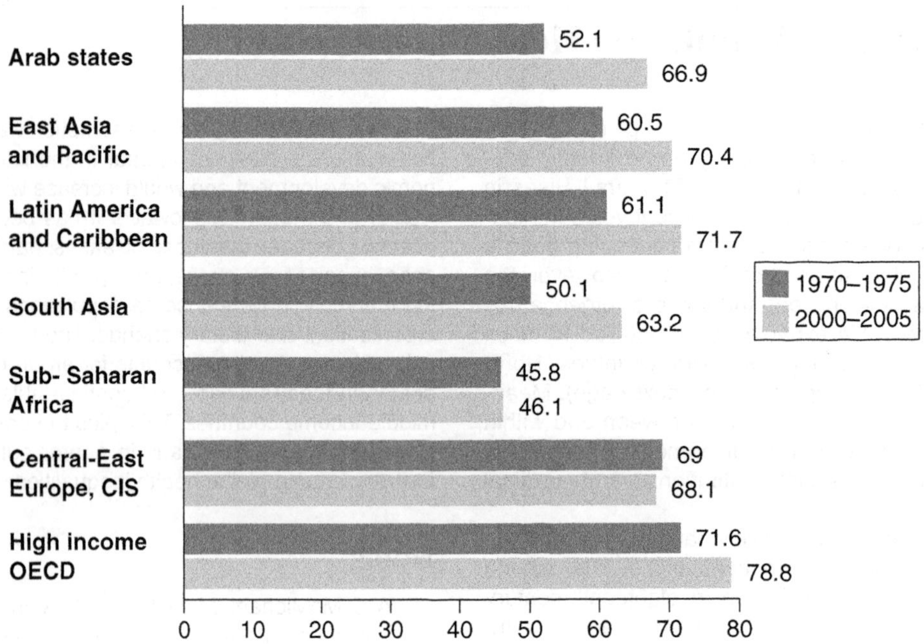

Changes in life expectancy by region, over the past three decades

Note: Differences are marked between regions—especially the lack of gains in sub-Saharan Africa and the central and eastern European (including ex-Soviet) countries.

Source: Based on M. Marmot, "Health in an Unequal World," *Lancet* 368, no. 9552 (2006): 2081–94.

Conclusion

The WCED was commissioned to examine critically the relationship between environmental resource use and sustainable development and to propose solutions for the tensions between environment (including the pressures of population growth and urbanization) and development. A prime task for the commission was to formulate a "global agenda for change" within the frame of ecologically sustainable development, while recognizing the aspirational goals of people and communities everywhere.[23]

During the time that the commission was developing its report, a widely held view, reinforced by the Green Revolution successes of the 1970s and early 1980s, was that continuing population growth need not have adverse environmental impacts. The commission was hesitant to embrace that view, which has recently been re-evaluated,[24] with renewed recognition of the adverse effects of rapid population growth, especially in developing countries, on both social and environmental conditions.[25]

In the 1980s, national governments and multilateral agencies began to see that economic development issues could not be separated from environment issues. Many forms of development erode the environmental resource base (including forests, fertile soils, and coastal zones) necessary for sustained development. And conversely, environmental degradation can jeopardize economic development. The WCED report rightly emphasized the futility of addressing environmental problems without alleviating poverty and international inequality. The report also recognized the needs for stronger social structures and legal processes to deal with tensions over environmental commons, and for more enlightened public agency structures at the international level to address these issues. It advocated partnerships with the private sector—a sector in which there is now a growing recognition that business-as-usual is no longer an option.

Those formulations remain important and valid, but they are an incomplete basis for future strategic policy. They overlook the fundamental role that sustaining an intact biosphere and its component systems plays in enabling the social and human developmental processes that can reduce poverty, undernutrition, unsafe drinking water, and exposures to endemic and epidemic infectious diseases. The report, if updated today, would seek a better balance between these sets of relationships.

The idea of "ecologically sustainable development" was, in the latter 1980s, ahead of its time. We had, then, neither the evidence nor the insight to know just how fundamental that framework was to achieving the other human goals that would be embraced over the next two decades. Today, the ongoing growth of the global population and—with economic development and rising consumer expectations—the increasingly great environmental impact of that population means that we may be less than one generation away from exhausting much of the biosphere's environmental buffering capacity.[13] Unless we can constrain our excessive demands on the natural world, the demographic and epidemiological transitions (faltering in some regions) will be further affected and human fulfillment will thus be eroded.

Twenty years on from the report of the World Commission on Environment and Development, we can see additional layers to the environment challenge that were little understood in the 1980s. Clearly, some fundamental changes are needed in how we live, generate energy, consume materials, and dispose of wastes. Population arithmetic will impose a further dimension of challenge: 4.8 billion in 1987; 6.7 billion in 2007; perhaps 8 billion by 2027. Beyond that, the numbers and outcomes will be influenced by what current and future "Brundtland reports" formulate, and how seriously and urgently we and our governments take their formulations and recommendations.

Notes

1. World Commission on Environment and Development, *Our Common Future* (Cambridge, UK, and New York: Cambridge University Press, 1987).
2. A. C. Kelley, "The Population Debate in Historical Perspective: Revisionism Revised," in N. Birdsall, A. C. Kelley, and S. W. Sinding, eds., *Population Matters: Demographic Change, Economic Growth, and Poverty in the Developing World* (Oxford, UK: Oxford University Press, 2001), 24–54.
3. P. McMichael, *Development and Social Change: A Global Perspective* (Thousand Oaks, California: Pine Forge Press, 2004).
4. A. J. McMichael, M. McKee, V. Shkolnikov, and T. Valkonen, "Mortality Trends and Setbacks: Global Convergence or Divergence?" *Lancet* 363, no. 9415 (2004): 1155–59; and R. Eckersley, "Is Modern Western Culture a Health Hazard?" *International Journal of Epidemiology* 35, no 5 (2006): 252–58.
5. United Nations, "Process of Preparation of the Environmental Perspective to the Year 2000 and Beyond," General Assembly Resolution 38/161, 19 December 1983.
6. WCED, note 1 above, page 1.
7. G. H. Brundtland, speech given at the launch of the WCED report, Oslo, Norway, 20 March 1987.
8. D. G. Victor, "Recovering Sustainable Development," *Foreign Affairs 85*, no. 1 (January/February 2006): 91–103.
9. WCED, note 1 above, page 98.
10. Intergovernmental Panel on Climate Change, *Climate Change. The IPCC Scientific Assessment* (Cambridge, UK: Cambridge University Press, 1990).
11. Ibid.; and C. M. Wackernagel et al., "Tracking the Ecological Overshoot of the Human Economy," *Proceedings of the National Academy of Sciences* 99, no. 14 (2002): 9266–71.
12. Worldwide Fund for Nature International (WWF), *Living Planet Report 2006* (Gland, Switzerland: WWF, 2006), http://assets.panda.org/dowloads/living_planet_report.pdf (accessed 23 Aug 2007).
13. S. Rahmstorf et al., "Recent Climate Observations Compared to Projections," *Science* 316, no. 5825 (4 May 2007): 709.
14. See R. L. Naylor et al., "The Ripple Effect: Biofuels, Food Security, and the Environment," *Environment* 49, no. 9 (November 2007): 30–43.
15. Millennium Ecosystem Assessment, *Ecosystems and Human Wellbeing. Synthesis* (Washington, DC: Island Press, 2005).
16. UN Department of Economic and Social Affairs, Population Division: http://esa.un.org/unpp/p2k0data.asp (accessed Nov 1, 2007).
17. WCED, note 1 above, page 95.
18. WCED, note 1 above, page 95. This statement has faint resonance with the ideas of the late U.S. economist Julian Simon, whose book *The Ultimate Resource* made the tendentious argument that the more people on Earth the greater the probability of occurrence of important new ideas. J. L. Simon, *The Ultimate Resource* (Princeton, NJ: Princeton University Press, 1981).
19. A. J. McMichael and C. D. Butler, "Emerging Health Issues: The Widening Challenge for Population Health Promotion," *Health Promotion International* 21, no. 1 (2006): 15–24.
20. McMichael, McKee, Shkolnikov, and Valkonen, note 4 above.
21. R. Smith, R. Beaglehole, D. Woodward, and N. Drager, eds., *Global Public Goods for Health* (Oxford: Oxford University Press, 2003).
22. M. Ezzati et al., "Rethinking the 'Diseases of Affluence' Paradigm: Global Patterns of Nutritional Risks in Relation to Economic Development," *Plos Medicine* 2, no. 5 (2005): e133.
23. Brundtland, note 7 above.
24. Kelley, note 2 above.
25. M. Campbell, J. Cleland, A. Ezeh, and N. Prata, "Return of the Population Growth Factor," *Science* 315, no. 5818 (2 February 2007): 1501–2.

Assess Your Progress

1. What are the health consequences of environmental degradation?
2. In what ways have western cultural and intellectual values influenced views on health and environment?
3. How does population growth affect social and economic conditions?
4. How would the Brundtland Commission Report differ from such a report issued today?

Anthony J. McMichael is a professor at the National Centre for Epidemiology and Population Health (NCEPH) at Australia National University in Canberra. From 2001 to 2007, he was director of NCEPH, where he has led the development of a program of epidemiological research on the environmental influences on immune disorders, particularly autoimmune diseases such as multiple sclerosis. Meanwhile, he has continued his pioneering research on the health risks of global climate change, developed in conjunction with his central role in the assessment of health risks for the Intergovernmental Panel on Climate Change. His work on climate and environmental change, along with longstanding interests in social and cultural influences on patterns of health and disease, also underlie his interests in understanding the determinants of the emergence and spread of infectious diseases in this seemingly "renaissant" microbial era. He may be contacted at Tony.McMichael@anu.edu.au.

Reversal of Fortune

Why Preventing Poverty Beats Curing It

ANIRUDH KRISHNA

Lifting people out of poverty has become a mantra for the world's political leaders. The first U.N. Millennium Development Goal is to halve the number of people whose income is less than $1 per day, currently about 1 billion people. And, in the past decade, millions around the world have been pulled out of poverty by economic growth, effective development aid, and sheer hard work.

Four years ago, I set out to discover which countries—and which local communities—were doing the best job of ending poverty. Using a varied sample of more than 25,000 households in 200 diverse communities in India, Kenya, Peru, Uganda, and the U.S. state of North Carolina, my colleagues and I traced which households have emerged from poverty and attempted to explain their success. At first, the data were very encouraging. In 36 Ugandan communities, 370 households (almost 15 percent of the total) moved out of poverty between 1994 and 2004. In Gujarat, India, 10 percent of a sample of several thousand households emerged from poverty between 1980 and 2003. In Kenya, 18 percent of a sample of households rose out of poverty between 1980 and 2004.

Looking at these figures, one could be forgiven for feeling a sense of satisfaction. But pulling people out of impoverishment is only half the story. Our research revealed another, much darker story: In many places, more families are falling into poverty than are being lifted out. In Kenya, for example, more households, 19 percent, fell into poverty than emerged from it. Twenty-five percent of households studied in the KwaZulu-Natal province of eastern South Africa fell into poverty, but fewer than half as many, 10 percent, overcame poverty in the same period. In Bangladesh, Egypt, Peru, and every other country where researchers have conducted similar studies, the results are the same. In many places, newly impoverished citizens constitute the majority of the poor. It's a harsh fact that calls into question current policies for combating poverty.

All sorts of factors—including financial crises and currency collapse—can push people into poverty. But our research indicates that the leading culprit is poor healthcare. Tracking thousands of households in five separate countries, my colleagues and I found that health and healthcare expenses are the leading cause for people's reversal of fortune. The story of a woman from Kikoni village in Uganda is typical. She and her husband lived relatively well for many years. "Then my husband was sick for 10 years before he died, and all the money that we had with us was spent on medical charges," she said. "My children dropped out of school because we could not pay school fees. Then my husband died. I was left with a tiny piece of land. Now I cannot even get enough food to eat."

Among newly poor households in 20 villages of western Kenya, 73 percent cited ill health and high medical costs as the most important cause of their economic decline. Eighty-eight percent of people who fell into poverty in 36 villages in Gujarat placed the blame on healthcare. In Peru, 67 percent of recently impoverished people in two provinces cited ill health, inaccessible medical facilities, and high healthcare costs. When families are hit by a health crisis, it's often hard to recover. In China, one major illness typically reduces family income by 16 percent. Successive illnesses ensure an even faster spiral into lasting poverty. Surveys in several African and Asian countries show that a combination of ill health and indebtedness has sent tens of thousands of households into poverty, including many that were once affluent. The phenomenon exists in the rich world as well; half of all personal bankruptcies in the United States are due to high medical expenses.

Millions of people are living one illness away from financial disaster, and the world's aid efforts are ill-suited to the challenge. An intense focus on stimulating economic growth isn't enough. Healthcare is not automatically better or cheaper where economic growth rates have been high. In Gujarat, a state in India that has achieved high growth rates for more than a decade, affordable healthcare remains a severe problem, and thousands have fallen into poverty as a result. Healthcare in fast growing Gujarat is no better than in other, often poorer, states of India. Indeed, Gujarat ranked fourth from the bottom among 25 states in terms of proportion of state income spent on healthcare. Perversely, rapid economic growth often weakens existing social safety nets and raises the danger of backsliding. In places as diverse as rural India, Kenya, Uganda, and North Carolina, we observed how community and family support crumbles as market-based transactions overtake traditional networks.

As economic growth helps lift people out of poverty, governments must stand ready to prevent backsliding by providing affordable, accessible, and reliable healthcare. Japan's recent history offers hope that enlightened policy can prevail. At 4 percent, Japan's poverty rate is among the lowest in the world. Sustained economic growth undoubtedly helped, but so too did an entirely different set of policies. Quite early in the country's post-World War II recovery, Japanese officials recognized the critical relationship between illness, healthcare services, and poverty creation, and they responded by implementing universal healthcare as early as the 1950s.

Regrettably, that insight hasn't traveled nearly as well as Japan's many other exports. It's well past time that political leaders put as much effort into stopping the slide into poverty as they do easing the climb out of it.

Assess Your Progress

1. What has been neglected in the emphasis on progress in pulling people out of poverty?
2. What is the biggest contributing factor to financial disaster among the poor?
3. What must governments do to prevent people from slipping back into poverty?

Anirudh Krishna is assistant professor of public policy and political science at Duke University.

Reprinted in entirety by McGraw-Hill with permission from *Foreign Policy,* May/June 2006, pp. 62–63. www.foreignpolicy.com.

UNIT 6
Women and Development

Unit Selections

Learning Outcomes

After reading this unit you should be able to:

- Describe the challenges which women face in developing countries.
- Identify the benefits of educating girls.
- Explain why women are particularly vulnerable in conflict situations.
- Recognize the importance of including women in post-conflict settlements.
- Discuss the consequences of recession and climate change for women.
- Outline the obstacles to ensuring women's rights.

Student Website

www.mhhe.com/cls

Internet References

WIDNET: Women in Development NETwork
www.focusintl.com/widnet.htm

Women Watch/Regional and Country Information
www.un.org/womenwatch

There is widespread recognition of the crucial role that women play in the development process. Women are critical to the success of family planning programs, bear much of the responsibility for food production, account for an increasing share of wage labor in developing countries, are acutely aware of the consequences of environmental degradation, and can contribute to the development of a vibrant, civil society and good governance. Despite their important contributions, however, women lag behind men in access to health care, nutrition, and education while continuing to face formidable social, economic, and political barriers. Women's lives in the developing world are invariably difficult. Often female children are valued less than male offspring, resulting in higher female infant and child mortality rates. In extreme cases, this undervaluing leads to female infanticide.

Those females who do survive face lives characterized by poor nutrition and health, multiple pregnancies, hard physical labor, discrimination, and in some cases violence. Clearly, women are central to any successful population policy. Evidence shows that educated women have fewer and healthier children. This connection between education and population indicates that greater emphasis should be placed on educating women. In reality, female school enrollments are lower than those of males because of state priorities, insufficient family resources to educate both boys and girls, female socialization, and cultural factors. Education is probably the largest single contributor to enhancing the status of women and promoting development, but access to education is still limited for many women. Sixty percent of children worldwide not enrolled in schools are girls. Education for women leads to improved health, better wages, and greater influence in decision making, which benefits not only women but the broader society as well. Educated women contribute more to their families, are less likely to subject their daughters to female genital mutilation, and are three times less likely to contract HIV.

Women make up a significant portion of the agricultural workforce. They are heavily involved in food production right from planting to cultivation, harvesting, and marketing. Despite their agricultural contribution, women frequently do not have adequate access to advances in agricultural technology or the benefits of extension and training programs. They are also discriminated against in land ownership. As a result, important opportunities to improve food production are lost when women are not given access to technology, training, and land ownership commensurate with their agricultural role.

The industrialization that has accompanied the globalized production has meant more employment opportunities for women, but often these are low-tech, low-wage jobs. The lower labor costs in the developing world that attract manufacturing facilities are a mixed blessing for women. Increasingly, women are recruited to fill these production jobs because wage differentials allow employers to pay women less. On the other hand, expanding opportunities for women in these positions contribute to family income. The informal sector, where jobs are small scale, more traditional, and labor-intensive, has also attracted more women. These jobs are often their only employment option, due to family responsibilities or discrimination.

© ArabianEye/PunchStock RF

Women also play a critical role in the economic expansion of developing countries. Nevertheless, women are often the first to feel the effects of an economic slowdown. The consequences of the structural adjustment programs that many developing countries have to adopt have also fallen disproportionately on women. When employment opportunities decline because of austerity measures, women lose jobs in the formal sector and face increased competition from males in the informal sector. Cuts in spending on health care and education also affect women, who already receive fewer of these benefits. Currency devaluations further erode the purchasing power of women. The global economic crisis is only going to worsen the plight of working women. Because of the gender division of labor, women are often more aware of the consequences of environmental degradation. Depletion of resources such as forests, soil, and water are much more likely to be felt by women, who are responsible for collecting firewood and water, and who raise most of the crops. As a result, women are an essential component of successful environmental protection policies, but they are often overlooked in planning environmental projects.

Enhancing the status of women has been the primary focus of several international conferences. The 1994 International Conference on Population and Development (ICPD) focused attention on women's health and reproductive rights, and the crucial role that these issues play in controlling population. The 1995 Fourth World Conference on Women held in Beijing, China, proclaimed women's rights to be synonymous with human rights. Along with the Convention on the Elimination of All Forms of Discrimination against Women, these developments represent a turning point in women's struggle for equal rights, and have prompted efforts to pass legislation at the national level to protect women's rights.

There are indications that women have made progress in some regions of the developing world. The election of Ellen John-Sirleaf as president of Liberia and Africa's first female head of state is the most visible indicator of a trend toward greater political involvement of women in Africa. In the Middle

East, the 2002 Arab Human Development Report highlighted the extent to which women in the region lagged behind their counterparts in other parts of the world. While there has been some progress in the region recently, it has been uneven. It remains the case that women in conflict zones are particularly vulnerable to violence. In Afghanistan, not only are women subject to the violence that comes with war but a recent family law has set back the progress on women's rights made after the ouster of the Taliban. There continues to be a wide divergence in the status of women worldwide, but the recognition of the valuable contributions they can make to society is increasing the pressure to enhance their status.

The Women's Crusade

The oppression of women worldwide is the human rights cause of our time. And their liberation could help solve many of the world's problems, from poverty to child mortality to terrorism. A 21st-century manifesto.

NICHOLAS D. KRISTOF AND SHERYL WUDUNN

In the 19th century, the paramount moral challenge was slavery. In the 20th century, it was totalitarianism. In this century, it is the brutality inflicted on so many women and girls around the globe: sex trafficking, acid attacks, bride burnings and mass rape.

Yet if the injustices that women in poor countries suffer are of paramount importance, in an economic and geopolitical sense the opportunity they represent is even greater. "Women hold up half the sky," in the words of a Chinese saying, yet that's mostly an aspiration: in a large slice of the world, girls are uneducated and women marginalized, and it's not an accident that those same countries are disproportionately mired in poverty and riven by fundamentalism and chaos. There's a growing recognition among everyone from the World Bank to the U.S. military's Joint Chiefs of Staff to aid organizations like CARE that focusing on women and girls is the most effective way to fight global poverty and extremism. That's why foreign aid is increasingly directed to women. The world is awakening to a powerful truth: Women and girls aren't the problem; they're the solution.

One place to observe this alchemy of gender is in the muddy back alleys of Pakistan. In a slum outside the grand old city of Lahore, a woman named Saima Muhammad used to dissolve into tears every evening. A round-faced woman with thick black hair tucked into a head scarf, Saima had barely a rupee, and her deadbeat husband was unemployed and not particularly employable. He was frustrated and angry, and he coped by beating Saima each afternoon. Their house was falling apart, and Saima had to send her young daughter to live with an aunt, because there wasn't enough food to go around.

"My sister-in-law made fun of me, saying, 'You can't even feed your children,'" recalled Saima when Nick met her two years ago on a trip to Pakistan. "My husband beat me up. My brother-in-law beat me up. I had an awful life." Saima's husband accumulated a debt of more than $3,000, and it seemed that these loans would hang over the family for generations. Then when Saima's second child was born and turned out to be a girl as well, her mother-in-law, a harsh, blunt woman named Sharifa Bibi, raised the stakes.

"She's not going to have a son," Sharifa told Saima's husband, in front of her. "So you should marry again. Take a second wife." Saima was shattered and ran off sobbing. Another wife would leave even less money to feed and educate the children. And Saima herself would be marginalized in the household, cast off like an old sock. For days Saima walked around in a daze, her eyes red; the slightest incident would send her collapsing into hysterical tears.

It was at that point that Saima signed up with the Kashf Foundation, a Pakistani microfinance organization that lends tiny amounts of money to poor women to start businesses. Kashf is typical of microfinance institutions, in that it lends almost exclusively to women, in groups of 25. The women guarantee one another's debts and meet every two weeks to make payments and discuss a social issue, like family planning or schooling for girls. A Pakistani woman is often forbidden to leave the house without her husband's permission, but husbands tolerate these meetings because the women return with cash and investment ideas.

Saima Muhammad, lives near Lahore, Pakistan. She was routinely beaten by her husband until she started a successful embroidery business.

Saima took out a $65 loan and used the money to buy beads and cloth, which she transformed into beautiful embroidery that she then sold to merchants in the markets of Lahore. She used the profit to buy more beads and cloth, and soon she had an embroidery business and was earning a solid income—the only one in her household to do so. Saima took her elder daughter back from the aunt and began paying off her husband's debt.

When merchants requested more embroidery than Saima could produce, she paid neighbors to assist her. Eventually 30 families were working for her, and she put her husband to work as well—"under my direction," she explained with a twinkle in her eye. Saima became the tycoon of the neighborhood, and she was able to pay off her husband's entire debt, keep her daughters in school, renovate the house, connect running water and buy a television.

Goretti Nyabenda Musiga Commune, Burundi

In Burundi, which is one of the poorest counteries in the world, Goretti Nyabenda used to be largely a **prisoner in her hut.** In Keeping with tradition in the region where she lived, she could not leave without the permission of her husband, Bernard. Her interactions with Bernard consisted in good part of being beaten by him. "I was wretched" she remembers. Then Goretti joined an empowerment program run by CARE, taking out a $2 microloan to buy fertilizer. The result was an excellent crop of potatoes worth $7.50—and Goretti began to build a small business as a farmer, goat breeder and banana-beer brewer. When Bernard fell sick with malaria, it was Goretti who was able to pay the bill. Today Goretti is no longer beaten, and she comes and goes freely. Her children, including her second daughter, Ancilla, have been able to afford school with Goretti's earnings.

"Now everyone comes to me to borrow money, the same ones who used to criticize me," Saima said, beaming in satisfaction. "And the children of those who used to criticize me now come to my house to watch TV."

Today, Saima is a bit plump and displays a gold nose ring as well as several other rings and bracelets on each wrist. She exudes self-confidence as she offers a grand tour of her home and work area, ostentatiously showing off the television and the new plumbing. She doesn't even pretend to be subordinate to her husband. He spends his days mostly loafing around, occasionally helping with the work but always having to accept orders from his wife. He has become more impressed with females in general: Saima had a third child, also a girl, but now that's not a problem. "Girls are just as good as boys," he explained.

Saima's new prosperity has transformed the family's educational prospects. She is planning to send all three of her daughters through high school and maybe to college as well. She brings in tutors to improve their schoolwork, and her oldest child, Javaria, is ranked first in her class. We asked Javaria what she wanted to be when she grew up, thinking she might aspire to be a doctor or lawyer. Javaria cocked her head. "I'd like to do embroidery," she said.

As for her husband, Saima said, "We have a good relationship now." She explained, "We don't fight, and he treats me well." And what about finding another wife who might bear him a son? Saima chuckled at the question: "Now nobody says anything about that." Sharifa Bibi, the mother-in-law, looked shocked when we asked whether she wanted her son to take a second wife to bear a son. "No, no," she said. "Saima is bringing so much to this house.... She puts a roof over our heads and food on the table."

Sharifa even allows that Saima is now largely exempt from beatings by her husband. "A woman should know her limits, and if not, then it's her husband's right to beat her," Sharifa said. "But if a woman earns more than her husband, it's difficult for him to discipline her."

What should we make of stories like Saima's? Traditionally, the status of women was seen as a "soft" issue—worthy but marginal. We initially reflected that view ourselves in our work as journalists. We preferred to focus instead on the "serious" international issues, like trade disputes or arms proliferation. Our awakening came in China.

After we married in 1988, we moved to Beijing to be correspondents for *The New York Times.* Seven months later we found ourselves standing on the edge of Tiananmen Square watching troops fire their automatic weapons at prodemocracy protesters. The massacre claimed between 400 and 800 lives and transfixed the world; wrenching images of the killings appeared constantly on the front page and on television screens.

Yet the following year we came across an obscure but meticulous demographic study that outlined a human rights violation that had claimed tens of thousands more lives. This study found that 39,000 baby girls died annually in China because parents didn't give them the same medical care and attention that boys received—and that was just in the first year of life. A result is that as many infant girls died unnecessarily every week in China as protesters died at Tiananmen Square. Those Chinese girls never received a column inch of news coverage, and we began to wonder if our journalistic priorities were skewed.

A similar pattern emerged in other countries. In India, a "bride burning" takes place approximately once every two hours, to punish a woman for an inadequate dowry or to eliminate her so a man can remarry—but these rarely constitute news. When a prominent dissident was arrested in China, we would write a front-page article; when 100,000 girls were kidnapped and trafficked into brothels, we didn't even consider it news.

Amartya Sen, the ebullient Nobel Prize-winning economist, developed a gauge of gender inequality that is a striking reminder of the stakes involved. "More than 100 million women are missing," Sen wrote in a classic essay in 1990 in *The New York Review of Books,* spurring a new field of research. Sen noted that in normal circumstances, women live longer than men, and so there are more females than males in much of the world. Yet in places where girls have a deeply unequal status, they vanish. China has 107 males for every 100 females in its overall population (and an even greater disproportion among newborns), and India has 108. The implication of the sex ratios, Sen later found, is that about 107 million females are missing from the globe today. Follow-up studies have calculated the number slightly differently, deriving alternative figures for "missing women" of between 60 million and 107 million.

The U.N. has estimated that there are 5 thousand honor killings a year, the majority in the Muslim world.

Girls vanish partly because they don't get the same health care and food as boys. In India, for example, girls are less likely to be vaccinated than boys and are taken to the hospital only when they are sicker. A result is that girls in India from

1 to 5 years of age are 50 percent more likely to die than boys their age. In addition, ultrasound machines have allowed a pregnant woman to find out the sex of her fetus—and then get an abortion if it is female.

The global statistics on the abuse of girls are numbing. It appears that more girls and women are now missing from the planet, precisely because they are female, than men were killed on the battlefield in all the wars of the 20th century. The number of victims of this routine "gendercide" far exceeds the number of people who were slaughtered in all the genocides of the 20th century.

For those women who live, mistreatment is sometimes shockingly brutal. If you're reading this article, the phrase "gender discrimination" might conjure thoughts of unequal pay, underfinanced sports teams or unwanted touching from a boss. In the developing world, meanwhile, millions of women and girls are actually enslaved. While a precise number is hard to pin down, the International Labor Organization, a U.N. agency, estimates that at any one time there are 12.3 million people engaged in forced labor of all kinds, including sexual servitude. In Asia alone about one million children working in the sex trade are held in conditions indistinguishable from slavery, according to a U.N. report. Girls and women are locked in brothels and beaten if they resist, fed just enough to be kept alive and often sedated with drugs—to pacify them and often to cultivate addiction. India probably has more modern slaves than any other country.

Another huge burden for women in poor countries is maternal mortality, with one woman dying in childbirth around the world every minute. In the West African country Niger, a woman stands a one-in-seven chance of dying in childbirth at some point in her life. (These statistics are all somewhat dubious, because maternal mortality isn't considered significant enough to require good data collection.) For all of India's shiny new high-rises, a woman there still has a 1-in-70 lifetime chance of dying in childbirth. In contrast, the lifetime risk in the United States is 1 in 4,800; in Ireland, it is 1 in 47,600. The reason for the gap is not that we don't know how to save lives of women in poor countries. It's simply that poor, uneducated women in Africa and Asia have never been a priority either in their own countries or to donor nations.

Abbas Be, a beautiful teenage girl in the Indian city of Hyderabad, has chocolate skin, black hair and gleaming white teeth—and a lovely smile, which made her all the more marketable.

Money was tight in her family, so when she was about 14 she arranged to take a job as a maid in the capital, New Delhi. Instead, she was locked up in a brothel, beaten with a cricket bat, gang-raped and told that she would have to cater to customers. Three days after she arrived, Abbas and all 70 girls in the brothel were made to gather round and watch as the pimps made an example of one teenage girl who had fought customers. The troublesome girl was stripped naked, hogtied, humiliated and mocked, beaten savagely and then stabbed in the stomach until she bled to death in front of Abbas and the others.

Abbas was never paid for her work. Any sign of dissatisfaction led to a beating or worse; two more times, she watched girls murdered by the brothel managers for resisting. Eventually Abbas was freed by police and taken back to Hyderabad. She found a home in a shelter run by Prajwala, an organization that takes in girls rescued from brothels and teaches them new skills. Abbas is acquiring an education and has learned to be a bookbinder; she also counsels other girls about how to avoid being trafficked. As a skilled bookbinder, Abbas is able to earn a decent living, and she is now helping to put her younger sisters through school as well. With an education, they will be far less vulnerable to being trafficked. Abbas has moved from being a slave to being a producer, contributing to India's economic development and helping raise her family.

Perhaps the lesson presented by both Abbas and Saima is the same: In many poor countries, the greatest unexploited resource isn't oil fields or veins of gold; it is the women and girls who aren't educated and never become a major presence in the formal economy. With education and with help starting businesses, impoverished women can earn money and support their countries as well as their families. They represent perhaps the best hope for fighting global poverty.

In East Asia, as we saw in our years of reporting there, women have already benefited from deep social changes. In countries like South Korea and Malaysia, China and Thailand, rural girls who previously contributed negligibly to the economy have gone to school and received educations, giving them the autonomy to move to the city to hold factory jobs. This hugely increased the formal labor force; when the women then delayed childbearing, there was a demographic dividend to the country as well. In the 1990s, by our estimations, some 80 percent of the employees on the assembly lines in coastal China were female, and the proportion across the manufacturing belt of East Asia was at least 70 percent.

The hours were long and the conditions wretched, just as in the sweatshops of the Industrial Revolution in the West. But peasant women were making money, sending it back home and sometimes becoming the breadwinners in their families. They gained new skills that elevated their status. Westerners encounter sweatshops and see exploitation, and indeed, many of these plants are just as bad as critics say. But it's sometimes said in poor countries that the only thing worse than being exploited in a sweatshop is not being exploited in a sweatshop. Low-wage manufacturing jobs disproportionately benefited women in countries like China because these were jobs for which brute physical force was not necessary and women's nimbleness gave them an advantage over men—which was not the case with agricultural labor or construction or other jobs typically available in poor countries. Strange as it may seem, sweatshops in Asia had the effect of empowering women. One hundred years ago, many women in China were still having their feet bound. Today, while discrimination and inequality and harassment persist, the culture has been transformed. In the major cities, we've found that Chinese men often do more domestic chores than American men typically do. And urban parents are often not only happy with an only daughter; they may even prefer one, under the belief that daughters are better than sons at looking after aging parents.

Why do microfinance organizations usually focus their assistance on women? And why does everyone benefit when women enter the work force and bring home regular pay checks? One reason involves the dirty little secret of global poverty: some of the most wretched suffering is caused not just by low incomes but also by unwise spending by the poor—especially by men. Surprisingly frequently, we've come across a mother mourning a child who has just died of malaria for want of a $5 mosquito bed net; the mother says that the family couldn't afford a bed net and she means it, but then we find the father at a nearby bar. He goes three evenings a week to the bar, spending $5 each week.

Our interviews and perusal of the data available suggest that the poorest families in the world spend approximately 10 times as much (20 percent of their incomes on average) on a combination of alcohol, prostitution, candy, sugary drinks and lavish feasts as they do on educating their children (2 percent). If poor families spent only as much on educating their children as they do on beer and prostitutes, there would be a breakthrough in the prospects of poor countries. Girls, since they are the ones kept home from school now, would be the biggest beneficiaries. Moreover, one way to reallocate family expenditures in this way is to put more money in the hands of women. A series of studies has found that when women hold assets or gain incomes, family money is more likely to be spent on nutrition, medicine and housing, and consequently children are healthier.

In Ivory Coast, one research project examined the different crops that men and women grow for their private kitties: men grow coffee, cocoa and pineapple, and women grow plantains, bananas, coconuts and vegetables. Some years the "men's crops" have good harvests and the men are flush with cash, and other years it is the women who prosper. Money is to some extent shared. But even so, the economist Esther Duflo of M.I.T. found that when the men's crops flourish, the household spends more money on alcohol and tobacco. When the women have a good crop, the households spend more money on food. "When women command greater power, child health and nutrition improves," Duflo says.

Such research has concrete implications: for example, donor countries should nudge poor countries to adjust their laws so that when a man dies, his property is passed on to his widow rather than to his brothers. Governments should make it easy for women to hold property and bank accounts—1 percent of the world's landowners are women—and they should make it much easier for microfinance institutions to start banks so that women can save money.

Of course, it's fair to ask: empowering women is well and good, but can one do this effectively? Does foreign aid really work? William Easterly, an economist at New York University, has argued powerfully that shoveling money at poor countries accomplishes little. Some Africans, including Dambisa Moyo, author of "Dead Aid," have said the same thing. The critics note that there has been no correlation between amounts of aid going to countries and their economic growth rates.

Our take is that, frankly, there is something to these criticisms. Helping people is far harder than it looks. Aid experiments often go awry, or small successes turn out to be difficult to replicate or scale up. Yet we've also seen, anecdotally and in the statistics, evidence that some kinds of aid have been enormously effective. The delivery of vaccinations and other kinds of health care has reduced the number of children who die every year before they reach the age of 5 to less than 10 million today from 20 million in 1960.

Abbas Be was held captive in a Delhi brothel. After she was freed, she returned to her home city of Hyderabad, became a bookbinder and now puts her sisters through school.

In general, aid appears to work best when it is focused on health, education and microfinance (although microfinance has been somewhat less successful in Africa than in Asia). And in each case, crucially, aid has often been most effective when aimed at women and girls; when policy wonks do the math, they often find that these investments have a net economic return. Only a small proportion of aid specifically targets women or girls, but increasingly donors are recognizing that that is where they often get the most bang for the buck.

In the early 1990s, the United Nations and the World Bank began to proclaim the potential resource that women and girls represent. "Investment in girls' education may well be the highest-return investment available in the developing world," Larry Summers wrote when he was chief economist of the World Bank. Private aid groups and foundations shifted gears as well. "Women are the key to ending hunger in Africa," declared the Hunger Project. The Center for Global Development issued a major report explaining "why and how to put girls at the center of development." CARE took women and girls as the centerpiece of its anti-poverty efforts. "Gender inequality hurts economic growth," Goldman Sachs concluded in a 2008 research report that emphasized how much developing countries could improve their economic performance by educating girls.

98 percent of people in Egypt say they believe that 'girls have the same right to education as boys.'

Bill Gates recalls once being invited to speak in Saudi Arabia and finding himself facing a segregated audience. Four-fifths of the listeners were men, on the left. The remaining one-fifth were women, all covered in black cloaks and veils, on the right. A partition separated the two groups. Toward the end, in the question-and-answer session, a member of the audience noted that Saudi Arabia aimed to be one of the Top 10 countries in the world in technology by 2010 and asked if that was realistic. "Well, if you're not fully utilizing half the talent in the country," Gates said, "you're not going to get too close to the Top 10." The small group on the right erupted in wild cheering.

Policy makers have gotten the message as well. President Obama has appointed a new White House Council on Women and Girls. Perhaps he was indoctrinated by his mother, who was one of the early adopters of microloans to women when she worked to fight poverty in Indonesia. Secretary of State Hillary Rodham Clinton is a member of the White House Council, and she has also selected a talented activist, Melanne Verveer, to direct a new State Department Office of Global Women's Issues. On Capitol Hill, the Senate Foreign Relations Committee has put Senator Barbara Boxer in charge of a new subcommittee that deals with women's issues.

Yet another reason to educate and empower women is that greater female involvement in society and the economy appears to undermine extremism and terrorism. It has long been known that a risk factor for turbulence and violence is the share of a country's population made up of young people. Now it is emerging that male domination of society is also a risk factor; the reasons aren't fully understood, but it may be that when women are marginalized the nation takes on the testosterone-laden culture of a military camp or a high-school boys' locker room. That's in part why the Joint Chiefs of Staff and international security specialists are puzzling over how to increase girls' education in countries like Afghanistan—and why generals have gotten briefings from Greg Mortenson, who wrote about building girls' schools in his best seller, "Three Cups of Tea." Indeed, some scholars say they believe the reason Muslim countries have been disproportionately afflicted by terrorism is not Islamic teachings about infidels or violence but rather the low levels of female education and participation in the labor force.

Claudine Mukakarisa Kigalf, Rwanda

Claudine Mukakarisa spent much of the genocide in Rwanda **imprisoned in a rape house.** She escaped, and afterward she found that she was the only one left alive in her family—she was pregnant, homeless and 13 years old. Claudine gave birth in a parking lot, and hating the child because its father was a rapist, she initially left him to die. But then she returned to the parking lot, picked up her son and nursed him. She survived by begging and washing laundry; eventually, another child followed—the father was a man who raped her after offering her shelter. Claudine, with her two children, received help from an aid organization called Women for Women International, which paired her with Murvelene Clarke, a bank employee from Brooklyn. Clarke began donating $27 a month, and that money (together with training in making beadwork, which can be sold) helped Claudine educate her children.

So what would an agenda for fighting poverty through helping women look like? You might begin with the education of girls—which doesn't just mean building schools. There are other innovative means at our disposal. A study in Kenya by Michael Kremer, a Harvard economist, examined six different approaches to improving educational performance, from providing free textbooks to child-sponsorship programs. The approach that raised student test scores the most was to offer girls who had scored in the top 15 percent of their class on sixth-grade tests a $19 scholarship for seventh and eighth grade (and the glory of recognition at an assembly). Boys also performed better, apparently because they were pushed by the girls or didn't want to endure the embarrassment of being left behind.

Another Kenyan study found that giving girls a new $6 school uniform every 18 months significantly reduced dropout rates and pregnancy rates. Likewise, there's growing evidence that a cheap way to help keep high-school girls in school is to help them manage menstruation. For fear of embarrassing leaks and stains, girls sometimes stay home during their periods, and the absenteeism puts them behind and eventually leads them to drop out. Aid workers are experimenting with giving African teenage girls sanitary pads, along with access to a toilet where they can change them. The Campaign for Female Education, an organization devoted to getting more girls into school in Africa, helps girls with their periods, and a new group, Sustainable Health Enterprises, is trying to do the same.

And so, if President Obama wanted to adopt a foreign-aid policy that built on insights into the role of women in development, he would do well to start with education. We would suggest a $10 billion effort over five years to educate girls around the world. This initiative would focus on Africa but would also support—and prod—Asian countries like Afghanistan and Pakistan to do better. This plan would also double as population policy, for it would significantly reduce birthrates—and thus help poor countries overcome the demographic obstacles to economic growth.

But President Obama might consider two different proposals as well. We would recommend that the United States sponsor a global drive to eliminate iodine deficiency around the globe, by helping countries iodize salt. About a third of households in the developing world do not get enough iodine, and a result is often an impairment in brain formation in the fetal stages. For reasons that are unclear, this particularly affects female fetuses and typically costs children 10 to 15 I.Q. points. Research by Erica Field of Harvard found that daughters of women given iodine performed markedly better in school. Other research suggests that salt iodization would yield benefits worth nine times the cost.

We would also recommend that the United States announce a 12-year, $1.6 billion program to eradicate obstetric fistula, a childbirth injury that is one of the worst scourges of women in the developing world. An obstetric fistula, which is a hole created inside the body by a difficult childbirth, leaves a woman incontinent, smelly, often crippled and shunned by her village—yet it can be repaired for a few hundred dollars. Dr. Lewis Wall, president of the Worldwide Fistula Fund, and Michael Horowitz, a conservative agitator on humanitarian issues, have drafted the 12-year plan—and it's eminently practical and built on proven methods. Evidence that fistulas can be prevented or repaired comes from impoverished Somaliland,

Do-It-Yourself Foreign AID

People always ask us: How can I help the world's needy? How can I give in a way that will benefit a real person and won't just finance corruption or an aid bureaucracy? There are innumerable answers to those questions, but it's becoming increasingly clear that many of them involve women. From among the examples in our book "Half the Sky," here are a handful:

Choose a woman to lend to on kiva.org. The minimum amount is $25, and you can choose from people all over the world. The money will be used to support a business and will be paid back. Or go to globalgiving .com, find a woman abroad whose cause you identify with and make a small gift. On GlobalGiving, for example, we have supported a program to prevent runaway girls from being trafficked into brothels.

Sponsor a girl abroad through one of the many child-sponsorship organizations. We do so through Plan USA (planusa.org), but there are many other great ones, including Women for Women International (womenforwomen.org).

Become an advocate for change by joining the CARE Action Network at care.org. CARE is now focused on assisting women and girls for the pragmatic reason that that is where it can get the best results. The network helps people speak out and educate policy makers about global poverty.

Find a cause that resonates with you, learn more about it and adopt it. For example, we send checks to support an extraordinary Somali woman, Edna Adan who has invested her savings and her soul in her own maternity hospital in Somaliland (ednahospital.org).

Even school kids can make a difference. Jordana Confino, an eighth grader in Westfield N.J., started an initiative with friends to help girls go to school in poor countries. The effort grew to become Girls Learn International (girlslearn.org), which now pairs American middle schools and high schools with needy classrooms in Africa, Asia and Latin America. An expanded list of organizations that specialize in supporting women in developing countries is at nytimes.com/magazine.

— N.D.K. and S.W.D.

a northern enclave of Somalia, where an extraordinary nurse-midwife named Edna Adan has built her own maternity hospital to save the lives of the women around her. A former first lady of Somalia and World Health Organization official, Adan used her savings to build the hospital, which is supported by a group of admirers in the U.S. who call themselves Friends of Edna Maternity Hospital.

For all the legitimate concerns about how well humanitarian aid is spent, investments in education, iodizing salt and maternal health all have a proven record of success. And the sums are modest: all three components of our plan together amount to about what the U.S. has provided Pakistan since 9/11—a sum that accomplished virtually nothing worthwhile either for Pakistanis or for Americans.

One of the many aid groups that for pragmatic reasons has increasingly focused on women is Heifer International, a charitable organization based in Arkansas that has been around for decades. The organization gives cows, goats and chickens to farmers in poor countries. On assuming the presidency of Heifer in 1992, the activist Jo Luck traveled to Africa, where one day she found herself sitting on the ground with a group of young women in a Zimbabwean village. One of them was Tererai Trent.

Tererai is a long-faced woman with high cheekbones and a medium brown complexion; she has a high forehead and tight cornrows. Like many women around the world, she doesn't know when she was born and has no documentation of her birth. As a child, Tererai didn't get much formal education, partly because she was a girl and was expected to do household chores. She herded cattle and looked after her younger siblings. Her father would say, Let's send our sons to school, because they will be the breadwinners. Tererai's brother, Tinashe, was forced to go to school, where he was an indifferent student. Tererai pleaded to be allowed to attend but wasn't permitted to do so. Tinashe brought his books home each afternoon, and Tererai pored over them and taught herself to read and write. Soon she was doing her brother's homework every evening.

The teacher grew puzzled, for Tinashe was a poor student in class but always handed in exemplary homework. Finally, the teacher noticed that the handwriting was different for homework and for class assignments and whipped Tinashe until he confessed the truth. Then the teacher went to the father, told him that Tererai was a prodigy and begged that she be allowed to attend school. After much argument, the father allowed Tererai to attend school for a couple of terms, but then married her off at about age 11.

Tererai's husband barred her from attending school, resented her literacy and beat her whenever she tried to practice her reading by looking at a scrap of old newspaper. Indeed, he beat her for plenty more as well. She hated her marriage but had no way out. "If you're a woman and you are not educated, what else?" she asks.

Yet when Jo Luck came and talked to Tererai and other young women in her village, Luck kept insisting that things did not have to be this way. She kept saying that they could achieve their goals, repeatedly using the word "achievable." The women caught the repetition and asked the interpreter to explain in detail what "achievable" meant. That gave Luck a chance to push forward. "What are your hopes?" she asked the women, through the interpreter. Tererai and the others were puzzled by the question, because they didn't really have any hopes. But Luck pushed them to think about their dreams, and reluctantly, they began to think about what they wanted.

Tererai timidly voiced hope of getting an education. Luck pounced and told her that she could do it, that she should write down her goals and methodically pursue them. After Luck and her entourage disappeared, Tererai began to study on her own, in hiding from her husband, while raising her five children. Painstakingly, with the help of friends, she wrote down her goals on a piece of paper: "One day I will go to the United States of America," she began, for Goal 1. She added that she would earn a college degree, a master's degree and a Ph.D.—all exquisitely absurd dreams for a married cattle herder in Zimbabwe who had less than one year's formal education. But Tererai took the piece of paper and folded it inside three layers of plastic to protect it, and then placed it in an old can. She buried the can under a rock where she herded cattle.

Then Tererai took correspondence classes and began saving money. Her self-confidence grew as she did brilliantly in her studies, and she became a community organizer for Heifer. She stunned everyone with superb schoolwork, and the Heifer aid workers encouraged her to think that she could study in America. One day in 1998, she received notice that she had been admitted to Oklahoma State University.

Some of the neighbors thought that a woman should focus on educating her children, not herself. "I can't talk about my children's education when I'm not educated myself," Tererai responded. "If I educate myself, then I can educate my children." So she climbed into an airplane and flew to America.

At Oklahoma State, Tererai took every credit she could and worked nights to make money. She earned her undergraduate degree, brought her five children to America and started her master's, then returned to her village. She dug up the tin can under the rock and took out the paper on which she had scribbled her goals. She put check marks beside the goals she had fulfilled and buried the tin can again.

In Arkansas, she took a job working for Heifer—while simultaneously earning a master's degree part time. When she had her M.A., Tererai again returned to her village. After embracing her mother and sister, she dug up her tin can and checked off her next goal. Now she is working on her Ph.D. at Western Michigan University.

Tererai has completed her course work and is completing a dissertation about AIDS programs among the poor in Africa. She will become a productive economic asset for Africa and a significant figure in the battle against AIDS. And when she has her doctorate, Tererai will go back to her village and, after hugging her loved ones, go out to the field and dig up her can again.

Edna Adan A former first lady of Somalia and World Health Organization official, she built her own maternity hospital in the enclave of Somaliland.

There are many metaphors for the role of foreign assistance. For our part, we like to think of aid as a kind of lubricant, a few drops of oil in the crankcase of the developing world, so that gears move freely again on their own. That is what the assistance to Tererai amounted to: a bit of help where and when it counts most, which often means focusing on women like her. And now Tererai is gliding along freely on her own—truly able to hold up half the sky.

Assess Your Progress

1. What abuses do women often suffer in developing countries?
2. What impact does empowering women have on their families?
3. How might governments and donor countries help to improve women's lives?
4. Aside from the economic benefits, what other reasons are there to educate and empower women?
5. What steps are needed to more fully involve women in the fight against poverty?

Nicholas D. Kristof is a *New York Times* Op-Ed columnist and **Sheryl WuDunn** is a former *Times* correspondent who works in finance and philanthropy. This essay is adapted from their book *"Half the Sky: Turning Oppression Into Opportunity for Women Worldwide,"* which will be published next month by Alfred A. Knopf. You can learn more about *Half the Sky* at nytimes.com/ontheground.

Gendercide

Killed, aborted or neglected, at least 100m girls have disappeared—and the number is rising.

Imagine you are one half of a young couple expecting your first child in a fast-growing, poor country. You are part of the new middle class; your income is rising; you want a small family. But traditional *mores* hold sway around you, most important in the preference for sons over daughters. Perhaps hard physical labour is still needed for the family to make its living. Perhaps only sons may inherit land. Perhaps a daughter is deemed to join another family on marriage and you want someone to care for you when you are old. Perhaps she needs a dowry.

Now imagine that you have had an ultrasound scan; it costs $12, but you can afford that. The scan says the unborn child is a girl. You yourself would prefer a boy; the rest of your family clamours for one. You would never dream of killing a baby daughter, as they do out in the villages. But an abortion seems different. What do you do?

For millions of couples, the answer is: abort the daughter, try for a son. In China and northern India more than 120 boys are being born for every 100 girls. Nature dictates that slightly more males are born than females to offset boys' greater susceptibility to infant disease. But nothing on this scale.

For those who oppose abortion, this is mass murder. For those such as this newspaper, who think abortion should be "safe, legal and rare" (to use Bill Clinton's phrase), a lot depends on the circumstances, but the cumulative consequence for societies of such individual actions is catastrophic. China alone stands to have as many unmarried young men—"bare branches", as they are known—as the entire population of young men in America. In any country rootless young males spell trouble; in Asian societies, where marriage and children are the recognised routes into society, single men are almost like outlaws. Crime rates, bride trafficking, sexual violence, even female suicide rates are all rising and will rise further as the lopsided generations reach their maturity.

It is no exaggeration to call this gendercide. Women are missing in the millions—aborted, killed, neglected to death. In 1990 an Indian economist, Amartya Sen, put the number at 100m; the toll is higher now. The crumb of comfort is that countries can mitigate the hurt, and that one, South Korea, has shown the worst can be avoided. Others need to learn from it if they are to stop the carnage.

The Dearth and Death of Little Sisters

Most people know China and northern India have unnaturally large numbers of boys. But few appreciate how bad the problem is, or that it is rising. In China the imbalance between the sexes was 108 boys to 100 girls for the generation born in the late 1980s; for the generation of the early 2000s, it was 124 to 100. In some Chinese provinces the ratio is an unprecedented 130 to 100. The destruction is worst in China but has spread far beyond. Other East Asian countries, including Taiwan and Singapore, former communist states in the western Balkans and the Caucasus, and even sections of America's population (Chinese- and Japanese-Americans, for example): all these have distorted sex ratios. Gendercide exists on almost every continent. It affects rich and poor; educated and illiterate; Hindu, Muslim, Confucian and Christian alike.

Wealth does not stop it. Taiwan and Singapore have open, rich economies. Within China and India the areas with the worst sex ratios are the richest, best-educated ones. And China's one-child policy can only be part of the problem, given that so many other countries are affected.

In fact the destruction of baby girls is a product of three forces: the ancient preference for sons; a modern desire for smaller families; and ultrasound scanning and other technologies that identify the sex of a fetus. In societies where four or six children were common, a boy would almost certainly come along eventually; son preference did not need to exist at the expense of daughters. But now couples want two children—or, as in China, are allowed only one—they will sacrifice unborn daughters to their pursuit of a son. That is why sex ratios are most distorted in the modern, open parts of China and India. It is also why ratios are more skewed after the first child: parents may accept a daughter first time round but will do anything to ensure their next—and probably last—child is a boy. The boy-girl ratio is above 200 for a third child in some places.

How to Stop Half the Sky Crashing Down

Baby girls are thus victims of a malign combination of ancient prejudice and modern preferences for small families. Only one country has managed to change this pattern. In the 1990s

South Korea had a sex ratio almost as skewed as China's. Now, it is heading towards normality. It has achieved this not deliberately, but because the culture changed. Female education, anti-discrimination suits and equal-rights rulings made son preference seem old-fashioned and unnecessary. The forces of modernity first exacerbated prejudice—then overwhelmed it.

But this happened when South Korea was rich. If China or India—with incomes one-quarter and one-tenth Korea's levels—wait until they are as wealthy, many generations will pass. To speed up change, they need to take actions that are in their own interests anyway. Most obviously China should scrap the one-child policy. The country's leaders will resist this because they fear population growth; they also dismiss Western concerns about human rights. But the one-child limit is no longer needed to reduce fertility (if it ever was: other East Asian countries reduced the pressure on the population as much as China). And it massively distorts the country's sex ratio, with devastating results. President Hu Jintao says that creating "a harmonious society" is his guiding principle; it cannot be achieved while a policy so profoundly perverts family life.

And all countries need to raise the value of girls. They should encourage female education; abolish laws and customs that prevent daughters inheriting property; make examples of hospitals and clinics with impossible sex ratios; get women engaged in public life—using everything from television newsreaders to women traffic police. Mao Zedong said "women hold up half the sky." The world needs to do more to prevent a gendercide that will have the sky crashing down.

Assess Your Progress

1. Why are male children often preferred over females in developing countries?
2. What are the consequences of a disparity between the number of males and females?
3. What three factors account for female gendercide?

Women in Developing Countries 300 Times More Likely to Die in Childbirth

UN report reveals 500,000 women in developing world die each year as a result of pregnancy.

SARAH BOSELEY

Women in the world's least developed countries are 300 times more likely to die during childbirth or because of their pregnancy than those in the UK and other similarly developed countries, a UN report says today.

The death toll is more than half a million women a year, according to Unicef, the UN children's emergency fund. Some 70,000 who die are girls and young women aged 15 to 19. Although it is the subject of one of the millennium development goals, the death toll is not going down.

The reasons are multiple, according to Unicef's annual state of the world's children report on maternal and newborn health. "The root cause may lie in women's disadvantaged position in many countries and cultures and in the lack of attention to, and accountability for, women's rights," it says.

"Saving the lives of mothers and their newborns requires more than just medical intervention," said Ann Veneman, Unicef's executive director. "Educating girls is pivotal to improving maternal and neonatal health and also benefits families and societies."

Women die as a result of infection and of haemorrhage. Some have obstructed labour and cannot get a caesarean section. Others die of preventable complications.

Both mothers and babies are vulnerable in the weeks after birth, the report points out. They need post-natal visits, proper hygiene and counselling about the danger signs for themselves and their baby.

Many developing countries have succeeded in reducing the death rate for children under five, but have failed to make much progress on mothers. Niger and Malawi, for example, cut under-five deaths by nearly half between 1990 and 2007.

In the developing world, a woman has a one-in-76 risk of dying because of pregnancy or childbirth in her lifetime. In developed countries, that risk is only one in 8,000.

Having a child in a developing country is one of the most severe health risks for women. For every woman who dies, another 20 suffer illness or injury, which can be permanent.

The 10 countries with the highest risk of maternal death, says Unicef, are Niger, Afghanistan, Sierra Leone, Chad, Angola, Liberia, Somalia, the Democratic Republic of Congo, Guinea-Bissau and Mali.

Deaths of newborns have also received too little attention, the report says. A child born in one of the least developed countries is nearly 14 times more likely to die within the first 28 days of life than one in an industrialised country such as the UK.

Assess Your Progress

1. What accounts for higher death rates during pregnancy and childbirth in developing countries?
2. Why are newborns also vulnerable to preventable death in poor countries?
3. Where is the risk of maternal mortality greatest?

Educating Girls, Unlocking Development

Compelling evidence, accumulated over the past 20 years . . . , has led to an almost universal recognition of the importance of focusing on girls' education as part of broader development policy.

RUTH LEVINE

One of the most important public policy goals in the developing world is the expansion and improvement of education for girls. Vital in its own right for the realization of individual capabilities, the education of girls has the potential to transform the life chances of the girls themselves, their future families, and the societies in which they live. Girls with at least a primary school education are healthier and wealthier when they grow up and their future children have much greater opportunities than they otherwise would; even national economic outcomes appear to be positively influenced by expanded girls' education.

Unlike some development outcomes that depend on multiple factors outside the control of policy makers (either in developing countries or among donor nations), significant improvement in girls' education can be achieved through specific government actions. Expansion of basic education, making school infrastructure and curriculum more girl-friendly, and conditional cash transfers and scholarships to overcome household barriers have all been used to improve key outcomes, with demonstrable success. Lessons from regions that have made rapid advances with girls' education, and from programs that have introduced successful financing and teaching innovations, can be applied to accelerate progress.

While public policy can make the difference, policies that ignore important gender-related constraints to education at the primary and, particularly, at the postprimary educational levels can have the opposite effect, reinforcing existing patterns of gender discrimination and exclusion. Those patterns are often deep-seated. Families in many societies traditionally have valued schooling less for girls than for boys. In most households, the domestic workload falls more to females than to males, leaving less time for school. If families are struggling to find income, the demand for girls' help around the house (or in wage labor) may increase. Many parents believe that the return on educational investments varies according to gender—particularly if girls, when they marry, leave their parents' households to join the husbands'.

When girls in developing countries do enroll in school, they frequently encounter gender-based discrimination and inadequate educational resources. Large numbers of girls in sub-Saharan Africa drop out, for example, when they reach puberty and the onset of menstruation simply because schools lack latrines, running water, or privacy. Parental concerns about girls' security outside the home can limit schooling where girls are vulnerable in transit and male teachers are not trusted. And in some countries, cultural aversion to the education of girls lingers. Afghanistan's Taliban insurgents, who believe that girls' education violates Islamic teachings, have succeeded in closing numerous schools, sometimes by beheading teachers. Afghanistan is an extreme case, but a reminder nonetheless of the challenges that remain on the path toward achieving the high payoffs from girls' education.

The Benefits

Why is the schooling of girls so critical? Education in general is among the primary means through which societies reproduce themselves; correspondingly, changing the educational opportunities for particular groups in society—girls and minority groups—is perhaps the single most effective way to achieve lasting transformations. A considerable body of evidence has shown that the benefits of educating a girl are manifested in economic and social outcomes: her lifetime health, labor force participation, and income; her (future) children's health and nutrition; her community's and her nation's productivity. Most important, education can break the intergenerational transmission of poverty.

Female participation in the formal labor market consistently increases with educational attainment, as it does for males. In at least some settings, the returns to education of girls are superior to those for boys. Several studies have shown that primary schooling increases lifetime earnings by as much as 20 percent for girls—higher than for their brothers. If they stay in secondary school, the returns from education are 25 percent or higher.

The inverse relationship between women's education and fertility is perhaps the best studied of all health and demographic phenomena. The relationship generally holds across countries and over time, and is robust even when income is taken into account. Completion of primary school is strongly associated with later age at marriage, later age at first birth, and lower lifetime fertility. A study of eight sub-Saharan countries covering the period from 1987 to 1999 found that girls' educational attainment was the best predictor of whether they would have their first births during adolescence.

Another study examined surveys across the developing world to compare female education and fertility by region. The higher the level of female education, the lower desired family size, and the greater the success in achieving desired family size. Further, each additional year of a mother's schooling cuts the expected infant mortality rate by 5 to 10 percent.

Maternal education is a key determinant of children's attainment. Multiple studies have found that a mother's level of education has a strong positive effect on daughters' enrollment—more than on sons and significantly more than the effect of fathers' education on daughters. Studies from Egypt, Ghana, India, Kenya, Malaysia, Mexico, and Peru all find that mothers with a basic education are substantially more likely to educate their children, especially their daughters.

Children's health also is strongly associated with mothers' education. In general, this relationship holds across countries and time, although the confounding effect of household income has complicated the picture. One study, for instance, compared 17 developing countries, examining the relationship between women's education and their infants' health and nutritional status. It found the existence of an education-related health advantage in most countries, although stronger for postneonatal health than for neonatal health. (In some countries the "education advantage" did appear to be eliminated when controlling for other dimensions of socioeconomic status.)

Other studies have found clear links between women's school attainment and birth and death rates, and between women's years of schooling and infant mortality. A 1997 study for the World Bank, which focused on Morocco, found that a mother's schooling and functional literacy predicted her child's height-for-age, controlling for other socioeconomic factors.

Although the causal links are harder to establish at the macrolevel, some researchers have made the attempt, with interesting results. For example, in a 100-country study, researchers showed that raising the share of women with a secondary education by 1 percent is associated with a 0.3 percent increase in annual per capita income growth. In a 63-country study, more productive farming because of increased female education accounts for 43 percent of the decline in malnutrition achieved between 1970 and 1995.

In short (and with some important nuances set aside), girls' education is a strong contributor to the achievement of multiple key development outcomes: growth of household and national income, health of women and children, and lower and wanted fertility. Compelling evidence, accumulated over the past 20 years using both quantitative and qualitative methods, has led to an almost universal recognition of the importance of focusing on girls' education as part of broader development policy.

The Trends

Given the widespread understanding about the value of girls' education, the international community and national governments have established ambitious goals for increased participation in primary education and progress toward gender parity at all levels. The Millennium Development Goals (MDG), approved by all member states of the United Nations in 2000, call for universal primary education in all countries by 2015, as well as gender parity at all levels by 2015.

There is good news to report. Impressive gains have been made toward higher levels of education enrollment and completion, and girls have been catching up rapidly with their brothers. As primary schooling expands, girls tend to be the main beneficiaries because of their historically disadvantaged position.

The rate of primary school completion also has improved faster for girls than for boys, again in large part because they had more to gain at the margins. Across all developing countries, girls' primary school completion increased by 17 percent, from 65 to 76 percent, between 1990 and 2000. During the same period, boys' primary completion increased by 8 percent, from 79 to 85 percent. Global progress is not matched, however, in every region. In sub-Saharan Africa, girls did only slightly better between 1990 and 2000, with primary completion increasing from 43 to 46 percent. (The primary completion rate for boys went in the opposite direction, from 57 to 56 percent.)

The overall good news about girls' progress must be tempered by realism, and a recognition that the goal is not to have boys' and girls' educational attainment "equally bad." Today, a mere nine years from the MDG deadline, it is clear that the important improvements over the past several decades in the developing world—in many instances, unprecedented rates of increase in primary school enrollment and completion—still leave a large number of poor countries very far from the target. While girls are making up ground rapidly, in many of the poorest countries the achievements on improved gender parity must be seen in the context of overall low levels of primary school completion.

An estimated 104 million to 121 million children of primary school age across the globe are not in school, with the worst shortfalls in Africa and South Asia. Completion of schooling is a significant problem. While enrollment has been increasing, many children drop out before finishing the fifth grade. In Africa, for example, just 51 percent of children (46 percent of girls) complete primary school. In South Asia, 74 percent of children (and just 63 percent of girls) do so.

Low levels of enrollment and completion are concentrated not only in certain regions but also among certain segments of the population. In every country completion rates are lowest for children from poor households. In Western and Central Africa, the median grade completed by the bottom 40 percent of the income distribution is zero, because less than half of poor children complete even the first year of school.

The education income gap also exacerbates gender disparities. In India, for example, the gap between boys and girls from the richest households is 2.5 percent, but the difference for children from the poorest households is 24 percent.

Girls are catching up quickly in most countries, but the level they are catching up to is still quite low.

In some countries the main reason for low educational attainment is that children do not enroll in school. In Bangladesh, Benin, Burkina Faso, Ivory Coast, India, Mali, Morocco, Niger, and Senegal, more than half of children from the bottom 40 percent of the income distribution never even enroll. Elsewhere, particularly in Latin America, enrollment may be almost universal, but high repetition and dropout rates lead to low completion rates. In both cases poor students are much more likely not to complete school.

In many countries the rural/urban education gap is a key factor explaining education differentials. In Mozambique, the rural completion rate is 12 percent, while at the national level 26 percent of children complete school. Burkina Faso, Guinea, Madagascar, Niger, and Togo all demonstrate a similar pattern. In rural areas, the gender gap in completion is pronounced in Africa: in Benin, Burkina Faso, Guinea, Madagascar, Mozambique, and Niger, a mere 15 percent of girls who start primary school make it to the end.

Policy makers increasingly are recognizing the importance of addressing the special needs and vulnerabilities of marginal populations, even in relatively well-off countries with education levels that, on average, look quite good. As my colleagues Maureen Lewis and Marlaine Lockheed at the Center for Global Development highlight in a forthcoming book, girls who are members of marginalized groups—the Roma in Eastern Europe, the indigenous populations in Central America and elsewhere, the underprivileged castes and tribes in India—suffer a double disadvantage. Low educational attainment for girls is an obvious mechanism through which historical disadvantage is perpetuated. In Laos, for example, more than 90 percent of men in the dominant Laotai group are literate, while only 30 percent of the youngest cohort of women belonging to excluded rural ethnic groups can read and write.

Beyond the primary school enrollment and completion trends, a complex problem is the quality of education. Although measurement of learning outcomes is spotty at best, analyses of internationally comparable assessments of learning achievement in mathematics, reading, and science indicate that most developing countries rank far behind the industrialized nations. This is all the more of concern because the tests are taken by the children in school who, in low-enrollment countries, are the equivalent in relative terms to the top performers in the high-enrollment developed nations. The data on national examinations is equally alarming. Student performance on national exams in South Asian and African countries shows major gaps in acquisition of knowledge and skills.

Thus, the picture of progress and gaps is a complex one: rapid improvements relative to historical trends, but far off the ideal mark in the poorest countries. Girls are catching up quickly in most countries, but the level they are catching up to is still quite low. In many nations, the "lowest hanging fruit" has already been reached; for all children, and for girls in particular, the ones now out of school come from the most economically and socially disadvantaged backgrounds, and will be the hardest to reach. Finally, even among those children in school, evidence about poor learning outcomes should be cause for alarm.

The Challenges

The central imperative for improving educational opportunities and outcomes for girls in the low enrollment countries, including in sub-Saharan Africa and parts of South Asia, is to improve overall access and the quality of primary schooling. In doing so, planners and policy makers should ensure that they are not perpetuating barriers to girls' participation.

Getting to universal primary education (either enrollment or the more ambitious goal of completion) in sub-Saharan Africa and South Asia will require large-scale expansion in physical infrastructure, the number of teachers, and teaching/learning materials. Moreover, it will require fundamental improvements in the education institutions: more attention to learning outcomes rather than enrollment numbers, greater incentives for quality teaching, and more responsiveness to parents. This is a huge agenda. The donor and international technical community can support it, but it must be grounded in the political commitment of national and subnational governments.

Secondary to the "more and better education for all" agenda, and of particular relevance in countries that have already made significant progress so that most children go to school, is the need to understand and address the needs of particular disadvantaged groups, where gender differentials are especially pronounced. Beyond the efforts to reach children from poor and rural households, public policy makers need to understand and pay attention to ethnic and linguistic minorities, reaching them with tailored approaches rather than simply an expansion of the types of educational opportunities provided to the majority population. In addressing this challenge, policy makers must accept that reaching these key populations implies higher unit costs, as well as the adoption of potentially controversial measures, such as bilingual curriculum.

Finally, success in moving close to universal primary school enrollment generates its own new challenges. As more children complete primary school, the private benefits, in higher wages, decline (though the social benefits remain high). Private rates of return—perceived and real—cease to be seen as much of a reason for sending children to primary school, unless there is access to postprimary education. In addition, both the expansion of the existing education systems in many developing countries and the "scaling-up" of other public sector functions (such as health services, water management, and general public administration) require a larger cadre of educated and trained workers, the products of postprimary education. For these reasons, attention must be given to expanded opportunities for girls at the secondary level.

While international attention and goal-setting have been directed almost exclusively at the primary level, and the donor community has been persuaded by arguments about greater economic returns from primary education and the potentially regressive effects of investments at the secondary level, a large agenda remains unattended. It is at the secondary level that many of the microeconomic, health, and fertility outcomes of girls' education are fully realized. And common sense alone suggests that the large (and growing) cohort of children moving through primary schooling will create unsustainable pressures for postprimary education opportunities. If those are severely rationed, as they are in much of sub-Saharan Africa, the negative feedback to parents who sacrificed to send their children through primary school may be profound. Sorting out the design, financing, and institutional arrangements for effective secondary schooling—that is also responsive to labor market demand—is an essential part of good policy making today.

The Way Forward

Beyond general expansion of enrollment, governments can get out-of-school children into school by crafting specific interventions to reach them, and by increasing educational opportunities (formal and informal) for girls and women. In designing these initiatives, success depends on understanding and taking into account powerful demand-side influences that may constrain girls' school participation.

Specific interventions have been shown, in some settings, to get hard-to-reach children into school. These include eliminating school fees, instituting conditional cash transfers, using school feeding programs as an incentive to attend school, and implementing school health programs to reduce absenteeism. Several interventions have proved particularly successful where girls' participation is low. These include actions that increase security and privacy for girls (for example, ensuring that sanitation facilities are girl-friendly), as well as those that reduce gender-stereotyping in curriculum and encourage girls to take an active role in their education.

While few rigorous evaluations have been undertaken, many experts suggest that literacy programs for uneducated mothers may help increase school participation by their children. Adult literacy programs may be particularly useful in settings where there are pockets of undereducated women, such as ethnic or indigenous communities.

It is tempting for policy makers to focus on specific programmatic investments. But sustained improvements in education are impossible to achieve without improving the way in which key institutions in the sector function, and without increasing parental involvement in decisions affecting their children's education. Many countries with poorly performing educational systems suffer from institutional weaknesses, including low management capacity, nontransparent resource allocation and accounting practices, and substandard human resources policies and practices. Incentive structures that fail to reward good performance create and reinforce the most deleterious characteristics of weak institutions.

Parents who are well informed of policies and resource allocations in the education sector and who are involved in decisions regarding their children's schooling exert considerable influence and help contribute solutions. Involved communities are able to articulate local school needs, hold officials accountable, and mobilize local resources to fill gaps when the government response is inadequate.

In Benin, Burkina Faso, Guinea, Madagascar, Mozambique, and Niger, a mere 15 percent of girls who start primary school make it to the end.

A Modest Proposal

Donor agencies have been at the leading edge of the dialogue about the importance of girls' education, often providing the financial support, research, and political stimulus that may be lacking in countries that have more than their hands full with the basics of "Education for All." There is a broad consensus in the international donor community about the value of girls' education, and innovations have been introduced through donor-funded programs under the auspices of UNICEF, the World Food Program, the US Agency for International Development, and other key agencies. These have been valuable contributions, and have supported the work of champions at the national and local levels.

The donor community could come together now to accelerate progress in a very particular way. Working with both governments and nongovernmental organizations in countries where specific excluded groups—ethnic and/or linguistic minorities—have much poorer education outcomes, donors could finance the design, introduction, and rigorous evaluation of targeted programs to improve access to appropriate educational opportunities, with a particular emphasis (if warranted by the baseline research) on the needs and characteristics of girls. While different bilateral and multilateral donors could take the lead in funding specific types of programs or working in particular countries on the challenge of the "doubly disadvantaged," a shared learning agenda could be coordinated across agencies to generate much more than the spotty anecdotes and case studies on which we currently depend.

The learning agenda would include three components: first, the enduring questions to be examined—for example, determining the most effective strategies to improve learning outcomes among children who come from households where the language spoken is not the language of instruction; second, the use of methods that permit observed results to be attributed to the program; and third, the features that will ensure maximum credibility of the evaluations, such as independence, dissemination of results (whether the findings are favorable or not), and wide sharing of the data for reanalysis.

Just as education can transform individuals' lives, learning what works can transform the debates in development policy. The beneficiaries in developing countries would include not only girls who receive the education they deserve and need, but also families and communities and future generations thereby lifted over time out of poverty.

Assess Your Progress

1. What are the advantages of educating women in developing countries?
2. How can expansion of educational opportunity be achieved?
3. What are the promising trends in educating women?
4. Where is greater emphasis on educating women required?
5. What are the challenges in improving educational opportunity?

Ruth Levine is director of programs and a senior fellow at the Center for Global Development.

Girls in War

Sex Slave, Mother, Domestic Aide, Combatant

RADHIKA COOMARASWAMY

"The attackers tied me up and raped me because I was fighting. About five of them did the same thing to me until one of the commanders who knew my father came and stopped them, but also took me to his house to make me his wife. I just accepted him because of fear and didn't want to say no because he might do the same thing to me too." This is the testimony of a young girl of 14 from Liberia as told to the *Machel Review* in a focus group conducted jointly by the United Nations Children's Fund (UNICEF) and the Office of the Special Representative of the Secretary-General for Children and Armed Conflict (OSRSG/CAAC).

This story shows how vulnerable girls are in armed conflict. Actually, they can be affected by war in five different ways. Firstly, they are often direct victims of violence—killed, maimed or sexually violated as war crimes are committed against them. Secondly, they can be recruited and used as combatants for fighting in the battlefield. Thirdly, as refugees and internally displaced persons (IDPS), they remain in insecure environments, often deprived of basic amenities. Fourthly, they are frequently trafficked and exploited, as perpetrators abuse their vulnerability. Finally, when they become orphans, some of them have to manage child-headed households, eking out a living for themselves and their siblings.

Direct Violence

The number of children who are victims of direct violence, especially killings, has greatly increased in the last few years. Many have lost their lives in the confrontation between terrorism and counter terrorism. We have seen the phenomenon of children being used as suicide bombers and we have seen children as victims of aerial bombardment, a part of what is euphemistically called "collateral damage".

In Afghanistan I met Aisha, a girl whose home had been destroyed during an air raid which killed many of her family members, and whose school had been attacked by insurgents opposing education for girls. But Aisha was determined to go on with her studies so that she could become a school teacher.

Sexual Violence

Girls are often raped or violated in situations of conflict. Raping girls and women is often a military strategy aimed at terrorizing the population and humiliating the community. At other times, the climate of impunity in war zones leads to rape and exploitation by individual soldiers who know they will not be punished. Eva was a young girl I met in the Democratic Republic of the Congo. She and her friend were walking to school when they were waylaid by armed members of the Democratic Liberation Forces of Rwanda. They were taken to the camp, repeatedly raped, compelled to live in a state of forced nudity and assigned to domestic chores for the members of the group. Eva finally escaped and found shelter in Panzi hospital, a refuge for victims of sexual violence, where she found out that she was pregnant. She was 13 years old. When I met her, Panzi hospital was taking care of her child while she was attending school. They were trying to trace her family, even though they knew that girls who are victims of rape are often shunned by their next of kin.

Girl Soldiers

Increasingly, girls are being recruited into fighting forces as child soldiers. Some are abducted and have to play the dual role of sex slave and child combatant. This was particularly true in the wars of Sierra Leone and Liberia. In other cases, girls join the fighting forces for a multitude of reasons because they identify with the ideology, they want to run away from home or they have no other option for survival. Maria was a former girl child soldier whom I met in Colombia. She joined the rebel groups because her brothers had joined before her. Subjected to domestic violence at home, she ran away. She fought with the rebels and was then captured during one of the confrontations. Today she feels very lost. She does not want to go back home and she feels she has neither the education nor the skills to survive alone. When I met her, she was being taken care of by a foster parent. She felt boys were frightened of her because of her past. She also told me that many girls who had left the movement finally end up in sex work as a survival strategy.

Internally Displaced

Eighty percent of the world's refugees and internally displaced are women and children. Displaced children are perhaps one of the most vulnerable categories. In many parts of the world they are separated from their families while fleeing, becoming orphans overnight. And living in camps, they are often recruited into the fighting forces. Displaced children also suffer from high rates of malnutrition and have little access to medical services. Many girls are victims of violence in the camp or when they leave the camp to gather firewood and other necessities. For those who advocate for the rights of displaced children, the first priority should be security. The objective is to ensure that children are safe, protected from sexual violence and recruitment, and that there are child-friendly spaces in the camp. The second priority is education. Recently, UN agencies and non-governmental organizations (NGOS) have partnered to advocate strongly that education is an integral part of emergency response and not a luxury development. This was one of the key messages of the General Assembly debate on Education in Emergencies, in March 2009. It is important to plan for schools and play areas for children as the camp is constructed and provisions are made for families to be settled. It gives children a sense of normalcy and routine when they live in the camps.

Trafficking and Sexual Exploitation

Another concern we have for girl children in situations of armed conflict is that they are often trafficked and sexually exploited. At the international level, commentators have always pointed to "waves" of trafficking: that is, particular groups being trafficked in large numbers at a particular time. These waves often occur in areas of armed conflicts; women flee in large numbers, and being sex workers is their only survival strategy. They become victims of terrible exploitation by ruthless international criminal gangs. So many of these stories have been chronicled and a great deal of effort has been made over the last two decades to tackle the phenomenon. Nevertheless, the ground realities of conflict still lead to the sexual vulnerability of girls and women. Our own peacekeepers have not been immune to these situations. The UN Department of Peacekeeping Operations has made it a priority through their zero tolerance policy and code of conduct and discipline to ensure that this type of activity ceases and that peacekeepers will only be seen as protectors.

In areas of armed conflicts women flee in large numbers, and being sex workers is their only survival strategy. They become victims of terrible exploitation by ruthless international criminal gangs.

Orphans and Child-Headed Households

The terrible toll of war also makes many children into orphans overnight. In many parts of the world, we are seeing child-headed households where children have to fend for themselves as well as for other children. This happens especially to girl children who have to take over the role of parents. Parentless children often live in deplorable conditions such as broken-down buildings with leaky roofs, or no roofs at all. They sleep together under torn plastic sacks and cook with old rusty cans and broken pottery. They are susceptible to all manner of diseases and their situation is terribly vulnerable and heartbreaking. UN agencies are trying ways of giving these children a future without institutionalizing them in centres. It is their aim to keep children in the community and make it the responsibility of the community to take care of its children. Through schemes that find foster homes and foster mothers, they hope to let the children enjoy the benefit of family life.

The terrible toll of war also makes many children into orphans overnight. In many parts of the world, we are seeing child-headed households where children have to fend for themselves and also other children. This happens especially to girl children who have to take over the role of parents.

The International Tribunals and the Fight against Impunity

How has the international community responded to these devastating descriptions of what girl children suffer during war time? Recently things are slowly beginning to change, especially in the fight against impunity. The first breakthrough for children was the establishment of international tribunals which began to hold perpetrators accountable for international crimes. The cases before the tribunals of the Former Yugoslavia and Rwanda that dealt with sexual violence, created a framework of international jurisprudence that will help us in the future. Individual women found justice, and there is always the deterrent effect that cannot be measured in an empirical manner. Recently, the Special Court for Sierra Leone found several commanders of the Revolutionary United Front guilty of 16 charges of war crimes and crimes against humanity including conscription and enlistment of children under 15 into the fighting forces. The setting up of the International Criminal Court was the culmination of this trajectory. Their first case, the Thomas Lubanga case, involved the recruitment and use of children as child soldiers, strengthening the cause for children. Our office submitted an amicus curiae to the court in that case, arguing that girl children should be brought into the ambit of protection. We advocate for the young, abducted girls who play multiple roles in camps, to receive the protection of the law against being recruited, used, as well as forced to participate in the hostilities. We hope to get our day in court to argue this point of view so that the enormous suffering of girl children does not remain invisible.

Involvement of the Security Council

In the area of children in armed conflict, another mechanism that has begun to chip away at impunity is Security Council resolution 1612. The resolution, passed in 2005, created a Working

Group on Children and Armed Conflict. It also established a monitoring and reporting mechanism involving a Task Force at the national level made up of all the UN agencies, assigned to report on the violations. The Task Force is chaired by either the Resident Co-ordinator or the Special Representative and is often co-chaired by UNICEF. Through this mechanism, OSRSG/CAAC receives bimonthly reports on grave violations against children in war zones. The Security Council process is informed by the Annual Report of the Secretary-General to the Council which lists parties that recruit and use child soldiers. Resolution 1612 recommends the prospect of targeted measures against persistent violators of children's rights. The hope in 2009 is to extend these measures, beyond the recruitment and use of child soldiers, to include sexual violence against children, such that those who persistently use sexual violence in war be listed, shamed and face the possibility of sanctions. Having received the full support of the UN system, it is hoped that Member States, especially those in the Security Council, will help our office deliver on this promise.

In a world where there is so much abuse against women and children, one may become cynical about these small steps that the international community has begun to take to fight impunity, but we must not underestimate their effects. Recently, I was in the Central African Republic and met three generations of women in one family who had been raped when Jean-Pierre Bemba's troops attacked the capital, Bangui. They were getting ready to go to The Hague to testify against him. Their elation at the possibility of justice, and their gratitude that these things have come to pass has convinced me that we are on the right path. Grave violations, war crimes and crimes against humanity must be taken seriously, so that the culture of impunity that often hangs over warfare be broken.

Reintegration of Former Child Soldiers

Another area where the international community can help is the field of rehabilitation and reintegration. Reintegrating children affected by war is a major task facing governments, UN agencies and NGO partners working in the field. The Paris Principles give us a framework on how to reintegrate children associated with armed groups, but these principles are also a guide to reintegrating all children. The call for community-based programming that works with the child, while developing the family and the community in an inclusive manner, must be the starting point for child-based programming. And yet, some children need special attention. Research shows that children who were forced to commit terrible crimes and children who were victims of sexual violence need special care and attention. Girl children often have different needs from boys. Treating children as important individuals while, at the same time, developing the community in a holistic manner, is the only sustainable way forward.

Finally we cannot even begin to speak of the psychological toll that war takes on children. When I was in Gaza, I went to a school and entered a classroom of nine year-old girls, who were drawing in an art class. I moved from one to the other, and then I just looked down at one girl's drawing, Ameena's. She had drawn a house and she explained to me that the two figures in the house were her mother and herself. Above the house there was a mangled object which I gather was a helicopter gunship; to the left of the house there was an imposing looking tank and to the right of the house, a soldier. All these were firing at the home. Her sad, dull eyes on her beautiful face told the rest of the story. Meeting the day to day reality of war is a terrible calling for all of my colleagues working in the field. But rebuilding the shattered lives of children is an even more daunting task; to make them smile again, care again and live with purpose is the challenge of the hour.

Assess Your Progress

1. In what ways are girls vulnerable in conflict situations?
2. How are internal displacement and vulnerability linked?
3. How has the international community responded to this vulnerability?

Radhika Coomaraswamy is the Special Representative of the UN Secretary-General for Children and Armed Conflict (www.un.org/children/conflict).

Remember the Women?

Women belong at the center of the debate over the Afghan war, not on the margins.

ANN JONES

Women are made for homes or graves.

—Afghan saying

Gen. Stanley McChrystal says he needs more American troops to salvage something like winning in Afghanistan and restore the country to "normal life." Influential senators want to increase spending to train more soldiers for the Afghan National Army and Police. The Feminist Majority recently backed off a call for more troops, but it continues to warn against US withdrawal as an abandonment of Afghan women and girls. Nearly everyone assumes troops bring greater security; and whether your touchstone is military victory, national interest or the welfare of women and girls, "security" seems a good thing.

I confess that I agonize over competing proposals now commanding President Obama's attention because I've spent years in Afghanistan working with women, and I'm on their side. When the Feminist Majority argues that withdrawing American forces from Afghanistan will return the Taliban to power and women to house arrest, I see in my mind's eye the faces of women I know and care about. Yet an unsentimental look at the record reveals that for all the fine talk of women's rights since the US invasion, equal rights for Afghan women have been illusory all along, a polite feel-good fiction that helped to sell the American enterprise at home and cloak in respectability the misbegotten government we installed in Kabul. That it is a fiction is borne out by recent developments in Afghanistan—President Karzai's approving a new family law worthy of the Taliban, and American acquiescence in Karzai's new law and, initially, his theft of the presidential election—and by the systematic intimidation, murder or exile of one Afghan woman after another who behaves as if her rights were real and worth fighting for.

Last summer in Kabul, where "security" already suffocates anything remotely suggesting normal life, I asked an Afghan colleague at an international NGO if she was ever afraid. I had learned of threatening phone calls and night letters posted on the gates of the compound, targeting Afghan women who work within. Three of our colleagues in another city had been kidnapped by the militia of a warlord, formerly a member of the Karzai government, and at the time, as we learned after their release, were being beaten, tortured and threatened with death if they continued to work.

"Fear?" my colleague said. "Yes. We live with fear. In our work here with women we are always under threat. Personally, I work every day in fear, hoping to return safely at the end of the day to my home. To my child and my husband."

"And the future?" I said. "What do you worry about?"

"I think about the upcoming election," she said. "I fear that nothing will change. I fear that everything will stay the same."

Then Karzai gazetted the Shiite Personal Status Law, and it was suddenly clear that even as we were hoping for the best, everything had actually grown much worse for women.

Why is this important? At this critical moment, as Obama tries to weigh options against our national security interests, his advisers can't be bothered with—as one US military officer put it to me—"the trivial fate of women." As for some hypothetical moral duty to protect the women of Afghanistan—that's off the table. Yet it is precisely that dismissive attitude, shared by Afghan and many American men alike, that may have put America's whole Afghan enterprise wrong in the first place. Early on, Kofi Annan, then United Nations secretary general, noted that the condition of Afghan women was "an affront to all standards of dignity, equality and humanity."

Annan took the position, set forth in 2000 in the landmark UN Security Council Resolution 1325, that real conflict resolution, reconstruction and lasting peace cannot be achieved without the full participation of women every step of the way. Karzai gave lip service to the idea, saying in 2002, "We are determined to work to improve the lot of women after all their suffering under the narrow-minded and oppressive rule of the Taliban." But he has done no such thing. And the die had already been cast: of the twenty-three Afghan notables invited to take part in the Bonn Conference in December 2001, only two were women. Among ministers appointed to the new Karzai government, there were only two; one, the minister for women's affairs, was warned not to do "too much."

The Bonn agreement expressed "appreciation to the Afghan mujahidin who... have defended the independence, territorial integrity and national unity of the country and have played a major role in the struggle against terrorism and oppression, and whose sacrifice has now made them both heroes of jihad and champions of peace, stability and reconstruction of their beloved homeland, Afghanistan." On the other hand, their American- and Saudi-sponsored "sacrifice" had also made many of them war criminals in the eyes of their countrymen. Most Afghans surveyed between 2002 and 2004 by the Afghan Independent Human Rights Commission thought the leaders of the mujahedeen were war criminals who should be brought to justice (75 percent) and removed from public office (90 percent). The mujahedeen, after all, were Islamist extremists just like the Taliban, though less disciplined than the Taliban, who had risen up to curb the violent excesses of the mujahedeen and then imposed excesses of their own. That's the part American officials seem unwilling to admit: that the mujahedeen warlords of the Karzai government and the oppressive Taliban are brothers under the skin. From the point of view of women today, America's friends and America's enemies in Afghanistan are the same kind of guys.

Though women were excluded from the Bonn process, they did seem to make strides in the first years after the fall of the Taliban. In 2004 a new constitution declared, "The citizens of Afghanistan—whether man or woman—have equal rights and duties before the law." Westerners greeted that language as a confirmation of gender equality, and to this day women's "equal rights" are routinely cited in Western media as evidence of great progress. Yet not surprisingly, Afghan officials often interpret the article differently. To them, having "equal rights and duties" is nothing like being equal. The first chief justice of the Afghan Supreme Court, formerly a mullah in a Pakistani madrassa, once explained to me that men have a right to work while women have a right to obey their husbands. The judiciary—an ultraconservative, inadequate, incompetent and notoriously corrupt branch of government—interprets the constitution by its own lights. And the great majority of women across the country, knowing little or nothing of rights, live now much as they did under the Taliban—except back then there were no bombs.

In any case, the constitution provides that no law may contravene the principles of Sharia law. In effect, mullahs and judges have always retained the power to decide at any moment what "rights" women may enjoy, or not; and being poorly educated, they're likely to factor into the judgment their own idiosyncratic notions of Sharia, plus tribal customary laws and the size of proffered bribes. Thus, although some women still bravely exercise liberty and work with some success to improve women's condition, it should have been clear from the get-go that Afghan women possess no inalienable rights at all. Western legal experts who train Afghan judges and lawyers in "the law" as we conceive it often express frustration that Afghans just don't get it; Afghan judges think the same of them.

The paper foundations of Afghan women's rights go beyond national law to include the Universal Declaration of Human Rights, the International Treaty of Civil and Political Rights, and the Convention on the Elimination of All Forms of Discrimination Against Women (CEDAW). All these international agreements that delineate and establish human rights around the world were quickly ratified by the Karzai government. CEDAW, however, requires ratifying governments to submit periodic reports on their progress in eliminating discrimination; Afghanistan's first report, due in 2004, hasn't appeared yet. That's one more clue to the Karzai government's real attitude toward women—like Karzai's sequestration of his own wife, a doctor with much-needed skills who is kept locked up at home.

Given this background, there should have been no surprise when President Karzai first signed off in March on the Shiite Personal Status Law or, as it became known in the Western press, the Marital Rape Law. The bill had been percolating in the ultraconservative Ministry of Justice ever since the Iranian-backed Ayatollah Asif Mohseni submitted it in 2007. Then last February Karzai apparently saw the chance to swap passage of the SPSL for the votes of the Shiites—that is, the Hazara minority, 15–20 percent of the population. It was just one of many deals Karzai consolidated as he kept to the palace while rival presidential candidates stomped the countryside. The SPSL passed without alteration through the Parliamentary Judicial Committee, another little bunch of ultraconservative men. When it reached the floor of Parliament, it was too late to object. Some women members succeeded in getting the marriageable age for girls—age 9—revised to 16. Calling it victory, they settled for that. The Supreme Court reviewed the bill and pronounced it constitutionally correct on grounds the justices did not disclose.

The rights Afghan women stood to lose on paper and in real life were set forth in the SPSL. Parliamentarian Shinkai Karokhail alerted a reporter at the *Guardian,* and the law was denounced around the world for legalizing marital rape by authorizing a husband to withhold food from a wife who fails to provide sexual service at least once every four days. (The interval assumes the husband has four wives, a practice permitted by Islam and legalized by this legislation.) But that's not all the law does. It also denies or severely limits women's rights to inherit, divorce or have guardianship of their own children. It forbids women to marry without permission and legalizes forced marriage. It legalizes marriage to and rape of minors. It gives men control of all their female relatives. It denies women the right to leave home except for "legitimate purposes"—in effect giving men the power to deny women access to work, education, healthcare, voting and whatever they please. It generally treats women as property, and it considers rape of women or minors outside marriage as a property crime, requiring restitution to be made to the owner, usually the father or husband, rather than a crime against the victim. All these provisions are contained in twenty-six articles of the original bill that have been rendered into English and analyzed by Western legal experts. No doubt other regressive rules will be discovered if the 223 additional articles of the law ever appear in English.

In April a few women parliamentarians spoke out against the law. A group of women, estimated to number about 300, staged a peaceful protest in the street, protected by Kabul's police officers from an angry mob of hundreds of men who pelted them with obscenities and stones, shouting, "Death to the enemies of Islam!" Under pressure from international diplomats—President Obama called the law "abhorrent"—Karzai withdrew it for review. The international press reported the women's victory. In June, when a large group of women MPs and activists met with Karzai, he assured them the bill had been amended and would be submitted to Parliament again after the elections.

Instead, on July 27, without public announcement, Karzai entered the SPSL, slightly revised but with principal provisions intact, into the official gazette, thereby making it law. Apparently he was betting that with the presidential election only three weeks away, the United States and its allies would not complain again. After all, they had about $500 million (at least half of that American money) riding on a "credible" outcome; and they couldn't afford the cost of a runoff or the political limbo of an interregnum. In August,

Brad Adams, Asia director of Human Rights Watch, observed that such "barbaric laws were supposed to have been relegated to the past with the overthrow of the Taliban in 2001, yet Karzai has revived them and given them his official stamp of approval." No American official said a word.

But what about all the women parliamentarians so often cited as evidence of the progress of Afghan women? With 17 percent of the upper house and 27 percent of the lower—eighty-five women in all—you'd think they could have blocked the SPSL. But that didn't happen, for many reasons. Many women parliamentarians are mere extensions of the warlords who financed their campaigns and tell them how to vote: always in opposition to women's rights. Most non-Shiite women took little interest in the bill, believing that it applied only to the Shiite minority. Although Hazara women have long been the freest in the country and the most active in public life, some of them argued that it is better to have a bad law than none at all because, as one Hazara MP told me, "without a written law, men can do whatever they want."

The human rights division of the UN's Assistance Mission in Afghanistan (UNAMA) published a report in early July, before the SPSL became law, documenting the worsening position of Afghan women, the rising violence against them and the silence of international and Afghan officials who could defend them. The researchers' most surprising finding is this: considering the risks of life outside the home and the support women receive within it, "there is no clear distinction between rural and urban women." Commentators on Afghanistan, myself included, have assumed—somewhat snobbishly, it now appears—that while illiterate women in the countryside might be treated no better than animals, educated urban Afghan women blaze a higher trail. The debacle of the Shiite Personal Status Law explodes that myth.

The UNAMA report attributes women's worsening position in Afghan society to the violence the war engenders on two domestic fronts: the public stage and the home. The report is dedicated to the memory of Sitara Achakzai, a member of the Kandahar Provincial Council and outspoken advocate of women's rights, who was shot to death on April 12, soon after being interviewed by the UNAMA researchers. She "knew her life was in danger," they report. "But like many other Afghan women such as Malalai Kakar, the highest-ranking female police officer in Kandahar killed in September 2008, Sitara Achakzai had consciously decided to keep fighting to end the abuse of Afghan women." Malalai Kakar, 40, mother of six, had headed a team of ten policewomen handling cases of domestic violence.

Women's worsening position is a result of the violence the war engenders on two fronts: the public stage and the home.

In 2005 Kim Sengupta, a reporter with the London *Independent,* interviewed five Afghan women activists; by October 2008 three of them had been murdered. A fourth, Zarghuna Kakar (no relation to Malalai), a member of the Kandahar Provincial Council, had left the country after she and her family were attacked and her husband was killed. She said she had pleaded with Ahmed Wali Karzai, head of the Kandahar Provincial Council, for protection; but he told her she "should have thought about what may happen" before she stood for election. Kakar told the reporter, "It was his brother [President Karzai], the Americans, and the British who told us that we women should get involved in political life. Of course, now I wish I hadn't."

Women learn to pull their punches. MPs in Kabul confessed that they are afraid of the fundamentalist warlords who control the Parliament; so they censor themselves and keep silent. One said, "Most of the time women don't dare even say a word about sensitive Islamic issues, because they are afraid of being labeled as blasphemous." Many women MPs have publicly declared their intention to quit at the end of the term. Women journalists also told UNAMA that they "refrain from criticizing warlords and other power brokers, or covering topics that are deemed contentious such as women's rights."

Other women targeted for attack are civil servants, employees of international and national organizations, including the UN, healthcare workers and women in "immoral" professions—which include acting, singing, appearing on television and journalism. When popular Tolo TV presenter Shaima Rezayee, 24, was forced out of her job in 2005, she said "things are not getting better.... We have made some gains, but there are a lot of people who want to take it all back. They are not even Taliban, they are here in Kabul." Soon after, she was shot and killed. Zakia Zaki, 35, a teacher and radio journalist who produced programs on women's rights, was shot to death in her home in Parwan Province on June 6, 2007. Actress Parwin Mushtakhel fled the country last spring after her husband was gunned down outside their house, punished for his failure to keep her confined. When the Taliban fell, she thought things were getting better, but "the atmosphere has changed; day by day women can work less and less." Setara Hussainzada, the singer from Herat who appeared on the Afghan version of *American Idol* (and in the documentary *Afghan Star*) also fled for her life.

Threats against women in public life are intended to make them go home—to "unliberate" themselves through voluntary house arrest. But if public life is dangerous, so is life at home. Most Afghan women—87 percent, according to Unifem—are beaten on a regular basis. The UNAMA researchers looked into the unmentionable subject of rape and found it to be "an everyday occurrence in all parts of the country" and "a human rights problem of profound proportions." Outside marriage, the rapists are often members or friends of the family. Young girls forced to marry old men are raped by the old man's brothers and sons. Women and children—young boys are also targets—are raped by people who have charge of them: police, prison guards, soldiers, orphanage or hospital staff members. The female victims of rape are mostly between the ages of 7 and 30; many are between 10 and 20, but some are as young as 3; and most women are dead by 42.

Women rarely tell anyone because the blame and shame of rape falls on them. Customary law permits an accused rapist to make restitution to the victim's father, but because the question of consent does not figure in the law of sexual relations, the victim is guilty of *zina,* or adultery, and can be punished accordingly: sent to jail or murdered by family members to preserve family honor. The great majority of women and girls in prison at any time are charged with *zina*; most have been raped and/or have run away from home to escape violence. It's probably safe to say, in the absence of statistics, that police—who, incidentally, are trained by the American for-profit contractor DynCorp—spend more time tracking down runaway women and girls than real criminals. Rapists, on the other hand, as UNAMA investigators found, are often "directly linked to power brokers who are, effectively, above the law and enjoy immunity from arrest as well as immunity from social condemnation." Last year Karzai pardoned political thugs who had gang-raped a woman before witnesses, using a bayonet, and who had somehow been convicted despite their good connections. UNAMA researchers conclude: "The current reality is that...women are denied their most fundamental human rights and risk further violence in the course of seeking justice for crimes perpetrated against them." For women, "human rights are values, standards, and entitlements that exist only in theory and at times, not even on paper."

Caught in the maelstrom of personal, political and military violence, Afghan women worry less about rights than security. But they complain that the men who plan the country's future define "security" in ways that have nothing to do with them. The conventional wisdom, which I have voiced myself, holds that without security, development cannot take place. Hence, our troops must be fielded in greater numbers, and Afghan troops trained faster, and private for-profit military contractors hired at fabulous expense, all to bring security. But the rule doesn't hold in Afghanistan precisely because of that equation of "security" with the presence of armed men. Wherever troops advance in Afghanistan, women are caught in the cross-fire, killed, wounded, forced to flee or locked up once again, just as they were in the time of the Taliban. Suggesting an alternative to the "major misery" of warfare, Sweden's former Defense Minister Thage Peterson calls for Swedish soldiers to leave the "military adventure" in Afghanistan while civilians stay to help rebuild the country. But Sweden's soldiers are few, and its aid organizations among the best in the world. For the United States even to lean toward such a plan would mean reasserting civilian control of the military and restoring the American aid program (USAID), hijacked by private for-profit contractors: two goals worth fighting for.

Wherever troops advance, women are caught in the cross-fire, killed, wounded, forced to flee or locked up just as they were under the Taliban.

Today, most American so-called development aid is delivered not by USAID, but by the military itself through a system of Provincial Reconstruction Teams (PRTs), another faulty idea of former Defense Secretary Donald Rumsfeld. Soldiers, unqualified as aid workers and already busy soldiering, now shmooze with village "elders" (often the wrong ones) and bring "development," usually a costly road convenient to the PRT base, impossible for Afghans to maintain and inaccessible to women locked up at home. Recent research conducted by respected Afghanistan hands found that this aid actually fuels "massive corruption"; it fails to win hearts and minds not because we spend too little but because we spend too much, too fast, without a clue. Meanwhile, the Taliban bring the things Afghans say they need—better security, better governance and quick, hard-edged justice. US government investigators are looking into allegations that aid funds appropriated for women's projects have been diverted to PRTs for this more important work of winning hearts and minds with tarmac. But the greatest problem with routing aid through the military is this: what passes for development is delivered from men to men, affirming in the strongest possible terms the misogynist conviction that women do not matter. You'll recognize it as the same belief that, in the Obama administration's strategic reappraisal of Afghanistan, pushed women off the table.

So there's no point talking about how women and girls might be affected by the strategic military options remaining on Obama's plate. None of them bode well for women. To send more troops is to send more violence. To withdraw is to invite the Taliban. To stay the same is not possible, now that Karzai has stolen the election in plain sight and made a mockery of American pretensions to an interest in anything but our own skin and our own pocketbook. But while men plan the onslaught of more men, it's worth remembering what "normal life" once looked like in Afghanistan, well before the soldiers came. In the 1960s and '70s, before the Soviet invasion—when half the country's doctors, more than half the civil servants and three-quarters of the teachers were women—a peaceful Afghanistan advanced slowly into the modern world through the efforts of all its people. What changed all that was not only the violence of war but the accession to power of the most backward men in the country: first the Taliban, now the mullahs and mujahedeen of the fraudulent, corrupt, Western-designed government that stands in opposition to "normal life" as it is lived in the developed world and was once lived in their own country. What happens to women is not merely a "women's issue"; it is the central issue of stability, development and durable peace. No nation can advance without women, and no enterprise that takes women off the table can come to much good.

Assess Your Progress

1. What is the status of women's rights in Afghanistan?
2. What has acted as a constraint upon women's rights as outlined in the 2004 Afghan constitution?
3. How did the Shiite Personal Status Law further undermine women's rights?
4. How are women in public life affected by a lack of status in Afghanistan?
5. In what ways are women vulnerable at home?

Ann Jones, author of *Kabul in Winter,* does humanitarian work in postconflict zones with NGOs and the United Nations.

Women in the Shadow of Climate Change

BALGIS OSMAN-ELASHA

Climate change is one of the greatest global challenges of the twenty-first century. Its impacts vary among regions, generations, age, classes, income groups, and gender. Based on the findings of the Intergovernmental Panel on Climate Change (IPCC), it is evident that people who are already most vulnerable and marginalized will also experience the greatest impacts. The poor, primarily in developing countries, are expected to be disproportionately affected and consequently in the greatest need of adaptation strategies in the face of climate variability and change. Both women and men working in natural resource sectors, such as agriculture, are likely to be affected.[1] However, the impact of climate change on gender is not the same. Women are increasingly being seen as more vulnerable than men to the impacts of climate change, mainly because they represent the majority of the world's poor and are proportionally more dependent on threatened natural resources. The difference between men and women can also be seen in their differential roles, responsibilities, decision making, access to land and natural resources, opportunities and needs, which are held by both sexes.[2] Worldwide, women have less access than men to resources such as land, credit, agricultural inputs, decision-making structures, technology, training and extension services that would enhance their capacity to adapt to climate change.[3]

Worldwide, women have less access than men to resources such as land, credit, agricultural inputs, decision-making structures, technology, training and extension services that would enhance their capacity to adapt to climate change.

Why Women Are More Vulnerable

Women's vulnerability to climate change stems from a number of factors—social, economic and cultural.

Seventy percent of the 1.3 billion people living in conditions of poverty are women. In urban areas, 40 percent of the poorest households are headed by women. Women predominate in the world's food production (50–80 percent), but they own less than 10 percent of the land.

Women represent a high percentage of poor communities that are highly dependent on local natural resources for their livelihood, particularly in rural areas where they shoulder the major responsibility for household water supply and energy for cooking and heating, as well as for food security. In the Near East, women contribute up to 50 percent of the agricultural workforce. They are mainly responsible for the more time-consuming and labour-intensive tasks that are carried out manually or with the use of simple tools. In Latin America and the Caribbean, the rural population has been decreasing in recent decades. Women are mainly engaged in subsistence farming, particularly horticulture, poultry and raising small livestock for home consumption.

Women have limited access to and control of environmental goods and services; they have negligible participation in decision-making, and are not involved in the distribution of environment management benefits. Consequently, women are less able to confront climate change.

During extreme weather such as droughts and floods, women tend to work more to secure household livelihoods. This will leave less time for women to access training and education, develop skills or earn income. In Africa, female illiteracy rates were over 55 percent in 2000, compared to 41 percent for men.[4] When coupled with inaccessibility to resources and decision-making processes, limited mobility places women where they are disproportionately affected by climate change.

In many societies, socio-cultural norms and childcare responsibilities prevent women from migrating or seeking refuge in other places or working when a disaster hits. Such a situation is likely to put more burden on women, such as travelling longer to get drinking water and wood for fuel. Women, in many developing countries suffer gender inequalities with respect to human rights, political and economic status, land ownership, housing conditions, exposure to violence, education and health. Climate change will be an added stressor that will aggravate women's

Oxfam International reported disproportional fatalities among men and women during the tsunami that hit Asia at the end of 2004. According to an Oxfam briefing, females accounted for about three quarters of deaths in eight Indonesian villages, and almost 90 percent of deaths in Cuddalore, the second most affected district in India. Of the 140,000 who died from the 1991 cyclone disasters in Bangladesh, 90 percent were women.[6]

Women and girls in many rural societies spend up to three hours per day fetching water and collecting firewood. Droughts, floods, and desertification exacerbated by climate change make women spend more time on these tasks, diminishing their ability to participate in wage-earning activities.[7]

During natural disasters, more women die (compared to men) because they are not adequately warned, cannot swim well, or cannot leave the house alone.

Moreover, lower levels of education reduce the ability of women and girls to access information, including early warning and resources, or to make their voices heard. Cultural values could also contribute to women's vulnerability in some countries. For example, in Bangladesh, women are more calorie-deficient than men (the male members in a family have the "right" to consume the best portions of the food, and the female members have to content themselves with the left-overs) and have more problems during disasters to cope with.

In Sudan, the increase in the migration of men from the drought-hit areas of western Sudan increased the number of female-headed households, and consequently their responsibilities and vulnerabilities during natural disasters.

—Balgis Osman-Elasha

vulnerability. It is widely known that during conflict, women face heightened domestic violence, sexual intimidation, human trafficking and rape.[5]

According to the IPCC in Africa, an increase of 5–8% (160–90 million hectares) of arid and semiarid land is projected by the 2080s under a range of climate change scenarios.

Improving Women's Adaptation to Climate Change

In spite of their vulnerability, women are not only seen as victims of climate change, but they can also be seen as active and effective agents and promoters of adaptation and mitigation. For a long time women have historically developed knowledge and skills related to water harvesting and storage, food preservation and rationing, and natural resource management. In Africa, for example, old women represent wisdom pools with their inherited knowledge and expertise related to early warnings and mitigating the impacts of disasters. This knowledge and experience that has passed from one generation to another will be able to contribute effectively to enhancing local adaptive capacity and sustaining a community's livelihood. For this to be achieved, and in order to improve the adaptive capacity of women worldwide particularly in developing countries, the following recommendations need to be considered:

- Adaptation initiatives should identify and address gender-specific impacts of climate change particularly in areas related to water, food security, agriculture, energy, health, disaster management, and conflict. Important gender issues associated with climate change adaptation, such as inequalities in access to resources, including credit, extension and training services, information and technology should also be taken into consideration.
- Women's priorities and needs must be reflected in the development planning and funding. Women should be part of the decision making at national and local levels regarding allocation of resources for climate change initiatives. It is also important to ensure gender-sensitive investments in programmes for adaptation, mitigation, technology transfer and capacity building.
- Funding organizations and donors should also take into account women-specific circumstances when developing and introducing technologies related to climate change adaptation and to try their best to remove the economic, social and cultural barriers that could constrain women from benefiting and making use of them. Involving women in the development of new technologies can ensure that they are adaptive, appropriate and sustainable. At national levels, efforts should be made to mainstream gender perspective into national policies and strategies, as well as related sustainable development and climate change plans and interventions.

Notes

1. ILO, 2008. Report of the Committee on Employment and Social Policy, Employment and labour market implications of climate change, Fourth Item on the Agenda, Governing Body, 303rd Session (Geneva), p. 2.
2. Osman-Elasha, 2008 "Gender and Climate Change in the Arab Region", Arab Women Organization, p. 44.
3. Aguilar, L., 2008. "Is there a connection between gender and climate change?", International Union for Conservation of Nature (IUCN), Office of the Senior Gender Adviser.
4. Rena, Ravinder and N. Narayana (2007) "Gender Empowerment in Africa: An Analysis of Women Participation in Eritrean Economy", New Delhi: *International Journal of Women, Social Justice and Human Rights,* vol.2. no.2., pp. 221–237 (Serials Publishers).
5. Davis, I. et. al. 2005, "Tsunami, Gender, and Recovery".

6. IUCN 2004 (a), "Climate Change and Disaster Mitigation: Gender Makes the Difference". Intergovernmental Panel on Climate Change, 2001. Climate Change: Impacts, Adaptation and Vulnerability, Contribution of Working Group II to the Third Assessment Report of the IPCC.
7. IUCN 2004 (b), "Energy: Gender Makes the Difference". Gender Action, 2008. Gender Action Link: Climate Change (Washington, D.C.), www.genderaction.org/images/Gender%20 Action%20Link%20-%20Climate%20Change.pdf
8. Third Global Congress of Women in Politics and Governance, 2008. Background and Context Paper for the Conference, Manila, Philippines, 19–22 October, www.capwip. org/3rdglobalcongress.htm IUCN 2007, "Gender and Climate Change: Women as Agents of Change"

Assess Your Progress

1. Why are women particularly vulnerable to climate change?
2. Why are they less able to deal with the consequences of climate change?
3. How do socio-cultural norms affect women's ability to meet the challenge of climate change?

Balgis Osman-Elasha is Principal Investigator with the Climate Change Unit, Higher Council for Environment and Natural Resources, Sudan; and a lead author of the Intergovernmental Panel on Climate Change's Fourth Assessment Report.

Recession Hits Women in Developing Countries

OLIVIA WARD

In Nepal, destitute parents sell their daughters to traffickers. In Pakistan, marrying off underage daughters relieves a family's financial burden. In parts of Asia and Africa, mothers are forced to choose which of their children they will feed, and which will starve.

Today, International Women's Day, women celebrate the gains made in achieving equal rights and highlight the widespread wrongs that damage the lives of the 3.3 billion females around the world.

But the issue foremost in women's minds is the global recession, which has hit the most vulnerable half of humanity with exceptional force.

Seventy percent of the poorest people on the planet are women and girls, and even in a wealthy country like Canada they are the majority of the poor.

Although the global downturn began in the financial sector, dominated by men, it is now bearing down on women, most often found in low-wage and part-time jobs.

The recession has plunged from wealthy to developing countries, where women lack safety nets to help them survive.

"As the economy slows, the disaster in the financial institutions is affecting the real economy," says Sylvia Borren, co-chair of the Global Call to Action Against Poverty, a coalition of groups in 100 countries.

"What happens is the informal sector suffers first—the cleaning women, gardeners and people who do the household jobs. They are mostly women."

As worldwide consumer confidence fades, says the International Labour Organization, traditionally female service jobs in cafes and retail stores are also disappearing. It predicts that 22 million of an estimated 51 million to lose their jobs this year will be women.

Adding to the problem is a global food crisis that has caused a spike in the price of dietary staples like rice, narrowing the line between malnutrition and starvation.

"The increase in hunger and economic stress is accelerating fast, and that affects women in a number of different ways," says Borren.

Because women earn less than men even in good times—a 16 percent global pay gap, according to the International Trade Union Confederation—they have less to fall back on when times turn bad.

Struggle in Iraq

The most shattering moment of Bushara's life arrived without warning: "One year ago when I went out to buy breakfast, I saw something written on the wall of our house," she said. "The graffiti told Shiites in the neighbourhood to get out."

Bushara, an Iraqi mother who lived near Abu Ghraib prison, knew there was no time to waste. The death squads were on the march. In bare feet, she fled with her husband and young daughters as the winter winds propelled them from their home. Her story, told to Oxfam International, is typical for Iraqi women, who have suffered loss and destitution since the U.S. overthrow of Saddam Hussein in 2003. Nor has the reported lessening of violence since 2007 improved their lives.

According to an Oxfam survey released last week, "despite fragile security gains and a decline in indiscriminate and sectarian violence over the past months, the day-to-day lives of many women in Iraq remain dire." Questioning 1,700 women in five provinces, Oxfam found:

- More than 40 percent said their security situation was worse than last year; 22 percent said it was about the same.
- 55 percent said they had become victims of violence since the invasion.
- More than 30 percent had family members who died violently.
- About 69 percent said access to water was worse; 25 percent had no daily access to drinking water.
- Two-thirds had electricity less than six hours a day, and one-third less than three hours a day.
- 40 percent said that their children were not attending school.

—Olivia Ward

But those at the bottom are also caught in a vicious circle of poverty and abuse. Women who held normal jobs are forced into the "shadow" economy of prostitution, drug smuggling and other criminal activity. Or they are drawn into the nets of vicious international traffickers.

They're also more at risk of domestic violence, when unemployed husbands and fathers take out their frustration at home.

At the same time, cuts in humanitarian aid budgets mean less money to spend on education, the key factor in lifting women out of poverty. Health care suffers, with devastating effects on pregnant women, HIV/AIDs victims, and those in conflict zones where women are targeted for sexual attack.

Some of the worst affected women are migrants, whose numbers grow as life gets harder in their original countries.

"Women and girls are disproportionately affected by the risks of migration because of their vulnerability to exploitation and violence," says Ndioro Ndiaye of the International Organization for Migration. And, he adds, lack of access to health care can have long-term effects for women and their children.

But as the economic storm clouds gather, the horizon is not entirely dark for women, says Borren.

"If you go to local solutions, you see room for hope," she says.

"To help in the food crisis, there's organizing and investing in microcredit so women can have plots of land. Unions are trying to solve the problem of lack of qualified teachers with fast-track training. Small water and electricity projects can work at the household level."

Along with increased risk there is great opportunity for women in the current crisis, Borren says. "We're concentrating on top-down solutions, which have proved unsustainable, and often stupid. Now it's time to put women at the centre, and work from the bottom up."

Assess Your Progress

1. Why did the global recession hit women in particular?
2. What impact did the recession have on women in the informal sector?
3. How have cuts in humanitarian aid worsened the problem?

Women's Rights as Human Rights

The Promotion of Human Rights as a Counter-Culture

ZEHRA F. KABASAKAL ARAT

Human rights are rights claimed against the State and society by virtue of being a human being. However, the human rights of most people have been continuously violated all around the world. Since all civilizations have been patriarchal,[1] regardless of the overall human rights conditions maintained in a society, women have been subject to more human rights violations than men. Women constitute the poorest and the least powerful segments of their communities. They are denied equal access to education, job training, employment, leisure time, income, property, health care, public office, decision-making power and freedoms, as well as control over their own body and life.[2] Cultural norms, laws and philosophies, including those that are considered progressive and emancipatory, have usually discriminated against women.

Omission of Women

The ancient Stoics' notion of natural rights, that human beings are created with certain inalienable rights, did not encompass women. When the Christian Church leader St. Thomas Aquinas (c. 1225–1274) was exposed to ancient Greek philosophy—largely through the writings of the Muslim philosophers Avicenna (Ibn Sina, 980–1037) and Averroes (Ibn Rushd, 1126–1198) who studied ancient Greek philosophy, reconciled reason with faith and championed equality and religious tolerance—he incorporated natural rights theory into his teaching. However, he ignored Averroes' egalitarian approach that opposed the unequal treatment of sexes and considered the reduction of women's value to childbearing and rearing as detrimental to the economic advancement of society and thus causing poverty.[3] Instead, Aquinas revived Aristotle's misogynous perception of woman as "misbegotten man" and wondered why God would create woman, a defective creature, in the first production of things;[4] while other church leaders later questioned if women had souls, that is, if they were fully human.

In modern times, progressive philosophers, such as Jean-Jacques Rousseau (1712–1778), could promote political freedoms and rights, but reject the notion of equality of the sexes. The revolutionary fervour of the eighteenth century that opposed oppression led to the French Declaration of the Rights of Man and Citizen (1789). However, the articulation of human rights in this document, which continued to inspire people all over the world for centuries, could not escape sexism prevalent at the time and omitted women. Nevertheless, a few elite women, such as French playwright and essayist Olympe de Gouges (1748–1793) and English philosopher Mary Wollstonecraft (1759–1797), raised their objections and defended women's rights by issuing The Declaration of the Rights of Woman (1790) and A Vindication of the Rights of Women (1791), respectively. The collaboration of Harriet Taylor Mill (1807–1858) with her husband John Stuart Mill (1806–1873) resulted in writings that advocated women's rights and political equality.[5]

Yet, gender biases prevailed throughout the twentieth century. Even members of the Commission that drafted the 1948 Universal Declaration of Human Rights were willing to employ the word "man" in reference to the holder of the rights. When the Soviet delegate, Vladimir Koretsky, objected to using the words "all men" as "historical atavism, which preclude us from an understanding that we men are only one half of the human species", the Commission Chair, Eleanor Roosevelt, defended the wording by arguing: [in English] "When we say 'all men are brothers', we mean that all human beings are brothers and we are not differentiating between men and women."[6] Thus, the language was maintained for some time. The final draft mostly employed the gender-neutral terms of "human being", "everyone" and "person", and the Preamble included a specific reference to the "equal rights of men and women", thanks largely to the efforts of two female Commission members, Hansa Mehta of India and Minerva Bernardino of the Dominican Republic.[7]

However, the Universal Declaration and the subsequent human rights documents adopted by the United Nations and other intergovernmental organizations have continued to employ the nominative and possessive pronouns "he" and "his", in line with the established tradition and understanding that male nouns or pronouns would stand for the female ones as well. Despite their clearly and repeatedly stated anti-discrimination clauses, which specify that sex as a characteristic or status cannot be used as grounds for discrimination or for denial of human rights, documents issued by the United Nations fell short of ensuring that human rights are equally applicable to both sexes.[8] Gender gaps were visible even in the United Nations, which did not have women in high office posts, as they were concentrated in clerical and lower-paying jobs, thus maintaining occupational segregation. Starting in the 1970s, however, some significant steps towards addressing gender disparities have been taken by various intergovernmental and non-governmental organizations and government agencies.

The Cedaw: An International Treaty for Women's Rights

A very important stimulus was the UN General Assembly resolution of December 1972, declaring 1975 as the International Women's Year. In 1975, the first UN world conference on women, held in Mexico City, declared 1976 to 1985 as the United Nations Decade for Women. The intensive efforts and actions undertaken during the Decade included organizing more conferences on women, the creation of specialized agencies, such as the United Nations Development Fund for Women (UNIFEM) and the UN International Research and Training Institute for the Advancement of Women (INSTRAW), elevating the Branch of the Advancement of Women to a "Division" status and putting women's rights and concerns on the agenda of other conferences and organizations. Arguably, the most important development that took place during the Decade was the preparation of the Convention on the Elimination of All Forms of Discrimination against Women (CEDAW), which was adopted by the Assembly in 1979.

CEDAW was the culmination of a long process, but was given impetus in 1973 by the UN Commission on the Status of Women (csw). In its working paper, the Commission stated that neither the Declaration on the Elimination of Discrimination Against Women (1967) nor the legally binding human rights treaties had been effective in advancing the status of women. It also argued for a single comprehensive convention that would legally bind States to eliminate discriminatory laws, as well as de facto discrimination. With 30 articles organized in six parts, CEDAW defines "discrimination against women" in its first article: "For the purposes of the present Convention, the term 'discrimination against women' shall mean any distinction, exclusion or restriction made on the basis of sex, which has the effect or purpose of impairing or nullifying the recognition, enjoyment or exercise by women, irrespective of their marital status, on a basis of equality of men and women, of human rights and fundamental freedoms in the political, economic, social, cultural, civil or any other field."

The subsequent 15 articles of the Convention (Articles 2 to 16) specify the areas of discrimination, such as laws, legal structure, political and public life, education, employment, health care, rural environment, marriage and family, in which States parties should take measures to eliminate discrimination. The last two parts (Articles 17 to 30) refer to the administration of the implementation of the Convention. "For the purpose of considering the progress made in the implementation", Article 17 creates a Committee on the Elimination of Discrimination against Women, which functions as a monitoring and advisory agency. The Committee evaluates the periodic reports submitted by States parties, questions government delegations that present the report, guides and advises States parties in meeting the objectives of the Convention, and issues general recommendations that help interpret the intention and scope of the Convention.

The general recommendations issued by the Committee have been important for elaborating on the provisions of the Convention and for drawing attention to some gender-specific human rights violations and the attitudes and practices that disregard the value of women. By stressing such issues as gender-based violence, unequal pay for work of equal value, undervalued and unremunerated domestic activities of women, polygamy and other marital practices that disadvantage women and violate their dignity, the general recommendations have broadened the scope of CEDAW and made it a living document. In other words, some limitations in the wording of the Convention, such as treating man as a measure by requiring States parties to ensure that women enjoy a series of rights "on equal terms with men", or failing to make explicit references to some violations that are experienced mainly by women, are redressed by CEDAW through the general recommendations.

The popularity of CEDAW, as reflected in its high rate of ratification, has been encouraging. It entered into force on 3 September 1981, less than two years after the General Assembly adopted it on 18 December 1979. According to the Office of the High Commissioner for Human Rights, as of 15 February 2008, 185 countries constituting 96 percent of UN Member States have become parties to the Convention. However, ratification, accession or succession by 78 countries (42 percent of States parties) involved declarations or reservations, which allow them to limit their treaty obligations.[9] Since more States have placed reservations on this Convention than on any other human rights treaties,[10] CEDAW appears to be "the human rights instrument least respected by its States parties".[11] Reservations can be withdrawn later; so far, 14 States parties have withdrawn their reservations and a similar number withdrew or modified theirs with regard to some provisions. However, reservations justified by the claim that the culture or religion of the country conflicts with the provisions of the Convention are not likely to be withdrawn in the near future. Such broad reservations undermine "the object and purpose" of the treaty and leave it inapplicable for all practical purposes.

Cultural or religious objections to the provisions can be challenged by two interrelated arguments: first, it should be pointed out that the United Nations human rights regime, including regional ones, are essentially counter-culture; and second, although there may be tensions between goals (e.g., the preservation of culture versus the elimination of discriminatory cultural norms) or between two or more human rights (e.g., people's right as opposed to women's rights to self-determination), the international human rights regime requires them to be resolved by upholding the principles of universality and equality in dignity.

Promotion of Human Rights as a Counter-Culture

Although recognition and respect for some rights articulated in the Universal Declaration on Human Rights can be found in the cultural references and religious texts of many communities, the traditional cultural norms and practices also include numerous discriminatory stipulations. The novelty of the Declaration and subsequent human rights documents is not only universalism—the notion that *all* people hold certain rights by virtue of being human—but is also the desire to end *all* forms of violations that have been allowed in existing cultures. In other words, international human rights follow a reactive pattern: as violations are noticed, the rights violated within prevailing cultures are enumerated in declarations and treaties to bring them under protection. In the case of women, many human rights violations and discrimination have been not only culturally permissible, but often encouraged or demanded by cultural norms. That is why CEDAW makes specific references to culture, as well as traditions and customs embodied in cultures, and emphasizes the need to change discriminatory cultural norms, values and practices.

- It stresses that "a change in the *traditional* role of men, as well as the role of women, in society and in the family is needed to achieve full equality between men and women" (Preamble);
- States Parties . . . agree . . . "to take all appropriate measures, including legislation, to modify or abolish existing laws, regulations, *customs and practices* which constitute discrimination against women" (Article 2(f));
- States Parties shall take in all fields, in particular in the political, social, economic and *cultural fields,* all appropriate measures, including legislation, to ensure the full development and advancement of women, for the purpose of guaranteeing them the exercise and enjoyment of human rights and fundamental freedoms on a basis of equality with men (Article 3);
- States Parties shall take all appropriate measures: (a) To modify the *social and cultural patterns of conduct* of men and women, with a view to achieving the elimination of *prejudices and customary and all other practices* which are based on the idea of the inferiority or the superiority of either of the sexes or on *stereotyped roles* for men and women (Article 5). (Emphasis mine.)

Tensions between Competing Rights

The universality of human rights, and especially women's rights, is often challenged by cultural relativists. Relativist arguments, especially when combined with charges of cultural imperialism, pose a major dilemma for the international human rights community. How can peoples' cultures and their right to self-determination be recognized when several aspects of those very cultures systematically violate a number of human rights? This question is particularly important for women's rights. Since all contemporary societies are patriarchies, promoting women's rights inevitably conflicts with patriarchal "cultural" values, religious norms and other hierarchical structures in all countries. Thus, following a strict rule of cultural relativism would keep women's rights "alien" virtually to all societies, and the emancipatory aspects of the international human rights regime would be undermined and jeopardized in the name of cultural preservation.

With regard to culture and religion, we need to ask the following questions: Who speaks on behalf of the people and religion? Who *defines* the meaning of culture or *interprets* the sources of religion and develops doctrines? Cultures, of course, are neither monolithic nor static, but within each culture there are people who would benefit from making it monolithic and keeping it static. In other words, cultures are based on power structures, and by setting norms and assigning values they also perpetuate those structures. Culturally (and officially) promoted values privilege some members of society and disadvantage others, and the privileged ones would tend to use their power to sustain those values that would justify and preserve their privileged positions. Thus, without any democratization of the interpretation and decision-making processes, cultural relativism and preservation of culture end up serving only as shields protecting the privileged people.

By the same token, all religious texts and oral traditions are received in a cultural context and filtered through and fused with the prevailing cultural norms. Always open to interpretation, their messages can be subverted and mitigated by the existing power structures. Thus, religions can embody contradictory norms, which are selectively used and reinterpreted both by the privileged and those who challenge their understanding of religion and its requirements. It is needless to note that in patriarchal systems, it is the voice of the privileged men that dictates cultural and religious norms, even though women may help in their transmission and perpetuation. Egalitarian and emancipatory interpretations by women and their advocates tend to be disregarded or suppressed.

What Needs to Be Done?

Human rights are closely linked to culture, and the expansion, full recognition and protection of rights would demand the transformation of cultural norms and their material foundations. Thus, compliance with international human rights would require a shift in cultural mores, as well as political commitment. The advocacy of human rights has to involve: (1) analyzing cultural norms in terms of their conformity with human rights principles; (2) acknowledging the diversity of the interpretation of cultures and religious sources; and (3) demanding that States parties to conventions be specific about their reservations, indicating when and how they will remove their reservations.

Universalists usually attempt to advance their arguments against relativist claims by pointing out that several rights embodied in the Universal Declaration and other human rights instruments have existed and have been respected in the cultural and religious traditions of most societies. Although such assertions can be empirically supported, as already noted, the traditional cultural norms and practices also include numerous discriminatory stipulations. Thus, both aspects of cultures (egalitarian-emancipatory and discriminatory-oppressive) should be acknowledged, and all cultures analysed as to where and how they observe the principle of universality. Since human rights are about human dignity, the principle of universality means establishing the dignity of all and calls for equal treatment. Cultures therefore should be examined to identify their contradictions with regard to the principle of equality. Once revealed, the "egalitarian" aspects of cultures can be highlighted and linked to international human rights in terms of principles.[12]

Critical assessment of cultures and egalitarian interpretation of cultural sources already exist, but these alternative voices tend to be repressed at home and ignored in international debates. Nations and other members of the international human rights community have to break away from the habits of tolerating cultural discrimination in the name of respect for differences, attributing violations solely to the culture, equating culture with religion and treating cultures as monolithic and static. While there has been considerable attention on interfaith and intercommunal conflicts and domination, e.g., rights of religious and ethnic minorities, their has been no effort to address *the intra-communal differences and hegemonies.* Acknowledging the diversity within a culture and religious community by States parties and in international forums would provide support to the alternative voices and help democratize the interpretation process.

The relativist arguments and reservations placed on treaties can be countered by pointing out that international human rights norms demand such a change of customs and traditions, and what is presented as religious requirement is open to interpretation. It should be demanded of States parties that make such claims, not only to fully explain and specify their reservations, but also to stipulate a programme that would lead to their removal. The expert committee that oversees the implementation of CEDAW has already taken some action on these lines. For example, it has issued several recommendations to press States parties that placed "blanket reservations", declaring they would implement CEDAW as long as its provisions do not contradict the Islamic law *Shari'a,* to clarify their points of reservation.[13] The Committee also problematized the issue of interpretation: " . . . at its 1987 meeting, the CEDAW Committee adopted a decision requesting that the United Nations and the specialized agencies promote or undertake studies on the status of women under Islamic laws and customs, and in particular on the status and equality of women in the family, on issues such as marriage, divorce, custody and property rights and their participation in public life of the society, taking into consideration the principle of El Ijtihad (interpretation) in Islam."[14]

Not surprisingly, the States parties affected by the decision denounced it as a threat to their religious freedoms and rejected the Committee's recommendation, but the Committee has been persistent in pressing this issue. In 1994, it amended the guidelines for the preparation of reports to provide additional and specific guidelines for States parties that have entered substantial culture-and religion-based reservations. Jane Connors provides a summary:[15] "Such States should report specifically with regard to their reservations, why they consider them to be necessary, their precise effect on national law and policy, and whether they have entered similar reservations to other human rights treaties which guarantee similar rights. Such States are also required to indicate plans they might have to limit the effect of the reservations or withdraw them and, where possible, specify a timetable for withdrawing them. The Committee made particular reference to . . . [some States], indicating that the Committee considers such reservations to be incompatible with the object and purpose of the Convention and requiring a special effort from such countries who are directed to report on the effect and interpretation of their reservations."

In its persistent effort, the Committee should also encourage shadow reports, which not only include the assessments of what has not been done by the reporting State towards implementing the Convention, but which also present alternative interpretations of the culture and religious sources. Inviting such reports would equip the Committee with the information needed to effectively question States parties' justification for their reservations and allow them to recognize the diversity within their society. It would also support women and women's rights advocates by validating their *right to interpret* their cultural and religious sources.

Notes

1. Here, "civilization" is employed as a sociological term in reference to societies that achieve high levels of economic productivity, which lead to specialization of labour, social stratification and institutionalization. A curious case is the Iroquois nations. The extent of power that the Iroquois matrons had over public affairs has led many impressed observers to classify these nations as "matriarchy". Although the Iroquois matrons enjoyed some authority, they could not be chiefs or serve on the Council of Elders—the highest ruling body of the six-nation Iroquois Confederacy. Women mainly maintained a veto power and exercised an indirect influence due to their control of food and other supplies. No matriarchal society—as exact opposites of patriarchy—has been recorded in history. Although some pre-civilized societies have demonstrated more egalitarian gender relations, even in those societies the power balance has been usually tilted in favour of men. See, Rayna R. Reiter, ed., *Toward an Anthropology of Women* (New York: Monthly Review Press, 1975).
2. For current statistical information on the gender gap in many areas, see *Human Development Report 2007/2008.* (New York: Oxford University Press, 2007) tables 28–33.
3. Majid Fakhry, *Averroes: His Life, Work,* (Oxford: Oneworld Publications, 2001).
4. St. Thomas Aquinas found women to be valuable (thus created in the first production) only for their reproductive role (in procreation). See, St. Thomas Aquinas, Summa Theologicae, Question XCII, art. 1, "Whether Woman Should Have Been Made in the First Production of Things", available at www.newadvent.org/summa/109201.htm.
5. John Stuart Mill and Harriet Taylor Mill, *Essays on Sex Equality.* Edited with and an introductory essay by Alice S. Rossi (Chicago: University of Chicago Press, 1970).
6. Mary Ann Glendon. *A World Made New* (New York: Random House, 2001), 68.
7. Glendon, (2001): 111–112 and 162.
8. Hilary Charlesworth, "Human Rights as Men's Rights", *Women's Rights Human Rights: International Feminist*

Perspectives. Edited by Julie Peters and Andrea Wolper (New York: Routledge, 1995): 103–113.

9. Article 28 allows the ratification of the Convention with reservations, as long as they are compatible "with the object and purpose" of the Convention. Thus, States may enter reservations or "interpretive declarations" when they sign or ratify the Convention. Although "declarations" are not referred to in the text, they tend to employ a language similar to the one used in reservations and play the same role in limiting State obligations. Thus, for the purposes of this essay, declarations are treated the same as reservations.
10. Henry J. Steiner and Philip Alston, *International Human Rights in Context: Law, Politics, Morals.* Second Edition (Oxford: Oxford University Press, 2000): 180.
11. Belinda Clark, "The Vienna Convention Reservations Regime and the Convention on the Discrimination against Women." *American Journal of International Law,* 85:2 (April 1991): 281–321, 318.
12. Such a study of *The Qur'an,* the sacred text and highest authority in Islam, shows that Muslim women are granted equality with men at the spiritual level, but denied equality at the social level, and argues for the elevation of the spiritual equality recognized in the sacred text to become the standard that would be used in the reformulation of social roles. See, Zehra Arat, "Women's Rights in Islam: Revisiting Qur'anic Rights", *Human Rights: New Perspectives, New Realities.* Edited by Peter Schwab and Adamanta Pollis, eds., (Boulder: Lynne Rienner Publishers, 2000): 69–94.
13. Michele Brandt and Jeffrey A. Kaplan, "The Tension between Women's Rights and Religious Rights: Reservations to CEDAW by Egypt, Bangladesh and Tunisia", *The Journal of Law and Religion* 12:1 (1995–96): 105–142; Connors, 1997; Clark, 1991.
14. UN Doc E/1987/SR 11.
15. Jane Connors. "The Women's Convention in the Muslim World", *Human Rights as General Norms and a State's Right to Opt Out: Reservations and Objections to Human Rights Convention.* Edited by J.P. Gardner (London: British Institute of International and Comparative Law, 1997): 85–103, 99–100.

Assess Your Progress

1. What is the history of human rights with respect to women?
2. Since the 1970s, what steps have been taken to address gender disparities?
3. How has CEDAW been undermined?
4. What are the tensions between women's rights and culture?
5. What needs to be done to more effectively protect women's rights?

Zehra F. Kabasakal Arat is Juanita and Joseph Leff Professor of Political Science at Purchase College of the State University of New York and is Chair of the Human Rights Research Committee of the International Political Science Association. She is the author of *Human Rights Worldwide.* Some of the arguments presented here appeared in her earlier publications.

Test-Your-Knowledge Form

We encourage you to photocopy and use this page as a tool to assess how the articles in *Annual Editions* expand on the information in your textbook. By reflecting on the articles you will gain enhanced text information. You can also access this useful form on a product's book support website at www.mhhe.com/cls.

NAME: DATE:

TITLE AND NUMBER OF ARTICLE:

BRIEFLY STATE THE MAIN IDEA OF THIS ARTICLE:

LIST THREE IMPORTANT FACTS THAT THE AUTHOR USES TO SUPPORT THE MAIN IDEA:

WHAT INFORMATION OR IDEAS DISCUSSED IN THIS ARTICLE ARE ALSO DISCUSSED IN YOUR TEXTBOOK OR OTHER READINGS THAT YOU HAVE DONE? LIST THE TEXTBOOK CHAPTERS AND PAGE NUMBERS:

LIST ANY EXAMPLES OF BIAS OR FAULTY REASONING THAT YOU FOUND IN THE ARTICLE:

LIST ANY NEW TERMS/CONCEPTS THAT WERE DISCUSSED IN THE ARTICLE, AND WRITE A SHORT DEFINITION:

We Want Your Advice

ANNUAL EDITIONS revisions depend on two major opinion sources: one is our Advisory Board, listed in the front of this volume, which works with us in scanning the thousands of articles published in the public press each year; the other is you—the person actually using the book. Please help us and the users of the next edition by completing the prepaid article rating form on this page and returning it to us. Thank you for your help!

ANNUAL EDITIONS: Developing World 11/12

ARTICLE RATING FORM

Here is an opportunity for you to have direct input into the next revision of this volume.
We would like you to rate each of the articles listed below, using the following scale:

1. **Excellent: should definitely be retained**
2. **Above average: should probably be retained**
3. **Below average: should probably be deleted**
4. **Poor: should definitely be deleted**

Your ratings will play a vital part in the next revision.
Please mail this prepaid form to us as soon as possible.
Thanks for your help!

RATING	ARTICLE
______	1. The New Face of Development
______	2. How Development Leads to Democracy: What We Know about Modernization
______	3. The New Population Bomb: The Four Megatrends that Will Change the World
______	4. The Ideology of Development
______	5. The Case against the West: America and Europe in the Asian Century
______	6. Industrial Revolution 2.0
______	7. A Tiger Despite the Chains: The State of Reform in India
______	8. The Poor Man's Burden
______	9. Cotton: The Huge Moral Issue
______	10. R.I.P., WTO
______	11. Taking the Measure of Global Aid
______	12. The New Colonialists
______	13. A Few Dollars at a Time: How to Tap Consumers for Development
______	14. The Politics of Hunger: How Illusion and Greed Fan the Food Crisis
______	15. The Micromagic of Microcredit
______	16. Many Borrowers of Microloans Now Find the Price Is Too High
______	17. Haiti: A Creditor, Not a Debtor
______	18. Fixing a Broken World
______	19. Afghanistan's Rocky Path to Peace
______	20. A Nation on the Brink
______	21. Africa's Forever Wars
______	22. The Most Dangerous Place in the World
______	23. Africa's New Horror
______	24. Behind Iran's Crackdown, an Economic Coup
______	25. Mexico's Drug Wars Get Brutal
______	26. Call in the Blue Helmets
______	27. Crying for Freedom
______	28. In Sri Lanka, the Triumph of Vulgar Patriotism
______	29. Bring Me My Machine Gun
______	30. Free at Last?
______	31. "Moderates" Redefined: How to Deal with Political Islam
______	32. The Islamists Are Not Coming
______	33. The Transformation of Hamas
______	34. Adios Monroe Doctrine: When the Yanquis Go Home
______	35. The Return of *Continuismo?*
______	36. Perilous Times for Latin America
______	37. Is a Green World a Safer World?: Not Necessarily
______	38. The Last Straw
______	39. The World's Water Challenge
______	40. Water Warriors
______	41. Soot from Third-World Stoves Is New Target in Climate Fight
______	42. Population, Human Resources, Health, and the Environment: Getting the Balance Right
______	43. Reversal of Fortune: Why Preventing Poverty Beats Curing It
______	44. The Women's Crusade
______	45. Gendercide
______	46. Women in Developing Countries 300 Times More Likely to Die in Childbirth
______	47. Educating Girls, Unlocking Development
______	48. Girls in War: Sex Slave, Mother, Domestic Aide, Combatant
______	49. Remember the Women?
______	50. Women in the Shadow of Climate Change
______	51. Recession Hits Women in Developing Countries
______	52. Women's Rights as Human Rights: The Promotion of Human Rights as a Counter-Culture

NO POSTAGE NECESSARY IF MAILED IN THE UNITED STATES

BUSINESS REPLY MAIL
FIRST CLASS MAIL PERMIT NO. 551 DUBUQUE IA

POSTAGE WILL BE PAID BY ADDRESSEE

McGraw-Hill Contemporary Learning Series
501 BELL STREET
DUBUQUE, IA 52001

ABOUT YOU

Name Date

Are you a teacher? ❒ A student? ❒
Your school's name

Department

Address City State Zip

School telephone #

YOUR COMMENTS ARE IMPORTANT TO US!

Please fill in the following information:
For which course did you use this book?

Did you use a text with this ANNUAL EDITION? ❒ yes ❒ no
What was the title of the text?

What are your general reactions to the Annual Editions concept?

Have you read any pertinent articles recently that you think should be included in the next edition? Explain.

Are there any articles that you feel should be replaced in the next edition? Why?

Are there any World Wide Websites that you feel should be included in the next edition? Please annotate.

May we contact you for editorial input? ❒ yes ❒ no
May we quote your comments? ❒ yes ❒ no

NOTES

NOTES

NOTES

NOTES

NOTES

NOTES